THE GREEKS

THE
GREEKS

EDITED BY
JEAN-PIERRE VERNANT

Translated by
Charles Lambert and
Teresa Lavender Fagan

THE UNIVERSITY OF CHICAGO PRESS
Chicago & London

Jean-Claude Vernant is professor emeritus at the Collège de France.

The University of Chicago Press, Chicago 60637
The University of Chicago Press, Ltd., London
© 1995 by The University of Chicago
All rights reserved. Published 1995
Printed in the United States of America

04 03 02 01 00 99 98 97 96   5 4 3 2

ISBN (cloth): 0-226-85382-9
ISBN (paper): 0-226-85383-7

Originally published as *L'Uomo greco,* © 1991, Gius. Laterza & Figli.

Library of Congress Cataloging-in-Publication Data

Uomo greco. English
    The Greeks / edited by Jean-Pierre Vernant : translated by Charles Lambert
and Teresa Lavender Fagan.
        p.   cm.
    Includes bibliographical references and index.
    ISBN 0-226-85382-9. — ISBN 0-226-85383-7 (pbk.)
    1. Greece—Social life and customs.   2. Greece—Civilization.
I. Vernant, Jean Pierre.   II. Title.
DF78.U5913   1995
949.5—dc20   94-32964
                                                                      CIP

CONTENTS

99227

CHAPTERS 5, 6, AND 7, originally written in English, have been given in their English versions with editing, including in chapter 6, some new material. The chapters originally written in French have been checked against the French texts; chapter 9 is new to this edition.

In chapters 5, 6, and 7, quotations from the works of classical writers have been given in the translations of the authors of the chapters. In other chapters, some modern translations into English have been used and are credited.

INTRODUCTION

Jean-Pierre Vernant

W HAT EXACTLY DO we mean when we speak of ancient Greek man, and how can we justifiably claim to paint a portrait of him?[1] The use of the singular form, "man," is immediately problematic. From Athens to Sparta, from Arcadia, Thessaly, or Epirus to the city-states of Asia Minor, to the colonies of the Black Sea, from southern Italy and Sicily, in many diverse situations, ways of life, and political regimes, will we always and everywhere find a single model for Greek man? And that man whose image we are seeking to draw, is he the one of the archaic period, the war hero celebrated by Homer, or the other one, different in so many ways, whom Aristotle defined in the fourth century B.C. as a "political animal"? Although the documents we have available lead us to focus our study on the classical period and to turn our spotlight most often on the city of Athens, the face of the subject whose portrait is sketched at the conclusion of this study is less a complete and whole visage than one that is broken up into a multitude of facets reflecting the different points of view that the authors of this collection have chosen to emphasize. We will thus discover, proceeding one after the other according to the chosen angle of vision, Greek man as a citizen, a religious believer, a soldier, someone engaged in economic activities, a servant, a peasant, as both a listener and a spectator, active in the characteristic forms of sociality, advancing from childhood to adulthood on a path fraught with trials and milestones to achieve full manhood, consistent with the Greek ideal of an accomplished being.

In this gallery of portraits painted by modern scholars, the series of representations, even if each takes up a point of view or a particular question—what did it mean for a Greek man to be a citizen, a solider, the head of a family?—does not form a mere series of juxtaposed items, but rather a unified whole whose elements support or complete each other and form a fresh unity, not duplicated elsewhere. Put together by historians, this model indeed hopes to reveal the characteristic traits of the activities undertaken by the ancient Greeks in the major realms of collective life. This design is not arbitrary: it is supported by documentation that is as complete and precise as possible.

Nor is it "commonplace," insofar as, leaving aside generalities on human nature, it is committed to identifying what was unique to the behavior of the Greeks, their specific ways of engaging in practices as universally widespread as those relating to war, religion, economics, politics, and domestic life.

Thus, we are dealing with what was uniquely Greek. To shed light upon such singularity means we must from the outset adopt a comparative point of view, and in this confrontation with other cultures, beyond any traits that might be shared, we must place the accent on divergences, separateness, and distances. The Greeks are distant from us, from the ways we act, think, and feel, ways that are so familiar to us that they seem to be natural, to go without saying, but from which we must detach ourselves when we turn toward the Greeks; otherwise we shall find them in our way when we make that turn. Also the Greeks are distant from men of other times that are not antiquity, from civilizations other than that of ancient Greece.

But the reader, if he is ready to grant us the singularity of the Greek case, will perhaps be tempted to shift his objection and question our use of the word "man." Why "man" and not Greek civilization or the city-state? It is, he might argue, the social and cultural context that is subject to constant changes; man adapts his behavior to those changes, but in himself he remains the same. How could the eye of the citizen of Athens in the fifth century B.C. have differed from that of our contemporaries? A valid question. Yet we are not dealing with eyes or ears in this book, but rather with the Greek way of using them: vision and hearing, their place, their forms, and their respective status. Here is an example that may clarify what I mean, with apologies for its personal nature: How could we see the moon today through the eyes of an ancient Greek? I was able to do just that as a young man during my first trip to Greece. I was sailing at night, from island to island; lying on deck, I watched the sky above me where the moon was shining, a luminous nocturnal face, casting its pale reflection, immobile or dancing, over the dark back of the sea. I was in awe, fascinated by the soft and strange light that bathed the sleeping waves; I was moved as if in the presence of a woman, someone both near and distant, familiar and yet inaccessible, whose brilliance had come to visit the darkness of the night. It is Selene, I told myself, nocturnal, mysterious, and brilliant; it is Selene I see. Many years later, while I was watching the images of the first lunar explorer on my television screen, jumping around heavily in his spacesuit over what looked like the vast empty lot of a desolate suburb, I had an impression of sacrilege as well as a painful sensation that something had ruptured that could never again be repaired: having witnessed those images, as the whole world had done, my grandson would never again be able to see the moon as I once had, through the eyes of the ancient Greeks. The word "Selene" has become a purely scholarly reference; the moon, as it appears in the sky, no longer answers to that name.

And yet there is the persistent illusion that, a man being a man, if historians managed to reconstruct perfectly the decor in which the ancients lived, they would have accomplished their task, and in reading their work, each of us would find ourselves standing in the sandals of a Greek. Saint-Just was not the only French revolutionary to believe that he had only to practice the ancient virtues of simplicity, frugality, and inflexibility for the republican of '89 to be identified with the Greek and Roman statesman. In the *Holy Family,* Marx discusses the issue clearly: "The illusion appears tragic when Saint-Just, on the day of his execution, pointed to the large [painting] of the 'Rights of Man' hanging in the hall of the *Conciergerie,* and said with proud dignity, 'And yet it was I who did that.' It was just this [painting] that proclaimed the *right* of a *man* who cannot be the man of the ancient commonweal any more than his *economic* and *industrial* conditions are those of *ancient* times" [Internal Publications translation, p. 122]. According to François Hartog, who cites this passage: "The man of rights cannot be a man of the ancient city"—nor can the citizen of modern states, the follower of a monotheist religion, the worker, the head of industry, or the financier, the soldier of world wars between nations, the head of a family with his wife and children, the private individual in his intimate personal life, or the young person today chasing after adulthood through an adolescence that seems never to end.

Having said this, what should the task of the presenter be in an introduction to a work on Greek man? Certainly not to summarize or comment on the texts that, within their respective fields of scholarly expertise, the most qualified Hellenists have graciously offered to us, and for which at the very beginning of this book we wish to thank them warmly. Rather than repeating or embellishing upon what they have been able to convey better than anyone else, I would like to adopt a slightly different perspective within the same comparative spirit, a transverse point of view in relation to theirs; each author has in fact taken great care to limit his analysis to a specific type of behavior and thus to outline a series of distinct facets in the lives of the ancient Greeks. Approaching the same subject of study from another angle and this time winding the entire network of threads they have untangled around the individual, I will address the question of what aspects, in ancient Greek man's relationships with the divine, with nature, with others, and with himself, should be most emphasized in order to see what made him "different" in his ways of acting, thinking, and feeling—one might just as easily say in his way of being in the world, in society, and in himself.

This is an ambitious plan that might cause some to smile if I did not have two justifications for trying my hand at it. First, the time certainly seems to have come, after forty years of research carried out in the footsteps and in the company of other scholars on what I have called the inner history of Greek man, for me to venture to take stock of what I have learned by risking some general conclusions. At the beginning of the 1960s I wrote, "Whether we look at religious facts (myths, rituals, figurative representations), at science, art, social institutions, technical and economic facts, we will always consider them as works created by men, as the expression of organized activities of the mind. Through those works we seek to find out what man himself might have been, that ancient Greek man who cannot be separated from the social and cultural framework of which he is both the creator and the result." A quarter of a century later, I still adhere to the terms of that programmatic declaration. However, even if the goal of my project—to be able to sketch some general traits—may appear too risky, the project itself, and this is my second justification, is more modest because it is more delimited. Leaving aside the results (which are of course incomplete and temporary, as is every historical study) of my research into the changes that occurred in Greek man from the eighth to the fourth century B.C. through the entire gamut of psychological activities and functions—frameworks of space, forms of temporality, memory, imagination, will, the person, symbolic practices, and the wielding of signs, modes of reasoning, intellectual tools—I shall attempt to sketch an outline properly titled, not "Greek Man," but "Greek Man and Us." Not Greek man as he was to himself—an impossible task because the very notion of it is devoid of sense—but Greek man as he appears to us today at the conclusion of an inquiry that for lack of direct dialogue has been carried out in endless advances and retreats, from us to him, from him to us, combining objective analysis and an effort at sympathy, bringing distance and proximity into play, stepping back in order to get closer without blending together, getting nearer in order to perceive distances as well as affinities better.

Let us begin by looking at the gods. What was the divine for Greek man, and how was he placed in relation to it? Phrased in these terms, the question risks being skewed from the outset. Words are not innocent. In our minds the word "God" does not simply evoke a single, eternal, absolute, perfect, transcendent being, the creator of all that exists, associated with a series of other notions closely related to it: the sacred, the supernatural, faith, the church and its clergy. It delimits a particular realm of experience in close association with those notions—religious experience—whose place, function, and status are clearly distinct from other aspects of life in society. The sacred is contrasted to the profane, the supernatural to the world of nature, faith to unbelief, clerics to laymen, just as God separates himself from a universe that at every moment depends entirely upon him because he created it and created it out of nothing. However, the multiple gods of Greek polytheism did not possess the characteristics by which we describe the divine. They were neither eternal, perfect, omniscient, nor all-powerful. They did not create the world; they were born in it and by it. Surging up in successive generations as the universe, through primordial powers such as "Chaos," the Abyss, and "Gaea," the Earth, was being created and organized, they dwelt within its bosom. Their transcendency was thus completely relative; it had worth only in relation to the human sphere. Like men, but living above them, the gods were an integral part of the cosmos.

This means that there was not the radical break between the earthly and the divine that for us separates the natural order from the supernatural. Understanding the world in which we live as it appears to us and a quest for the divine did not comprise two divergent or contrasting interests, but rather attitudes that could be joined or merged together. The moon, the sun, the dawn, the light of day, the night, and also a mountain, a grotto, a spring, a river, a forest could be perceived and experienced on the same level as one of the great gods of the Greek pantheon. They evoked the same forms of respect and of admiring deference that marked man's relationship with the divinity. Where, then, lay the dividing line between humans and the gods? On one side of it were men, uncertain, ephemeral beings, subject to illness, aging, and death—there was nothing in them of what gave existence its value and brilliance: youth, strength, beauty, grace, courage, honor, glory; nothing in them that did not soon fade and disappear forever, nor anything that did not include, implicated in every desirable good, a corresponding evil, its opposite and counterpart: there was no life without death, no youth without old age, no effort without fatigue, no abundance without labor, no pleasure without suffering. Every light here on earth had its shadow, every beam its reverse side of darkness.

The opposite was true among those who were called nonmortals (*athanatoi*), fortunate (*makarēs*), powerful (*kreittous*): the divinities. Each residing in his own realm, the gods embodied the strengths, abilities, virtues, and benefits that men, throughout their transitory lives, could obtain only in the form of a fleeting and darkened, dreamlike reflection. There was a gulf, therefore, between the two races, the human and the divine. Greek man of the classical period was always keenly aware of that disparity. He knew that there existed an impassable border between men and the gods: in spite of the resources of the human mind and of all that it had managed to discover or invent throughout time, the future remained indecipherable, death had no cure, and the gods were beyond man's reach, beyond his intelligence, just as the brilliance of their faces was too strong to be endured. Thus one of the primary rules of Greek wisdom concerning man's relationship with the gods was that he could never claim to be their equal in any way whatsoever.

Accepting all the deficiencies that accompany man's condition as a fact inscribed in human nature and against which it would be useless to argue had several consequences. First, Greek man could not expect the gods—nor ask them—to grant him any form whatsoever of that immortality they were so privileged to possess. The hope that an individual might survive after death—other than as a shadow without strength or consciousness in the darkness of Hades—did not enter into the framework of man's dealings with the gods as established through his forms of worship; in any event, it represented neither the main principle nor a major element within that framework. The idea of individual immortality must have seemed quite strange and incongruous to fourth-century Athenians, judging from the precautions Plato felt obliged to take before asserting through the voice of Socrates in the *Phaedo* that in each one of us there exists an immortal soul. Yet that soul, insofar as it is imperishable, is conceived as a sort of god, a *daimon:* far from being connected with the human individual, with what makes him a unique being, the soul is like a small particle of the divine that has temporarily strayed down on earth.

The second consequence is that however great it may have been, the distance between the gods and men did not preclude a form of kinship between them. They were beings of the same world, but of a tiered and strictly hierarchized world. From the bottom to the top, from the inferior to the superior, the difference was one from the least to the most, from scarcity to abundance on a scale of values that extended without any real break, without that complete change of design required, by reason of an incommensurability, by a passage from the finite to the infinite, from the relative to the absolute, from time to eternity. The perfections with which the gods were endowed were extensions of those manifested in the order and beauty of the world, the positive harmony of a city ruled with justice, the elegance of a life led with restraint and self-control; the piety of Greek man did not follow the path to a renunciation of the world, but rather one that led to making it more beautiful.

Men were subject to the gods as a servant is to the master upon whom he depends. This meant that mortal existence was not self-sufficient. For each individual, being born immediately involved something beyond himself; parents, ancestors, founders of the lineage all came directly from the ground or were born of some god. As soon as his eyes opened to the light of life, man was thus in a state of indebtedness. He paid back that debt by rendering the homage to the divinity that it rightfully demanded through a scrupulous observance of traditional rituals. While incorporating an element of fear upon which the obsessive anxieties of the superstitious could ultimately feed, Greek religious devotion included another, quite different aspect. By establishing contact with the gods and by making them present in a certain sense among mortals, divine worship introduced a new dimension into the lives of men, one of beauty, of grace, of positive communion. The gods were celebrated through processions, songs, dances, choruses, games, competitions, and banquets where together members of the community ate the meat of animals offered up in sacrifice. At the very time it venerated the immortals in the way they deserved, the ritual festival, for those who were destined to die, appeared as the ornament of their days, an ornament that, by conferring grace, joy, and mutual accord upon them, illuminated them with a burst of light, a bit of divine splendor. As Plato said, in order to become accomplished men, children had to learn as early as possible how "to live by playing and by playing games such as sacrifices, songs, and dances" (*Laws* 803c). For it is to us other men, he explains, "that the gods have been given not only to share our festivals but to grant us a sense of the rhythm and the harmony accompanied by pleasure, through which they inspire us by instituting our choruses and by intertwining us all together through song and dance" (*Laws* 653d). In that intertwining of celebrants accomplished through the ritual, the gods, through the pleasant game of the festival, were also associated and in accord with men.

Men depended on the gods: without their consent nothing could be accomplished on earth below. Thus, at all times, one had to put oneself right with the divinity by constantly being at its service. But service was not servitude. To distinguish himself from the barbarian, Greek man loudly proclaimed that he was a free man, *eleutheros,* and the expression "slave of god," which one finds widely stated among other peoples, was unknown in ancient Greece, not only in the prevailing forms of worship, but even in the way religious functions or the priesthoods of a divinity were described, since it was a matter of citizens' exercising their priestly functions in an official capacity. Freedom/slavery: for those who conferred their full and precise meanings upon these two terms, within the framework of the city, those notions appear too exclusive of each other for both to be applied to the same individual. He who was free could not be a slave, or rather, one could not be a slave without immediately ceasing to be free. On this point, other reasonings come into play. The world of the gods was distant enough so that the world of men could maintain its autonomy in relation to it; it was not, however, so far that man felt powerless, crushed, reduced to nothing before the infinitude of the divine. So that success would crown his efforts, in peace as in war, to gain wealth, honor, excellence, so that peace would reign in the city, virtue in men's hearts, intelligence in their minds, the individual had to be an active participant; it was up to him to take the initiative and to pursue his task without sparing any effort. In the entire realm of things human, it was each person's responsibility to initiate action and to persevere in order to succeed. By accomplishing one's task appropriately, one had the best chance of assuring oneself divine benevolence.

Distance and proximity, anxiety and joy, dependence and autonomy, resignation and initiative—between these opposite poles all kinds of intermediate attitudes could crop up, depending upon the moment, the circumstance, the individual. But however diverse, however contrasting they may have been, they were in no way incompatible. All were inscribed within the same field of possibilities; their range drew the limits inside of which the religious devotion of the ancient Greeks could operate, in the form that was unique to it, indicating multiple, but not indefinite, paths authorized by this type of relationship with the divine, which was characteristic of ancient forms of worship.

I say "forms of worship" and not religion or belief. As Mario Vegetti has correctly pointed out, the first of those latter two terms had no equivalent in ancient Greece, where there was no religious domain incorporating institutions, codified behavior, and intimate convictions into an organized whole clearly distinct from other social practices. The religious could be found in all aspects of life; every daily act embodied, alongside other aspects and blended with them, a religious dimension. This was true from the most banal to the most solemn, from the private sphere to public life. Vegetti recalls a highly significant anecdote: some guests who have come to visit Heraclitus stop outside his door when they see he is busy warming himself by the fire of his oven. According to Aristotle, who wished to prove that, just like the observation of the stars and celestial movement, the study of even the humblest things possessed dignity, Heraclitus, inviting his guests to enter, is supposed to have said to them: "There, too, [in the kitchen oven] there are gods" (*De partibus animalium* 1.5.645a). But since it was present everywhere and on every occasion, the religious ran the risk of no longer having either a place or a way of appearing that was unique to it. Therefore, we must speak of "religion" among the ancient Greeks only with the same precautions and reservations we used when discussing the notion of God.

Regarding belief, things become a bit more complicated. Today, on a religious level we are either believers or unbelievers: the dividing line is clear. To belong to a church, to be a regular participant, to accept a body of truths formed into a credo having the value of dogma—these are the three elements of religious involvement. There was nothing similar in ancient Greece: there was no organized church or clergy; there was no dogma. Belief in the gods therefore did not take on the form either of belonging to a church or of accepting a group of propositions set forth as truths that escaped, through their revelatory nature, all discussion and criticism. Greek man's "believing" in the gods did not fall within a strictly intellectual framework;

it did not aim to form a knowledge of the divine; it had no doctrinal character. In this sense, the path was clear for there to develop, beyond religion and without open conflict with it, forms of inquiry and reflection whose precise goal was to develop knowledge, to attain truth, in and of itself.

Thus, Greek man did not find himself at one time or another faced with a choice between belief and unbelief. By honoring the gods in conformity with the most established traditions, and by having confidence in the efficacy of the form of worship practiced by his ancestors as well as by all the members of his community, the faithful could demonstrate either an extreme credulity, like the superstitious man mocked by Theophrastus, or a cautious skepticism (like Protagoras, who believed that one was unable to know whether the gods existed or not, or indeed anything about them), or complete incredulity, like Critias, who maintained that the gods had been invented to keep men in subservience. But incredulity was not unbelief, in the sense that a Christian might give the term. Questioning on an intellectual level did not strike directly at the heart of Greek piety in order to destroy it. One cannot imagine Critias refusing to participate in ceremonies of worship or to perform sacrifices when appropriate. Was this hypocrisy? Rather, one must understand that since "religion" was inseparable from civic life, to exclude oneself from it was the same as putting oneself outside society, as ceasing to be what one was. There were, of course, people who wanted no part of civic religion, who wanted to exist outside the *polis;* their attitude had nothing to do with their greater or lesser degree of incredulity or skepticism. To the contrary, it was their faith and their involvement in sectarian movements with mystical inclinations, such as Orphism, that made them marginal in both religious and social contexts.

It is time to look at another of the themes I mentioned earlier: the world—although, since it was "full of gods," according to the famous formula, the world was already at issue when we were discussing the divine. It was thus a world in which the divine was implicated in each of its parts as in its whole and in its general organization. Not in the way the Creator is concerned with what he formed out of nothingness, which, outside and far from him, bears his mark, but otherwise directly and intimately, it contained a divine presence pervasive wherever one of its manifestations appeared. The term *phusis,* which we translate as "nature" when we discuss what Aristotle said about the philosophers of the Miletus school, who in the sixth century B.C. were the first to begin a *historia peri phuseōs,* an inquiry into nature—that *phusis*-nature had little in common with the subjects of our natural sciences or of physics. Whether it made plants grow, caused living beings to change location, or moved stars around in their celestial orbits, *phusis* was an animate and living power. For the "physicist" Thales, even inanimate things like rocks participated in *psychē,* which was both breath and soul, whereas the first of these terms has a "physical" connotation for us, and the second a "spiritual" one. Animate, inspired, living—through its dynamism nature was close to the divine, through its animation close to the essence of man himself. To repeat the expression Aristotle uses regarding the phenomenon of dreams that come to inhabit our sleep, nature was strictly speaking *daimonia,* "demonic" (*On Divination in Sleep* 2.463b.12–15); and since at the heart of each man the soul was a *daimon,* a demon, there was between the divine, the physical, and the human more than continuity: there was a kinship, a conaturalness.

The world was beautiful, like a god. By the end of the sixth century, the term that was used to describe the universe as a whole was *kosmos;* in more ancient texts it is applied to whatever, positively ordered and ruled, had the value of ornament, conferring upon the one who was thus adorned a surplus of grace and beauty. Unified in its diversity, permanent throughout fleeting time, harmonious in the arrangement of the parts that formed it, the world was like a marvelous jewel, a work of art, a precious object similar to one of those *agalmata* whose perfection qualified them to serve as offerings to a god within the confines of his sanctuary. Man contemplated and admired that great living thing, the world in its entirety; he was incorporated into it. From the start the universe uncovered and imposed itself upon man, in its unimpeachable reality, like a primal given, prior to any experiment that might have been carried out on it. In an attempt to know the world, man could not place the starting point of his project inside himself, as if to reach something one had to pass through the consciousness one had of it. The world man's knowledge focused on was not attained "in his mind." There was nothing farther from Greek culture than the Cartesian *cogito,* the "I think" set forth as a condition for and a foundation of all knowledge of the world, of oneself, and of God; or than the Leibnizian concept according to which each individual is an isolated monad, without a door or window, containing inside himself, as in an enclosed movie theater, the entire unfolding of the film that recounts his existence. To be understood by man, the world did not have to undergo that transmutation that would turn it into a conscious fact. To have a representation of the world did not consist of rendering it present *in* man's thoughts. It was his thoughts that were of the world and present in the world. Man belonged to the world to which he was related and that he knew through shared feeling or complicity. From the start, man's being was a being-in-the-world. If that world had been foreign to him, as we suppose to be the case today, if it had been a pure object, made of size and movement, in contrast to a subject made of judgment and thought, man could in fact have communicated with it only by assimilating it into his own consciousness. But for ancient Greek man, the world was not that objectified external universe, cut off from man by the impassable barrier that separates matter from the mind, the physical from the psychic. Man was in a relationship of intimate community with the animate universe to which everything connected him.

Here is an example that may help us to understand better what Gerard Simon calls "a form of presence in the world and of presence in oneself that we can no longer grasp without a serious effort of methodical distancing, demanding a true archaeological reconstruction" ("L'ame du monde," *Le temps de la réflexion* 10 (1989): 123). I wish to speak about sight and vision. In Greek culture, "seeing" had a privileged status. It was valued to the point of occupying an unparalleled position in the range of human capabilities. In a certain sense, man's very nature was sight. And this was for two reasons, both decisive. Foremost, to see and to know were as one; if *idein,* "to see," and *eidenai,* "to know," are two verbal forms of the same term, if *eidos,* "appearance, visible aspect," also means "the specific character, the intelligible form," this is because knowledge was interpreted and expressed through one's way of seeing. Knowing was a form of vision. Second, to see and to live were also one and the same. To be living, one had at the same time to see the light of the sun and to be visible to the eyes of all. To leave this life meant both to lose one's sight and one's visibility, to abandon the clarity of day to delve into another world, that of Night, where, lost in the Darkness, one was stripped simultaneously of one's face and one's ability to see.

But this "seeing," all the more precious in that it was knowledge and life, was not interpreted by the Greeks the way it is today—ever since Descartes and the rest have been there. We distinguish three levels in the visual phenomenon: first light, physical reality, whether it be wave or corpuscle; then the eye as a physical organ, an optical fixture, a sort of black box whose function is to project an image of the object onto the retina; and finally, the strictly psychic act of perceiving the viewed object at a distance. Between the final act of perception, which assumes a spiritual instance, a consciousness, an "I," and the material phenomenon of light, there is the same gulf that separates the human subject from the external world.

Conversely, for the Greeks, vision was only possible if there existed a total reciprocity between what was seen and the one who saw, conveying if not a complete identity between the two, then at least a very close kinship. Because the sun in the sky illuminated all things, it, too, was an eye that saw everything; and if one's eye saw, it was because it radiated a sort of light comparable to that of the sun. The ray of light that emanated from the object and made it visible was of the same nature as the optical ray that issued from the eye and enabled it to see. The emitting object and the receiving subject, the light rays and the optical rays, belonged to the same category of reality, about which we can say that the physical-psychic opposition was foreign to it, or that it was both on a physical and psychic order. Light was vision, and vision was luminous.

As Charles Mugler notes in a study entitled "La lumière et la vision dans la poésie grecque" [Light and vision in Greek poetry] (*Revue des études grecques* (1960): 40–70), the language itself testified to this ambivalence. The verbs that described the acts of seeing and watching, *blepein, derkesthai, leussein,* used as direct objects not only the thing the gaze focused on, but also the igneous-luminous substance projected by the eye just as one might throw a projectile. And these rays of fire, which we would call physical, carried with them the feelings, passions, and conditions of the soul, which we would call psychic, of the one who was looking. The same verbs also use as grammatical objects terms denoting terror, savagery, murdering fury. The gaze, when it reached the object, transmitted to it what the viewer, upon seeing it, experienced.

Of course, the language of poetry has its own rules and conventions. But this concept of the gaze plunged its roots into Greek culture so deeply that it appears again transposed onto certain philosophical remarks, sometimes shocking to us, such as those of Aristotle. In his *De insomniis,* the Lyceum master maintains that if sight is affected by its object, "it also acts upon it in a certain way," as do all brilliant objects, for sight falls into the category of brilliant and colorful things. As proof of this he says that if women look at themselves in a mirror at the time of their menstrual periods, the polished surface of the mirror becomes covered with a sort of haze the color of blood; this blemish stains new mirrors so deeply that it cannot easily be removed (*De insomniis* 2.459b.25–31).

But it is perhaps in Plato that the "kinship" between light, the ray of fire emitted by the object, and the one the eye projects outside itself is asserted most clearly as the cause of vision. How, indeed, did the gods fashion "light-bearing eyes," *phosphora-ommata?*

> For the pure fire contained within us and related to [the external fire] (*adelphos*) they caused to flow smoothly through the eyes, and in dense quantities throughout. . . . When, therefore, the light of day (*methēmerinon phos*) surrounds the stream of vision, then, by the mutual falling of similar bodies on each other, one well-adapted body is constituted, according to the direction of the eyes, wherever the light proceeding from within resists that which falls on it from without. But the whole becoming similarly affected through similitude, when it either touches anything else or is itself touched by another. (*Timaeus* 45b f. [Davis translation])

Let us summarize: instead of three distinct facts—physical reality, sensory organ, mental activity—there was, to explain vision, a sort of luminous arm like a tentacle, which through the eyes extended one's organism outside itself. By reason of the kinship between the three phenomena, which all consisted equally of a very pure fire giving light without burning, the optical arm combined with the light of day and with the rays emitted by objects. Blending with them, it formed a single body (*sōma*), perfectly continuous and homogeneous, which belonged as a whole both to oneself and to the physical world. Thus one could touch, wherever and however far it might be, the external object by sending out an extensible bridge made of the same matter as the thing that was seen, as the one who was seeing, as the light that enabled sight. One's gaze operated in the world where it found its place like a piece of that world.

Therefore, we are not surprised to read Plotinus, who in the third century A.D. writes that when we perceive any object through sight,

> the object is grasped there where it lies in the direct line of vision; it is there that we attack it [*prosbalomen*]; there,

then, the perception is formed; the mind looks outward; this is ample proof that it has taken and takes no inner imprint, and does not see in virtue of some mark made upon it like that of the ring on the wax; it need not look outward at all if, even as it looked, it already held the image of the object, seeing by virtue of an impression made upon itself. It includes with the object the interval, for it tells at what distance the vision takes place: how could it see as outlying an impression within itself, separated by no interval from itself? Then, the point of magnitude: how could the mind, on this hypothesis, define the external size of the object or perceive that it has any—the magnitude of the sky, for instance, whose stamped imprint would be too vast for it to contain? And, most convincing of all, if to see is to accept imprints of the objects of our vision, we can never see these objects themselves; we see only vestiges they leave within us, shadows: the things themselves would be very different from our vision of them. (*Enneades* 4.6.1.14–32 [MacKenna translation])

Why should we cite this passage in its full length? Because it reveals the distance that separates us from the ancient Greeks insofar as our concepts of sight are concerned. As long as the interpretive field in which their concept of vision is located has not ceded its place to another, completely different one, the issues of visual perception as they are debated in modern times, in particular that of vision at a distance, in which binocularity comes into play, and that of the constancy of the apparent size of objects despite their being separated from each other, which involves multiple factors, will not even have to be raised. Everything is settled from the time our gaze wanders among objects in the world to which it belongs, leading us in its wake into the expanse of the sky. The difficulty in such a situation is not in understanding how it is that we see as we do—in a certain way that goes without saying—but how we can see otherwise than what is, or see the object elsewhere than where it is, for example, in a mirror.

What formula should be chosen to characterize this particular style of being-in-the-world? Undoubtedly the best would be to define it negatively in relation to our own by saying that in it man is not separated from the universe. The Greeks certainly knew that there existed a "human nature," and they readily reflected on the traits that distinguished man from other creatures, inanimate things, beasts, and gods. But recognizing his singularity did not cut man off from the world; it did not lead him to establish, in the face of the entire universe, a realm of reality irreducible to any other and that his form of existence radically pushed into the margins: man and his mind as a world in themselves, entirely separate from everything else.

Bernard Groethuysen wrote that the ancient wise man never forgot the world, that he thought and acted in relation to the cosmos, that he was a part of the world, that he was "cosmic" (*Anthropologie philosophique* [Paris, 1952], p. 80). One might say of the Greek individual that, in a less reflective and theoretical way, he, too, was spontaneously cosmic.

Cosmic did not mean lost, drowning in the universe; however, that human subject's involvement in the world implied a particular form of relationship to himself and to others. The maxim of Delphi, "Know thyself," did not praise, as we might have a tendency to assume, a turning to oneself to attain, through introspection and self-analysis, a hidden "I," invisible to all others, that would be set forth as a pure act of thought or as the secret realm of personal intimacy. The Cartesian *cogito,* the "I think therefore I am," was no less foreign to the knowledge Greek man had of himself than it was to his experience of the world. Neither one was obtained in the interiority of his subjective consciousness. For the oracle, "Know thyself" meant: learn your limits; know that you are a mortal man; do not attempt to be the gods' equal. Even for Plato's Socrates, who reinterprets the traditional formula and gives it a new philosophical significance by saying, "Know what you truly are, what in you is yourself, that is, your soul, your *psychē*"—this in no way intended to urge his listeners to turn their gaze inward to discover themselves inside their "I." If there was an incontestable fact, it was that the eye could not see itself: it always had to direct its rays toward an object located outside it. Likewise, man could never contemplate himself the visible sign of his identity, the face he offered to the gazes of all in order for them to recognize him, except by seeking in the eyes of others the mirror that externally reflects one's own image. Let us read Socrates' dialogue with Alcibiades:

> Have you observed that the face of the person who looks into another's eye is shown in the optic confronting him, as in a mirror, and we call this the pupil, for in a sort it is an image of the person looking?—That is true.—Then an eye viewing another eye, and looking at the most perfect

part of it, the thing wherewith it sees, will thus see it-self. . . . And if the soul, too, my dear Alcibiades, is to know herself, she must surely look at a soul and especially at that region of it in which occurs the virtue of a soul—wisdom, and at any other part of a soul which resembles this. (*Alcibiades* 1.133a–b [Lamb translation])

What were those objects similar to wisdom? Intelligible forms, mathematical truths, or even—according to the undoubtedly inter-polated passage that Eusebius mentions in his *Praeparatio evangelica,* immediately following the text we have just cited—God, for "he is the best mirror of human things for whoever wishes to judge the quality of one's soul, and it is in him that we can best see and know ourselves." But whatever these objects may have been—the soul of others, intelligible essences, God—it was always by looking, not within one's soul, but outside it, at another being related to it, that one's soul could know itself the way the eye could see an external lighted object owing to the natural affinity between the gaze and the light, the complete similitude between the one who saw and that which was seen. Thus, what one was, one's face and soul, could be seen and known only by looking at the eye and the soul of another. Each person's identity was revealed through his relationship with oth-ers, through the intersecting of gazes and the exchanging of words.

Here, again, as in his theory of vision, Plato proves to be a good source. Even if, by placing the soul at the center of his notion of the identity of each person, he marked a turning point whose conse-quences were ultimately decisive, he did not step outside the frame-work in which the Greek representation of the individual was in-scribed. First, because that soul, which was us, did not convey the uniqueness of our being, its fundamental originality, and conversely, as a *daimon,* it was impersonal or suprapersonal—being in us, it was beyond us, its function not to ensure our uniqueness as human be-ings, but to liberate us from that concept by integrating us into the cosmic and divine order. Next, because self-knowledge and a rela-tionship to oneself could not always be directly, immediately, estab-lished, because they remained caught in that reciprocity of seeing and of being seen, of the self and of the other, that forms a characteristic trait of cultures of shame and honor as opposed to cultures of blame and duty—shame and honor, instead of feelings of guilt and obliga-tion, which necessarily, in a moral subject, relate to his intimate per-sonal consciousness. In this regard, there is a Greek word that should be taken into consideration: *timē*. It denotes the "worth" attributed to an individual, that is, both the social markings of his identity (his name, his lineage, his origins, his status within the group along with the honors connected to it, the privileges and respect that he may rightfully expect) and his personal excellence, all of his qualities and merits (beauty, strength, courage, nobility of behavior, self-mastery) that on his face, in his demeanor, his bearing, indicate to everyone his adherence to the elite group of *kaloikagathoi,* the beautiful-and-good, the *aristoi,* the excellent ones.

In a face-to-face society where to be recognized one had to surpass one's rivals in constant competition for glory, each person was placed under the gaze of others; each person existed because of that gaze. One was what the others saw in one. The identity of an individual coincided with his social evaluation: from derision to praise, from scorn to admiration. If a man's worth remained thus connected to his reputation, any public attack on his dignity, any act or word that cast aspersions on his status, was felt by the victim, as long as it was not openly recanted or made right, as a disparagment or annihilation of his very being, his intimate virtue, and as a way of bringing about his fall from grace. Dishonored, he who was unable to make his offender pay for his insult lost face, he gave up his *timē,* his renown, his rank, his privileges. Cut off from ancient solidarities, from his peers, what remained of him? Having fallen below the vile, below the *kakos,* which itself still had a place in the ranks of the people, he found himself, according to Achilles, who was offended by Agamemnon, a wanderer, without a country or roots, a despicable exile, a man of nothing, to quote the words of the hero (*Iliad* 9.648 and 1.293). To-day we would say, That man no longer exists; he no longer has an identity.

On this point, there is an issue that seems to insist on being raised. Even in democratic Athens of the fifth century, the aristocratic values of competition for glory remained dominant. Rivalries were pursued between citizens who on a political level were considered to be equals. But they were not equals as holders of the rights that every man was naturally believed to possess. Every person was equal, the same as everyone else through his full participation in the common affairs of the group. But outside those communal affairs, alongside the public domain, there was a private space in personal behavior and in social relations where the individual was the master of the game. "The freedom which we enjoy in our government," proclaims Pericles in the praise of Athens which Thucydides attributes to him, "extends also to our ordinary life. There, far from exercising a jealous surveillance over each other, we do not feel called upon to be angry with our neighbour for doing what he likes, or even to indulge in those injurious looks which cannot fail to be offensive, although they inflict to positive penalty. But all this ease in our private relations does not make us lawless as citizens. Against this fear is our chief safeguard" (Thucydides 2.37.2–3 [Crawley translation]). Thus, the individual had a place all his own in the ancient city-state, and this private aspect of existence was extended to the intellectual and artistic life, where each person claimed to be certain he was doing things differently and better than his predecessors and neighbors; to criminal law, where each person was accountable for his own misdeeds depending on the greater or lesser degree of his guilt; to civil law, with the institution, for example, of the inheritance by testament; and to the realm of religion, where it was individual worshipers who made entreaties to the divinity. But this individual never appeared either as the embodiment of inalienable universal rights or as a person in the modern sense of the term, with his singular inner life, the secret world of his subjectivity, the fundamental originality of his "me." This was an essentially social form of the individual, marked by a desire to win fame, to gain enough renown in the eyes of his peers through his lifestyle, his merits, his generosity, and his deeds to turn his singular existence into the common good of the entire city, indeed of all Greece. Therefore, when the individual confronted the issue of his own death, he could not fall back on the hope of continuing to live in the other world the way he had in this one, in all his singularity, as a soul unique to him, belonging to him alone, or through his resuscitated body. For those ephemeral creatures, destined to the decrepitude of old age and to death, what means were there to preserve their name, renown, beautiful countenance, youth, virile courage, and excellence in the beyond? In a civilization of honor in which every person throughout his life was identified by what the others saw and said of him, in which he "existed" all the more when the glory that celebrated him was greater, he would continue to exist if that glory remained imperishable instead of disappearing into the anonymity of oblivion. For ancient Greek man, nondeath signified the permanent presence of one who had left the light of the sun in the collective social memory, in the two forms it might assume: continued remembrance through the songs of poets repeated indefinitely from generation to generation, and a memorial structure erected to stand forever on his tomb; the collective memory functioned as an institution ensuring certain individuals the privilege of survival under the heading of a glorious death. Instead of an immortal soul, therefore, there was imperishable glory and the lamenting of everyone forever; in place of a paradise reserved for the just, there was the assurance, for the man who deserved it, of an everlasting remembrance established in the very heart of the society inhabited by the living.

In the epic tradition, the warrior who, like Achilles, chose a brief life and devoted himself entirely to deeds in war, falling in the spring of his youth on the battlefield, ultimately acquired a heroic dimension through a "beautiful death" that would never again be forgotten. The city echoed this theme in particular, as Nicole Loraux has shown, in the funeral oration for the citizens who also chose to die for their country. Mortality and immortality were connected and intertwined, and were embodied in those stout-hearted men; those *agathoi andres,* rather than being in opposition. As early as the seventh century, Tyrtaeus celebrated in his poems the warrior as "the common property of the city and all the people," he who was able to hold firm in the first row of the phalanx. If he fell to the enemy, "young and old mourn him alike and the whole city is prostrated with great lamentations. . . . Never do his noble glory or his name perish, but, even though he remains underground, he is immortal" (9 D.27 f. Prato). At the beginning of the fourth century, Gorgias also found in that paradoxical association of the mortal and the immortal an opportunity to satisfy his taste for antitheses: "Although they are dead, sorrow for their absence is not dead with them; but immortal, although it resides in bodies which are not immortal, that sorrow does not cease to live for those who are no longer alive." In his funeral oration for the Athenian soldiers who fell during the so-called Corinthian War (395–386), Lysias echoes the theme and develops it in a better argued form:

> If it were possible for those who escaped the dangers of warfare to be immortal forever, it would be right for the living to mourn for the dead for all time, but as it is, our nature is subject to both diseases and old age, and the deity who presides over our lot in life is inexorable. So that it behooves us to hold these to be the most fortunate, who, facing dangers for the greatest and the noblest cause, thus ended their lives not entrusting themselves to chance,

nor awaiting a natural death, but choosing the most glorious. And, indeed, their memory does not grow old, and the honors they receive are envied by all men, who are mourned on account of their nature, as mortals, but are praised in song as immortals, on account of their valor. . . . And therefore I praise them happy for this death, and envy them, and I believe that to these alone of men it was a privilege to have been born, who, after they received mortal bodies, yet left behind them undying remembrance through their valor. [Roth translation]

Is this rhetoric? Undoubtedly in part, but certainly not rhetoric alone. The speech finds strength and support in a configuration of identity in which each person appeared inseparable from the social values recognized in him by the community of citizens. In what made him an individual, ancient Greek man remained as integrated into society as he was in the cosmos.

From the freedom of the ancients to that of the moderns, from ancient democracy to that of today, from the citizen of the *polis* to the man of rights, going from Benjamin Constant to Moses Finley and Marx, it is indeed a world that has changed. But it is not simply a transformation of political and social life, of religion, or culture; man has not remained what he once was, no more in his way of being himself than in his relationships with others and with the world.

Notes

1. [The following sources were used for quotations from classical writers: *Select Orations of Lysias*, trans. Edward Roth et al. (Philadelphia, 1899); the International Publications edition of Karl Marx and Frederick Engels, *Collected Works*, vol. 4 (1844–45; New York, 1975); *The Works of Plato*, vol. 2, *The Republic, Timeus, and Critias*, trans. Henry Davis (London, 1900), and *Plato*, vol. 8, trans. W. R. M. Lamb (Cambridge, Mass., 1955); Plotinus, *The Enneads*, trans. Stephen MacKenna, 2d ed. revised by B. S. Page (London, 1956); and the Modern Library edition of the *Complete Writings of Thucydides: The Peloponnesian War*, unabridged Crawley translation, with an Introduction by J. H. Finley, Jr. (New York, 1951)—trans.]

CHAPTER ONE

The Economist

Claude Mossé

IN HIS POLITICS, Aristotle defines Greek man using the well-known term, *zōon politikon,* a political animal.[1] In fact this translation of the term limits the true meaning the philosopher wanted to convey, namely, that what distinguished Greek man from his contemporaries was the fact that he lived within that superior form of human organization—the city-state. And to be a citizen meant precisely that one possessed *aretē politikē,* the quality that enabled one alternately to *archein* and to *archestai,* to govern and to be governed, and to participate in the decision making that involved the entire civic community. *Oikonomikē,* the knowledge of *oikonomia,* was primarily the art of managing well one's *oikos,* one's household. And what we call economics, that is, all phenomena concerning the production and exchange of material goods, had not acquired the autonomy among the ancient Greeks that has distinguished it in the modern world since the eighteenth century. As Karl Polanyi has stressed, economics were still "embedded," integrated within the social and political aspects of ancient Greek society.

This is precisely what makes the historian's task difficult when he attempts to place Greek man in an economic context, and to reveal, from behind the *homo politicus* of the philosophers, *homo economicus,* the man who produced, exchanged, managed, even speculated, with the goal for some of accumulating goods and wealth, and for others of ensuring their daily sustenance. The task is difficult not only because the sources available to us are mostly fragmentary and thus do not enable us to reconstruct a picture of the different economic activities that characterized the world of Greek cities in as much detail as we would like to; but above all because the Greeks did not separate those many diverse activities from the rest of their lives, of which, moreover, they were an integral part, and therefore did not feel the need to describe them. Or rather, they took pains to describe the only activity that, in addition to war and politics, they deemed worthy of a free man, that is, the working of the land. And if, as we shall see, we have more precise information about craftsmen or maritime trade that might shed some light upon what we have inferred from objects found in archaeological digs (pottery shards, coins, etc.), this is because those activities underwent an important development in Athens, primarily in the fourth century, sometimes giving rise to disputes among those who were involved in maritime trade, for example, occasions for public trials, the speeches of which have come down to us.

All of this must indeed be repeated, so paradoxical does it seem a priori: the ancient Greek world was a world of cities, urban life occupied an essential place in it, and yet it was agriculture that constituted the primary activity of most of the members of the civic community. Even in cities such as Athens, Corinth, Miletus, or Syracuse, it was above all the land that ensured each person his livelihood. The Greek world in the archaic and classical periods was first and foremost a world of peasants, which explains the importance throughout history of the agrarian issues and the conflicts that divided cities regarding the issue of landownership. The ideal of autarchy, which fourth-century philosophers would defend in their utopian constructs, was the translation of that reality: Greek man lived foremost off of the fruit of his land, and the proper functioning of the city-state required that all those who were members of the civic community had some land to their name. The connection between land and the citizen was such that not only could landowners alone be citizens in many cities, but it was also true that in all cities only citizens could own land.

However, that land was not exactly fertile, and the Greek world has always been dependent on imports from Egypt, Cyrenaica, or the Euxine (Black Sea) for its supplies of grain. Only certain Peloponnesian cities and western colonial cities produced enough grain to meet their needs. Nevertheless, in addition to the fruits and leguminous plants typical of Mediterranean regions, everywhere one tried to grow a little wheat or barley from out of a relatively mediocre soil. Only grapevines and olive trees provided more abundant harvests, resulting in surpluses that could be exported. But beyond these very general considerations, what sources are available to us in our attempt to sketch a profile of the Greek peasant? A few representations portrayed on vases, a few pieces of pottery enable us to view peasants at work, pushing their plows (simple wooden-jointed swing-plows, with or without metal plowshares), gathering olives, or pressing grapes. Yet these representations provide no precise information on the social status of those who engaged in those activities. For such information we must look to literary sources. Fortunately, for the reasons mentioned above, the life of the peasant inspired at least three of the most famous writers of ancient Greece. First, there is the great poem by Hesiod, the *Works and Days,* a religious calendar that, while revealing the very serious crisis the Greek world was experiencing at the end of the eighth century, a crisis that prefigured the violent struggles that marked the history of the following century, nonetheless describes the daily life of the Boeotian peasant, the friendly or hostile relationships he maintained with his neighbors, and the different activities that gave rhythm to each year. To start, there was the time for farming, when the peasant attached his plow to his oxen and prepared the earth for sowing. Then came the time "when you hear the cry of the crane / going over, that annual / voice from high in the clouds, you should take notice / and make plans. / She brings the signal for the beginning of planting, / the winter / season of rains" [*Works and Days,* lines 448–50, Lattimore translation].

For the peasant, winter was the occasion to repair his tools. At that time men and beasts lived closed up in their houses to escape the blowing of Boreas, the icy north wind from Thrace. But let the thistle flower, let the cicada sing, and those were the joys of summer: "Then is when goats are at their fattest, / when the wine tastes best, / women are most lascivious, but the men's strength / fails them / most, for the star Seirios shrivels them, knees / and heads alike, / and the skin is all dried out in the heat; then / at that season, / one might have the shadow under the rock, / and the wine of [Byblos]; / a curd cake, and all the milk that the goats / can give you, / the meat of a heifer, bred in the woods, / who has never borne a calf, / and of baby kids also" [ibid., lines 585–94]. But one also had to think about bringing in the harvest, then of ordering the slaves "to winnow the sacred yield of Demeter." After this the grain would be put into the bins that were stored in the house, and fodder and hay would be stored for the animals. Then came the time for picking the grapes and making wine, "the gifts of bountiful Dionysus."

Hesiod's poem has often been interpreted as a cry of revolt against "the kings devouring gifts," as the expression of peasant misery in Boeotia at the end of the eighth century. And it is indeed true that there are many allusions in the poem to the poverty and hunger of the farmer who, if he did not work hard and neglected his duties to the gods, had to borrow from his neighbor or was forced to go begging. But the peasant life the poem describes is led on a relatively large property. There are many servants, and the harvest is diverse and carefully stored away. What is more, the person with whom the poet is speaking, either real or imaginary, that so-called brother, has surplus produce, which he loads onto a large ship when the time is right for sailing. Granted, navigation was dangerous, but it was also a source of profit, and whoever undertook it might thus increase his wealth. Throughout the poem, therefore, an image of a relatively well-off peasantry is drawn. It is difficult to know whether that image corresponds to a precisely dated and situated reality, or to an ideal derived from reality in order to construct a representation of peasant life most likely to satisfy the gods.

Three centuries after Hesiod, it is a slightly different image of the peasant that the comic poet Aristophanes presents to us. We are no longer in Boeotia, but in Athens, at the time of the Peloponnesian War, when the countryside was regularly ravaged by incursions of Peloponnesian armies. Aristophanes' peasant is no more poverty-stricken, no more of a *ptōchos* than Hesiod's peasant is. He, too, owns a few slaves, and even though the war forces him to flee to the city to seek shelter inside its walls, he nevertheless misses his village, like Dicaeopolis in the *Acharnians,* who yearns for his "country home, which never told me to 'buy fuel, vinegar, or oil'; there the word 'buy,' which cuts me in two, was unknown; I harvested everything at will" [Athenian Society translation]. As for Strepsiades, who in the *Clouds* makes the mistake of marrying a woman from the city, he longingly evokes his earlier life as a peasant: "I lived so happily in the country, a commonplace, everyday life, but a good and easy one—had not a trouble, not a care, was rich in bees, in sheep, and in olives" [ibid.]. And he remembers the time when he smelled of "the wine-cup, of cheese and of wool," of abundance—an idyllic image of a peasant life that must have been less easy and less prosperous than the comic poet claims, but that nevertheless conveys a reality: the importance of peasants in a city such as Athens, of those *autourgoi,* owners of the land they worked themselves under often difficult conditions, even if they had a few slaves who undertook the hardest work. It was this small and middling landowning peasantry that formed the bulk of the civic population, and it was from among its ranks that the hoplites, upon whom the security of the city depended, were recruited. We must still examine the geographical extension of this type of peasantry, as well as the true amount of time that peasant society existed in the course of Greek history. Athens, of course, once again offers a model for these inquiries: emancipated through Solon's reforms, the peasants of Attica formed the basis for the democracy that was established with Cleisthenes and was strengthened under Ephialtes and Pericles. Of course, many questions remain concerning the distribution of land and the lifestyle of that rural population. The most recent research suggests a massive parcellation of land in Attica, even if that does not necessarily imply the absence of large estates owned by a single individual incorporating scattered properties either within a single deme [an administrative division of ancient Attica and of modern Greece] or across different demes. The few surveys carried out in the Attic countryside do not enable us to reach any conclusions concerning the existence of isolated farms. Houses grouped in a village—generally located in the center of the deme—seem to have been the usual type of agrarian habitation, a pattern that has remained more or less standard around the Mediterranean. The Attic peasantry did not live in complete self-sufficiency, contrary to what is asserted by Dicaeopolis of the *Acharnians*. In another comedy by Aristophanes, the hero, who is also a peasant, sends his slave to buy some flour. What was said above concerning the need to import grain implies that in fact many peasants did not harvest enough wheat to meet their needs and those of their *oikos*—wives, children, and servants.

But Aristophanes' plays, like Thucydides' remarks, demonstrate that the Peloponnesian War, by forcing the peasants to abandon their houses and fields, dealt harsh blows to that small Athenian peasantry. Aristophanes' later comedies, the *Ecclesiazusae* and *Plutus,* are eloquent in this regard. Praxagora, the revolutionary who plans to put power back into the hands of women, justifies making all goods common property, by pointing out those who don't even have a plot of land on which to be buried. And Chremylus, the peasant in *Plutus,* reproaches Poverty for inflicting misery on peasants who no longer have anything but rags to wear and "leaves of withered radish" to eat. However, the misery of peasants in Athens did not give rise to the same type of revolutionary demands, the dividing up of land and the abolishment of debts, that were encountered elsewhere in the Greek world. And today there is no longer very much support for the argument that the Peloponnesian War would have caused a concentration of land in Attica, even if a passage in the *Oeconomicus* reveals that it was possible, like Ischomachus' father, the man with whom Socrates is speaking, to speculate on land bought uncultivated and resold after cultivation.

If, indeed, agriculture was the means by which the small peasant of Attica assured his daily sustenance, for someone who owned more land it could be a true source of income. As was noted earlier, large estates in Attica were most often made up of scattered parcels of land, either within a single deme or across different neighboring demes. Nevertheless, there did exist even larger estates, such as the one Xenophon describes in the *Oeconomicus,* our third source on rural life in Greece, or the one owned by Phaenippus, the landowner whom we know of through a speech of the Demosthenean corpus. Whereas the owner of scattered parcels of land farmed them with reliable slaves who, once the harvest was brought in, paid their master the *apophora* [rent], either in kind or in money, the owner of a vast contiguous estate had to have a team of slave workers headed by a steward, who was usually a slave as well. However, as we learn from a passage of the *Memorabilia,* also by Xenophon, a free man might have been driven, owing to his poverty, to accept that sort of work. The *kaloskagathos* of the *Oeconomicus* is obviously the ideal image of the perfect landowning citizen. And apart from the allusions to his father's speculations, one doesn't see that the proper management of the estate had as its goal any sort of ambition to make a profit by commercializing the harvest of the estate. The grain, wine, and olive harvests were to be stored in Ischomachus' household reserves. All the same, Ischomachus, like Critobulus, the first man Socrates speaks to in the dialogue, was a rich citizen, who had to offer sacrifices to his fellow citizens in the deme, to carry out the *eisphorai* and liturgies [tax obligations], duties that weighed heavily on the richest, implying that part of the harvest of the estate brought in monetary income. The speech against Phaenippus confirms that for a large landowner, agriculture could be a source of considerable income. Phaenippus sold his wood, wheat, and wine, and even profited from the difficulties Athens was having obtaining supplies at the end of the 30s in the fourth century by speculating on the prices of the latter two commodities. That was a new phenomenon, however, perhaps characteristic of the end of the century: we will return to this question.

This Athenian model of a largely dominant landowning peasantry—a commentary by Dionysius of Halicarnassus suggests that only five thousand Athenians out of the twenty-five to thirty thousand citizens of the city at the beginning of the fourth century did not own land—was certainly widespread in a large part of the Greek world. The great movement of colonization that had begun around the middle of the eighth century and was pursued for another two centuries had ended with the creation of new city-states whose *chōra,* or countryside, had been divided up among the colonists, who had often been forced from their city of birth by *stenochōria,* a scarcity of land. The research carried out by archaeologists in southern Italy, Sicily, and Crimea, with the help of aerial photography in particular, has attempted to shed light on the way land was distributed in some of these colonial cities. Later texts, such as the founding decree for the colony of Brea in the Adriatic, or the tale of the founding of Thurii in southern Italy, told by the historian Diodorus Siculus, testify to the importance of the distribution of the land, which was conferred upon special magistrates, geometers and distributors of land. Many problems nevertheless arise from this: did the colonists themselves work their *kleroi,* their allotment, or did they have it worked by more or less servile natives, such as the Cillicyrians of Syracuse, and then sat back to collect the income from it? This is in any event what must have occurred in the Athenian cleruchies, those military colonies set up by the Athenians on the territory of some of their recalcitrant allies. Regarding the colonists who settled in Mytilene on the island of Lesbos, after the surrender of the inhabitants who had attempted to leave the Athenian alliance, Thucydides specifies that "the Lesbians continued to cultivate the land themselves, agreeing to pay the cleruchs a rent of two minae a year for each allotment."

Not only the colonies but cities in general must have been based on a landowning peasantry. Otherwise it would be difficult to understand the importance of the demand for dividing up lands in the struggles that ravaged the cities from the seventh to the fourth century and later. If, as we have seen, thanks to Solon's reforms Athens maintained a relative balance during that entire period, the same was not true elsewhere. The movement that resulted in the flourishing of tyrannies in a large part of the Greek world between the middle of the seventh century and the end of the sixth indeed seems to be connected to the unequal distribution of landed properties, and the *dēmos* on which, according to tradition, most of those tyrants depended was primarily a rural *dēmos*. Moreover, it was not by chance that the theoreticians at the end of the fifth century who conceived of plans for ideal cities were concerned first with the problem of the organization of the *chōra* and of the distribution of land. And Aristotle saw in what a contemporary historian has called "the republic of peasants" the type of city closest to the ideal he envisioned.

But among the cities of the real world, the political theoreticians of the fourth century also cited as an example the one that to them seemed to have the best laws and the best social organization—Sparta. Sparta was also a city of landowners. But these landowners were not peasants. In Laconia and Messenia it was Helots who cultivated the earth, servile peasants whom other Greeks considered slaves of a different type than those they had in their own cities. Of the same origin, speaking the same language, they represented a permanent danger for the Spartans, and their revolts mark the history of the Lacedaemonian city. There are still many things we don't know about them. Specifically, we don't know whether the rent they owed their masters was fixed or proportional to the harvest, nor whether they were isolated on their master's *kleroi* or formed village communities. The Messenians freed themselves from Spartan jurisdiction in the fourth century with the help of the Theban Epaminondas. The Helots of Laconia remained enslaved, with the exception of those who, in the course of the Spartan revolutions of the third century, were freed to provide the reformer kings the soldiers they needed to stand up to the Macedonians and their Achaean allies.

Thus, free or not, Greek man appeared above all as a peasant, cultivating his own land or that of those more powerful than he, or having it farmed by others, but connected in any event to agricultural work, or in the case of the Euboean or Thessalian cities, to raising animals, chiefly horses. The connection between the land and the city was not just an "economic" one. It was also a religious connection, and in most Greek cities, political as well, since not only could citizens alone be landowners, but because often one had to be a landowner to be a citizen.

One can then understand why the craft professions were held in such low esteem. In his *Oeconomicus*, Xenophon has Socrates say:

> [The professions] that are called mechanical (*banausic*, or artisanal) are spoken against everywhere and have quite plausibly come by a very bad reputation in the cities. For

they utterly ruin the bodies of those who work at them
and those who are concerned with them, compelling them
to sit still and remain indoors, or in some cases even to
spend the whole day by a fire. And when the bodies are
made effeminate, the souls too become much more diseased. Lack of leisure to join in the concerns of friends and
of the city is another condition of those that are called mechanical; those who practice them are reputed to be bad
friends as well as bad defenders of their fatherlands. Indeed
in some of the cities, especially those reputed to be good at
war, no citizen is allowed to work at the mechanical arts.
[Lord translation, p. 17]

Was Xenophon, in mentioning that prohibition, referring only to
Sparta, or was he voicing a wish shared by an entire aristocratic intel-
ligentsia in the face of a completely different reality? There is in fact
no doubt that in a certain number of cities there were craftsmen
within the civic community. But it had undoubtedly not always been
thus. In Homeric poems the *dēmiourgoi* appear as specialists who go
from *oikos* to *oikos* to offer their services for payment, which at that
time was obviously in kind. They were thus outside the community
being formed by the nascent city. We must also remember that some
of what we call craftwork was at that time done within the *oikos*. We
need only recall the bed Odysseus fashioned with his own hands, or
Hesiod's directions for making a plow. Thread was spun and cloth
woven at home by the mistress of the house and her servants. However, certain trades would soon become the domain of specialized
craftsmen: primarily metalworking, ceramics, tanning, and in cities
located along the sea, shipbuilding. Then, of course, there was stone-
and marble-cutting when cities began to raise religious or public
monuments and decorate them with bas reliefs and statues.

Once again, it is obviously Athens that provides us with the most
information regarding, on the one hand, the status of craftsmen and,
on the other, the importance of the craft trades. Very early on, Athens
was an important center for the ceramics industry: the large Dipylon
vases are proof of this. But is was during the tyranny of the Peisistratids that an increasingly important crafts industry developed in Athens, one favored by the politics of the tyrants, who undertook a vast
program of public construction, issued the first coins and consequently began to extract systematically the silver deposits from the

mines of Laurium, and finally inaugurated a maritime policy that prefigured the one Themistocles and Pericles adopted in the following century. It is not by chance that in the second half of the sixth century, Attic pottery, first black-figure then red-figure vases, appeared over the entire Mediterranean basin, definitively superseding Corinthian pottery.

How many artisans were there then in Athens, and how did they live? It is difficult to answer such a question. It has been suggested that in the fifth century, when there was the greatest production of red-figure vases, there were no more than four hundred ceramics workers. Earlier we mentioned there were some five thousand citizens who had no land at the beginning of the fourth century. But they were not all necessarily artisans or merchants. Furthermore, many of the artisans were undoubtedly foreigners who came to Athens to exercise their trades, attracted by the advantages offered by a rich and powerful city. Tradition has it, moreover, that Solon had been the instigator of a call for foreign labor. And we must not forget that some of that artisanal labor force was made up of slaves working alongside their masters in workshops or on the sites of public construction projects. The artisanal activities we know most about are those that, in one way or another, were under the control of the city, for example, the construction of public buildings. Indeed, many accounts have come down to us that enable us to follow the organization of work fairly closely. The decision to undertake the construction of a public, religious, or civic building in fact depended on a vote from the citizens' Assembly. A commission of *epistatai* drew up the specifications and concluded a series of individual contracts with the various suppliers, after which the descriptive estimate, of *syngraphē*, was submitted to the Assembly. If it was approved, one or several architects were chosen to be responsible for coordinating the different phases of the project. Thus there were Callicrates and Ictinus for the Parthenon, and only Callicrates for the Long Walls, which connected Athens to Piraeus. These architects received a salary that was scarcely higher than that earned by the skilled workers whom they were responsible for recruiting: stonecutters, sculptors, carpenters, and blacksmiths. This uniformity of salary—salaries were most often fixed as a lump sum for a specific task—making very little distinction not only between the architect and the worker, but also between the citizen or the metic [any resident alien including freed slaves] and the slave, is revealing. It conveys the fact that labor was not seen as a measurable activity and producer of goods, but as a "service." And it is no coincidence that the same term, *misthos,* denoted the salary paid for a public activity, including military service, and productive labor and that the amounts of these different *misthoi* were noticeably similar, varying threefold at most—from three obols for the salary of a judge to one or one and one-half drachmas [that is, six or nine obols] for that of the prytanis or the architect. Inscriptions enable us to measure the respective place of citizens, metics, and slaves among the laborers working on the public construction sites. In 409 B.C. on the construction site of Erechtheion, there were twenty citizens out of the seventy-one contracted workers, and among the workers roughcasting the columns, seven citizens, six metics, and twenty-one slaves. In 329 on the construction site of Eleusis, nine citizens out of twenty-seven contractors and twenty-one citizens out of ninety-four skilled workers. The others were metics or slaves. The latter worked alongside their masters and in principle received the same salary, a part of which was returned to the master. Some of those slaves were undoubtedly public slaves, who received food from the city as compensation.

In contrast, slaves made up the largest portion of the labor force in the mines of Laurium. As we saw earlier, mining had started in very ancient times, but its true expansion began around the middle of the sixth century, when Athens began to stamp the coins that would become the most valued in the Aegean world. From the fifth century, with the discovery of the rich deposits on Maronea, the mining industry underwent rapid development, which did not stop until the final years of the Peloponnesian War, when the Spartan occupation of the fortress of Decelea incited the flight of the twenty thousand slaves who had been working in the mines and in the workshops above ground. Mining resumed with some vigor only in the middle of the fourth century, and it is also for that period that we know the most about how the mines functioned. Mines were in fact owned by the state, which rented them out to certain individuals. At least this is what we can infer from inscriptions, almost all of which date from the third quarter of the fourth century and provide the accounts of *poletai,* magistrates responsible for the allocation of mining concessions. Some scholars also believe that there were mines owned by individuals, but there is very little proof of this. On the other hand, a recent study has shown that concessionaires were often men whose inherited property was located in demes near the mining district.

Much remains unknown, nevertheless, about the nature of the rent paid by the concessionaires and the frequency of payments. But it seems almost certain that mining was a source of real profit for the concessionaires, especially since the rent they paid in general seems to have been quite reasonable. Of the seventy-six mining rents known through inscriptions, twenty-two were 20 drachmas, and thirty were 150 drachmas. And Demosthenes mentions a concession that included three separate groups whose total worth reached 3 talents. But the interpretation of his text is doubtful. In his *On Revenues,* Xenophon cities the example of three rich Athenians, Nicias, Hipponicus, and Philemonides, who earned appreciable income from renting out slave miners. Nicias was the famous politician and strategist of the Peloponnesian War, who died during the Sicilian expedition. In the fourth century his descendants appear among the mining concessionaires, which suggests that he did not simply rent out his slave workforce, but also held interests in the working of the mines themselves. Hipponicus, the son of Callias, belonged to one of the richest families in Athens. In the fourth century one of his descendants owned properties in Besa, in the mining district. The lists of concessionaires, as well as orators' speeches, indicate that most of those who held interests in the mines belonged to what the English historian John K. Davies has called the "Athenian propertied families." Even the man who gave the speech *Against Phaenippus,* who complains of the misfortunes of the time, admits having made a fortune by working a mining concession in Laurium. And the rich Meidias, the enemy of Demosthenes, also derived part of his income from mining, since the orator accuses him of having put his trierarchy to profit to obtain gallery wood for silver mines.

But the mining industry did not just involve the extraction of ores. Excavations carried out in the mining district, in particular in the region of Thoricus, have brought to light the presence of treatment workshops above ground. These shops might have been owned by the concessionaire, but they might also have belonged to others. A speech from the Demosthenean corpus, *Against Pantaenetus,* concerns a *dikē metallikē,* a mining lawsuit brought against a certain Pantaenetus who had come forward as the acquirer of a mine and works in Maronea and of thirty slaves for the sum of 10,500 drachmas. It is not clear whether Pantaenetus had also been a concessionaire: he had his slaves treat the ore extracted by others. One can assume with some likelihood that whoever owned the workshops generally also owned the connected land. This explains why the mining industry was the concern of citizens alone, and most often of well-to-do citizens. A speech by Hyperides, *For Euxenippus*, mentions the fortunes made by certain mining concessionaires: 60 talents for a certain Euthycrates, 300 talents for Epicrates of Pallene and his associates, who were among the richest men (*plousiotatoi*) of the city. The confiscation of the fortune of Diphilus, who had become rich by extracting from the silver mines piles of ore reserved as supports, brought the city 160 talents. These considerable sums confirm that in the second half of the fourth century silver mining had become increasingly active, and that the workers and concessionaires earned substantial income from it. Let us note once again, however, that those considerable fortunes only occurred at a time in Athen's history when the city was prey to difficulties of all kinds. This is an issue to which we shall return.

If the mining industry and the processing of ore involved both the city, through the control it exercised and the taxes it levied, and the richest among the citizens, the same was not true for other artisanal activities we have learned about through our sources. Shipbuilding was certainly also strictly controlled by the city, insofar as each year the Council chose the *triēropoioi* responsible for putting such construction to public bidding. But the shipyards themselves were undoubtedly scattered, and the labor force made up of small free craftsmen and slaves. The weapons industry was an ancient one that required those involved to expend a large investment in raw materials and labor. Citizens and metics worked together here, if one may judge by the few indications provided by our sources. Thus the metic Cephalus, the father of the orator Lysias, who settled in Athens at the instigation of Pericles, owned a workshop of 120 slaves. When at the time of the Thirty Tyrants the agents of the oligarchs arrested his sons, they found in the house, in addition to the 120 slaves, 700 shields and gold, silver, copper, and gems. At the beginning of the fourth century, Demosthenes' father owned a knife-making workshop employing 30 slaves, which each year earned an income of 3,000 drachmas. Here, too, Demosthenes mentions in his father's estate the presence of ivory and iron, the raw materials used in that industry. Another well-known manufacturer of weapons was the banker and former slave Pasion, who had left in his will a shield-making workshop. The weapons industry was perhaps not as diversified as Aristophanes claims when, in his *Peace,* he presents helmet, aigrette, sword, and pike makers. It is nevertheless true that in this industry, which was particularly important for the defense of the city, there was a rather advanced degree of specialization: Cephalus and Pasion made only shields, Demosthenes' father made sharp weapons, a certain Pistias, mentioned by Xenophon in the *Memorabilia*, was known for the quality of his armor. Whether citizens or metics, those who engaged in the manufacture of weapons were rich men. These rich men were not themselves workers: they simply supervised the work of their slaves or, most often, like the large estate owners, passed that supervision on to a steward, who was himself a slave or a freedman. Thus Aphobus, who was hired by Demosthenes' father to manage the weapons workshop, which had been reduced after the sale of half the slaves that worked in it, managed it for a certain time, then passed it on to a freedman, Mylias, and finally to the other overseer, Therippides. One might assume that Pistias, the armor maker mentioned by Xenophon, supervised his workshop himself and controlled the quality of the articles that came out of it. Furthermore, these "workshops" were not just places for manufacturing. Generally located in the home of the owner, they were also stores where the articles were sold. We can then understand why Xenophon included in his scornful assessment of the banausic professions the workers who exercised them and those who supervised the workers. Although the owner of the workshop of metalworking slaves was an income-earning property owner in the same right as the owner of landed property, he was nevertheless included in the same social category as the small craftsman who worked with his hands. Aristotle, who refused to grant the artisan the status of citizen in the ideal city, admitted, however, that there might be artisan citizens in an oligarchical city, since there were rich men among them. And the orator for whom Lysias composed the speech against the proposition of Phormisius asserts that among the five thousand citizens who would have been denied citizenship because they did not own land, there were a number of rich men. We know, moreover, that some of those rich *banausoi,* manual workers or artisans, attained positions of leadership in the city during the last third of the fifth century, attracting the sarcasm of Aristophanes. The tanners Cleon and Anytus, the potter Hyperbolus, were quite obviously not manual workers. Like the earlier-mentioned metalworkers, they merely supervised, or more likely collected the income from their workshops filled with slaves.

We must, however, refrain from viewing the Athenian crafts industry as something reserved for slaves working for wealthy free men. Many free craftsmen in fact worked with their hands, in the shops that surrounded the agora or in the Cerameicus workshops. Although tanners were generally rich men, having the raw leather worked by their slaves, the shoemakers on the other hand were small craftsmen, working on demand, such as the shoemaker figured on a vase painting, measuring the sandal he has just completed on the foot of his client. The potters who clustered in the northwest of the agora were also small artisans. A few figured representations enable us to imagine what those small workshops were like. The potter himself worked at the wheel while his slaves worked the clay, prepared the enamel and glazing, put the vases into the kiln, and watched over the firing. There were undoubtedly kilns shared by several workshops. The potter and the painter were free men who signed their work. There were surely foreigners among them, and the profession of potter or of vase painter was scarcely more valued than were the other craft trades: thus Demosthenes hurls at his adversary Aeschines, as a sign of his low birth, the fact that his brother exercised that trade. It would obviously be impossible to list all the many small trades that existed in a city like Athens. Small trades exercised by poor citizens, metics, or slaves, such as the perfume maker who had a shop in the agora who is the subject of the speech by Hyperides, *Against Athenogenes*. It was difficult to tell the free men from the slaves, since as the anonymous author of the *Athenian Republic* notes, they were all dressed the same. Did the citizens among them find the time to "be involved with the city and their friends," to repeat Xenophon's formula? Historians differ on this point. One must, however, admit that small tradesmen did participate in the life of the city, at least as members of the Assembly, otherwise one could not understand the criticism of the adversaries of democracy nor this remark by Socrates to the young Charmides, who hesitated to take the floor before the Assembly: "Who are those people who intimidate you? Fullers, cobblers, carpenters, blacksmiths, farmers, merchants, traders who think only of selling at a high price what they bought at a low one; for they are the men who make up the Assembly of the people." One notes that in this list peasants are submerged amid a crowd of artisans and merchants. And we may recall that Aristotle preferred peasant democracy because, burdened by their daily work, farmers attended assemblies less often.

In the philosopher's mind, this peasant democracy was quite obviously unlike Athenian democracy, even though, when he generalizes on radical democracy, Aristotle does not cite Athens in particular. Can we do the same, that is, apply the Athenian model to other cities such as Corinth, Megara, Miletus, or Syracuse? Archaeological sources suggest the existence of much artisanal activity in many maritime cities. But we are most often forced to admit our ignorance concerning the structure of those activities, and the social status of the people who engaged in them. We know that Corinth exported vases, that Syracuse was renown for the quality of its coins, and Miletus for that of its fine fabrics. One may therefore assume there existed in those cities and in a few others a craft industry comparable to that of Athens. But we lack the information that literary sources and inscriptions have provided for the latter city. Only public constructions are somewhat better known owing to inscriptions. They reveal the working conditions on all the large work sites, conditions analogous to those found in Athens on the sites of the Acropolis or of Eleusis. This is not surprising if one considers that often work teams, and even individual artists, traveled from one site to another: for example, there was Phidias, working at Olympia, or the travels of Praxiteles in the fourth century.

Greek man was therefore also a craftsman. And as such he enjoyed, as Pierre Vidal-Naquet has pointed out so well, an ambiguous status. The holder of a *technē,* he was thus indispensable for liberating men from the constraints of nature. But because he isolated himself to do it, he could not reach the superior *technē,* which was *technē politikē.* Protagoras alone granted that everyone could possess the knowledge of politics. But we must not forget that the theory the philosopher of Abdera was developing was the one upon which democracy was established, that democracy within which, as Xenophon's Socrates repeated, craftsmen and merchants shared the power to make decisions with the peasants at the time of the assemblies.

This leads us to the third aspect of the economic activity of ancient Greek man: trade. It is the one upon which debates among moderns have been the loudest, also the one about which our knowledge has not ceased to grow, owing to the progress of research, particularly in archaeology. The vast distribution of ceramics testifies to the fact that very early on there were commercial exchanges in the Greek world. In the Mycenaean era, vases manufactured on the Hellenic continent reached southern Italy and the Orient. The collapse of the Mycenaean palaces put an end to such trade, and when merchants are mentioned in Homeric poems, they are usually Phoenicians or even those mysterious Taphians who appear in the *Odyssey*. In the world of heros, as Moses Finley reminds us, exchanges primarily emerged from the practices of gift giving and of counter–gift giving, and trade in the strict sense remained foreign to it. But in his *Works* Hesiod mentions the voyages of his father, forced through necessity to take to the sea on a "black vessel" to seek uncertain profit, ending up in Accra. The poet presents trade (*emporia*) as a remedy to escape "debts and bitter hunger," as a last resort that could, however, earn one profit (*kerdos*), provided one took care to sail only during the fifty days in the middle of summer when the sea was not too dangerous. It is therefore obvious that in the eighth century the Greeks participated in the awakening of trade in the Mediterranean. Of course, we must mention here what is traditionally called colonization, that swarming of Greeks onto the northern and eastern shores of the Mediterranean. It serves little purpose to return to the misguided issue of the commercial or agrarian origin of those "colonies." We have already mentioned the *stenochōria,* the lack of land that compelled some of the members of the civic community to take to the seas in search of new lands. But apart from the fact that those expeditions, which were often organized by the city with the consent and the advice of the Delphic clergy, assumed a minimal knowledge of maritime matters, the commercial dimension must have been a factor. On the one hand, the expeditions often involved obtaining certain raw materials that the Greeks had in short supply, primarily iron and tin. On the other hand, the settling of Greeks in southern Italy, on the shores of Gaul or Spain, in Egypt or Syria, on the shores of the Euxine, could not help but encourage the development of trade, although not necessarily between mother and daughter cities. The excavations that have been done by archaeologists in Pithecussae (Ischia) have shown the importance of metalworking establishments where the ore undoubtedly imported from Etruria was refined. The founding of Marseille at the dawn of the sixth century on a site that evidently did not provide access to rich cultivatable lands, but appeared as the natural outlet of the Gallic rivers by which the tin from the mysterious Cassiterides islands arrived, is significant from this point of view. Equally significant was the installation, in the seventh century, of a Greek commercial base in Naucratis, in Egypt, where the merchants from Greece or from the Greek cities of Asia Minor could obtain wheat from the valley of the Nile in order to resell it to Aegean cities.

If, therefore, the existence of Greek maritime trade in the archaic period cannot be contested, two important problems regarding it are nevertheless raised: who organized it, and what role did money play or would it play in that trade? The first question has given rise to often contradictory responses. According to some, and the example of Hesiod's father cited above might be an illustration of this, only marginal types engaged in trade, peasants overwhelmed by debts, youngest sons excluded from the family inheritance, who, unable to make a living from the harvest of a land holding, took to the seas, with the hope of making a profit, by selling high what they had obtained at a low price. According to others, however—and here, too, Hesiod might be called upon, when he invited Perses to go to sea to sell the surplus of his harvest—engagement in trade implied on the one hand the possession of a ship, and on the other, a cargo of goods to exchange. The first "traders" could therefore only be those who held some power in the cities, people who lived both from the income of their land and from the profit assured them by the possibility of having any surplus. One can cite the brother of the poet Sappho who sailed independently and frequented the entrepôt in Naucratis, or those Phocaeans who traded by using fast penteconters that took them as far as the shores of Iberia. In certain coastal cities of Asia Minor, in Miletus, Halicarnassus, Phocaea, in certain islands of the Aegean such as Samos, Chios, or Aegina, there must thus have existed a merchant aristocracy that evolved from the aristocracy of landowners, but who were more adventurous, and more interested in making money by taking to the seas.

It is perhaps unnecessary to choose between these two images of the Greek merchant in the archaic period. Although we must point out that at that time trade was still largely the domain of adventurers, it could also have been practiced by rich and powerful property owners as well as by marginal types forced by necessity. Because sailing remained subject to the caprices of winds and storms, trade could be the source of profit as well as the cause of ruin for those who engaged in it. The story told by Herodotus of the Samian Colaeus, who was turned away by a storm from Egypt where he was undoubtedly going to get some wheat, running aground on the shores of Andalusia after an unbelievable journey, is perhaps fictional, but it conveys well the dangers of that adventurous trade, its uncertainties, and the extremely diverse status of those who engaged in it.

One then notes, regarding the second question raised above about the place of currency in commercial exchanges, that it is impossible to provide a definitive response. We know that the question of the origin of money has been the subject of many debates among the moderns, in particular stemming from two texts by Aristotle. The first, in book I of the *Politics,* expressly links the invention of money to the necessities of trade: "For a convenient place from whence to import what you wanted, or to export what you had a surplus of, being often at a great distance, money necessarily made its way into commerce" [Ellis translation, 1.1257a]. In contrast, the second text, from book 5 of *Nicomachean Ethics,* emphasizes money as an instrument for measuring and placing a value on the goods exchanged, an indispensable tool for maintaining equality in reciprocal relationships within the civic community. Granted, it is still a matter of exchanges, Aristotle citing as an example the relationship that was established between an architect and a shoesmith, but we see well that that particular exchange has only a small connection with the development of maritime trade. If one holds to the facts, one notes that the first coins appeared in the Greek world only at the end of the seventh century, that is, more than a century after the awakening of commercial exchanges in the Mediterranean. Moreover, the study of monetary treasures has shown that the circulation of coins, at least until the fifth century—and again we are dealing primarily with Athenian coins—remained relatively limited, beyond the place they were issued. Without denying that money played an important role in trade, especially beginning in the classical period, today emphasis is placed on its other functions, fiscal and military, (much money was issued in order to pay the salaries of mercenary armies), and also political, insofar as money was the symbol of independence and a civic emblem. All the same, if money was not invented to respond to the needs of trade, over the years it nevertheless became the privileged instrument of trade. And this is evident from what we know about Athenian trade in the classical period, owing in particular to speeches of the Demosthenean corpus, but also to a few literary texts that in this context insist upon the predominance of Athens, toward which we must once again turn.

Athenian trade developed starting in the sixth century. Solon is traditionally believed to be responsible for a reform in weights and measures and for the adoption of a new monetary standard. We know today that the first Athenian coins, stamped on the back with the

Laureot Owl, go back no farther than the second half of the sixth century. It was at that same time that the diffusion of black-figure vases made in the Cerameicus workshops was at its height, and that under the influence of the Peisistratids Athens began to turn toward the Euxine and the Straits to ensure the replenishment of grain stocks for the city whose population was increasing. In the fifth century, the construction of a port to be used in wartime, but also for trade in Piraeus, the development of a powerful navy, also the domination that, following the Persian Wars, Athens exercised over the Aegean cities, contributed in making Piraeus a sort of hub of trade in the Mediterranean. "We see arriving toward us," Thucydides has Pericles say, "thanks to the size of our city, all products from all over the earth, and the goods provided by our land are no longer only ours to enjoy any more than are those from the rest of the world." The anonymous author of the oligarchic pamphlet known by the name of the *Athenian Republic* echos that idea: "The Athenians alone are able to gather together the wealth of the Greeks and the barbarians. If a state is rich in wood needed to build ships, where would it sell it if it did not get along with the nation that is master of the sea? And if a city is rich in iron, copper, or linen, where would it sell them if it did not get along with the master of the sea? Now it is from those very materials that I build my ships. From one country I obtain wood, from another copper; another provides me with linen, another wax." Three quarters of a century later Xenophon repeats the same thing in *On Revenues:*

> At this point I propose to offer some remarks in proof of the attractions and advantages of Athens as a centre of commercial enterprise. In the first place, it will hardly be denied that we possess the finest and safest harbourage for shipping, where vessels of all sorts can come to moorings and be laid up in absolute security as far as stress of weather is concerned. But further than that, in most states the trader is under the necessity of loading his vessel with some merchandise or other in exchange for his cargo, since the current coin has no circulation beyond the frontier. But at Athens he has a choice: he can either in return for his wares export a variety of goods, such as human beings seek after, or, if he does not desire to take goods in exchange for goods, he has simply to export silver, and he cannot

have a more excellent freight to export, since wherever he
likes to sell it he may look to realise a large percentage on
his capital." ([Dakyns translation, p. 331]

As we can see, not only does Xenophon underscore the centrality of
Athens and of its port in Mediterranean trade, as well as the advantages of its geographic position (it is "accessible to every wind that
blows, and can invite to its bosom or waft from its shore all products"), but in addition he links Athens' commercial preeminence to
the value of its currency.

We can imagine what goods were in fact traded. Included among
the imports, as we have already mentioned, was the grain that was
indispensable for feeding the population, since local production of
grain was only partially sufficient. Wheat came from Egypt and Sicily, but primarily from the northern regions of the Black Sea. According to an assertion made by Demosthenes, more than half of the
wheat imported originated in the Euxine, and the honorary decrees
made to the local petty kings indicate that the merchants from Athens
benefited from particularly favorable conditions there. Athens also
imported wood for shipbuilding, wood that for the most part came
from northern Greece and from Macedonia. Andocides, during his
years in exile following his sentencing for having participated in the
plot to mutilate the herms, became involved in the trading of wood
for construction, and Demosthenes accused Meidias of having put his
trierarchy to profit for importing wood to build retaining walls in the
silver mines of Laurium.

The third most important import was slaves, who for the most part
came from the eastern regions, Caria, Cilicia, the Pontic areas, and
also from the north of the Aegean, from Thrace in particular. As we
have seen, Athens also needed to import iron and copper. In addition,
the merchants who unloaded their cargo of necessities in Piraeus also
unloaded luxury items such as fine fabrics, perfumes, spices, wines,
etc. In exchange, not only did Athens reexport to the rest of the Aegean world part of the merchandise that came into Piraeus, but it also
exported wine, oil, marble, and above all, as Xenophon stressed in
the passage cited above, coined money. It is important to make clear
that the problem of what today we call the balance of foreign trade
was not an issue, and that exporting coined money was not a sign of
a trade deficit. The city, moreover, only intervened to regulate traffic
coming into and leaving the port, to oversee the honesty of transac-

tions and to levy the taxes that were imposed on all merchandise that entered or left. Only the trading of wheat was the object of controls to which certain texts allude, as is confirmed by the existence of special officials posted for the surveillance of that trade, the *sitophylakai*. Yet these controls, which were imposed to ensure an adequate supply for the city and to discourage the speculation in which certain merchants could be involved in times of difficulty, were perhaps not truly effective until after the fourth century, when Athens had lost some of its strength in the Aegean.

If we seek to understand the world of merchants, the world of the *emporion*, we must rid ourselves of many preconceived notions. The Athenian merchant was neither a rich importer nor a humble metic. Citizens and foreigners rubbed elbows on the docks of Piraeus and in the Great Hall where the merchandise was put on display. At the top of the social scale, we find those rich citizens who made "bottomry loans" but who most often remained uninvolved in the transaction itself, intervening only if it went badly for them, or if they were denied the high interest brought in by maritime loans. Some also owned mines or workshops, Demosthenes' father, for example, politicians like Demosthenes himself, or former merchants retired from business, such as the man who made the speech Lysias prepared, *Against Diogiton*. Often the transaction was negotiated through the intervention of a banker, who drew up the contract, the *syngraphē*, which connected the lender and his debtor or debtors, and which was presented before the court in the event of a dispute. The true merchants, the *emporoi*, were either citizens, foreigners passing through, or permanent residents. In general, they were people of relatively modest means, forced to go into debt in order to buy a shipment, with the hope that the profit they might make would enable them, once their debt and the interest had been paid off, to save enough to go back to sea with a new cargo. Indeed, most of these *emporoi* themselves went to sea. Only the richest could entrust their cargo to an employee, usually a slave, and remain on land. Some *emporoi* owned their own ships. But most had to pay their passage and that of their cargo on a ship owned by a fitter, a *naukleros,* who most often got together with several merchants for a trip to Pontus or Sicily. The speeches of the Demosthenean corpus thus bring back to life a whole world of merchants, of shipowners, of more or less honest agents, ready to hire their services to one man or another. The difficulties of navigation, the risks of being shipwrecked or of pirate attacks made these maritime undertakings quite hazardous. Eventually, a law was enacted that provided the lender guarantees in the form of a mortgage on the ship or the cargo. But in the case of shipwreck, the lender lost all his rights and the debtor was freed of his debts. This gave rise to fraudulent shipwrecks, occasions for trials where it is difficult to know, by reading the speeches alone, which side was telling the truth. These trials, from the middle of the fourth century, were subject to an accelerated procedure before the tribunal presided over by the thesmothetes [one of the six ancient Athenian junior archons, or magistrates], and—a fact characteristic of the importance of maritime trade—foreigners and even slaves, who were often used as commercial agents, could bring a suit without using a "patron" citizen as an intermediary. Nevertheless, foreigners were always viewed by their partners with a certain distrust, and without going so far as to suggest xenophobia, it was not uncommon to hear a citizen throw his adversary's place of birth at him as an insult before the tribunals. We must also note that these associations between lenders, *emporoi*, and *naukleroi* were most often ephemeral, created for the duration of a round-trip journey to Pontus or Sicily, Egypt or Marseille. We must therefore once and for all reject the notion of a merchant class controlling Athenian trade. What was the situation elsewhere? We are forced to admit our almost complete ignorance here. But we may assume that in the large maritime cities there were analogous forms of merchant activity in which the city itself was not involved, even though in every port taxes were imposed on incoming and outgoing ships and cargo. Likewise, it is impossible to assess, even approximately, the volume of goods traded, which must have varied significantly, moreover, from one year to the next. Finally, we must not forget that, even at the end of the fourth century, a good deal of commodity exchange was informal and not part of commerce properly speaking. This was true of exchanges on the local level, but it was even true of long-distance exchanges.

We have not yet mentioned the role of bankers within this world of the *emporion*. Rather, we have seen that the banker sometimes acted as an intermediary between the lender and the merchant, in particular holding the contract that fixed the terms of the loan. In fact the word "bank," by which we are translating the Greek term *trapeza*, must not be taken in the wrong sense. In the world of the Greek city-states, bankers did not play the role played by a modern bank, that is, of a credit establishment able to finance productive investments. The banker's table was primarily one for changing money, where the foreign merchant passing through a port could obtain local currency and obtain an assessment of the foreign money he brought with him. However, undoubtedly from the end of the fifth century, and at least in Athens, bankers also received money on deposit, which they gave back to their clients if the latter wished to advance a loan—and not only for commercial purpose—but which, it appears, the bankers themselves could not put to work. This role of intermediary and moneychanger undoubtedly enabled those who performed it to make substantial profits, but it did not make them "influential men," to repeat a formula recently applied to a banker in the last century. Thus the bankers whose names we know through our sources are found for the most part to have been former slaves. The best known of these slave bankers, the famous Pasion, was surely a man of means. But it is significant that, once freed, and having become a citizen under circumstances about which we know very little, he used part of his fortune to purchase land. This allowed his son Apollodorus to play the gentleman farmer, leaving the management of the bank to a former slave, Phormion, and preferring to the profits that he could make by exchange transactions the heavy expenditures expected of one who wanted a political career.

Before leaving the world of trade, there are a few things left to say about local exchanges. Given the nature of the Greek landscape and the difficulty of the terrain, overland trade was relatively limited. It was always easier to load cargo onto ships, even for a short distance, and to take a sea route. Trade may have been rare from city to city, but within the boundaries of a city-state there was frequent exchange between the countryside and the city. Peasants from the *chōra* came to the town to sell any surplus they might have had in order to buy what only the urban craftsmen could provide them. Thus Aristophanes made fun of the mother of the poet Euripides, who came to the marketplace to sell the parsley from her garden. But alongside the small peasants who traveled to the market, or who sent their wives or slaves there, there were also professional merchants at the agora, those *kapēloi* at whom the comedies of Aristophanes poke fun and who obviously came from among the poorest ranks of the population. Here, too, citizens and foreigners, the latter most often being metics who had settled permanently in Athens, worked side by side; and if we continue to believe Aristophanes, there were also women *kapēloi,* sellers of ribbon, perfume, flowers, and so on. Often these women were forced, like the mother of a speaker in the Demosthenean corpus, to engage in activities considered unworthy of a free woman, out of poverty or owing to the absence of a husband who was kept far away by a war.

This portrayal of the economic activities of Greek man, already limited for the most part to the example of Athens, would be incomplete if we did not mention in conclusion an activity that fell neither in the category of crafts nor of trade—fishing. Unfortunately, we do not know very much about these humble people, who must, however, have been numerous in a land surrounded in all directions by the sea. We know only that there were large fishing grounds in certain parts of the Greek world, such as the region of the Euxine, which supplied large quantities of dried fish. We know nothing of the organization of fishing, about which we can only assume that everywhere it was a small-scale and individual activity.

This quick review of the economic activities of Greek man thus confirms the validity of the model proposed by the great English historian Moses Finley in his book the *Ancient Economy*. However, we must now question the permanence of that model. Indeed, on several occasions it has appeared that the fourth century, often presented as a century of crisis and decline—which indeed it was on a political level, for cities such as Sparta or Athens—demonstrated, if not true transformations in various aspects of economic life, at least a more effective appreciation of the problems raised by the production and exchange of goods. We have already mentioned certain treatises by Xenophon, such as the *Oeconomicus* or *On Revenues,* to which one may add the second book of the *Economics* attributed to Aristotle. Granted, the first of these treatises, which is presented in the form of a Socratic dialogue, is primarily a manual of advice aimed at the perfectly honest man. But the concern with organizing the administration of the estate in a rational way, by having slaves specialize in specific tasks, conveys a new mentality, the desire to produce more and better-quality goods. Similarly, if the treatise *On Revenues* has as its final goal the utopian dream of ensuring each Athenian his daily triobol, by renting a number of slaves three times the number of citizens at an average rate of one obol per man per day, it nevertheless remains that a development of mines was proposed, primarily by the city itself, that would increase the production of silver, the volume of which, as Xenophon notes, could be endlessly increased. It is in this regard, moreover, that he provides us with information that certainly comes out of simple good sense, but that nonetheless conveys a true and new perception of economic facts. Proposing to increase the number of slaves working in the mines, and consequently the amount of metal extracted, he notes:

> There is no analogy between this and other industries. With an increase in the number of bronze-workers articles of bronze may become so cheap that the bronze-worker has to retire from the field. And so again with ironfounders. Or again, in a plethoric condition of the corn and wine market these fruits of the soil will be so depreciated in value that the particular husbandries cease to be remunerative, and many a farmer will give up his tillage of the soil and betake himself to the business of a merchant, or of a shopkeeper, to banking or money-lending. But the converse is the case in the working of silver; there the larger the quantity of ore discovered and the greater the amount of silver extracted, the greater the number of persons ready to engage in the operation. [Dakyns translation, p. 335]

This text is interesting, for it reveals both new concerns among theoreticians and also the limits of their economic thinking. Xenophon knew the law of supply and demand and the speculations to which it could give rise. But he doesn't wonder why that law did not apply to silver. Similarly, the famous passage from *Cyropaedia* on the division of trades in the large cities arises more from a qualitative conception of production than from an understanding of the laws of the marketplace. And yet those laws were not completely unknown since that division was related to demand. As for the *Economics,* a treatise issued from the Aristotelian school that has come down to us in a composite form, its interest lies in the second book, not so much because it provides us a series of anecdotes about the thousand and one ways of earning income, as because the notion of *oikonomia* is enlarged to the dimensions of the city and the kingdom, and because the fiscal strategies that illustrate it no longer come out of the management of an *oikos*.

Does this concrete evidence of economic matters in theoretical writings—and the Aristotelian analyses of the origin of money and of chrematistics go in the same direction—convey a change in the mentality of those engaged in economic activities? A change of what magnitude? We must answer this question with caution. The answer appears to be found on several levels. First of all—and of course this once again primarily concerns Athens—it seems a given that we must henceforth renounce that mode of obtaining goods that goes back to the beginning of time, that is, the exploitation of the weakest. Deprived of its empire, Athens found itself deprived of the income earned from it in the form of tributes and legal fees, not to mention the land confiscated from recalcitrant allies. As both Isocrates and Xenophon noted, Athens could no longer live off the exploitation of its allies. It thus had to find in itself the income necessary for the smooth functioning of its institutions. The fourth century thus brought the development of an early fiscal organization in Athens and the growth of taxation of the richest citizens. Since there was no question of the latter toning down their traditional way of life—quite to the contrary, private wealth, if we are to believe literary sources, but also archaeological evidence, continued to assert itself—it was necessary to begin finding new sources of revenue. Maritime lending at usurious rates was one of them. But it implied that one had cash on hand, that is, in excess. In other words, even if one did not conceptualize the relationship between an increase in production and a growth in revenues, even if one thought first of increasing the number of slaves rather than perfecting production techniques, one still ended up wanting to produce more. Granted, one must be careful not to generalize using fragmentary information. But there was the incontestable awakening of the mining industry in the third quarter of the fourth century. And there was the no less real development of economic activity in Piraeus, which forced the city to pay more attention to commercial affairs and to create a more rapid procedure for the business of the *emporion*. And perhaps even more significant, there was the increased importance of the financial magistracies and the role that the "technicians" of financial affairs, such as Callistratus, Eubulus, and especially Lycurgus were called upon to play at the head of the city, the latter of whom was responsible for the *dioikēsis*, the entire administration of the city, a true manager who didn't hesitate to bring dishonest or careless mining concessionaires before the courts.

We must also mention the reproach repeated by the orators of the second half of the century: the increasing lack of interest among the citizens in the business of the city, which went hand in hand with a greater interest in their own private affairs, their *idia*. Certainly that was true of the poorest among the citizens, whom the loss of the empire and the cleruchies had deprived of many advantages in the form of salaries, booty, or the allocation of land, and who henceforth had to try to live off their meager property and the few distributions of the theoric, the sum distributed at the time of dramatic performances that became, according to Demosthenes, a sort of financial aid for the most unfortunate. But that reproach was also addressed to the rich who were more concerned with making money than with participating in political debates, which were increasingly becoming the exclusive activity of professional speechmakers or of technicians of war and finances. We have a precious source available on this subject in the plays of Menander, that representative of the New Comedy, a disciple of the Peripatetic school whose apogee occurred in the last two decades of the century, when Athens, defeated and controlled by a Macedonian garrison, had ceased to play a primary role in the Aegean. In Menander's comedies there is never the slightest reference to political events. The heroes he puts on stage are rich young men, often opposed to their fathers, who are revolted by their sons' dissolute life and the amorous intrigues in which they go astray. These "bourgeois" characters are often called away on business, and it is often upon their return that the action comes to a head. They have slaves, expensive homes, and, when at the end of the play everything falls into place with the desired marriage, the domestic help is mobilized, a reputed chef is called upon to prepare the wedding supper. We are far here from Aristophanes' vigorous and strongly politicized world of the peasant. And if the poor are sometimes mentioned—and they are often peasants—they remain in the background, unless they are found to be of noble origin. But everywhere the importance of money is asserted, the importance of wealth, which enables young men to maintain courtesans and the latter to buy back their freedom. We must certainly be careful not to see in "Meander's people" an exact image of the contemporary social reality. The fact nonetheless remains that the features of a new society were being drawn, that of the Hellenistic age.

It would be excessive and risky to say that Greek man at the end of the fourth century had become a *homo economicus*. But we can say without too much hesitation that he was truly no longer that *zōon politikon* whom Aristotle sought in vain to resuscitate. Clearly the Greek world, partially enslaved, was still a world formed essentially of cities, and political life subsisted there in a formal way. But the conquests of Alexander opened an immense world to the Greeks, which they would rule over under the aegis of the Macedonian rulers who divided up the spoils of it. Even if we must be careful not to apply to the economy of the Hellenistic world the extent of development that Rostovtzeff believed he discerned, it nevertheless remains true that a real Mediterranean market was created in this period, stimulating a growth in production and a development, if not of production techniques, at least of administrative and financial ones. But the Greeks who administered the finances of the Ptolemies or the Seleucid kings no longer had anything in common, beyond the language in which they expressed themselves and a few religious practices, with the Athenians of Marathon or the Spartans of Thermopylae. Greek man made way for Hellenistic man.

Notes

1. [The following sources were used for quotations from classical writers: the Athenian Society edition of Aristophanes, *The Eleven Comedies* (1912; London, 1930); Hesiod, *The Works and Days,* trans. Richmond Lattimore (Ann Arbor, Mich., 1991); the Carnes Lord translation of the *Oeconomicus* in Leo Strauss's *Xenophon's Socratic Discourse: An Interpretation of the "Oeconomicus"* (Ithaca, N.Y., 1970); *A Treatise on Government, or The Politics of Aristotle,* trans. William Ellis (New York, 1912); *The Works of Xenophon,* trans. H. G. Daykns (London, 1892)—trans.]

Bibliography

Andreyev, V. N. "Some Aspects of Agrarian Conditions in Attica in the Fifth to the Third Centuries B.C." *Eirenè* 12 (1974): 5–46.
Austin, Michel, and Pierre Vidal-Naquet, eds. *Economies et sociétés en Grèce ancienne. Périodes archaique et classique.* Paris, 1972.
Burford, Alison. *The Greek Temple Builders at Epidauros: A Social and Economic Study of Building in the Asklepian Sanctuary during the Fourth and Early Third Centuries B.C.* Liverpool, 1969.
———. *Craftsmen in Greek and Roman Society.* Ithaca, N.Y., 1972.
Detienne, Marcel. *Crise agraire et attitude religieuse chez Hésiode.* Brussels, 1964.
Finley, M. I. *Economy and Society in Ancient Greece.* New York, 1982.
———. *The Ancient Economy.* 2d ed. Berkeley, 1985.
———, ed. *Problèmes de la terre en Grèce ancienne.* Paris, 1973.
Frontisi-Ducroux, F. *Dédale: Mythologie de l'artisan en Grèce ancienne.* Paris, 1975.

Garlan, Yvon. *Slavery in Ancient Greece.* Revised and expanded edition. Translated by Janet Lloyd. Ithaca, N.Y., 1988.

Garnsey, Peter, Keith Hopkins, and C. R. Whittaker, eds. *Trade in the Ancient Economy.* Berkeley, 1983.

Healy, J. F. *Mining and Metallurgy in the Greek and Roman World.* London, 1978.

Humphreys, S. C. "Archaeology and the Social and Economic History of Classical Greece." *La Parola del Passato* 116 (1967): 374–400.

———. "Economy and Society in Classical Athens." *Annali della Scuola Normale Superiore di Pisa* 39 (1970): 1–26.

———. "Homo Politicus and Homo Economicus: War and Trade in the Economy of Archaic and Classical Greece." In *Anthropology and the Greeks,* pp. 159–74. Boston, 1978.

Lauffer, S. *Die Bergwerksklaven von Laureion.* 2d ed. Wiesbaden, 1979.

Lepore, E. "Economia antica e storiografia moderna." In *Ricerche storiche ed economiche in memoria di Corrado Barbagallo,* vol. 1, pp. 3–33. Naples, 1970.

Mele, Alfonso. *Società e lavoro nei poemi omerici.* Naples, 1968.

Mossé, Claude. *La colonisation dans l'Antiquité.* Paris, 1970.

———. *Le travail en Grèce et à Rome.* 3d ed. Paris, 1980.

Osborne, Robin. *Demos: The Discovery of Classical Attika.* New York, 1985.

Lowry, S. T. *The Archaeology of Economic Ideas: The Classical Greek Tradition.* Durham, N.C., 1987.

Vernant, Jean-Pierre. *Mythe et pensée chez le Grecs: Études de psychologie historique.* Revised and expanded edition. Paris, 1985.

———. *Myth and Society in Ancient Greece.* Translated by Janet Lloyd. New York, 1990.

Vidal-Naquet, Pierre. "Economie et société dans la Grèce ancienne: L'oeuvre de Moses Finley." *Archives européennes de sociologie.* 6 (1965): 111–48.

———. *The Black Hunter: Forms of Thought and Forms of Society in the Greek World.* Translated by Andrew Szegedy-Maszak. Baltimore, 1986.

Will, Edouard. "Trois quarts de siècle de recherches sur l'économie grecque antique." *Annales E.S.C.* 9 (1954): 7–22.

———. "Réflexions et hypothèses sur les origines de la monnaie." *Revue de numismatique* 17 (1955): 5–23.

———. *Le monde grec et l'Orient.* With the collaboration of Claude Mossé and Paul Goukowsky. Vol. 1, 4th ed. Paris, 1991. Vol. 2, 3d ed. Paris, 1990.

CHAPTER TWO

War and Peace

Yvon Garlan

THERE CAN BE little doubt that ancient Greek man was not only accustomed to war, but was even quite bellicose.[1] This can easily be demonstrated using various means. From the documentation available to us, we can assess the frequency of wars and see, for example, that in the classical period Athens was at war on an average of more than two years out of three, without ever enjoying peace for more than ten years in a row. In addition, there was the chronic insecurity caused by several more or less legal forms of violence that occurred on land and even more so on sea (acts of retaliation, rights of salvage, private, semi-public, or clearly state-supported piracy). Drawing on archaeology, we similarly note the existence of fortifications erected at great expense around the principal residential and political centers (while attempting to imagine what living in an enclosed city must have been like), and various other types of fortifications located in the country-side (watch towers in which people lived, control posts, defense positions)—keeping in mind that the vast majority of monuments and works of art that decorate the great sanctuaries and public squares were in fact offerings made by the conquerors. From epigraphic documentation, we see the temporary and precarious nature of the treaties that put an end to hostilities for a period that was often limited to five, ten, or thirty years, as if peace were automatically seen as precarious, if not simply as a sort of prolonged truce.

To the Greek historians, war alone appeared to be a subject truly worthy of remembrance: it provided them with the unifying theme of their works (the Persian Wars in Herodotus, the Peloponnesian War in Thucydides, Roman imperialism in Polybius) or at least gave a rhythm to their accounts of the events. War was a constant source of concern in the daily lives of citizens: in Athens, citizens were required to participate in wars from the age of nineteen to fifty-nine (men were in the active army until the age of forty-nine, then in the reserves); everywhere deciding to wage war was one of the minimal duties of popular assemblies. On all levels and in all realms of society, the significance of the warrior model was asserted: within families the soldier, as portrayed on Attic vases, was the central figure around whom the internal relationships of the *oikos* were organized; in the religious realm the divinities of Olympus were each endowed with a specific military function; in the realm of morality the worth of a good man (*agathos*), his *aretē,* consisted above all in the reasoned courage he showed both in his inner being, by struggling against the baser passions, and on the battlefield, where "beautiful death" awaited him, the only death with any social significance.

In spite of his eagerness for war, Greek man cannot, however, be defined as *homo militaris,* if by that we mean a man who loves violent acts for their own sake, independent of the forms they assume and the ends for which they are performed.

Civil war (*stasis*), which opposed members of the same political community, conceived in the image of the family, was unequivocally considered disastrous and ignominious. A value could only be placed on a war between two opposing communities, a *polemos,* and yet there were still conditions imposed. Unbridled and savage war, akin to that of wolves, was in fact considered a scandalous transgression (*hybris*) of the norms of appropriateness, in other words, of justice, which men were expected to respect in their dealings with each other as well as with regard to the gods. On the contrary, the true *polemos* could not dispense with observing certain rules: declaring war in good and due form; making appropriate sacrifices to the gods; respecting sites (sanctuaries), people (heralds, pilgrims, suppliants), and actions (oaths) connected to the divine; granting permission to the defeated to gather up their dead; and to a certain extent, abstaining from gratuitous cruelty. This was true above all of wars between Greeks, which would finally be criticized in principle (without any apparent effect) by the apostles of Panhellenism in the fourth century. But it was also more or less true of the wars, considered just by definition, waged against the "barbarians." When the rules of war were followed, those wars brought no shame for the blood shed and demanded no final purification of the fighters. Such "laws," believed to be common to all Greeks, indeed to all of humanity, in spite of their ambiguities and their being stretched on numerous occasions, were helpful in reducing the extent of conflicts.

However, it would be giving in to an optical illusion to believe that the entire Greek world was constantly being torn apart by war. Indeed, we must always keep in mind that, simply owing to the content of the texts we have available, the man who is familiar to us, who will be our chief focus, is the Greek of classical Athens, and to a lesser extent of classical Sparta, who was engaged in vast, imperialistic confrontations, and not the Greek of the "back country" that spread out over more than a thousand small city-states that generally existed secluded and sheltered in the shadows of the great powers. There we are able to observe localized conflicts in which adjacent cities battled each other with very limited objectives and means. In spite of their frequency, they must have caused only minor, quickly resolved tears in a tightly woven social fabric. The same was true of the various acts of "piracy." Contracting an alliance could easily widen the rifts: but here, too, we must be careful not to exaggerate. In general, forming an alliance meant only that one was expected to contribute by sending support troops for the defense of the allies' territory, and did not imply entering into direct hostilities with the aggressors. Nor is there any evidence, for example, that the archaic period over all was as bellicose as the centuries that followed. All these limitations, de jure or de facto, help us understand that the omnipresence of war in ancient Greece in no way meant that all of that land was constantly under fire and sword.

Contrasted to a militaristic view of Greek history, there is also the eminent place reserved for the praise of peace in both public opinion and in the works of theoreticians. Of the texts celebrating its benefits, one could make an abundant, quite repetitive collection, from the writings of Homer to those at the end of the Hellenistic period. There was always the same refrain: peace was abundance, the sweetness of life, joy, the enjoyment of the simple pleasures of life; war was abstinence, effort (*ponos*), pain, and suffering. Similarly, on a conceptual level, there is Plato's assertion that "one must live as best one can, the longest part of one's life in peace" (*Laws* 7.803d), or Aristotle's that "peace is the ultimate goal of war, just as leisure is that of work" (*Politics* 7.1334a)—which prevented them from using Sparta as a model, where those truths seemed reversed.

Are we to deduce from this that two opposing factions, one made

up of warmongers and the other of pacifists, both equally convinced
out of principle that their cause was just, continually fought and alternately triumphed? Certainly not. First, quite simply because the
most clear-cut assessments on this subject are either only descriptions
of specific events, sometimes contradicted by the same author by entirely different assertions, or deal only with the opportuneness of a
specific war, and not with war in general (thus we know of no Athenian in the fifth century who opposed imperialism in and of itself).
Next, and above all, because peace was considered only from a personal, hedonistic, and we might say existential point of view, with no
strictly humanitarian considerations, nor any desire in that connection to see changes made in the social structure or in human nature.
Peace was only a particularly delectable end point to cap the trials of
war. It corresponded to the moment when the peasant could delight
in storing away and enjoying the fruits of his hard labor. Such an
attitude thus in no way detracted from seeing the necessity, the rationality, and the grandeur of war; on the contrary, it tended to justify
war by seeing happiness as its final goal.

Disastrous in itself, socialized war was thus able to assume in a
positive way all the values invoked by the civic elite.

The Causes of War

"Assuming one wishes to wage war on those who are doing what is
just, he would be very careful not to admit as much," declared Alcibiades (who had not been at the Sophists' school for nothing) in the
Platonic dialogue that bears his name (109c).

Out of this principle, complementary to the "laws" mentioned
above, or rather from that *petitio principii* that is not specifically
Greek, there developed an entire casuistry that resulted in the creation
of repertoires of pretexts for war, such as the one proposed by the
Aristotelian author of the *Rhetoric for Alexander* at the beginning of
the third century B.C.: "After having been the victims of past injustice
we must henceforth, when circumstances warrant it, punish those
who have committed such injustice; or being the victims of an injustice at the present time one must wage war for oneself, or for one's
benefactors, or lend support to allies who are victims of an injustice,
either in the interest of the city or for its glory, or for its power, or for
any other reason of this kind. When we declare war, we must present
the greatest possible number of these pretexts" (1425a).

Judging from what the Greek historians tell us about the grievances officially cited by the belligerents as reasons to engage in a conflict, we recognize that there was no lack of imagination employed and that in their justifications they eagerly left no stone unturned: a territorial infringement, an attack on supply routes, not respecting established agreements, the establishment of a disgraced regime, any sort of true or potential threat, impiety, an affront sullying the glory of the city—any excuse was valid to exercise one's rights and to defend oneself, if possible by attacking first.

Into this incongruous collection of arguments and quibbles, Greek historians attempted to impose some order and to introduce a somewhat wider view of events: Herodotus, employing different means, combined divine will, revenge for offenses endured in a more or less distant past, and political motives; Thucydides, beyond the "complaints and differences" accumulated on the eve of the Peloponnesian War, pointed out the "truest and least admitted motive" formed by the fear the Spartans felt in the presence of increasing Athenian power; Polybius went so far as to distinguish the profound causes of a conflict, the pretext for it, and its point of departure. But their reflections stop short at this point and never result in an explicit judgment on the causes of the phenomenon of war in general.

Such judgment is not, however, completely absent from Greek texts. It is primarily, but not exclusively, found in Plato and Aristotle, who, since they do not exclude war (any more than they do slavery) from their plans for ideal societies, could not avoid explaining its existence. Their discussions are convergent and apparently simple: For Plato the cause of war would be the desire to "have more," to acquire wealth, and possibly slaves, and for Aristotle, above all to acquire slaves—and for both of them, to obtain food in the animal world and at the pre-civic stage of humanity (once the natural abundance of the Golden Age or the simplicity of primitive customs had disappeared). I am well aware that the words "wealth" and "slaves" might take on a more or less metaphorical meaning. But this in no way changes the global perspective of our two philosophers: in their opinion, war was essentially the art of acquiring through force supplemental means of existence, in the form of food, money, or working bodies, just as peace was the art of enjoying those acquisitions.

Modern historians have hence found themselves faced with the following dilemma: should the existence of war in ancient Greece be attributed to a single, essentially economic cause, or were there many heterogeneous causes (political, religious, ideological, as well as economic)? Most historians, taking eclecticism as a virtue, have opted for the latter solution—even though they admit the importance of the economic conditions and consequences of war, and sometimes also submit a uniform explanation by grouping the diversity of grievances under the same basic impulse, such as the agonistic spirit of the Greeks, or even the natural combativeness of the human race. But is it good methodology to carve up the heart of ancient texts in this way, choosing one point of view over another? Would it not be best to attempt to understand their coexistence, distinguishing the levels on which they are both located in the totality of social structures?

In order to do this, let us first recall in very broad terms the fundamental role played in the Greek world by physical and legal constraints, which are generally described as being extra-economic: they existed on the one hand inside the cities to extort any surplus production that enabled citizens to flourish at the expense of a servile workforce; on the other hand, they existed outside the cities in the form of territorial expansion, which formed the principal mode of economic growth and the primary way to resolve internal conflicts. All of this was carried out by virtue of a "law" that was never questioned, one that implied that the right of the victor to seize the person and the goods of the defeated provided the best title to ownership.

In this context, one characteristic of precapitalist societies (which is also found, for example, in past centuries in the Sahel region of Niger), the notions of wealth and power could be linked only intimately, organically. Together they formed the foundation of politics in the Greek sense of the term (the art of living in the *polis*), where each notion often appeared in the form of the other and was achieved through the intervention of the other. Thus a tangled series of unique intrigues proliferated within the political arena (in the modern, restricted, sense of the word), feeding on all the forms of sublimation engendered by a sense of honor and a will for competition—with all the risks that occurred through chance and the relative talent of those involved. As the Greek historians were more or less aware, international relations, in all their transformations, were "loaded" with economic meaning, even if their superficial appearance was generally of an entirely different nature. This, in my opinion, is the only way of seeing things that avoids an artificially firm distinction between economic and noneconomic causes of war. The politico-military complex, with the specific values connected to it, is thus inserted perfectly within the socioeconomic structures of the Greek city-states.

The Motivations of Warriors

Whatever the ostensible causes of a conflict may have been, what seems in any case to have counted most to those involved were the foreseeable, concrete, and immediate repercussions war had in their lives.

In the best scenario, that of an offensive and victorious war, one calculated the profit that could be made from it less in terms of military pay than in diverse and lucrative spoils of war: prisoners whom one chose to free in return for ransom or to sell to slave merchants rather than adding them to one's own herd of slaves; livestock captured in the countryside; the produce from fields already harvested or still standing; valuable objects (worked or coined metal, fabrics), and even all sorts of useful objects (tools, woodwork, etc.). The distribution of these spoils, to which were added territorial conquests and more or less regular tributes was a primary and always delicate problem to resolve, as seen in documents that regulate in advance the pro rata distribution of booty to allies according to the number of their contingents or the nature—either movable or not—of the goods seized. Unfortunately, we have very few details of how such regulations were carried out once the "shares of honor" that were eventually granted to the most valorous warriors, as well as the weapons, the riches, and sometimes the land consecrated to a certain divinity in the form of first fruits and tithes, had been distributed. It seem the state received (in addition to tributes and territorial conquests) the precious metals obtained during sacking or from the sale of prisoners. The soldiers themselves received edible goods and equipment; their superiors received a few items of their choice—if only to compensate for the sums they might have personally spent to improve the food of their troops, sometimes to ensure that they were armed and taken care of. It is all the more difficult for us to assess the situation with any precision since each of the parties involved sought to profit from circumstances and went beyond their rights, and since customs must have varied depending on the period and the city in question. Thus it was the custom in Sparta that a king received one-third of the booty obtained under his command. Even if such facts were almost never stated in official declarations, all these prospects for individual and collective gain, when it appeared reasonable to take advantage of them, encouraged war and greatly influenced the troops. Such was the case in Athens in 415 at the time of the departure of the Sicilian expedition: "All alike," reports Thucydides, "fell in love with the enterprise. The older men thought that they would either subdue the places against which they were to sail, or at all events, with so large a force, meet with no disaster; those in the prime of life felt a longing for foreign sights and spectacles, and had no doubt that they should come safe home again; while the idea of the common people and the soldiery was to earn wages at the moment, and make conquests that would supply a never-ending fund of pay for the future [of the State]" (6.24.3 [Crawley translation]).

But it is with regard to quite different situations that the motives of fighters are most often described to us: when they had to ward off an enemy invasion and ensure their own safety.

What was foremost and often uniquely at stake in a military operation was the territory, which the aggressors plundered and ravaged as much as was technically possible, and politically opportune, for them to do. Thus there was no city that did not react strongly, if only for purely material reasons, for most citizens were landowners to a greater or lesser extent, even in a city as "commercial" as Athens was at the end of the fifth century. Any attempt to seize land thus undermined the economic balance and consequently the social balance of the community, raising the threat, if not of food shortages, then at least of internal conflicts between those who would suffer from the situation and those who would not. This problem was so great that in order to ensure peace among citizens better, legislators were known to rule that property was to be equitably distributed along the frontiers so that everyone would feel equally concerned with its defense. In this sense all social values, notably religious ones, connected to the ownership of land had a bearing on the issue.

Leaving aside how the opposing forces compared to one another, defensive responses varied according to the idea one had of the best interests of the city. For a long time in a more or less autarkic social framework, citizens sought to put an end to incursions as quickly as possible, either by opening up negotiations with the aggressors or by provoking a decisive battle in the open countryside. This is what Pericles resolutely opposed at the beginning of the Peloponnesian War, to the great frustration of the invaders led by the Spartan king,

Archidamus, and to the great anger of the Athenians, who were very reluctant to retreat in mass inside the Long Walls that linked Athens to Piraeus: it was stressed to them that this was the only way, as painful as it might be, to protect what was most essential to them, namely, their maritime empire. We could point out other examples of "Periclean" strategy used by cities that had every reason or who saw themselves forced by a third party to sacrifice the defense of their territory to that of the urban fortifications, just as from time to time after the fifty century cities continued to resort to pitched battles. On the whole, however, a more subtle and more complex strategy aiming to reconcile both defense imperatives tended to prevail: the defense of the territory was assured as much as possible through the construction of rural fortifications and by sending out commandos without compromising the security of the urban nucleus. That strategy was difficult to put into practice, as is evident in particular in the little treatise *Siegecraft,* written by Aeneas Tacticus around the middle of the fourth century: in it we see citizens at first eager to go individually into their fields to save what they could of them, then impatient to cross swords with the enemy at the risk of running into ambushes, before their leaders could manage to regroup them into battle formations and urge them to use a few elementary precautions.

As a last resort, the only possible course of action remaining was to ensure at all costs the protection of the urban center, the fortifications of which were increasingly called for as a result of the military changes of the fourth century, and which continued to grow in strength and complexity to adapt to the increasing perfection of the machines used in sieges and to the development of assault tactics. Only Sparta took pride, until the beginning of the Hellenistic period, in being able to dispense with such accoutrements and to owe its security to "a crown of warriors, and not of bricks" (Plutarch *Moralia* 228E). Plato approved of Sparta's stance, since he consented at most to the adapting of exterior walls of houses on the periphery for defensive means. But Aristotle, who must have been a better voice of public opinion, did not approve: "To consider it wise not to build walls around cities is the same as looking for a site easy to invade and to leveling mountainous areas; it is also the same as not building walls around private homes for fear that their inhabitants might become cowards" (*Politics* 7.1331a [Ellis translation]).

Even more than a pitched battle waged in the open countryside, a siege was a crucial trial that mobilized the energies of the soldiers and those of all the inhabitants: for being captured by storm by definition meant blind massacres and sacking, and often also the annihilation of the conquered community by the enslavement of its inhabitants. Thanks again to the work by Aeneas Tactitus, we can witness the anguish and the exaltation of the besieged, as well as the ingenious nature of the measures taken in such circumstances: not only against the external enemy, its machines and ploys, but also against the internal enemy, that is, the opponents of the local regime, who were inclined to betray it in order to take over. In a climate of such extreme tension, a feeling of patriotism in the hearts of all citizens was identified fully with the immediate protection of their lives, their families, their social position, and their property.

Thus a materialistic notion, both substantive and emotive, of the fatherland ruled the motives of the fighters—which obviously does not mean that they were unable to rise above their personal interests to a higher degree of abstraction. To our contemporaries, who are accustomed to more mystification in the matter, that notion might perhaps appear a bit limited. Let us at least be able to enjoy its freshness and authenticity.

Military Function and Social Status

This notion had as a corollary, very different from modern understanding, that the military rank of members of the community was in principle proportional to their social status.

One can certainly find in ancient Greece some traces and fragments of the Indo-European trifunctionality analyzed so well by Georges Dumézil, which conceives of the cosmic and social orders as the result of the superposition of the three functions of sovereignty, strength, and fertility.

In the mythical universe in particular, we can thus distinguish divinities, such as Ares and Athena, whose original attributes are connected to the second function; many heroes, such as Heracles, Tydeus, Parthenopeus, and Achilles, whose stories illustrate the destiny of the warrior; as well as groups of clearly military character, such as the Spartans of Thebes, the Phlegyae of Orchomenus in Boeotia, the Aegidae of Sparta, the Gegeneis in Colchis, or the giants, enemies of the gods. The duality of the warrior function compared to the function of sovereignty, depending on whether it unfolds for itself or agrees to collaborate in a position subordinate to the maintenance of the whole, whether it performs in a disorganized or an organized way, will serve to explain the antithesis of Ares and Athena, of Heracles and Achilles, or the Hesiodic opposition [in *Works and Days*] between the race of bronze and that of the heroes. Fossilized in a ritual of the classical period, we might believe we recognize some sort of significant tripartition, such as in the offering to the young Cretan by his lover of a cup, a war costume, and a steer.

But there is something else entirely that predominates in Greek history, beginning with the Mycenaean tablets of the thirteenth century and the Homeric poems of the eighth century: it is a concentration at the top of the social hierarchy of military abilities and responsibilities within the hands of an elite that played a determining role on the battlefield, one on a par with the role it also played in the political and economic arenas. It was that elite's place to flaunt its wealth, power, and courage in the first row of battle formations, while the "lesser" people huddled together in the background in compact formations to support and applaud the exploits of the champions. It was the elite's privilege to have weapons forged by the gods who assisted them, gigantic shields and, above all, chariots of war (even though in Homer they used them in bizarre ways or as simple means of transport!). Of course, they also received the choice shares of the spoils, beautiful captives and precious objects taken from the common booty. The aristocratic societies at the forefront of Greek history were thus subjected to an all-encompassing and functionally undifferentiated hegemony, even if it was defined by the warrior virtues that they valued most highly and that were expressed with the greatest autonomy.

The formation of city-states, beginning in the eighth century, gradually resulted in the fixing of new community relationships. But that transformation, about which we know very few of the details, did not alter the principle guiding the distribution of military functions among the members of a civic body that grew larger or smaller throughout the centuries depending upon the regime in power.

Henceforth it was as a citizen, and in one's capacity as such, that one was a soldier—and not the reverse. The exercise of armed force constituted, not the source, but the privileged expression of a whole integrated system of status positions representative of the different aspects of citizenship. Foremost were the economic abilities of individuals to provide themselves personally as the need arose with adequate weaponry. But it was not this ability in itself that determined their social ranking. Thus in Athens the census classifications of citizens and the political functions connected to them were based on the amount of their income, and not on criteria of a military nature. It simply went without saying that a certain service was expected from those who attained a certain census ranking. Sparta, which in the fourth century earned an exaggerated reputation for militarism, was no exception in this regard. What determined one's entrance into the corps of the "equals" (*homoioi*) was (apart from birth) the possession of a large estate worked by helots and the resulting ability to spend a share of the income from it on common meals—behavior in combat was considered only in a negative way, as a source of disqualification: it is significant that when Hellenistic Sparta wanted to remedy its "oliganthropy" [decline in the number of citizens] by integrating helots into its army, it proceeded to recruit them on the basis of their census ranking, not of their bravery.

This principle having been set forth, let us now see how it was transposed in a concrete manner into military life.

The Hoplite Model

The most noticeable manifestation of the urban development process is the appearance of a new type of warrior—the hoplite.

He was protected by greaves, a bronze helmet, and cuirass, as well as by a round shield measuring 80 to 90 centimeters in diameter, also made of bronze or a combination of wood, wicker, and animal skins. The primary innovation of that *hoplon,* which was to become the symbolic weapon of the hoplites, was that it no longer hung from the neck by a strap, but was carried on the left forearm by a center loop made of bronze, and was held by a thin strap on the edge. This had two important consequences. First, the hoplite could then use only his right arm to wield attack weapons—a wooden lance, approximately 2.5 meters long, bearing an iron or bronze tip and butt, as well as a short sword for hand-to-hand fighting. Second, his right flank, which was relatively exposed, had to be protected by the man next to him in line within a closely formed phalanx (also taking into account the limits imposed on the vision and the agility of soldiers by the helmet and the cuirass). One can then understand how this double technical and tactical innovation went hand in hand with a broader recruitment of anyone who was able to afford such equipment, and therefore with a certain enlargement of the civic body beyond the limits of the traditional aristocracy.

The protohistory of this hoplite phalanx remains largely controversial: When did it appear (middle of the seventh century?), all of a sudden or following a period of experimentation? Did it represent a complete revolution compared with earlier combat methods? Was it the cause or the consequence of contemporary sociopolitical changes, in particular of the appearance of tyranny? What then became of the cavalry that, according to Aristotle, was the favorite weapon of the first aristocratic cities? These are a few of the questions that modern historians continue to ask and that I can do no more than mention here in order to concentrate on the much better documented classical period.

In the meantime, the hoplite panoply was made somewhat simpler and lighter. Henceforth the armbands, thighpieces, and anti-arrow aprons generally disappeared, as did the second lance used as a javelin, which sometimes appears on archaic representations. The cuirass of molded bronze was replaced by a linen or leather coat reinforced with pieces of metal. This ensemble was no less costly: soldiers spent at least a hundred or so Attic drachmas, representing approximately one-fourth of the annual salary of a moderately skilled worker. In fifth-century Athens, such a financial outlay was required only of citizens belonging to one of the first three census classes, among which the third, the *zeugitai,* provided most of the manpower for armed conflicts. Such selection criteria within the civic body must have existed pretty much everywhere, at least in places where the civic body was not in fact limited, as in Sparta, to those who had the means to arm themselves as hoplites.

The decisive trial that awaited them was a pitched battle, which was commonly called an *agōn* (competition), not unlike an athletic competition, and followed the same pattern everywhere, with preliminary sacrifices (at different stages of the progression), confrontation on a closed field, and acts of thanksgiving accompanied by often analogous offerings (wreaths, three-footed structures, crowns). The battle itself unfolded according to plan, in conformity with highly ritualized practices, without incorporating any element of surprise.

Once an appropriately level battleground had been more or less tacitly agreed upon with the enemy, a site best provided by farm fields, the phalanx spread out over several rows (generally eight) in order to be able to exert a collective pressure and to ensure the automatic filling of any gaps. There was less than a meter between any two soldiers, so that an average-sized army, let us say around 10,000 men, spread out over some 2,500 kilometers. A few contingents of light-armed troops and cavalry were positioned in the wings; they were responsible for holding back any attempt at outflanking and, at the beginning and the end of the battle, for stirring up trouble within the enemy lines. After being assured of divine favor by making a final sacrifice, the warriors started off in an ordered march toward the enemy, who were some 100 meters away, and they often ended in a run: the Spartans carried this out in an impressive silence broken only by the sound of a flute, whereas others punctuated it with the sounding of trumpets, shouts, and peals of attack in honor of Ares and Enyalios. The clash took place head on and subsequently gave rise only to very few lateral maneuvres: with the exception that the phalanx naturally tended to advance in an oblique line to the right, for the simple reason that each member of the phalanx imperceptibly veered toward the side opposite his shield so as to be covered by the man next to him in line. Unless there was an accidental break in the center, the outcome of a battle was decided on the flanks: the first right flank to prevail gradually provoked the dislocation of the opposing phalanx. Since the commanders were unable to have any real effect on the course of events, especially without reserves, the result was panic, a disorderly retreat, and a brief chasing down of runaways. The fight ended on the conqueror's side with a peal of victory in honor of Dionysus and Apollo, the immediate raising of a trophy (a simple wooden monument decorated with weapons taken from the enemy), permission given to the defeated to collect their dead, and once back home, with prayers accompanied by sacrifices and banquets.

Expected to produce a judgment without appeal in a very short amount of time—most often in just a morning—the hoplite battle kept citizens from their normal activities only momentarily: for it occurred at the end of a brief campaign lasting only a few days or at most a few weeks, held judiciously in good weather so that citizens would secure their own harvests and might seize those of the enemy. Concerns with logistics were thus reduced to a minimum: conscripts had only to be asked to show up with a few supplies for the road and, for the rest, to count on what would be obtained from plundering and on the spontaneous influx of merchants seduced by the windfall.

Nor was there any equipment to provide, since each man showed up with his weapons, his battle gear, which did not resemble a uniform except in the case of the red tunics worn by the Spartans, and his personal effects loaded onto a mule or carried by a slave. Any break with normal civic life was truly minimal.

Nor was the pervasive atmosphere of the army unlike that found back home. The art of persuasion was used there, as in the Assembly, in the form of heart-felt exhortations addressed to the front line of troops right before they attacked. Supreme command was bestowed upon magistrates elected by the people, such as the ten Athenian *stratēgoi*, who often acted collegially, and their principal assistants, the taxiarchs who were placed at the head of tribal contingents—except in Sparta where command was carried out by kings or by certain of their entourage, surrounded by "tent companions," who among others included elected polemarchs who were placed at the head of different regiments. Again, Sparta was an exception, since its army, according to Thucydides (5.66.4), "save for a small part, consists of officers under officers." In principle, there were few subaltern officers, and during battles they remained on the first line of their units, wore only a few distinctive insignia (plumes or feathers on their helmets), and did not automatically serve the same function from one campaign to the next: thus they did not truly form a professional caste. The rank and file, all carrying identical weapons, formed interchangeable units, with the exception that those who were in the prime of their lives were placed in the first rows, and the most motivated, those who were most interested in the success of the operation, willingly held the right flank position. Under these conditions, obeying orders was essentially a matter of consent: punishment, especially corporal punishment, was subject to a judgment in good and due form before a tribunal of the army or, insofar as was possible, before the regular tribunals of the city.

The hoplites' courage was therefore not the result of a strictly military discipline—nor, as we have seen, was it the result of a warrior frenzy leaving no place of fear (as is demonstrated by their readiness to admit defeat). Aiming above all to ensure the cohesion of the phalanx, their courage was based upon a well-understood solidarity: it consisted of not abandoning one's comrades in arms and, therefore, of remaining steady in one's position. Consequently, an esprit de corps was systematically cultivated. It was continually infused into the Spartan *homoioi* through the entire community organization of their daily lives. In Athens it was also reinforced by grouping soldiers into tribes, or more precisely, into *trittues*. Thus natural relationships of mutual support based on kinship, friendship, and on being neighbors could come into full play within the hoplite phalanx.

By putting too much emphasis on the ludic and gregarious aspects of the hoplite battle, we risk forgetting how violent the individual confrontations that occurred really were, with relatively severe losses estimated at 14 percent for the defeated and at 5 percent for the conquerors. Quite far from simply having to push shoulder to shoulder to contain and make the enemy line retreat, as in a rugby skirmish, the hoplites also had to fight individual duels, using their lances, then their swords, against the adversary closest to them. At least at the height of the battle, the collective confrontation thus broke down into a series of one-on-one fights. The difference with the heroic period is that single combat was no longer permitted for its own sake, as a search for personal glory, as we see in the case of the Spartan who wanted to redeem himself in Plataea for having survived at Thermopylae: accused by his compatriots of having "left his place in the line and behaving like a madman," because "on account of the blame which attached to him, he had manifestly courted death," he was deprived of all honors (Herodotus 9.71). As a good citizen, he should have submitted his action to a certain moral discipline (*sōphrosynē*), taking into account the interests of the collectivity.

Ultimately, it is appropriate to note that this hoplite model, one strictly defined on a political level and that tended to underscore the preeminence of a certain social elite, was in fact limited in time. Even though the merits of this type of warrior continued more than ever to be celebrated, particularly as represented by those who had fought at Marathon, by the end of the fifth century, hoplite recruitment began to be extended, in fact if not by law, to other social classes, for example, in Sparta to include certain inferiors, and in Athens to include *thetēs*, who made up the fourth and final census category. On the other hand, on a military level the hoplite phalanx (which, true, had rarely acted alone as in Marathon) had increasingly to reckon with the light-armed infantry and especially with the semi-light corps of peltasts, before having to admit its inferiority before the Macedonian phalanx. At the same time, the role of surprise, cunning, treachery, and technical capabilities in warcraft increased: contemporaries were well aware of this, men such as Demosthenes, who in 341 in his *Third Philippic* (47–50) drew up a bitter report on this evolution. Let us avoid, however, placing too much emphasis on those developments: up to the time of the Hellenistic city-states, the hoplite infantry was to remain the noble weapon par excellence and was to continue for a long time to play an essential role in the pitched battles that decided the course of important historical events.

Military Duties at the Top and Bottom of the Social Scale

There were also other participants in the military life of a city found elsewhere on the above-mentioned axis.

In ancient Greece, owning a horse was an obvious sign of wealth, and belonging to the cavalry a social distinction; even in the vast plains, such as Thessaly, Boeotia, or Campania, which were natural places in which to raise horses. In Athens it seems that for a long time having a cavalry depended upon the good will of the young aristocrats who alone had the means to maintain a mount and the time to practice riding, for parades and victories at competitions at least as much as for war. It was on the advice of Pericles, around the middle of the fifth century, that the Athenians organized a regular cavalry, made up of 500, then 1,000, citizens (and also 200 archers on horseback), although it could have been earlier, at the beginning of the century, as vases from that period portray the first scenes of tryouts for entrance to the cavalry. Perhaps Pericles can be credited with having instituted the system of recruitment that prevailed in the classical period. This system consisted of paying a select group of young men from the first two census classes (especially the second one, whose name in fact was *hippeis*) a certain sum of money, which was enough or at least helped to buy a charger whose worth was periodically reassessed and recorded on lead tablets, a great many of which have been found on the site of the agora. In addition, a daily allowance was paid for the maintenance of the horse. Enlistment into the cavalry was thus reserved for a well-defined elite census class, whose reputation was displayed, for example, on the inner frieze of the Parthenon around 440, before it was diminished after the democratic restoration of 401, in spite of the arguments Xenophon published on its behalf around 360.

Militarily speaking, the Greek cavalry was, however, always limited by its inability to open a breach in the hoplite phalanx. Carrying short lances that were used as javelins, sometimes using spurs and light cuirasses, but without stirrups or hard saddles, handicapped in addition by the weakness of a tackle not made of iron, in general the cavalry was used only for exploration and harassment, with troops whose numbers in most cities were equivalent at best to one-tenth of those of the phalanx. The Spartans appeared particularly negligent in this area, since they waited until 424 to form a small cavalry of 400 men.

The richest Athenians, those who for the most part belonged to the first census class of *pentakosiomedimnoi,* were uniquely responsible for manning the fleet: in the beginning, perhaps, by themselves providing the ships within the little-known framework of the naucraries and, after the founding of the trierarchy, by overseeing the maintenance and functioning of the triremes built by the state. This liturgy, which was carried out periodically depending on need, was quite burdensome, since it sometimes reached a cost of close to 6,000 drachmas. Thus it had to be rearranged so as to distribute the financial responsibility better: first by dividing it up, at the end of the Peloponnesian War, between two trierarchs, then in 357 by assigning responsibility for it to groups called "symmories." Other taxes for military purposes were even imposed on the *zeugitēs:* these were contributions (*eisphorai*) that were in principle requested only rarely, but that became more or less common after the Peloponnesian War. Collecting these contributions was facilitated in 378/7 by the creation of "symmories," models for the symmories of trierarchies in which the richest citizens took on the role of guarantors. Voluntary gifts (*epidoseis*), which were recognized through beautiful honorific decrees, were also expected of the same social classes, especially beginning in the second half of the fourth century. These were the principal internal means of financing the military in the cities whose regular revenues left very little surplus.

On the other hand, of the many Athenian citizens who belonged to the last census class (a good half of the civic body) only personal duty could be expected, duty that for a long time was confined to the most despised areas of combat. Such was the case of light-armed troops, of javelin throwers, archers, and slingers, whose intervention in the margins of the hoplite phalanx until the fifth century was of very little use and whose activity at a distance seemed morally so undesirable that it was banned in the early archaic period through an agreement made between the Chalcidians and the Eretrians, who were contesting the small Lelantine plain. Archers in particular had a bad reputation from Homer to Euripides, one of whose characters stigmatizes Heracles in these terms: "He has never held a shield on his left arm nor confronted a lance; holding the bow, the most cowardly of weapons, he was always ready to flee. For a warrior archery is no proof of courage; courage consists of remaining in the ranks and seeing, without cowering or turning one's face, running toward you a whole field of poised lances, always staying firm in one's ranks" (*Heracles* 5.159–64).

After the Peloponnesian War, and above all with the growing number of peltasts carrying javelins and a small shield (*pelta*), it became increasingly obvious that the light-armed troops could sometimes overcome the hoplites and that using them would be advantageous in many circumstances (protecting territorial borders, during sieges). The prejudices against them began to fade in light of their deeds, but did not, however, disappear completely.

Oarsmen, who, stuck on their thwarts, propelled the triremes before and during battles, belonged to the same social classes—at least many of them came from those classes, since the Athenian *thetēs* alone, without the addition of foreigners, would not have been able to fill two or three hundred ships. The success of ramming, the foundation of naval tactics, depended on their maneuvering skills—the dozen or so hoplites sailing on each trireme were there only to bring the effects of ramming to a favorable conclusion. One might say that the oarsmen acted as a kingpin in the development of Athenian maritime imperialism begun by the prestigious victory of Salamis in 480. And yet they hardly enjoyed a good reputation in the opinion of aristocrats, as we see expressed on the eve of the Peloponnesian War in the *Constitution of the Athenians* by the "Old Oligarch," or later in Plato's work. Other cities, such as Sparta, simply embarked noncitizens, rural dependents, or foreigners onto their ships—there were very few cities, such as Hellenistic Rhodes, that seemed to have held service in the navy in high esteem.

Urban Marginals

This law of making military roles proportional to social status is again seen in the case of those living on the margins of the civic body.

Those who had the most affinities with citizens were their minor sons; they belonged to citizens "in power" and were educated and treated as such. Being on the middle ground between childhood and adulthood, they were, in Greece as elsewhere, assimilated respectively into nature and culture, in a transitional phase strongly marked by ancient rites of passage. They engaged in exercises that sometimes contrasted them with hoplites and sometimes prepared them for hoplite warfare. The first of these rituals has been of great interest to modern historians, in the light of many ethnological parallels provided by other archaic societies, such as those in nineteenth-century Africa.

It was seen particularly clearly in Spartan education (*agōgē*), which, for more than ten years, increasingly challenged young men grouped into "herds" with tests of endurance and simulated battles that above all employed cunning as a tactic. At the end of this probative period, the best of the *eirēnes* entered into the institution known as the *krypteia*. Members of the *krypteia*, that is, the "hidden ones" were sent in the middle of winter into the most remote regions of the territory, without supplies and armed only with a simple dagger, instructed not to let themselves be seen, to feed by looting, and to spend the night hunting down helots against whom the ephors had already declared war. During this phase of segregation, which preceded their definitive admittance into the community of adults, they thus behaved, so to speak, as anti-hoplites.

In Athens, young men were taken in hand by the state much later than in Sparta, only at the end of their adolescence. They were then subjected to the *ephēbeia*, the existence of which must date at least from the beginning of the classical period, undoubtedly in the form of a single year of training reserved for the first three census classes. But the detailed information we have about it is of a much more recent date, after its reorganization and reinforcement by Epicrates around 335–4, at the time Lycurgus attempted to restore Athen's military power, which had been greatly compromised shortly before by the defeat of Chaeronea by the Macedonians. A chapter in Aristotle's *Constitution of the Athenians* (42) and some inscriptions reveal the principal aspects of its functioning. At the time, the *ephēbeia* included the sons of all citizens, regardless of their census class, aged nineteen and twenty years old. During the first year, the ephebes, after a tour of the sanctuaries, were installed as garrisons in Piraeus and received complete military training there: the wielding of hoplite weapons, archery, javelin throwing, working a catapult. The second year they passed in review and received the shield and the lance of the hoplite from the state before marching through Attica and being stationed in rural fortresses. Thus they found themselves, although in a less pronounced way than members of the Lacedaemonian *krypteia*, occupying a marginal position both spatially and politically—even though they had already been entered in the deme register—by their absence from the Assembly of the people and by being barred from testifying in court, except in cases involving the family. Even in times of war, the ephebes were not full-fledged warriors, since their role, like that of the age-class of fifty- to fifty-eight-year-olds, was theoretically limited to defending Attica.

The same antithetical position of the young compared to adults is found again elsewhere, in more or less evanescent forms and on different levels. It reappears, for example, in the distinction (Platonic in particular) between hunting at night, with traps recommended to the young and a hunt by pursuit using spears reserved for the others. It also often crops up in the universe of myths rich in perpetual adolescents like Hyppolytus, who are immature and made wild by not having successfully integrated into the world of adults. Another good representative of this youth that pushes its specific nature to the limit before blending into the adult community is the Athenian hero Melanthus, "the dark," who uses cunning (*apatē*) to triumph over the Theban champion Xanthus, "the fair," in hand-to-hand combat for the possession of a small frontier zone. The festival of the Apaturia is believed to have derived its name from this, a festival during which adolescents sixteen years old, having reached physiological maturity, were presented to the phratries (clans) of their fathers (this is the true etymology of the word "Apaturia") and cut off their long hair as a divine offering.

The rest of the population shared the distinction of being deprived of all political rights and of not being part of the city in the strict sense of the term. But these noncitizens were nevertheless an indispensable element in its survival, just as in times of war they indirectly shared its successes and especially its failures. They therefore could not live completely outside military activities. In fact if not by law, passively or actively, more or less regularly and always in a subordinate position, they were implicated in them, according to the concrete modes that depended, for each category, on its variable distance, or rather its original position, with respect to the civic body.

Thus in Athens the resident foreigners who had been integrated to a certain extent by being granted the privileged status of metic in principle only contributed in separate units to the defense of the territory (as hoplites or as light infantry, depending on their income, but not as cavalry) and served most often in the navy as oarsmen or as specialized sailors (but not as pilots). They were also subject to the *eisphorai,* of which they provided the sixth part, but were not affected by the trierarchy, inasmuch as it had for a long time implied the command of a trireme. And the Lacedaemonian army included contingents of perioecic hoplites [free noncitizens], as well as scouts called "Skiritae," who had been raised in a mountainous region formerly conquered by Sparta in its struggle against Tegea.

The military role of slaves normally consisted only of seeing to the personal needs of their masters while in the army, just as they did in civic life. It was only at critical times, indeed desperate ones, that some of them were armed. The decisions made in those moments varied on the one hand depending on the status of those concerned, for example, depending on whether one was dealing with slaves/merchandise of the Athenian type or with indigenous populations reduced on the spot to slavery, such as the Spartan helots. They varied on the other hand depending on the honorableness of the function that was granted to them: oarsmen or light infantrymen rather than hoplites. Correlatively, they may or may not have been freed, before or after military operations. On the whole, it is significant that the helots, who were considered particularly treacherous, were clearly more in demand than Athenian slaves: this is because their residual vocation as a formerly free people explained both their defiant spirit and their relative military aptitude.

Even women who were citizens, although courage was by definition an essentially masculine trait, were more or less involved in war: either as exemplary victims incarnating the last chances of perpetuating the community and knowing best how to conjure away its annihilation through their lamentations, their prayers, and their encouragement to the soldiers; or in a completely unusual way, as makeshift soldiers fighting directly for the protection of their homes. In this case, we see them carrying weapons appropriate to their condition (sometimes kitchen utensils!) and using all sorts of ruses, very unlike hoplites, inspired by their feminine nature. It is only in the mythical universe of the Amazons or in the utopian world of the Platonic *Republic* that they are transformed into women–soldiers: but that conversion was then either conditioned by their partial desexualization (the removal of the left breast to better wield a bow) or lim-

ited to virgins (*parthenoi*), who had not yet found the normal fulfillment of their being through marriage.

Military Amateurism

This system of status distribution of military functions, which existed
everywhere in variable forms, appears to have disregarded any qualification acquired through a specific training and to have accepted a
universal amateurism.

This is a common subject of the official rhetoric of funeral orations,
which tended in particular to absorb the warrior function into the
political function. The best example of this is found at the very beginning of the Peloponnesian War in Pericles, who superbly declares:
"Our confidence is founded less on preparations and trickery, but
rather on the strength of our souls from which we draw when it is
time to act" (Thucydides 2.39.1 [Crawley translation]).

Of all the social professions that predisposed men for military action the most highly valued was that of farmer. It was thought to
provide the best training for war, for several reasons set forth in particular by Xenophon in his *Oeconomicus* (5) because owning land
"stimulates in some degree the farmers to armed protection of the
country by nourishing her crops in the open for the strongest to
take"; because farming "teaches us to rule others," by inculcating a
sense of order, opportunity, justice, and piety; finally, because it
"makes the body strong" [Lord translation]. In this respect, it combined its effects with the practice of hunting, considered in the *Cyropaedia* (1.2) as "the best possible training for the needs of war": Indeed, hunting "accustoms a man to early rising; it hardens him to
endure heat and cold; it teaches him to march and to run at the top of
his speed; he must perforce learn to let fly arrow and javelin the moment the quarry is across his path; and above all, the edge of his spirit
must needs be sharpened by encountering any of the mightier beasts:
he must deal his stroke when the creature closes, and stand on guard
when it makes its rush: indeed, it would be hard to find a case in war
that has not its parallel in the chase" [Daykns translation].

In contrast, the craftsmen's trades ruin "the bodies of those who
work at them and those who are concerned with them, compelling
them to sit still and remain indoors, or in some cases to spend the
whole day by the fire. And when the bodies are made effeminate, the

souls too become much more diseased" so that those people "are reputed to be bad defenders of their fatherlands" (*Oeconomicus* 4 [Lord translation]). These ideological considerations were sometimes reflected in institutions, if it is true, for example, that to be elected a *stratēgos* in Athens it was necessary to own land within the frontiers.

Another condition for holding that office might have been (for we don't really know to what degree and until when this was in force) that the candidate also be the head of a family. The concern with preserving the freedom of his children indeed gave a soldier an additional reason to fight, just as according to Plato "every animal fights its best when its children are present" (*Republic* 5.467a). By fully realizing his social being, a citizen reached a supreme degree of responsibility and availability that predisposed him to sacrifice for the survival of the community, as was the case in 480 with the fathers whom the Spartans included in the elite corps of 300 men sent to Thermopylae.

The amateurism of the leaders and commanders corresponded to that of the fighters. The members of the Athenian Assembly who went on in great detail about the course of operations had no particular military competence. Nor did most of the *stratēgoi*, at least in the fifth century, for they owed their having been elected above all to the reputation they had made for themselves in the debates of the Assembly or in another sector of public life, as in the case of Sophocles. Consequently, until the end of the classical period, military leaders were for the most part rich nobles who through family tradition had an innate sense of leadership and could if necessary contribute to the maintenance of their troops: for example, one notes that 61 percent of the known Athenian *stratēgoi* are included in the list of large landowners.

Modern historians have correlatively emphasized the place held in military training by various social practices of a cultural and religious nature that were characteristic of those citizens who were not overwhelmed by the necessity of daily tasks and could enjoy leisure time (*scholē*). Foremost were the athletic trials for which men trained in the palaestrae and gymnasiums, which were traditionally closely linked to military life, and which were included in the program of competitions organized within the framework of civic or Panhellenic sanctuaries: races (including a race with hoplite weapons), jumping, throwing, fighting, and pancratium. A champion in these areas could only be an excellent soldier, as seen in an anecdote by Diodorus Siculus about Milon of Croton: "This man, six times the winner at Olympia, as brave a soldier as he was a good athlete, went into combat, they say, covered with Olympic wreaths and wearing the symbols of Heracles, the lion skin and the club; victorious, he won the admiration of his fellow citizens" (12.9.6). Also in Sparta, those who had won a wreath in the games fought alongside the king himself. In addition, there were processional dances with hoplite weapons and other sorts of armed dances, the most famous of which was the Pyrrhic: according to Plato, "on the one hand it imitates the movements one makes to avoid all the blows delivered close by or at a distance, dashing to the side, backing up, jumping high, crouching down, and on the other hand, the opposite movements, those which bear down on defensive behavior and attempt to imitate the path of the bow or the javelin or the gesture of striking any blow" (*Laws* 7.815a).

We must be careful, however, not to push this vision to the point of absurdity.

In fact, it has always had its antidotes: the constant interest everyone had in military operations, for the fundamental reasons we have already mentioned, and the general competence acquired through experience (as is proven particularly in Athens by the fact that the high military offices tended to be concentrated hereditarily within a limited number of important families).

Let us not forget that only the hoplite method of combat was in question there: it is only with regard to that method that the Persian Pheraulas, in Xenophon's *Cyropaedia* (2.3.9), said "all men naturally understand, just as in the case of other creatures each understands some method of fighting that it has not learned from any source other than instinct: for instance, the bull knows how to fight with his horns, the horse with his hoofs, the dog with his teeth, the boar with his tusks. And all know how to protect themselves, too, against that from which they most need protection, and that though they have never gone to school to any teacher" [cited in Garlan, *War in the Ancient World,* p. 164]. However, no one would have denied, even though they might deplore it, that the opposite was true of projectiles and especially of the navy, which, according to Thucydides (1.142) "is a professional matter."

On the other hand, many indications lead us to believe that in real life military training was not as neglected as the ideologues of the aristocracy maintained. Even in fifth-century Athens, the hoplites must have received a certain training during their *ephēbeia* and then been periodically called to reviews where their superiors verified the good condition of the individual equipment and where there were undoubtedly exhibitions of maneuvres in close formation. Some even advocated calling upon professional instructors who for a salary would go from city to city to teach the wielding of hoplite weapons in the private palaestrae: this art, *hoplomachia,* is believed to have been invented in Arcadia around the middle of the sixth century. Other instructors, of strategy and tactics (by this we mean the way to perform one's function as *stratēgos* and to arrange troops in battle), were included in Socrates' entourage, according to Xenophon's *Memorabilia.* In any case, there is no doubt that the Spartans, in spite of their distrust of that type of sophist specialized in the military arts, were better trained than the Athenians in the arms profession, to the great scorn of Pericles, who in his funeral oration makes fun of those people who "from their very cradles by a painful discipline seek after" courage (Thucydides 2.39.1 [Crawley translation]). We know almost nothing of the methods used by these "technicians of war" (as Xenophon called them), except that they placed great importance on the development of tactics, among which a particular countermarch was included that was to remain known as the "Laconian Countermarch."

We must above all note that in the course of the classical period an increasingly greater importance was granted to the technical aspects of warcraft. This evolution is already evident when we compare Herodotus, in whom the *technē* has scarcely any place between cunning and strength, to Thuycydides, where it emerges, linked to intelligence, in a commander's performance of his duties. There are too many manifestations of it in the fourth century to mention them all here: the appearance of technical treatises relating above all to siege warfare (such as the *Siegecraft* by Aeneas Tacticus); Plato's insistence on the necessity of military exercises, paralleling a tendency seen in many cities (particularly in Thebes in the time of Epaminondas and Pelopidas); the priority granted to experience in the choice of *stratēgoi* as seen in Aristotle's *Politics* and in an anonymous pamphlet from the early Hellenistic period (the *De eligendis magistratibus*) that cites as an example "a few small well-ruled cities" where "there are three elected men among those who have already carried out strategy and two among the young"; the specialization of the Athenian *stratēgoi* in various spheres of activity and a growing distinction between them and the orators, the men of war, and the men of the Assembly, often acting in collusion, and so on.

Mercenaries

Into the evolution we have just described a phenomenon was introduced that at first might appear completely incompatible with the deep civic roots of the military function: the cities' use of mercenaries, in other words, of professionals of war serving a foreign power for a salary.

In the archaic period Greeks, primarily from Ionia, had rented their services as "men of bronze" to Oriental rulers or had served as personal bodyguards to tyrants in Greece itself. After a period of calm the mercenary system became increasingly active, starting with the Peloponnesian War, to the benefit first of the Persian satraps of Asia Minor, then of the entire Greek world and its periphery. The famous expedition of the Ten Thousand recounted by Xenophon in his *Anabasis* is characteristic of this period. During the entire fourth century, Greeks of all origins set off by the tens of thousands on that path as hoplites, light infantry, and peltasts. With their confederates from the Balkans, they played an essential role in Alexander's conquest of the Persian empire and even more so in the establishment of the Hellenistic kingdoms.

There are many complex causes of the mercenary system. The primary ones must have been those that ended up separating the individual from his fatherland, either because it had been shattered apart (chiefly through war), or because he had been banished from it, or above all because he had been reduced to poverty there as a result of overpopulation, natural disasters, or a change in the sociopolitical regime. But he might also have allowed himself to be led onto the path of adventure by the potential for making good use of his military qualifications abroad (there were Peloponnesian hoplites, Cretan archers, Thracian peltasts) and for benefiting from the largesse of a victorious and prosperous employer.

The cities' extensive use of mercenaries was not without consequences for them, as well: an increased technical nature of military operations; financial difficulties; a tendency among citizens to pass on the less attractive tasks (distant expeditions, garrison duty); a resurgence of tyranny; a destabilization of traditional international relationships in favor of the richer states.

From this dual perspective, the rise of the mercenary system in the fourth century played a major role in what has been called the "crisis" of the city. But so as not to go too much beyond our fixed framework, what we will limit ourselves to pointing out here are the reasons for which the cities were able to agree to call upon mercenaries. The first reason undoubtedly has to do with the personality of those soldiers. Insofar as they came from Greek or Hellenized areas, they did not appear as absolute foreigners, like the Mamluks in the Ottoman empire. Many of them maintained the hope of regaining their status as citizen back home at the end of their adventures. While performing as mercenaries, they were often seen attempting to reproduce a civic model in various forms: by having themselves granted the freedom of the city for their good and loyal services; by usurping it in the conquered cities or from their own employers; sometimes even by establishing new cities on their own, in the best colonial tradition; or quite simply, by creating all sorts of professional organizations that functioned as cities on a small scale (voting on honorific decrees, sending out ambassadors). In this regard, it is quite significant that pirates, who in many ways were similar to mercenaries, often also slipped into a governmental mold by using existing structures or by forging new ones.

In the opposite direction it must be said that the soldier-citizen always had a bit of the mercenary in him. For both, war was expected to be a lucrative undertaking: to all appearances they received the same pay and the same share of the spoils. The patriotic passion of the citizen must have been blurred when he was sent to give aid to a foreign power: it was fairly common not to know very well whether auxiliaries were fighting as allies or as mercenaries. The regular system of recruitment could in the end tend to turn certain citizens into true professionals of war: thus in Athens, before they began to call upon different age groups in turn, for a long time the composition of the list of conscripts had been conferred upon the *stratēgoi,* who had every reason to give priority to volunteers and then to take individual abilities into serious account.

From the end of the fifth century, in certain cities one even saw the formation of a small permanent army, often made up of from 300 to 1,000 "chosen" citizens, who were, so to speak, "mercenaries of the interior." In 422 the Argives, for example, selected "a thousand of their co-citizens, the youngest among them, the most robust, and the richest; excusing them from all other duties and providing them with food at the expense of the State, they were asked to commit to a continuous training" (Diodorus 12.75.7). Of greater fame was the sacred battalion of the Thebans, which was reorganized in 379 by

Gorgidas: "He had 300 elite men join up, whose training and maintenance was paid for by the State, and who were camped in Cadmea" (Plutarch *Pelopidas* 18.1). In the same period, the Arcadian league also employed "public guardians" called "eparites," while just about everywhere the elite soldiers called *epilektoi* grew in number (in general we know very little about the method of their recruitment and the status of those soldiers).

It is within this historical context that we must situate contemporary plans for functionally based societies, rather than simply seeing a resurgence of the old Indo-European ideology or an imitation of the Egyptian model in them. They always granted an axial position to the warrior class. For Hippodamus of Miletus, it coexisted with two other classes, those of craftsmen and farmers, and it was supported by public land. Obviously, the Platonic *Republic* is even more famous, for in it the warrior elite, fed by the anonymous mass of producers reduced to a state of dependency, led a communal life entirely subordinate to the interests of the city, under the wing of the wisest among them.

These various tendencies toward a military professionalism force us not to insist too much on the contrast between mercenaries and the soldier-citizens, and not to dissociate them, at the end of this chapter, in the study of the problems raised by the harmonious integration of the warrior function into the political framework.

The Military and the Political

From this point of view, the chronic insubordination of mercenaries was not the only thing to cause problems. Their citizen counterparts, the "chosen ones," were in most cases second to none in their wish to impose their law on their compatriots. But those were only the most noteworthy manifestations of a structural propensity, so to speak, by the representatives of armed force to intervene directly in the internal life of cities—in the absence of any other organized force able to bring about the triumph of particular interest groups or maintain public order.

Any domestic dissent that turned toward civil war was immediately translated into military terms, dividing soldiers into two opposing camps along a line that as a general rule passed between the different official bodies: the cavalry against hoplites, hoplites against light infantry and sailors. The talents of leaders consisted precisely of preventing the malcontents from organizing along those lines, by being able to disarm them preventively or to temporarily distance them under some pretext, by submerging them into loyalist units, by banning the recruitment of mercenaries, etc. The confrontation normally took place in the city in the usual gathering places (agora, acropolis, theater, gymnasium) and ended with the massacre or the banishment of the defeated, who might have pursued the battle by settling in a foreign city or at a frontier post from which they could control a part of the territory. The events that occurred in Athens in 411 are a prime example of this: standing up to the oligarchs of the city, who were being supported by the cavalry, the hoplites and sailors stationed in Samos proceeded by themselves to replace their *stratētgoi* before settling in Piraeus and ultimately forcing the restoration of democracy.

What sometimes ignited things was precisely a chance alteration in the relationship of forces inside the army. Thus, at the time of the siege of Mytilene in 427, the man in power, a certain Salaethus, "armed the commons with heavy armor, which they had not before possessed, with the intention of making a sortie against the Athenians. The commons, however, no sooner found themselves possessed with arms than they refused any longer to obey their officers; and forming in knots together, told the authorities to bring out in public the provisions and divide them amongst them all" (Thucydides 3.27.2–3 [Crawley translation]). But it also happened that the effects of this were felt in the relatively long term, without unleashing any violence. Here are a few examples taken from Aristotle's *Politics:* "At Tarentum a little after the [Persian] war, where so many of the nobles were killed in a battle by the Iapygi, that from a free state [*politeia, moderate democracy*] the government was turned into a [radical] democracy; . . . At Athens, through the unfortunate event of the infantry battles, the number of the nobles was reduced by the soldiers being chosen from the list of citizens in the Lacedaemonian wars" (5.1303a [Ellis translation]). Also in favor of democracy, there was the fact, which had earlier come into play in Athens, that "the people, being the cause of the naval victory over the [Persians], assumed greatly upon it, and enlisted themselves under factious demagogues, although opposed by the better part of the citizens" (2.1274a [ibid.])— which must have occurred again in the fourth century when *thetēs* were integrated into the hoplite army.

The sustained attention Aristotle pays to these events proves that we are not dealing here with simple epiphenomena of a pathological nature (as modern historians have a tendency to believe), but rather with tendencies inherent in the life of a city. Even though different regimes have rested on criteria of wealth and distinction, it was necessary in all cases that they ensure the establishment of a strict correspondence between the political and military functions of citizens: an oligarchy was to rely upon the cavalry and a *politeia* was made up of hoplites (to the point of reserving, as the Malians did, the functions of magistracies to those who were the right age to see active duty), whereas a democracy could count only on the light infantry and on sailors. This was also true with regard to fortifications, in which "what is proper for some governments is not proper for all; as, for instance, a lofty citadel is proper for a monarchy and an oligarchy; a city built upon a plain suits a democracy; neither of these for an aristocracy, but rather many strong places" (7.1330b [ibid.]).

By reason of constraints endemic to warcraft, such harmony was not always easy to establish, in particular for the oligarchs: to call upon the poor to make up their light-armed infantry was "to form it against itself: But as a city is composed of persons of different ages, some young and some old, the fathers should teach their sons, while they were very young, a light and easy exercise; but when they are grown up, they should be perfect in every warlike exercise" (6.1321a [ibid.]). In the case of distortion, either structural or gratuitous, it was the military factor that won out: because "it is impossible to oblige those who have arms in their hands, and can insist on their own terms, to be always under command. . . . Those who have arms in their hands have it in their option whether they will or will not assume the supreme power" (7.1329a [ibid.]).

All these infringements, more or less legal and normal, of the military upon the political, and the care Aristotle takes to ward off the danger of them, fit well into our preliminary concept of war in ancient Greece. Insofar as the principal methods of exploitation and development were based essentially on the use of extra-economic constraints, war could only appear as a rational phenomenon, closely connected to the birth of the order guaranteed by justice, as was proven already at the beginning of time by the archetypal battle of the gods and the giants that had caused the cosmos to surge out of chaos. War remained the great midwife of political communities. It was therefore natural that those communities were constantly in military practice within their cities as they were threatened from without by armed force.

Notes

1. [The following sources were used for quotations from classical writers: the Modern Library edition of the *Complete Writings of Thucydides: The Peloponnesian War*, unabridged Crawley translation, with an Introduction by J. H. Finley, Jr. (New York, 1951); Xenophon, *The Education of Cyrus*, trans. H. G. Daykns (New York, 1914); Yvon Garlan, *War in the Ancient World: A Social History*, trans. Janet Lloyd (London, 1975); the Carnes Lord translation of the *Oeconomicus* in Leo Strauss's *Xenophon's Socratic Discourse: An Interpretation of the "Oeconomicus"* (Ithaca, N.Y. 1970); *A Treatise on Government, or The Politics of Aristotle*, trans. William Ellis (New York, 1912)—trans.]

Bibliographical Notes

This is not the place to provide a lengthy bibliography, although one could easily construct one from a certain number of general studies on the subject.

Among the more concrete and factual texts that appeared primarily in Germany in the nineteenth and early twentieth century, the most usable are those by Hans Delbruck, *History of the Art of War within the Framework of Political History*, translated from the German by W. J. Renfroe, Jr. (Westport, Conn., 1975–85), and by J. Kromayer and G. Veith, *Heerwesen und Kriegfuhrung der Griechen un Römer*, in volume 4 of W. Otto, *Handbuch der Altertumswissenschaft*, 3d ed. (1928). See also Paul Couissin, *Les institutions militaires et navales des anciens Grecs* (Paris, 1932).

A few recent syntheses propose a more "sociological" interpretation of war: F. E. Adcock, *The Greek and Macedonian Art of War* (Berkeley, 1957); Jean-Pierre Vernant, ed., *Problèmes de la guerre en Grèce ancienne* (La Haye, 1968); Yvon Garlan, *War in the Ancient World: A Social History*, trans. Janet Lloyd (London, 1975); Pierre Ducrey, *Warfare in Ancient Greece*, trans. Janet Lloyd (New York, 1986), which provides abundant illustrations. One should also add Raoul Lonis, "La guerre en Grèce: Quinze années de recherche, 1968–1983." *Revue des études grecques* 98 (1985): 321–79.

Many more specialized works bear the mark to a lesser or greater degree of this new orientation: *Armées et fiscalité dans le monde antique*, [Actes du colloque national], Paris, 14–16 October 1976 (Paris, 1977); J. K. Anderson, *Military Theory and Practice in the Age of Xenophon* (Berkeley, 1970); André Aymard, *Etudes d'histoire ancienne* (Paris, 1967), pp. 418–512; Angelo Brelich, *Guerre, agoni, e culti nella Grecia arcaica* (Bonn, 1961); Patrice Brun, *Eisphora—syntaxis stratiotika: Recherches sur les finances militaires d'Athènes au IVe siècle av. J.C* (Paris, 1983); Perre Ducrey, *Le traitement des prisonniers de guerre dans la Grèce antique, des origines à la conquête romaine* (Paris, 1968); Yvon Garlan, *Recherches de poliorcétique grecque* (Athens, 1974), and *Guerre et économie en Grèce ancienne* (Paris, 1989); P. D. A. Garnsey and C. R. Whittaker, eds., *Imperialism in the Ancient World: The Cambridge University Research Seminar in Ancient History* (New York, 1978); P. A. L. Greenhalgh, *Early Greek Warfare: Horsemen and Chariots in the Homeric and Archaic Ages* (Cambridge, 1973);

V. D. Hanson, *Warfare and Agriculture in Classical Greece* (Pisa, 1983); Virgilio Ilari, *Guerra e diritto nel mondo antico*, vol. 1, *Guerra e diretto nel mondo greco-ellenistico fino al III secolo* (Milan, 1980); Marcel Launey, *Recherches sur les armées hellénistiques* (1951), reprinted in two volumes with postscript by Yvon Garlan, Philippe Gauthier, and Claude Orrieux (Paris, 1987); J. F. Lazenby, *The Spartan Army* (Chicago, 1985); Pierre Leriche and Henri Tréziny, eds., *La fortification dans l'histoire du monde grec,* Actes du colloque international, "La Fortification et sa place dans l'histoire politique, culturelle, et sociale du monde grec," Valbonne, December 1982 (Paris, 1986); Raoul Lonis, *Les usages de la guerre entre Grecs et Barbares: Des guerres médiques au milieu du IVe siècle av. J.C.* (Paris, 1969), and *Guerre et religion en Grèce à l'époque classique; Recherches sur les rites, les dieux, l'idéologie de la victoire* (Paris, 1979); Nicole Loraux, *The Invention of Athens: The Funeral Oration in the Classical City,* trans. Alan Sheridan (Cambridge, Mass., 1986), and many articles on the ideology of war; L. P. Marinovic, *Le mercenariat grec au IVe siècle avant notre ère et la crise de la polis,* translated from the Russian by Jacqueline and Yvon Garlan (Paris, 1988); J. S. Morrison and R. T. Williams, *Greek Oared Ships, 900–322 B.C.* (London, 1968); W. K. Pritchett, *The Greek State at War,* vols. 1–4 (Berkeley, 1971–85); A. Scnapp, *La duplicité du chasseur* (1989); A. M. Snodgrass, *Arms and Armour of the Greeks* (Ithaca, 1967); Marta Sordi, ed., *La pace nel mondo antico* (Milan, 1985); Pierre Vidal-Naquet, *The Black Hunter: Forms of Thought and Forms of Society in the Greek World,* trans. Andrew Szegedy-Maszak (Baltimore, 1986), and "The Black Hunter Revisited," *Proceedings of the Cambridge Philological Society* 212 (1986): 126–44 (cf. *Mélanges Pierre Lévêque,* vol. 2 [1988]).

For a better problematical approach, see Ettore Ciccotti, *La guerra e la pace nel mondo antico, un saggio* (Turin, 1901); M. I. Finley, "Empire in the Greco-Roman World," *Greece and Rome* 25 (1978): 1–15, and "War and Empire," in *Ancient History* (1985). For works that look beyond the classical world, see Jean Bazin and Emmanuel Terray, eds., *Guerres de lignages et guerres d'etats en Afrique* (Paris, 1982); Claude Meillassoux, *The Anthropology of Slavery: The Womb of Iron and Gold,* trans. Alide Dasnois (Chicago, 1991); W. V. Harris, ed., *The Imperialism of Mid-Republican Rome* (Rome, 1984).

Among some recently published articles, I wish to point out W. R. Connor, "Early Greek Land Warfare as Symbolic Expression," *Past and Present* 119 (1988): 3–29; Peter Krentz, "The Nature of Hoplite Battle," *Classical Antiquity* 4 (1985): 50–61; F. Lissarague, "Autour du guerrier," in *La cité des images* (Paris, 1984), pp. 35–47; D. Miculella, "Ruolo dei militari e consenso politico nella *polis* aristotelica," *Studi Classici e Orientali* 34 (1984): 83–101.

I wish to thank Pierre Ducrey, Raoul Lonis, and Pierre Vidal-Naquet here for their contribution in reading and providing critiques of my manuscript.

CHAPTER THREE

Becoming an Adult

Giuseppe Cambiano

"WHICH BEING WITH a single voice has sometimes two feet, sometimes four, and sometimes three?"[1] By replying "man" Oedipus solved the riddle of the Sphinx. The changing modes of movement seemed an obvious reference to the three crucial phases in human life: infancy, maturity, and old age. An erect stature, which many philosophers from Plato and Aristotle on considered the essential feature distinguishing humanity from other animals, also marked the primacy of adulthood and the distance that the newborn child, so similar to the four-legged animal, would have to cover in order to become an adult. Naturally, the first requirement was survival. Infant mortality was high in ancient Greece as a result of premature or irregular births and illnesses caused by inadequate diets and insanitary conditions, not to speak of the therapeutic impotence of most ancient medicine. In Eretria, between the end of the eighth and the beginning of the seventh century B.C., the distance between infant and adult was further emphasized by the fact that those who died before the age of sixteen were interred in tombs, whereas adults were cremated, a process that sanctioned their passage from nature to culture.

However, not only nature operated in the selection process. Being born healthy made it possible to escape elimination, the inevitable fate of deformed infants, who were seen as a form of divine punishment of evil omen by parents and community alike. In Sparta, the decision to allow the newborn child to live was reserved for the oldest members of the tribe (*phylē*) to which the father belonged. Any child who appeared to be deformed or sickly could be abandoned on the slopes of Mount Taygetus. In Athens and other cities, the infant was exposed in a terracotta pot or some other container, far from home and frequently in uncultivated places a long way from the city, where, assuming it was not found by someone, it would die of hunger or be torn to shreds by wild animals. Not only deformed children were exposed but also, on occasion, healthy infants. The audiences of tragedies or the comedies of Menander frequently witnessed cases of exposed children who were later discovered: Oedipus himself had suffered such a fate. In order to control births, Aristotle preferred abortion to exposure, but insisted on the need for a law that would prohibit the rearing of deformed children. In Athens, the decision to expose a child was left to the father, while in the Cretan city of Gortyn, a freeborn woman who had a child after being divorced had to take it, with witnesses, to the home of her ex-husband. If he refused the child, it was up to him to decide whether it should be exposed or reared. In ancient times an Athenian father had the right to sell his child in order to pay off debts. This practice was outlawed by Solon, and exposure was adopted as an alternative, especially among the poorest. In Menander's *Perikeiromene,* a father describes how he exposed his son and daughter, following the death of their mother in childbirth and his own financial ruin after the sinking of a cargo in the Aegean.

Although there are no certain data, it is possible that most exposed babies were not unwanted legitimate children, but the illegitimate offspring of parents of mixed nationalities or irregular marriages, in particular of marriages between children of slaves. Even among the poor, it is unlikely that legitimate firstborn sons were exposed, although the exposure of daughters was more probable. It should not be forgotten that in Athens girls had to receive a dowry in order to be married, unlike the situation described by Homer and existing among aristocratic families in the archaic period, when the future husband offered gifts to the father of the bride. Exposure was therefore also a way of avoiding too many unmarried daughters, who would have weighed heavily on the economic resources of the father. Above all in the Hellenistic period, when most families had only one child and there was a decrease in the birthrate—the result, according to Polybius, of decadence—the exposure of female infants reached new proportions. Toward 270 B.C., the poet Posidippus claimed: "Anyone, even if he is poor, brings up a son; even if he is rich, he exposes a daughter."

An exposed child could be taken home by others, who had the

right to treat it as freeborn or as a slave; treating the infant as freeborn, however, did not mean that it was adopted. In Attic law, adoption was a transaction between the adopter and the father or guardian of the adopted and was usually intended to ensure a male heir. The most widespread practice was probably to treat the foundling as a slave for personal use—females were sometimes reared as prostitutes—or to sell the child at the appropriate time. Aelian mentions a law in Thebes that forbade citizens to expose their own children, obliging poor fathers to take the newborn child, male or female, to the magistrates, who would entrust the infant to anyone willing to pay a small fixed sum. In return for the expense of bringing up the child, the purchaser would be able to use him or her as a slave.

In ancient Greece, becoming a man did not just mean becoming an adult. The status of the parents was an essential factor in deciding who could, and who could not, become a real man. Not only Greek aristocracies, but also democracies, were based on a fixed number of citizens, whose inclusion in the civic body was determined by their birth. This had been sanctioned in Athens by a law proposed by Pericles in 451–450 b.c., which stated that for one to become a citizen both parents had to be Athenian. This law was reinstated in 403–402, after a period of relaxation during the Peloponnesian War. Adam Smith already saw that Athenian restrictions on granting citizenship depended on the need to maintain the economic advantages Athens derived from the tributes it received from other cities. Obviously, slaves also had parents, but this relationship was not legally recognized. Most slaves came from barbaric, or non-Greek, countries, but it is possible that some freeborn Greeks also became slaves. War was a prime source of slaves: the practice in conquered cities was usually to slaughter the adult males and bear the women and children into slavery. During the Peloponnesian War, Athens had done this to the inhabitants of Mytilene, Torone, Scione, and Melos. Peace treaties sometimes included the restitution of enslaved children. But the appeal made by Plato or Isocrates to the Greeks not to enslave fellow Greeks confirms that the practice still existed in the fourth century b.c. In previous centuries, good-looking male infants and boys in Ionian cities conquered by the Persians stood a good chance of becoming eunuchs. Herodotus talks of the revengeful deed of Periander, the tyrant of Corinth, who sent three hundred boys, sons of the leading citizens of Corcyra, from Alyattes to Sardis to be castrated. But during their journey, at Samos, the boys were rescued by the inhabitants of the island and returned to their home. The boys who fell into the hands of the slavedealer Panionius of Chios were less fortunate. According to Herodotus, he castrated them himself, before taking them to Sardis and Ephesus, where they were sold to barbarians at high prices.

Being a slave in a Greek city meant being denied participation in political life, many civil rights, and most religious festivals, as well as entry to the gymnasia and *palaistrai* in which future citizens were educated. For a slave, the process of becoming adult involved neither a qualitative leap nor a gradual preparation, as it did for the sons of free citizens. If the word *andrapodon*, foot man, used to describe the slave, tended to be assimilated to that used to indicate quadrupeds, *tetrapoda*, the frequent use of the term *pais* also underlined the permanent subjection of the slave. As Aristophanes said in the *Wasps*: "It is right to call someone who gets beaten *pais*, even when he's old." In Athens, it was legally acceptable to use corporal punishment with slaves and children, but not with freeborn adults. Child attendants, or *paidagōgoi*, who accompanied their master's sons to school, were probably the only slaves who could learn indirectly how to read and write, since they were present at lessons. As a general rule, however, the only training slaves received was connected to the work they did for their master, ranging from relatively light domestic duties to the far heavier work in the mines. This work was carried out exclusively by slaves, some of them children, not only in the mines of Nubia described by Diodorus Siculus, but also in the Athenian mines of Laurium. Aristotle mentions a teacher at Syracuse who gave paid lessons to slaves in the domestic sciences, probably including the culinary arts, given the reputation enjoyed by Sicilian cuisine. A master could send his young slaves to workshops in order to learn a trade, from which he would then receive an income. The most widespread practice, however, was probably that of apprenticing the slave in the master's own workshop. Such an apprenticeship must have begun early. Athenian vase paintings of workshops show many children at work, and it cannot be excluded that some of these were slaves. An artisan could also buy slaves in order to train them, especially if he had no children to whom he could hand down the business. This is what happened in the fourth century to Pasion and Phormion, who became so skilled at the art of banking that they were freed and eventually became owners of the bank. In his speech *Against Neaera*, Demosthenes talks of the freedwoman Nicarete, who bought seven baby girls after having carefully assessed their physical endowments. She brought the girls up as prostitutes, even passing them off as her own children in order to obtain higher prices from her clients, and finally sold them off as a single lot.

However, the crafts were not exclusively in the hands of slaves. Many foreigners and some citizens, especially the less well-off, worked as craftsmen. Their sons could receive physical and primary education, since teachers' fees were low, but as Protagoras pointed out in the Platonic dialogue named after him, the sons of the rich started school earlier and finished later. Aristotle is said to have stated clearly that poor men, unable to own slaves, treated their women and children as slaves in order to carry out their work. Even for the sons of the poorest citizens, becoming a man coincided for the most part with working at a craft or in the fields, although, especially in democratic cities such as Athens, this did not deprive them of their future right to participate in political life.

This also held true for sectors such as medicine. In a brief section of the Hippocratic writings, entitled *Law* and written before the second half of the fourth century, it is stated that an aspiring doctor must learn as a boy (*paidomathia*). This was not the case in imperial times, when a doctor like Galen, soaked in philosophical and scientific lore, appears to have begun his medical apprenticeship at the age of sixteen. Home and workshop were often the same thing, and it was here that, almost always, fathers passed the secrets of their trade on to their sons. We have knowledge of entire dynasties of painters and sculptors. The Hippocratic oath contains, among other things, the promise to transmit written and verbal learning to one's sons, to the sons of one's teacher, and to all other pupils who take the oath. If someone had no sons, or if sons revealed no particular talent—as was the case, according to Plato, with the sons of the sculptor Polyclitus—it was possible to adopt as heirs the sons of relatives or friends, to take on as apprentices the sons of freeborn citizens who lacked the means of subsistence, or to buy slaves and train them. In each case, the only way to learn a trade was in the workshop, rather than by means of the educational channels provided by the city.

As with slaves and metics, an early apprenticeship tended to isolate the children of poor citizens from their peers and bind them immediately to an adult world, with little or no experience of the gradual process that integrated the latter into the social, political, and military fabric of the city. This was not the case with a city like

Sparta, where all laboring activities were delegated to helots and *per-ioikoi*. Generally, however, apprenticeship to these activities was not considered part of *paideia* and the process of becoming a man. It would be well to remember that the term *paidia* (game), deriving from *pais* (child), was not opposed to terms describing work, but to *spoudē*, the "serious" activity of adults. In Aristophanes' parody, the *Clouds*, the ability of the young Pheidippides to build small houses, ships, and carts was regarded by his father as a sign that the boy was suited to higher education, not that he would become a skilled craftsman. In the *Laws*, however, Plato would have considered games of this type an imitation of, and preparation for, the crafts activities that would later be practiced by the adult. But in Plato's eyes, these games had very little to do with *paideia:* it is no coincidence that farming and the crafts are left entirely in the hands of slaves and foreigners in the *Laws*. According to Plutarch, no young man from a good family would have envied Phidias. It was not until the Hellenistic period that drawing became part of the educational curriculum, and even then the training provided was not regarded as preparation for a profession. The content and methodology of the arts could also be studied by nonpractitioners. This was also true of medicine, which was regarded as valuable knowledge by Plato and Aristotle since it enabled people to reach informed judgments and to make a theoretical use of medical results. It did not mean that they would become doctors.

The other decisive factor in determining who would become an adult citizen in the fullest sense was gender: women were excluded. Naturally, there were some exceptions, above all during the Hellenistic period and outside Athens, but generally, and in Athens in particular, a woman was integrated into the city as the daughter or wife of a citizen, rather than as a citizen in her own right. It was not until the Hellenistic period that we have evidence of a girl committing herself personally to a marriage contract with her future husband; such a commitment was generally assumed by the father or guardian of the girl. For most free Greek girls, becoming an adult was marked by the decisive event of marriage. The difference in status between female and male infants is well expressed by an alternative presented in Xenophon's *Memorabilia:* to whom should we entrust male children to be educated (*paideusai*) and virgin daughters to be guarded (*diaphy-laxai*)? The alternative to *paideia* for female children was safekeeping. The term "virgin" (*parthenos*) was principally an allusion to the state preceding marriage, rather than to that of physical integrity. A law attributed to Solon established that if a father discovered that this daughter had had sexual relations before marriage—the unequivocal sign of which was pregnancy—she ceased to be a member of the family and could be sold. The prospect of marriage in such a situation vanished, thus explaining the importance of safekeeping as a means of ensuring access to marital status.

From their birth, girls spent most of the time at home, in the care of their mothers or female slaves. The growth of the city following the creation of the *polis*—documented as not having occurred before the second half of the seventh century—significantly shifted female activity into the house, leaving the complete freedom of the outer world to men. Only the poorest women were obliged to leave their homes to work in the fields or as vendors. Inside the home, girls quickly learned the domestic tasks of spinning and cooking. The city's religious festivals provided them with their only opportunity to go out. Symposia, on the other hand, were forbidden to all women except prostitutes, dancers, and flautists. In ancient Athens, these religious festivals coincided with the initiation into adulthood of entire age-groups of boys. This was not the case, however, with girls, whose initiation took place in small groups, chosen to carry out a ritual preparation for marriage. Thus each year, on the occasion of the Arrhephoria, two girls of noble birth, aged between seven and eleven, began to weave the *peplos* that would be offered nine months later to Athena at the Panathenaea. The weaving of a *peplos* by girls is also documented in other places, such as Argos in honor of Hera. It is possible that, in Sparta, girls also wove the chiton consecrated annually to Apollo during the Hyakinthia festival. During the months preceding the Panathenaea, the two girls followed a special routine, at the end of which they were divested of their clothes and gold jewelry. The Arrhephoria was a rite of passage for them; they learned women's work, such as spinning and weaving, and prepared themselves to become wives and mothers. They also assumed the task of carrying under cover of night a basket, balanced on their heads, from the Acropolis to an underground place in a garden dedicated to Aphrodite. Inside the basket, unknown to the girls, was a simulacrum of the baby Erichthonius and the serpent, symbolizing sexuality and generation. They would then emerge from the holy place with other sacred objects wrapped in a cloth. Out of thousands of girls, only two were chosen: what had probably once constituted a collective rite of passage for an entire age-group, by means of a period of segregation and a test, was nothing more than a symbolic representation by the classical period. Thus there is evidence of girls of premarital age becoming priests in Arcadia and Calauria; girls from Locri were even forced to serve for life in the temple of Athena. Normally, however, female participation in religious rituals and tasks was symbolically linked to the decisive turning point in their life represented by marriage. This was the case with the Athenian festival of Artemis Brauronia. A number of girls aged between five and ten were consecrated to the service of Artemis at the sanctuary of Brauron, outside Athens, for a period of time unknown to us. In memory of the sacred she-bear of Artemis, killed after seeking refuge in her temple, the girls were known as bears and were obliged to atone for this sacrilegious act by their service. At the same time, they enacted the passage of the bear, freeing themselves from their wild state as a preparation for marriage and the integration of sexuality into culture.

Processions, dances, and choirs of girls were an essential element of many civic festivals. During the Panathenaea processions in the fourth century B.C., more than a hundred girls, chosen from the noblest families, bore the implements required for sacrifice. Nonetheless, most Athenian girls probably took part in these festivals as spectators rather than protagonists.

In classical Athens, as in many other cities, no schools were provided for female children or adolescents. They would listen to the myths associated with the religious rituals of their city from their mothers, older female relatives and female slaves, and they would sometimes have the opportunity to learn to read and write. But the view held by much of the male world cannot have been far removed from that expressed in these lines by Menander: "Teaching a woman to read and write? What a terrible thing to do! Like feeding a vile snake on more poison." Even in the Hellenistic period, illiteracy seems to have been more common among women than men, judging by the percentage of women who turned to others to write for them. In Teos a school existed for pupils of both sexes, and at Pergamum there were competitions in poetic recitation and reading for girls. But these were uncommon phenomena, and even physical education was an essentially male prerogative. The most notable exception was in Sparta, where girls were not taught to spin, weave, and cook since these were tasks of the servant rather than the wife. As well-nourished as boys, they soon began to take part in footraces, fighting, and discus and javelin throwing, naked in the presence of their male counterparts. We do not know if it was this Spartan example that led to the inclusion in the Olympic games of footraces for women, albeit on different days from the main events. According to Pausanias, these races involved three different age-groups, although whether Athenian girls took part is unknown.

It was even more unusual for girls to receive advanced education. One exception was Aspasia, the mistress of Pericles and, significantly, a foreigner rather than an Athenian citizen. Another was the circle of Sappho on Lesbos at the beginning of the sixth century B.C., a case for which there is no documented counterpart in classical Greece during the fifth and fourth centuries. This circle was an association composed of girls from Lesbos, as well as from cities along the Ionian coast. These girls practiced the arts of dance and song, learning to play the lyre and participating in wedding feasts, religious festivals, and, possibly, beauty contests in order to acquire the qualities they would need to marry noblemen. This appears to confirm the greater liberty enjoyed by girls of noble birth during the archaic era compared to the segregation that was characteristic of classical Athens. This circle also provided the occasion for the development of the kind of homoerotic ties that, in seventh-century Sparta, are documented by the *partheneia* of Alcman. This does not mean, however, that premarital sexual education was also provided.

In the life of a freeborn Greek girl, the decisive rite of passage was marriage. Marriage for a woman, far more than for a man, involved a radical change in situation. Exchanging the status of *parthenos* for that of woman coincided with becoming a wife and the potential mother of male citizens. Unlike sons, daughters did not remain in their parents' house for long. They married young, often before they were sixteen, and their husbands were at least ten years older. Betrothal took place even earlier: Demosthenes' sister was less than five. The law code from Gortyn in Crete established the beginning of marriageable age at twelve. Such a difference in age did not encourage the growth of intellectual or affective bonds between the bride and groom. Xenophon attributed the lack of education in wives to their youth at marriage.

In order to understand the nature of Athenian marriage, we must remember that it was a contract between two men, the father or guardian of the bride and the future husband. For the woman, marriage meant little more than moving from the father's house to that of the husband, from the custodial segregation of one to the custodial segregation of the other, in a handing over of all legal responsibility. In Egypt, on the other hand, regarded by both Herodotus and Sophocles as the absolute antithesis of the Greek world, it was the woman's job to leave the house in order to obtain food while the man stayed at home to weave. The Greek bride-to-be prepared for her wedding day by offering her childhood toys to Artemis and by cutting her hair, a sign that her adolescence was over. At Troezen, she consecrated her girdle to Athena Apatouria.

On the eve of the wedding day, both bride and groom took a ritual bath to wedding hymns in honor of Hymen and intended to favor the birth of healthy children, while the father of the bride made sacrifices to Zeus, Hera, Artemis, Aphrodite, and Peitho. The actual ceremony, the procession bearing the bride from the house of her father to that of her husband, confirmed that the real protagonist of the rite of passage and change of status, was the woman herself. The ceremony began with a feast at the home of the bride's father, where a child passed among the guests offering bread and saying, "They have escaped evil; they have found the good." The bread stood for the transition from a wild to a civilized state. Throughout the feast, the bride was veiled and surrounded by her friends, possibly uncovering her face only at the end. After wedding hymns, libations, and blessings, a torchlit procession accompanied the bride's nuptial cart to the house of the groom. Bearing a sieve of barley, which symbolized her new role as preparer of food, she entered the house and was taken to the hearth, where she received offerings of sweetmeats and dried figs to sanction her arrival. Finally, the bride and groom entered the wedding chamber, the door of which was guarded by a friend of the husband, and the marriage was consummated. The wedding ceremony itself took the form of a transfer from one house to another, rather than from the private space of one house to the wider and more public space of the city. By her mobility, the bride allowed a bond to be created between two families.

"Marriage, for a girl, played the same role as war for a young man" (Vernant). In a situation of constant war or threat of war, a factor that also decisively influenced prosperity and economic decay, military ability was essential. For the son of a citizen, becoming a man not only meant becoming a husband and father but, above all, a citizen capable of defending his city and of guiding it politically. Until at least the fourth century B.C., war and hoplite combat in compact ranks were entrusted, not to professional soldiers, but to citizens who were expected to show the same determination and courage that enabled them to rule the city during times of peace. This was the case for all cities, whether they were aristocratic or democratic. However, particularly after its victory over Athens in the Peloponnesian War, Sparta became a model for many intellectuals of the city best able to prepare its young men for war. Xenophon attributed this supremacy to the public nature of Spartan upbringing, which denied the family control over its children. Newborn infants were immediately put to the test by nurses, who washed them with wine instead of water so that weaklings would suffer from fits. It was the task of nurses, rather than mothers, to raise children, without swaddling them and accustoming them to an austere diet. Children were expected to avoid tantrums and not to be afraid of the dark or of being left alone. There is a certain degree of idealization in the descriptions of Spartan education provided by Xenophon and Plutarch. Undoubtedly, however, its aim was to strengthen and physically prepare Spartan children from infancy. The turning point came at the age of seven, when the boys were organized into groups, *agelai*—a term that usually described flocks of animals requiring a leader. They became used to living communally away from home and to being subject to the *agōgē*, a training program intended to impart discipline, obedience, and aggressiveness. Subjection to the *agōgē* enabled boys to become *homoioi*, "equals": full-fledged citizens exempt from labor of any kind. For this reason, both helots and *perioikoi* were excluded. Children were shaved and accustomed to being barefoot. From the age of twelve, they wore the same tunic all year round and slept on rushes they had plucked themselves. During the summer festivals, the Gymnopaidia, they performed exercises in the agora, naked beneath the burning sun. They were given very little food, in order to train them to use their cunning to procure it by theft. If they were caught, the punishment was a beating. Obedience was instilled by a system of rewards and punishments. At each stage of his life, the boy was under the control of someone older, who was always, unlike the slave child attendants of Athens, freeborn. Such pervasive social control created enormous conformism and tended to reinforce a desire for integration with the social body. But this was accompanied by the need of the military squads to choose the best leaders and to constitute select groups of soldiers. Contests between members of the same age-group during festivals and, in particular, the typical institution of staged battles satisfied this need.

Music was not excluded from Spartan education. During the Gymnopaidia, competitions in choral dance, often with masks, were held between members of both sexes. These competitions were also part of the Carnea, in honor of Apollo, from the seventh century on. However, the central element of the *agōgē* was not reading, writing, or gymnastics, but the games. It is no coincidence that many Olympic winners during the archaic period of the games were Spartans. The staged battles, which ritualized aggression and expressed a complementary mixture of cooperation and conflict, were a continuation of contests and actual war. These battles took place on an island formed by the Eurotas River, beside a temple to Artemis—a goddess with special links to the world of adolescence and to the tension that existed between the domesticated and the wild—between two teams of boys; each team was allocated one of the two bridges that led to the island. The night before the battle, both teams sacrificed a dog to Ares, god of war. After that two boars were made to fight, and the future winner of the battle was predicted. The struggle began at dawn and consisted in occupying the island and flinging one's opponents into the river. The actual conflict was a mixture of hoplite fighting in squads and a free-for-all, since all moves, including biting and hitting people in the eyes, were permitted.

The real process of initiation, however, with its moments of separation and segregation followed by reintegration, took place in the so-called *krypteia*. This concerned only an elite of ephebes and was undertaken by isolated individuals rather than groups, in difficult conditions, deprived of shelter, clothing, and food and armed with a single knife. By day they were expected to hide, while by night they operated as a kind of secret police, organizing ambushes against the helot population. It should be remembered that adult male Spartans were obliged to eat together daily at communal messes, and that they did not generally live on their own property. Furthermore, helot revolts were not infrequent, explaining the importance of surveillance and policing. It was in this way that the ephebes began to prepare themselves for public service. As an institution, the *krypteia* was the direct opposite of hoplite combat. It was carried out in the mountains at night, involved isolated unarmed individuals, and took the form of hunting, far from agricultural land. It dramatized the abandonment of childhood and the preparation for war. As soon as they had become men, those who had been subjected to the *krypteia* were probably enrolled in the select corps of the Three Hundred Knights, who actually fought on foot.

In Sparta, however, the transition to adult life, the exact moment of which is difficult to determine, revealed greater continuity with the past precisely because each phase was dominated by war. "It is difficult to say whether adult life in Sparta is a prolonged childhood or whether childhood is a premature training for life as an adult and soldier" (Vidal-Naquet). Marriage was considered obligatory, an essential condition for the reproduction of future soldiers, and those who did not marry were punished. For the young, however, marriage was not a rite of passage that marked the end of adolescence and the beginning of a new way of life. The wedding ceremony involved the abduction of the bride. Her head was shaved; she was dressed in men's clothing and made to lie on a straw pallet alone and in the dark. For the ephebe, isolation was a preparation for becoming a hoplite, while for the bride, it prepared her for a marriage that was rapidly consummated, after which the groom returned to sleep with the other young men of his own age. Unlike in Athens, the *oikos* had no significance in Sparta. Even after marriage, and up to the age of about thirty, the groom did not live with his bride but, as in Crete, led a communal existence with his contemporaries. He saw his wife on brief occasions for purely procreative purposes. She, in any case, could also be fertilized by others. The communal messes and prolonged cohabitation of the men were very closely linked to the pedagogic role played by homosexual relationships in Spartan society. *Paides,* too, ate at the adults' communal messes, where they learned the behavior and speech appropriate to the free adult male, also by means of such relationships.

Communal messes were found throughout the Greek world. They have also been documented in Miletus, Thurii, Megara, Thebes, and other cities, particularly in Crete, where homosexuality played an essential role in the passage to adulthood. Classical writers derived many Spartan institutions from Crete. The division into age-groups in Sparta was essential for the organization of society and the renewal of the select corps of ruling aristocratic warriors, because of its training program and coopting of new members. In Crete as well, after being looked after by women for a certain period, children joined their fathers at the communal messes, sitting on the floor and serving at the tables of the adults. They learned to read, write, and play music and were trained in gymnastics and staged battles by a *paidonomos*. At the age of seventeen, the *paides* of the best families each recruited other boys of their own age to form *agelai,* to be fed at the city's expense. The head of each *agelē* was almost always the father of the boy who had formed the group. He took them hunting, trained them, and administered punishment. At the age of approximately twenty-seven, after ten years in the *agelē,* they were regarded as adults and began to eat with the other men at communal messes and to sleep in the men's house, or *andreion,* where they were also trained in pyrrhic war dances. In Crete, the homosexual relationship between a boy and his older lover was an essential stage in becoming a man. However, it assumed the form of ritual abduction rather than courtship. The lover who intended to abduct the boy informed the boy's friends three days earlier. It was up to them to decide whether the abduction was acceptable, their decision being based on the rank of the lover. A lover who was equal or superior to the boy was regarded as suitable. In this case, the lover, accompanied by friends, could take the boy into the countryside, where they feasted and hunted—the favorite sport of the gods and a model for ephebes—for two months. After this period, it was no longer permitted to detain the boy. The typical pattern of an initiation rite, a period of segregation accompanied by aggregation, can be seen. On returning to the city, the boy regained his liberty after having received as a gift his military uniform, an ox, and a goblet. He sacrificed the ox to Zeus and gave portions to those who had escorted him to the city, declaring his satisfaction, or lack of it, with the period of intimacy he had spent in the company of his lover. The failure to find a lover, however, was unbecoming for sons of noble families. It signified the lack of those qualities that made it possible for a boy to enter the group of adult warriors, symbolized by the gift of arms following the homosexual rite of passage. Furthermore, abducted boys were given places of honor in choirs and gymnasia and wore the clothes their lover had given them as a sign of distinction. They thus became part of the elite composed of those known as the *kleinoi,* or "celebrated."

Compared to this educational model, Athens already appeared to classical writers to be the place in which fathers could decide on how their sons were to become men. This is only partly true, however, since the life of Athenian infants and children was also enmeshed in a web of religious festivals through which the city celebrated its values.

These festivals required the consensus of the entire community. The author of the *Constitution of Athens* complained about the excessive number of festivals in Athens, higher than in any other Greek city, and the fact that the sacrifice of so many victims meant that the entire *polis* could eat, even the poor. Athenian fathers did not have the right to decide the life or death of their children. However, it was their decision to admit their sons into the family or, until the age of majority had been reached, to transfer them to another family by means of adoption. They could also assign their sons to a guardian in the event of their own death. An orphan was primarily someone who had lost his father.

Between the fifth and tenth day after the birth of a male child, the Amphidromia took place in the presence of members of his family. During this ceremony, the newborn child was carried at a run around the hearth of his home, signifying his official entry into the family. On the tenth day there was a sacrifice and a feast, and the child was given his name. For the first few years, he was entrusted to the care of his mother or a nurse, generally a slave, while his father spent most of the day away from home. Herodotus praised the Persian custom of not allowing a son to see his father before he was five years old, so that the father would not suffer if the child died prematurely.

Games and stories from the body of traditional myths filled the child's days. During the Anthesteria, a festival in honor of Dionysus, they played a direct part in a rite that involved opening jars and tasting the new wine. These festivals included drinking contests, with slaves and children over the age of three taking part. During the second day of the festival, the so-called day of the pitchers, the children received gifts, such as toy carts or terracotta animals. They were also given a small pitcher with which, crowned with flowers, they participated in the contest. Access to wine represented the first step in the process of integration into the adult world, one of the most significant expressions of which was the symposium, from which women were excluded. A small pitcher was placed in the tomb of children who died before their third birthday, as if to signify passage into the world beyond.

Initiation into the Eleusinian mysteries was also open to children, and one of the honorary positions envisaged was that of the so-called *pais aph'hestias,* or hearth-child. This post was occupied annually by the elected child of a noble Athenian family, who was initiated at the community's expense in order to gain the city the favor of Demeter.

Two other boys, chosen for their birth and wealth, carried boughs of vine covered with grapes in the Oschophoria, a procession in honor of Dionysus. Since they were dressed in women's clothes, this is clearly a typical rite of passage in which the dramatized access to the new state of male adulthood was attenuated by a link with the "feminine" state of infancy, passed at home in the company of women and about to be abandoned. The cutting and dedicating of hair to Artemis during the Apaturia had a similar function. On this occasion, which took place at the age of sixteen, the father swore his son's legitimacy in the presence of his phratry, or "brotherhood."

An essential part of every festival was the series of musical and gymnastic games, which also demonstrated to adults the skills their children had acquired. These games, divided according to age-group, were an instrument used by the city to ensure that conditions were suitable for its reproduction and survival. Thus in classical Athens, during the Oschophoria, twenty adolescents from the best families were set to race in pairs over a distance of seven kilometers. Each pair represented one of the ten tribes into which the city was divided, which thus became the real protagonist of the event. The end of the race was followed by a procession of the ten victors. Athletic games for the three age-groups of children, adolescents, and adults had already been introduced into the Panathenaic games in 566–565 B.C. They were mostly contests that would have been familiar to Homer, as well as the pentathlon, which comprised wrestling, running, the long jump, discus, and javelin. There is no evidence of swimming competitions, although races in armor and on horseback and relay races with torches are well documented during the games dedicated to Theseus, founded around 475 B.C.

The games were actually a reality that exceeded the boundaries of individual cities. They provided young people with a space beyond the city and encouraged a sense of competition with other cities in Greece, particularly in the Pythian, Isthmian, Nemean, and Olympic games. Contests for the young had already been introduced into these games by the second half of the seventh century, with the exception of the pancration, a mixture of wrestling and boxing that was only admitted around 200 B.C. During the afternoon of the second day of the Olympic games, races involving the legitimate children of free Greek citizens between the ages of twelve and eighteen were held, even though it was not always easy to establish effective age in the absence of birth certificates. Naturally, aristocrats had most opportunity to train, and horse races, which required more expensive equipment, remained their prerogative. The city or private patrons provided the money to train no more than a handful of promising youngsters. Competitors at the games came from every social class, even though sport was not a habitual element in the activities of all young people.

Aristocratic combat in archaic Greece was a test of individual courage, whereas hoplite combat introduced deployment and cooperation as decisive elements. To a certain extent, the games absorbed the sense of individual competitiveness that was by now either absent or secondary in war. The object was not to establish records, but to beat the adversary personally in order to share the glory of victory with one's family and city. This was also true of the musical contests, which took place in many parts of the Greek world. We have evidence of a shipwreck toward the end of the fifth century B.C. in which thirty-five boys of Messene, members of a choir on its way to Rhegium, all perished. Their city dedicated bronze statues to their memory at Olympia, and Hippias of Elis composed an inscription.

As military activity ceased to be the prerogative of the aristocracy and the new figure of the hoplite citizen emerged, the need for systematic physical training became paramount. In the sixth century B.C., gymnasia and *palaistrai* began to spring up almost everywhere in Greece. Along with the theater, the gymnasium became a familiar building in Greek cities. When the Greeks began to establish themselves in Egypt and the East as a result of Alexander's conquests, the gymnasium became a badge of identity, distinguishing the newcomers from the indigenous population. In an attempt to integrate with the culture of his conquerors, the high priest of Jerusalem, Jason, appears to have founded a gymnasium for young Jews, with the approval of King Antiochus Epiphanes. At the age of twelve, and possibly earlier, boys began their athletic training under the supervision of a teacher, the *paidotribēs*. They practiced all the events included in city and national games, naked, oiled, and accompanied by music. During the Hellenistic period in Pella, no one could become a citizen without having attended a gymnasium. Generally, however, this was not a legal requirement, even though it gave an undoubted social distinction. It is no accident that in Athens slaves were forbidden to do gymnastic exercises or cover themselves with oil in the *palaistrai*. This meant that they were also excluded from military training. In a law attributed to Solon, this exclusion was accompanied by a ban on homosexual relations between slaves and freeborn boys. In a law made in Beroea in the middle of the second century B.C., the ban on frequenting gymnasia was extended to freed slaves and their children, to disabled people, to prostitutes and those involved in commerce, to drunks, and to the mad. This also helped to avoid pederastic relations unworthy of free men. There is no doubt that homosexuality played an important role in communities of a marked military character such as Crete or Sparta, not to speak of fourth-century Thebes. Here the lover gave his loved one a soldier's uniform when he became an ephebe, and the sacred band was composed entirely of pairs of lovers. But in communities like Athens, too, homosexual relations played a decisive role in the introduction to adult life. Having abandoned his house filled with women, a boy spent most of his time in the gymnasium, and it was here that his sexual life began. It was difficult for a young Athenian to have the opportunity for sexual contact with free girls or women, especially among the upper classes. Furthermore, the greater availability of sexual contact with slave girls lessened its significance and emotional hold. Even though it is impossible to exclude the possibility that homosexual relationships occurred between boys of the same age, the norm established a difference in age between the lover and the loved one. This asymmetry made it possible to distinguish between active and passive roles, not only in a physical sense. It also provided the relationship with an educational dimension. Apart from boys, the gymnasium could only be frequented by adult citizens with time to spare; in other words, men who were wellborn and wealthy. These men were able to watch the boys train and talk with them in order to arouse their interest. Classical writers often use hunting metaphors to describe the courtship; a prey earns respect and admiration by not allowing himself to be captured immediately. The boy was expected to display caution and to put his would-be lover to the test. The passivity of the loved one must never become slavery. In this way, models of conduct were developed whose aim was to prepare the future citizen both to govern and to be governed. A freeborn boy who prostituted himself for money was expelled from the community, since the only people who accepted the passive role of the prostitute were generally slaves or foreigners. In Athens, fathers, relatives, and guardians who prostituted a freeborn child, as well as those who paid for the child's services, were liable to be punished. As soon as a boy's beard began to grow, he abandoned his status as loved one. As he became an adult, he would assume the role of lover, even when he was married. Homosexual and heterosexual relationships were thus not considered mutually exclusive. The heterosexual relationship of marriage permitted the breeding of future citizens, while the educational aspect of the homosexual relationship contributed to the individual's moral and intellectual growth.

The other place in which the sons of free citizens gathered, in Athens and elsewhere, was the *didaskaleion,* or school, possibly even before they began to frequent the gymnasium. The existence of these schools, where children learned to read and write, is already documented at the beginning of the fifth century B.C., when the roof of a school on Chios caved in, killing 119 students who were studying—explicitly—*grammata.* Mass deaths of children such as this were greeted with particular perturbation, since they deprived small Greek cities of future generations at a stroke. In the same century, the athlete Cleomedes of Astypalaea, deprived of his prize at the games for having killed his adversary, pushed away in a rage the pillar that held up the roof of a school containing fifty children. Thucydides describes a Thracian attack on the most popular school in Mycalessus during which all the students were massacred. There is no proof that education was compulsory for the legitimate sons of Athenian citizens before the Hellenistic age. Nonetheless, in practice, such children could all receive some education, and fathers tended to send their sons to *grammatistai* or *paidotribēs* for as long a period as they could afford. Among the obligations of the guardian of a propertyless orphan was that of paying for his education.

The care of orphans in Athens and elsewhere did not coincide with the care provided for the poor. The only privileged orphans were those whose fathers had died in battle, for whom, since the middle of the fifth century B.C., Athens had provided maintenance and education at the city's expense until they came of age. The decree of Theozotides appears to have extended this right to the sons of Athenians who had suffered violent death during the tyranny of the Thirty. During the great Dionysia, immediately before the tragedies, the orphans of war victims were presented to the people; a herald announced that their fathers had died courageously and that the *polis* would raise the children as its own. These orphans would then have the right to front seats at the theater. This was obviously a political measure, intended to ensure social cohesion and military commitment. It also meant that the poorest members of the propertyless citizen class—thetes—might receive an education that was generally reserved in its entirety for the sons of the rich. Alexander also arranged for the orphans of fallen Macedonians to receive their fathers' army pay. Some inscriptions from the Hellenistic era speak of private donations to the cities of Teos and Miletus to pay the salaries of the teachers of all freeborn children. In the second century B.C., the kings of Pergamum sent corn and money to Rhodes for the same reason. But these are exceptions. It was generally the responsibility of the father to pay for his sons' education. Nor did education in itself ensure social promotion. Although the sons of metics could go to school, this had no effect on their legal status.

Sending one's son to the private house of a teacher rather than to the gymnasium, a public building built by the city, was related in a sense to the mythical tradition, which describes the hero being educated by a guardian away from home. This was the case with Achilles and Phoenix. A *didaskaleion,* however, was able to gather a group of pupils under a single teacher. The boy was taken to school by one of his father's slaves, the *paidagōgos,* who had to keep an eye on him and administer punishment if needed. In Athens, it was forbidden for a teacher to open his school or a *paidotribēs* his gymnasium before dawn and to close it before sunset. Teachers who had been authorized or appointed by the city on the basis of competence or qualifications, however, did not exist. The only control the city exercised over schools was moral. It was not until a more advanced age had been reached that a public space like the gymnasium could permit homosexual relationships on a sound educational basis.

The *didaskaleion* taught boys to read, write, and play music, although not for professional purposes as was the case with Oriental scribes. As the drafting of laws and decrees for the city assumed written form, literacy ensured that people became citizens in a complete sense. Learning to read aloud, moving from letters to syllables to words, then learning to write in the same way, could take a number of years. After that, pupils committed to memory lines and longer extracts from the poets, above all from Homer, who was always considered an unequaled reference point for models of behavior and values. Foreign languages, on the other hand, played no part in the educational priorities of the Greeks. A papyrus, dating from the third century B.C. and aimed at schools, contains some elementary arithmetical exercises. Mathematics at a higher level, however, apart from the practical purposes of calculation and measuring, remained limited to a somewhat restricted group of specialists.

A competitive approach permeated not only gymnastics but all types of education. Many documents, above all during the Hellenistic era, speak of reading and recitation contests, and there was even a mental arithmetic contest at Magnesia. These events frequently coincided with religious festivals celebrated at the gymnasium or in the city. This was particularly true for the other basic ingredient, apart from physical exercise, in education: music. Music was an essential feature in the choirs and dances that accompanied these festivals, in both Athens and Sparta. In Arcadia, according to Polybius, music played a part in education up to the age of thirty. Music teaching consisted primarily in learning how to play the lyre while singing in accompaniment. Apart from the lyre, there was a wind instrument known as the *aulos,* more similar to an oboe than to a flute. But the lyre left the mouth free to sing, whereas the *aulos* deformed the face and was regarded by the aristocratic Alcibiades as unfitting for a free man, since it deprived its player of speech. Apollo's victory over Marsyas, the virtuoso of the *aulos,* was not only a mythical event. By the fourth century B.C., the instrument was already being left more and more to specialists. Learning to sing and play, important skills in both religious worship and the self-celebration of the city, and thus in the integration of its youngest members, was done by ear, without written texts. On the occasion of contests, choirs of boys were prepared by teachers under the watchful eye of *chorēgoi.* These were citizens over the age of forty chosen for that purpose, with enough money to pay for the choir's preparation and training, who provided their own house for the purpose.

Exercise and music were recognized by the city as the ingredients that formed the model citizen. The stage immediately preceding transition to the adult state was that of the *ephēbeia.* In Athens, the *ephēbeia* was codified as a form of military service from 338 B.C., although the institution probably existed earlier. It lasted two years and was compulsory for the legitimate sons of all Athenians, irrespective of class. Ephebes were maintained by the city. For the period 261–171 B.C., inscriptions record a substantial decrease in the number of ephebes, to between 20 and 40 a year, compared to an earlier average of 650 a year. During this period, service was reduced to one year, it was no longer compulsory for everyone, and the city no longer financed it, thus automatically excluding the poorest. In the second and first centuries B.C., ephebes also contributed to expenses, with preference being given to rich citizens. In a period during which the military and political significance of Athens was inevitably diminished, the *ephēbeia* increasingly assumed the role of a cultural institution until, under Roman control, it began to attract foreigners from Italy and the East. From 161 B.C. on, this led to an increase in the number of ephebes. During the age of Aristotle, however, only citizens could become ephebes: young men who had reached the age of eighteen were enrolled in the register of the deme, the area of the city to which one's father belonged. The council of demesmen had to decide, by a secret vote, on the new citizen's age and legitimate descent from Athenian parents. The council could then accept, or reject as irregular, the candidacy. In some cases, it was in the interest of the guardian to delay enrollment and in that of the candidate to bring it forward. A young man whose candidacy was rejected returned to the class of *paides,* but he could also appeal. If the appeal was lost, however, he ran the risk of being sold into slavery.

Enrollment in the deme register and, as a result, the right to be considered a full citizen was a delicate step. It preceded the period of military service as an ephebe under the direction of a *kosmētēs* and ten *sōphronistai,* one for each tribe. The Assembly elected two teachers, a master of arms, and three instructors in the use of the bow, the javelin, and the catapult to train the ephebes. On the occasion of the festival of Artemis Agrothera, the ephebes took part in the procession and swore their loyalty to the state, its borders and institutions, and to their comrades in the sanctuary of Agraulos. They then went to Piraeus, where they performed guard duty in two barracks. During their second year of service, a review of the ephebes was held before the Assembly in the theater of Dionysus, during which they demonstrated their military prowess. By presenting them with a shield and lance, the city marked their transition to the adult state of hoplite. Under the leadership of generals, they served as patrolmen in Attica, carrying out garrison duty in the border forts and serving as bodyguards to Assembly meetings, clad in a black *chlamus.* Patrol duty along the borders and at the edges of the city, sometimes with foreigners, placed the ephebe in an intermediate position. Thus the ephebe, before occupying, as a citizen in the full sense, the space central to the city, was placed in a position of intermediacy—perhaps in memory of or even as an inheritance from a time when initiations had been by age-classes—even though he had already sworn allegiance as a hoplite at the beginning of this period.

Ephebes were fully integrated into the city's festivals. They participated at sacrifices and the games and, in particular, acted as escorts for sacred objects or statues of gods during processions, following preestablished routes that passed through the symbolic spaces of the city. This did not only happen in Athens. There is evidence of ephebes in a hundred Hellenistic cities. The urn containing the ashes of Philopoemen, killed by the Messenes in 183 B.C., was carried in procession at Megalopolis by the future historian Polybius, then a young ephebe of noble family.

From the third century B.C., however, the military aspect of the *ephēbeia* was increasingly absorbed by a kind of higher education. The gymnasium also continued to be the center of an ephebe's life. Athens had three gymnasia outside the city, the Lyceum, the Academy, and the Cynosarges. Two more were added toward the end of the third century B.C., the Ptolemaeum and the Diogeneium, possibly erected in honor of private benefactors. But these gymnasia provided more than physical exercise. They were the home of lessons and conferences given by philosophers, rhetoricians, and, sometimes, doctors. In the first century B.C., an astronomer held a conference in the gymnasium of Delphi. Between 208 and 204, a statue to the stoic philosopher Chrysippus was erected at the Ptolemaeum, where he might have taught. A new institutional dimension thus entered the life of young Athenians and of those foreigners who increasingly came to Athens to listen to its philosophers and rhetoricians. The book also made its appearance at this time. Libraries for ephebes are documented at Teos, Cos, and Athens. An Athenian decree of 117–116 B.C. established that the ephebes of each year should make a donation of books.

The public recognition given to the significance of philosophy, rhetoric, and higher education in general, as well as books, in the process of becoming an adult was not an obvious fact. In order to appreciate its importance, we need to take a step back. Even though, by the end of the sixth century B.C., Xenophanes of Colophon had already protested against the unjustified primacy given to gymnastics, which, in his opinion, contributed to neither the good order nor the well-being of the city, in most Greek cities the formation of the citizen-soldier was sustained by a substantial balance between gymnastics and music. However, with changes in the way political life was conducted and the growing centrality of language as an instrument for making decisions, imposing opinions, and achieving victory in law courts, above all in democratic cities, this balance had begun to deteriorate. In the second half of the fifth century B.C., the Sophists had appeared as an indication of, and factor in, such a process. They did not teach in a regular or continuous way in a single place, but wandered from city to city, making sample speeches in order to attract students and giving courses of lessons, initially in how to make convincing public speeches. Their teaching was mostly formal, explaining differences in style, language, and rhetorical figures, but they did not disdain to address political, ethical, and religious issues of general interest. Hippias of Elis demonstrated awareness of a number of specialist fields, from astronomy to mathematics. It was precisely during this period that such fields were being treated as practical subjects, as we can see from the work of Hippocrates of Chios. The Sophists taught privately and charged a fee, which meant that their pupils inevitably came from wealthier families. Their teaching was essentially concerned with the formation of a governing elite. Young people in particular were extraordinarily attracted to them. The teaching of the Sophists must have seemed premature when compared to the traditional division of duties appropriate to each stage of human life since it regarded the art of learning how to speak as something that could be acquired at an early age. Since the time of Homer, this art—along with skill in battle—had been the prerogative of the adult, if not of the old man. Age, in fact, was essential to the award of power in all Greek cities. Young men were expected to train for war. Learning how to speak would come later, with experience. Sophistic teaching, however, appeared to shoot ahead alarmingly. The failures and final defeat of Athens in the Peloponnesian War helped to weaken the authority of the elder generation and of the traditional educational channels they had favored in order to ensure that sons would become like their fathers. A typical subject for debate during the second half of the fifth century B.C. was whether wicked fathers could produce good sons, and vice versa.

Generational conflict is at the center of Aristophanes' *Clouds*. Here Socrates seems to be regarded as a Sophist, capable of teaching astronomy, geometry, and sacred things, but also of making objections and of convincing people that the weaker argument is the more valid. Unlike the wandering Sophists, however, he was placed in a kind of "thinking shop" rooted into the soil of the city, making it both more familiar and more dangerous to the citizens. Following his teaching, the young Pheidippides learns how to argue with his father, Strepsiades: You beat me as a child, so why can't I do the same to you? I was born free as well. In this kind of argument, age ceased to differentiate. Aristophanes' comedy expressed exactly the way in which advocates of the past contrasted the ancient *paideia* with the youth of today by means of the antithesis between the gymnasium and the agora. The gymnasium of the past, with its world of music and exercise, made boys modest, strong, and faithful to tradition, producing the men who had fought at Marathon. The new *paideia,* on the other hand, was focused on the agora and the baths, now filled with boys who had deserted the gymnasia. They no longer learned measure, but techniques for improving their speech to such a point that they argued with their fathers. In the *Frogs,* Aristophanes blamed Euripides for teaching boys the chattering, *lalia,* that had emptied the gymnasia. In the *Knights,* the Sausage-maker said that he had been educated in the agora, surrounded by dispute and fraud to such an extent that a rhetorician was able to predict his future career as a demagogue. In his speech *Against Alcibiades,* Andocides also refers to the conflict between the gymnasium and the tribune in terms of a reversal in the roles attributed to each age-group. Now it was the old who fought and the young who addressed the people. This reversal could be seen in Alcibiades, who, even to Thucydides, seemed to champion equality between young and old by opposing the older Nicias when he decided on a military expedition against Syracuse.

The portrait of Socrates drawn by Aristophanes in the *Clouds* also indicates that another important change had taken place. In this comedy, the old Strepsiades is ironically presented attending Socrates' thinking shop. One of the most striking differences between Socrates and the Sophists—a difference that emerges above all in Plato—was the fact that his philosophical teaching was extended into adulthood and that it practically never came to an end. The school of philosophy founded by Plato in the fourth century B.C. and situated near the suburban gymnasium of the Academy rather than in the agora made no distinction according to age. A predecessor, the Pythagorean community at Croton, had also addressed itself to adults, distinguishing between two progressive stages of initiation on the model of the mystery cults, with increasingly complex levels of knowledge. In Plato's dialogues, Socrates is presented first as a youth, then as an adult, and finally as an old man with a constant desire to learn—to such an extent that his music master, Connos, was mocked for being a teacher of the old. Socrates was also surrounded by adult disciples, such as Crito. In the *Apology,* Socrates' activity is seen to be a sort of endless *paideia* for all ages and types of citizen, aimed at the constant improvement of their souls. Socrates' accusers, Meletus in the *Apology* and Anytus in *Meno,* regarded the Athenian citizens who sat in the Assembly, the Council, and the courts as the real teachers of the young. In *Protagoras,* for different reasons, the Sophist praised the Athenian educational system. The idea of Athens as a school for democracy and justice, however, was opposed by the radical thesis of Plato that the Athenian citizens were far from being educators. On the contrary, they needed to be educated. Transposing the model of nutritional medicine from the body to the soul made it possible for Plato to regard philosophy as a technique of educational therapy indispensable at all ages.

In the *Republic,* historically existing cities, in particular Athens, were even presented as corrupters of philosophical natures. According to Plato, a real city should be concerned with philosophy, quite the opposite of the actual case. There was a widespread belief—expressed by Callicles in *Gorgias* and Adeimantus in the *Republic*—that philosophical discussion was suited to boys, but not to adult men. It could contribute to a boy's *paideia* but only on condition that it was then abandoned. For an adult citizen, on the other hand, philosophy was considered unworthy since it encouraged him to operate at the margins of the city, whispering in a corner with three or four boys. The adult's place was in the city's center, in the agora, where he could concern himself with political affairs. Effectively, even in Plato's *Republic,* the school of philosophy was seen as a place where people could protect themselves from the harmful teaching of the city and the Sophists, who merely restated its dominant values and thus perpetuated its malaise. Even physically, the school should be placed as far as possible from the city center.

In contrast with the viewpoint of this time, Plato's just city excluded an early study of dialectic, the most complex element in philosophy, since it could be used to contradict and cast doubt on traditional values, as the Sophists had shown. He felt that thirty was soon enough to begin to study philosophy, after having spent many years studying mathematics. This does not mean that Plato's Academy did not admit students under the age of thirty, but simply that the Academy was not in the just city. Aristotle also appears to have been aware of a difference in levels as far as the ability to learn was concerned. He recognized that although young people could easily become good mathematicians, it was less easy for them to acquire the wisdom they needed to guide them through life or the competence required by inquiries into natural philosophy, since both these fields depended on a wide experience of particulars that could only be gained with time. It is interesting to note that, in the *Characters,* Theophrastus mocked the figure of the *opsimathēs,* someone who had started to study at a later age, or those adults who still wanted to do gymnastics, dance and run with the boys, but said nothing at all about higher education and philosophy. In general, classical philosophers seem to have shared the opinion expressed by Epicurus, who said that no age was unsuitable if one wanted to concern himself with the state of the soul, that is, to philosophize.

During the fourth and third centuries B.C., the figure of the philosopher tended to be seen as a new role model, at times as an alternative to the traditional citizen. This was made possible by the fact that the philosopher absorbed and transposed onto another plane those qualities that had characterized the hoplite: strength, self-control, and cooperation. In the *Phaedo,* Socrates is shown serenely confronting death without renouncing his philosophy, in exactly the same way as a hoplite would face up to death while fighting for his country. This integration of military into philosophical morality appears to mark the triumph of stoicism, the figure of the wise man, insensible to suffering and able to withstand whatever blows fortune might impose. Even the procreative urge could be reabsorbed and transposed to a higher plane. In Plato it was expressed by the metaphor of the pregnant soul of knowledge being induced to give birth by skillful philosophical inquiry. The school of philosophy became the place in which this new model was reproduced and perpetuated. This allowed Plato's notion of *erōs,* as a vehicle for philosophical growth and thus an essential part of becoming a complete man, to recuperate the relationship between man and boy represented in the Greek world by the educational role of homosexual relationships. However, it also allowed him to insist on a less rigid distinction between the sexes. In both the *Republic* and the *Laws,* male and female children follow the same educational route in order to fulfill the same functions as adults. This was true not only for music and exercise, but also for military and philosophical training. In the *Laws,* the significant difference between the two sexes seems to consist in the fact that women married at least ten years before men and could occupy public office ten years later, when they were almost forty.

The presence of women is documented in Plato's Academy and the school of Epicurus, as well as among the Cynics, although it is difficult to establish whether they also taught or wrote. Even if this did occur, it would have been extremely unusual and, despite Plato's statements, philosophy remained a predominantly male activity. Aristotle later defused the most explosive elements of Plato's dispute with the historical city. In order to become a man, that is, a good citizen capable of governing the city, it was not necessary to become a philosopher. It remained true for Aristotle, however, that philosophy was the best kind of life, and that it could be achieved without necessarily becoming a citizen, with all the implied rights and duties, of the city where one's philosophical activity took place. Learning and doing philosophy were also fully compatible with the metic's state, as can be seen from the case of Aristotle himself, a native of Stagirus. Many Hellenistic philosophers left other Greek cities to study in Athens, where they settled down and began to teach, following the path that Anaxagoras had taken in the fifth century B.C. when he left his native Clazomenae to move to Athens. The Stoics even suggested that doing philosophy was compatible with the state of slavery.

Despite the variety of assumptions and approaches among the different schools, philosophy was considered to be the most effective way of becoming a man. But becoming a man now meant more than merely becoming a citizen. The city was unable to cope with this flight away from it toward philosophy and the growing divide between becoming a citizen and becoming a philosopher. The flight came to a head with the Cynics, by means of a radical transformation in the image of childhood. Most philosophers, the most notable exception being the Cynics, shared the contemporary view of the child as a being without reasoning or language, widely documented from Homer to the orators of the fourth century B.C. It was these features in children that made their situation initially so delicate, if they were to arrive at the state of adulthood. Plato actually believed in the need for a kind of indirect gymnastics within the womb produced by the mother's movements, followed by a childhood that was not confined to the house, with games that imitated and foreshadowed the activities and qualities of adult life. In Plato's view, only a *paideia* could produce men. This explains the need for public education—as in Sparta, but without the lopsided emphasis on gymnastics—for all children, composed of writing, reading, playing the lyre, and dancing.

Similar assumptions can be seen in Aristotle's discussion of the *paideia* in the *Politics*. In addition to the advice contained in the medical literature of the time, however, he says that more attention should be paid to the health of children. Within a view of nature as something organized according to a scale of constantly increasing complexity, culminating in the full reasoning ability and erect stature of the adult man, Aristotle regarded the child as dangerously close to the animal state. This was demonstrated by its "dwarflike" state, in which the upper limbs were more developed than the lower ones, forcing it to walk on all fours in the same way that animals do. This disproportion was also connected to the rising heat produced as food was digested, making babies sleep most of the time and only begin to dream by the time they were four or five. During the first forty days, according to Aristotle, babies are unable to cry, laugh, or respond to being tickled, even when awake. In other words, they lack those traits that distinguish the adult human being from other animals. During the first period of its life, the soul of the future human being is indistinguishable from that of an animal. Like other animals, babies cannot be described as happy or as capable of those activities that require an ability to reason and deliberate. Unlike animals, however, they are able to develop and to move away from the animal state, both in their physical proportions, which gradually achieve harmony, and in their mental faculties. The educational process must be grafted onto the natural growth from infant potential to the realization of human qualities in the adult, since it is education that sustains this growth. "No one," said Aristotle in the *Nicomachean Ethics*, "would choose to spend his entire life with the reasoning ability (*dianoia*) of a child." This was by far the most widely held view.

Nevertheless, the Cynics seemed to come very close to holding the opposite view. One of their premises was the abandonment of the metaphorical relation between different ages in human life and the "history" of the human race. This metaphor had led Aeschylus in *Prometheus* to describe men before the arrival of Prometheus—who gave them knowledge of the stars and seasons, of navigation and the alphabet, of medicine, the gods, and more generally, all the *technai*—with the Homeric term *nēpioi*, "infants," incapable of speech. The Cynics' position, in contrast, was presented as a deliberate regression to infancy, parallel to a return from culture to nature. Clearly, exceptions to the negative image of childhood can be found before the arrival of the Cynics. The Homeric *Hymn to Hermes,* for example, described the precocious child god as a thief and skillful trickster, capable of inventing a lyre by using the shell of a tortoise. Even in this case, however, the positive model was based on qualities that belong more properly to the adult state. In any case, the description is that of a god.

The concept of a child's innocence, spontaneity, and simplicity does not seem to have been present in the popular mind, any more than the idea that one can become good by returning to a childlike state. Some anecdotes describing Diogenes the Cynic, who, imitating the child's habit of drinking from his hands or balancing his lentils on bread, threw away bowls and cups, however, reflect the opposite attitude. The same mood can be seen in the rejection of the city and the artificial needs that are generated by it, in order to return to essential natural functions. It is no accident that the Cynics adopted, not only children, but also animals as a model for the ideal man, a somewhat rare figure in Diogenes' view. A positive image of the good child was created in this way, an image that was able to teach the adult, corrupted by city life, how to regain his goodness.

This concept of the good child and of an originally uncorrupted human nature was shared by the Stoics, even though it was in conflict with their conviction that most adults were stupid and evil. At least some of the Stoics were able to avoid blaming the city directly for this corruption by stating that the delicate process was set in motion by the work of mothers and nurses. Warm baths given to children eliminated from their bodies the *tonos,* or tension, that would later distinguish the entire moral life of the adult, as well as creating the false belief that what was pleasant coincided with what was good. Stoicism, in fact, was able to integrate itself more and more successfully into the city's institutions. Even though the inspiration came from King Antigonus Gonatas, Athens issued a decree in honor of Zeno, the founder of the Stoics, for having educated "the young men who entrusted themselves to him in order to be instructed in virtue and moderation" and for having led them "to the highest goals, using his own life as an example." Apart from the very brief interruption of 307, when a decree was issued outlawing philosophers, Athens and scholastic philosophy were soon reconciled. The inclusion of philosophy teaching in the period of military service was the sign that the city recognized the importance of philosophy during the *paideai.*

In some ways, the Platonic dream of philosophy as an integral part of the city seems to have come true, despite the essentially private nature of his teaching, to which foreigners were also admitted. But just as philosophy was institutionalized as part of an ephebe's training, this dream was radically abandoned. Most philosophical schools, and Plato in particular, felt that a long apprenticeship was necessary in order to become a philosopher, and that very few were capable of undergoing it. This did not mean that, for philosophers, other adults were not in need of education. Plato reconstructs, along with the laws and institutions of the city, its myths; these are first to be told by the children's nurses and then endlessly retold by storytelling elders. Thus they would become the means whereby the city as a whole, in all its age-classes, would become spellbound to itself (as by an *epōdē* or charm). The values on which the city was based were internalized and accepted in this way. Aristotle also understood that most people, whose lives were based on *pathē,* could not be persuaded by the force of the *logos* or by teaching and recognized that legislation was the most efficient way of providing a permanent education for adults. He believed that laws were endowed with greater power and excited less hostility than regulations imposed by individuals.

In practice, Athens was able to accept philosophy, not so much as a model for human life, but as a training that helped to produce the kind of person who still found his embodiment, even if increasingly notionally, in the figure of the citizen-soldier. The most successful line turned out to be that expressed by people like Callicles and Adeimantus, reformulated with particular vigor by Isocrates in the *Areopagiticus* shortly before the middle of the fourth century B.C. He contrasted the careful education of the past with the new system, which, once again, was said to be found in the agora and the gaming houses filled with flute players. In the past, education had been based on the recognition of social differences and the need to discipline youthful passions in order to direct them toward noble occupations. The least well-off found work in agriculture and commerce, thus protecting themselves from the harmful effects of indolence, while the rich were occupied with horse racing, gymnastics, hunting with dogs, and philosophy.

Isocrates adopted the educational approach that he attributed to the classical *paideia,* appealing to an elite with enough money to pay for his expensive courses, which lasted for three or four years. Toward the end of his life, he recorded that over a period of approximately forty-five years, his courses had been followed by a hundred pupils, many of whom had become illustrious figures in the political world of Athens and elsewhere. But what Isocrates called philosophy had nothing to do with what the Socratics, Plato, and the Academy meant by the term. For Isocrates, their philosophy was concerned with discussing the number of beings and the like—the kind of discussion to be found, for example, in Plato's *Sophist,* the first book of Aristotle's *Metaphysics,* or his *Physics.* Isocrates did not entirely reject such an approach, but cast it in a merely preparatory or additional role, linking it to geometry and astronomy. These disciplines were considered useless from a practical viewpoint. Nonetheless, they were profitable in the context of a "muscular conception" (Finley) of mental faculties, as part of a gymnastic training program for the brain. As such, however, these activities were more suited to children than adults. Adults received a different kind of philosophy, far more virile than that taught to boys in school. According to Isocrates, a science capable of determining with precision how one should speak and act could not be achieved. The skills of speaking, deliberating, and acting in the interests of the community that Isocrates taught, on the other hand, consisted in the ability to bring together with one's own opinions whatever seemed most suitable in the individual circumstances. Rhetoric, as the art of speaking, was freed from its negative associations with personal gain and fully integrated into the value system of the upper classes. It became capable of referring to the past in order to plan the future, to provide moral examples, and to justify political decisions, proposing the good citizen once again as a model and presenting itself as a privileged way to achieve the state of being a man. Although philosophers, on their part, did not renounce the primacy of the philosophical life, their voluntary integration into the fabric of the city of Athens meant that they were inevitably aligned with the choice made by Isocrates. The incompatibility between rhetoric and philosophy, which had been reinforced in the work of Plato and relaxed by Aristotle, was further weakened. When Athens sent an embassy to Rome in 155 B.C., in order to be let off a fine, representatives from three philosophy schools pleaded the city's case: the Academic Carneades, the Peripatetic Critolaus, and the Stoic Diogenes of Babylon. The finest orators were philosophers. The antagonism between philosophy and rhetoric no longer existed. Jointly they could permeate the teaching and preparation of young people in the upper classes of Greek and Roman society.

Notes

1. [The Penguin edition translations have been used, with some editing, for quotations from the works of classical writers—trans.]

Bibliography

Anderson, W. D. *Ethos and Education in Greek Music.* 2d ed. Cambridge, Mass., 1968.

Angeli, B. P., ed. *Lo Sport in Grecia.* Rome and Bari, 1988.

Arrigoni, G., ed. *Le donne in Grecia.* Rome and Bari, 1985.

Beck, F. A. G. *Greek Education, 450–350 B.C.* London, 1964.

Den Boer, W. *Private Morality in Greece and Rome.* Leiden, 1979.

Brelich, A. *Paides e parthenoi.* Rome, 1969.

Buffière, F. *Eros adolescent: La péderastie dans la Grèce antique.* Paris, 1980.

Burket, W. *Homo necans.* Berlin and New York, 1972.

Calame, C., ed. *L'amore in Grecia.* 3d ed. Rome and Bari, 1984.

Cambiano, G. *La filosofia in Grecia e a Roma.* 2d ed. Rome and Bari, 1987.

Cantarella, E. *L'ambiguo malanno.* 2d ed. Rome, 1985.

———. *Secondo natura: La bisessualità nel mondo antico.* Rome, 1988.

Clarke, M. L. *Higher Education in the Ancient World.* London, 1971.

Detienne, M. *Les jardins d'Adonis.* Paris, 1972.

Dover, K. J. *Greek Popular Morality in the Time of Plato and Aristotle.* Oxford, 1974.

———. *Greek Homosexuality.* London, 1978.

Finley, M. I., and H. W. Pleket. *I giochi olimpici.* Rome, 1980.

Flacelière R. *La vie quotidienne en Grèce au siècle de Périclès.* Paris, 1959.

Foucault, M. *Histoire de la sexualité. vol. 2, L'usage des plaisirs.* Paris, 1984. English translation, *History of Sexuality,* vol. 2, *The Use of Pleasure* (New York, 1985).

Gardiner, E. N. *Greek Athletic Sports and Festivals.* London, 1910.

Gernet, L. *Anthropologie de la Grèce ancienne.* Paris, 1968.

Harrison, A. R. W. *The Law at Athens: The Family and Property.* Oxford, 1968.

Jaeger, W. *Paideia: Die Formung des Griechischen Menschen.* 3 vols. Berlin, 1934-47.

Jeanmaire, H. *Couroi et courètes: Essai sur l'éducation spartiate et sur les rites d'adolescences dans l'antiquité héllénique.* Lille, 1939.

Johann, H.-T., ed. *Erziehung und Bildung in der heidnischen und christlichen Antike.* Darmstadt, 1976.

Kühnert, F. *Allgemeinbildung und Fachbildung in der Antike.* Berlin, 1961.

Lacey, W. K. *The Family in Classical Greece.* London, 1968.

Loraux, N. *Les enfants d'Athéna: Idées athéniennes sur la citoyenneté et la division des sexes.* 2d ed. Paris, 1984.

———. *Les expériences de Tirésias: Le féminin et l'homme grec.* Paris, 1989.

Marrous, H.-I. *Histoire de l'éducation dans l'antiquité.* 6th ed. Paris, 1965.

Nilsson, M. P. *Die hellenistische Schule.* Munich, 1955.

Pélékidis, C. *Histoire de l'éphébie attique des origines à 31 avant Jésus-Christ.* Paris, 1962.

Sissa, G. *Les corps virginal.* Paris, 1987.

Sweet, W. E. *Sport and Recreation in Ancient Greece: A Sourcebook with Translation.* Oxford, 1987.

Vatin, C. *Recherches sur le mariage et la condition de la femme mariée à l'époque héllénistique.* Paris, 1970.

Vegetti, M. *Passioni e bagni caldi: Il problema del bambino cattivo nell'antropologia storica.* In *Tra Edipo e Euclide,* pp. 71–90. Milan, 1983.

Verant, J.-P. *Mythe et pensée chez les Grecs.* Paris, 1965.

————. *Mythe et société en Grèce ancienne.* Paris, 1974. English translation, *Myth and Society in Ancient Greece* (New York, 1990).

————. *L'individu, la mort, l'amour: Soi-même et l'autre en Grèce ancienne.* Paris, 1989.

Vidal-Naquet, P. *Le chasseur noir: Formes de pensée et formes de société dans le monde grec.* Paris, 1981.

Willetts, R. F. *Aristocratic Society in Ancient Crete.* London, 1955.

CHAPTER FOUR

The Citizen

Luciano Canfora

Introduction

IN MANY GREEK cities during the sixth century B.C., the aristocracy, with the help of Spartan troops, expelled the so-called tyrants and took control of their city's politics.[1]

As far as we can tell, tyrannies generally had a popular base, and the tyrant had originally been a demagogue. Nevertheless, in the literary and political tradition that has come down to us, the image of tyranny is decidedly negative, and has even become confused with the idea of oligarchic domination (as we shall see below).

It is well-known that the epicenter and prototype of Greek aristocracies was Sparta. Here the notion of an elite (the Spartans) coincides with the notion of free men, and thus of citizenship. The dominion of this perfect aristocracy, devoted primarily to the virtue of war, was based on the existence of a large dependent underclass (*perioikoi* and helots). In Sparta, therefore, the polarity between slavery and freedom coincides with that between the elite and the masses. Considerable class and racial tension existed between these two worlds, the Spartans and the rest, a tension that was seen and experienced as a state of war. Each year the Spartan ephors "declared war" on the helots in a gesture that was more than merely symbolic. Spartan youngsters served their apprenticeship as warriors by organizing nocturnal hunting expeditions against the helots, whose murder clearly had a ritual sacrificial significance, quite apart from its desired terrorizing effect.

A. H. M. Jones has observed that the Athenian aristocracy, while constantly professing admiration for the Spartan system (we only have to recall the name of Critias, not to mention his nephew, Plato), would have found it extremely difficult to adapt to such a closed and spiritually sterile community. The oldest Attic text to have reached us, the *Constitution of the Athenians,* found among the works of Xenophon (although certainly not written by him), seems to be the first in a series of tributes to the Spartan ideal. The author, for example, expresses envy of the harsh treatment that can be meted out to slaves in Sparta and approval for a political system of "good government," or *eunomia,* in which the people, ignorant, incompetent, and thus incapable of holding power, are "reduced to slavery."

In Athens, however, this ideal, while appealing profoundly to an aristocracy that was anything but resigned and unarmed, was never transformed into reality. Or rather, it became a fact twice, briefly and unsuccessfully, in 411 and 404–403, when the military defeat of Athens by Sparta seemed to open up the possibility of installing the "Spartan model" in the city. Why did these attempts fail, if failure is the right word for what happened? Even the author of the *Constitution of the Athenians,* while emphasizing the main drawback of democracy (the fact that it opened up public office to incompetents), recognized that in Athens the people left the most delicate military responsibilities to their "superiors." The Athenian aristocracy had effectively adapted itself, as we shall see, to an open political system of democratic assembly, which had provided a new basis for the central problem of citizenship.

Thus, although the political situation in Athens was more confused than in Sparta, the city's aristocracy had been able to maintain its right to run the state. This right was based on the possession of certain abilities (not only military) and on the lasting prevalence of an aristocratic value system. This was even sanctioned by the political vocabulary: *sōphrosynē* did not only mean "wisdom" but also "oligarchic government" (Thucydides 8.64.5).

In eighteenth-century Europe, up to and beyond the French Revolution, it was customary to couple Rome with Sparta. There were certainly grounds for this. Polybius had already compared the two cities' constitutions and recognized that the Roman political system possessed a perfect balance of powers. He did not conceal, however, that the hub of this balance was an aristocracy that coincided with the very body (the Senate) through which its power was exercised.

The fact that the aristocracy will emerge as the main element in the political experience described in the following pages is therefore not surprising. If one wished to express briefly the reason behind such a long-lasting grasp of power, one might focus on the ability of the aristocracy to adapt and to co-opt. It is from this point of view that the model Spartan aristocracy shows itself to have been the least farsighted.

The Greeks and the Others

"The cities were smaller in those days, and the people lived in the rural areas, entirely occupied by farming." This is the situation that gave rise to tyrannies, according to Aristotle in the fifth book of his *Politics* (1305a18). "Given the size of the city, not all the citizens knew one another." In the opinion of Thucydides, this was one of the main factors in the climate of suspicion and difficulty created in Athens during the days leading up to the oligarchic takeover in 411 B.C. (8.66.3). The archaic city was small, making direct democracy—the participation in decision making of all "citizens"—an inevitable outcome, and one that could not be contradicted when an ever-growing number of "citizens" (or would-be citizens), no longer completely absorbed by their work in the fields, converged on the agora. As long as the situation was that described by Aristotle ("the people lived in the rural areas, entirely occupied by farming"), the struggle for power was the business of the aristocracy. These "lords" were permitted to bear arms and exercised their hegemony as a result of this privilege, one that can actually be seen in the funeral objects of Attic tombs (in the ancient tombs of the demes of Aphidnae, Thoricus, and Eleusis, nobles are buried with their weapons, other people without). The *sidērophoria,* the barbaric custom of walking around armed, was, according to Gustave Glotz, "a sign of nobility that accompanied the aristocrat to his tomb."

During the archaic era, these lords determined the alternating forms of government—aristocracy, tyranny, and the "interregnum" of a "mediator" (*aisymnētēs* or *diallaktēs*). Despite their different names, often due to the viewpoint of the person describing them, these forms were actually very difficult to distinguish from one another. We have only to consider the events on Lesbos described by Alcaeus and figures such as Pittacus, *diallaktēs* in the furious struggle between aristocratic clans yet labeled "tyrant" by Alcaeus before being elevated to the divine sphere of the Seven Wise Men of Greece along with his Athenian counterpart Solon. According to Aristotle, the people described by Alcaeus and others as "tyrants" were those who assumed the "leadership of the people" (*prostatai tou dēmou*).

They enjoyed the trust of the people, Aristotle wrote in the passage quoted previously, and the "proof" (*pistis*) of this trust was "hatred against the rich." This hatred, in Aristotle's view, was expressed in such events as the slaughter of the livestock of the rich, discovered near the river of the "tyrant" Theagenes of Megara, a man trusted by the people. Peisistratus, mentioned by Aristotle in the same context, was equally trusted.

At a certain point, however, the constant labor in the fields (*ascholia*) became lighter. Theognis complained (in approximately 540 B.C.) about a rabble that knew nothing of law and justice and wore goat-skins round their loins *pouring into the city,* where they counted for more than the newly impoverished nobles. He remarks with nostalgic regret that these people had once lived—or rather, to use his contemptuous term, "grazed"—outside the city. Now they had arrived, and the face of the city had changed (1.53–56). It is obvious that the spur toward direct democracy begins with this gradual movement of people into the city. The escape from *ascholia* coincided with the move toward democracy. The phenomenon was made possible by the fact that the community was small and because the alternative to personal power was, so to speak, within easy reach. There is thus no need to fantasize about some innate thrust toward politics in the Greek character, in comparison with the vast world they considered "barbaric," even though the Greeks themselves have claimed the existence of such a tendency.

The guiding thread in the slow creation of a "trend toward isonomy" in the Greek world between the eighth and the fifth century B.C. was the affirmation of "political presence" (Meier) by *all those who bore arms* and were thus "citizens."

The idealization of this development has produced the widely held belief that the Greeks "invented" politics. An Asian Greek like Herodotus, however, with considerable experience of the Persian world, attempted to claim (and, he observed, "was not believed") that the democratic hypothesis "of putting politics in common" (*es meson katatheinai prēgmata,* 3.80), as he expresses it, was also proposed in Persia at the death of Cambyses, when Athens was still being ruled by the sons of Peisistratus. Herodotus also noted that when Darius marched against Greece in 492, Mardonius, his relation and ally in the enterprise, "overthrew the tyrants in Ionia and installed democracy in the cities" as he traveled along the Ionian coast to the Hellespont (6.43). Herodotus feared that this, too, would be disbelieved by the Greeks, since "they did not believe that [during the crisis following the death of Cambyses] Otanes had proposed democracy to the Persians."

It is hard to see why Herodotus should not be believed. The invaluable information he gives brings Greeks and Persians more closely together. The abyss that seems to exist between them has been created by the ideological picture that the Greeks created of themselves; in practice, the two worlds were far more closely intertwined, in political experience as well. Proof of this can be found in the ease with which politicians such as Themistocles, Alcibiades, and Lysander entered into relations with Persia. They had been preceded by the Alcmeonidai, even though Herodotus attempts to draw a patriotic veil over the affair (5.71–73; 6.115 and 121–24). We are therefore entitled to conclude that the language adopted by Otanes (democratic hypothesis), Megabyzus (oligarchic hypothesis), and Darius (the successful monarchic hypothesis) during the constitutional debate described by Herodotus (3.80–82) was familiar to educated Persians, and not the exclusive preserve of the Greeks.

The Citizen-Soldier

Classical democracy is therefore the regime in which those who count—those people, that is, with access to the decision-making Assembly—possess citizenship. The problem is to establish exactly who these people were. If we consider the most well known, and certainly most characteristic, example—Athens—we can see that relatively few people were fortunate enough to be in this enviable state: freeborn adult males whose mother and father were both Athenian. The need to be freeborn was undoubtedly the most restrictive of these conditions when we remember that, according to even the most conservative estimates, there were four slaves for every freeborn Athenian. Nor should we forget the significant number of people with only one "purebred" parent in a commercial city open to constant contact with the outside world. Finally, at least until the age of Solon (sixth century B.C.), full political rights—the essence, that is, of being a citizen—were withheld from people with no property. There is still scholarly discussion as to whether even Solon really did extend the right of access to the Assembly to people without property, as Aristotle claimed in the *Constitution of Athens*. In a word, citizenship in the classical age came down to the figure of the citizen-soldier. Only those people who were able to fulfill the main function of a freeborn adult male—waging war—were regarded as citizens, free to take an active part in the community by participating in the decisions made at meetings of the Assembly. Work was the realm of slaves and, to a lesser extent, women.

For a considerable period, being a soldier meant being able to afford to equip oneself with arms. The concept of the citizen-soldier was thus identified with the property owner who had a sufficient income (generally from land) to arm himself at his own expense. As a result, people without property found themselves in a condition of political and civil powerlessness not far removed from that of slaves. Not until approximately a century after Solon, when Athens began to turn to the sea and a stable war fleet grew up to conquer the Persians, did the city need a massive military labor force: sailors, who were not expected "to arm themselves." This was the political and military event that opened up citizenship in the maritime democracies to people without property (the *thetēs*), who finally achieved the status of citizen-soldiers, as sailors, in Athens, the most powerful naval force in the Greek world. It is no coincidence that such a bitter critic of democracy as the anonymous author (possibly Critias) of the *Constitution of the Athenians* should have divided political models of the state into two categories (2.1–6): those that wage war by sea (Athens and her allied counterparts) and those that wage war on land (Sparta and similar states).

It is not, therefore, the nature of the political system that changed, but the number of those who were able to benefit from it. This explains why, when the Athenians, or rather, some Athenian doctrinaires with an interest in political forms, attempted to see exactly what the difference was between their own system and that of Sparta, they concluded by focusing on insignificant elements, such as Thucydides' oft-repeated distinction between the "slow" Spartans and the "fast" Athenians (1.70.2–3; 8.96.5). As we look through the political writing of Athens, we can also come across praise of Spartan "democracy," and even Isocrates, in his *Areopagiticus,* declares the existence of a profound similarity between the Spartan and Athenian systems (61).

Opening up citizenship—which is generally defined as "democracy"—is therefore intimately linked in Athens to the birth of its maritime empire, an empire that the democratic sailors themselves generally regarded as a world of subjects to be exploited as though they were slaves. A bond of solidarity with Athens' subject-allies was seen as an extension, among the allied communities as well, of the democratic system. Despite Athens' imperialist exploitation, the existence of this bond meant that there was always a social group in the allied communities that saw the alliance with Athens as valuable, since it implied the adoption of the governing city's political system. In other words, there also existed a social base for democracy in the subject cities of Athens.

Furthermore, extending citizenship to men without property in Athens had its effects at the top of the system. Those people who ruled the city because their social class gave them access to political education, the art of speaking, and therefore power were suddenly divided. Most of them agreed to rule a system in which non–property owners were in the majority. Those who accepted the situation (the most important families, rich landowners, knights, etc.) provided the city with its "political class," which ruled Athens from Cleisthenes to Cleon. A political dialectic that was often founded on personal conflict and prestige developed within this group. Each member of the group was convinced that he embodied the general interest. This can clearly be seen in every political activity of Alcibiades, who held the belief that his own supremacy of the political scene was also in the best interests of the community. A minority of "gentlemen," on the other hand, refused to accept the system. Organizing themselves into more or less secret groups (the so-called *hetaireiai*) they represented a constant threat to Athens, waiting for moments of uncertainty, particularly when the city was at war, in order to act. These men were known as the "oligarchs." They did not declare their desire for government by a restricted clique (they obviously never defined themselves as "oligarchs," preferring to talk about the need for "good government," *sōphrosynē,* etc.). They proposed a drastic reduction in the number of citizens, immediately excluding all non–property owners from the benefits of citizenship and returning the city to the state in which the only full "citizens" were those "capable of arming themselves at their own expense." The very term *oligoi* ("few"), observed Aristotle, creates confusion: what is important is not the number of people who possess "citizenship," so much as whether they are property owners or not. The respective numbers are "a matter of accident" (*Politics* 1279b35), and in any case, "the majority is also sovereign in oligarchies" (1290a31).

Drawing on this observation by Aristotle, Arthur Rosenberg makes an analogy that is both illuminating and contemporarily relevant: "The application of these definitions by Aristotle to the present would produce some curious, yet also very realistic, results: Soviet

Russia in 1917 and 1918 would be a democracy; the modern French republic would be an oligarchy. Neither evaluation should be seen as expressing praise or blame, since they would merely be statements of fact."

Basing his argument on controversial yet undoubtedly indicative estimates, Rosenberg stresses the fact that the numerical prevalence of non–property owners over the rest of society was anything but certain: "The ratio of non–property owners to property owners was only four to three. This meant that the latter only needed to encourage even a tiny proportion of the lower classes, by whatever means they chose, to join their party in order to acquire an absolute majority at the popular assembly." Rosenberg also points out the role played by an intermediate class, defined by him as the "small middle class" (*der kleine Mittelstand*), in the political and social dynamic of Athens. The support of this class considerably extended the social base for democracy, yet it could easily be withdrawn, as can be seen at moments of crisis. The class was essentially made up of small property owners (represented by Dicaeopolis of the *Acharnians*). Rosenberg is quite right to observe that, for this class, democracy "meant unrestricted access to cultural conquests and the opportunity to free oneself from the fatigue of one's daily labors by holding public office from time to time."

When Athens was defeated in its struggle with the Macedonian monarchy (the Lamian war at the end of the fourth century), the city's property owners, with the support of the victors, were finally able to deprive the 12,000 non–property owners of citizenship (Diodorus Siculus 18.18.5 and Plutarch *Phocion* 28.7), the latter being defined as those with less than 2,000 drachmas. This temporary defeat of the democratic system was expressed in the *isolation of the non–property owners*. The middle class allied itself at that moment with Phocion, Demades, and the other "reformers" with Macedonian sympathies.

The central importance of citizenship can be seen in the fact that the Athenian oligarchs, after some months in power, began by reducing the number of citizens to 5,000 and that they attempted to appease the fleet in terms of propaganda by insisting that in practice such a large number of people had never taken part in decisions of the Assembly (Thucydides 8.72.1). Its importance is equally evident in the democrats' decision, once they had regained power, to deprive those who had supported the oligarchs of full citizenship, reducing them to the rank of "disenfranchised" citizens (*atimoi*).

The phenomenon is so significant that a great dramatist like Aristophanes, taking advantage of the liberty offered by the parabasis for making political comment, launched an appeal to the city to readmit these *atimoi,* fallen into the "bird-traps of Phyrinicus" (one of the principal figures behind the 411 takeover), to full citizenship (*Frogs* 686–705). When the oligarchs were restored to power under the Spartan aegis in 404, they were not satisfied with creating an even further reduced civic body (3,000 full citizens). They also encouraged democrats, popular leaders, and whoever was linked to the democratic system for political or class reasons to go into exile, even at the cost of "depopulating" Attica, as Socrates pointed out to Critias and Charicles, in a dramatic dialogue reported by Xenophon in his *Memorabilia* (1.2.32–38).

"Purebred" citizens were always ready to take up arms against one another in order to defend their precious right to citizenship. They were all, however, agreed that it should never be extended to people outside the community. It was only in moments of the greatest danger or desperation that they realized the potential of radically extending citizenship. After the loss of the final fleet to be assembled at the climax of the exhausting war with Sparta (Aegospotami, summer 405), Athens made the unprecedented gesture of conceding citizenship to her closest ally, Samos. In doing so the city made a tardy, and desperate, attempt to "double" the size of the community. This short-lived measure (Tod *Greek Historical Inscriptions* 96) was obviously upset by Athens' surrender (April 404) and the expulsion of the democrats of Samos by the victorious Lysander a few months later (Xenophon *Hellenica* 2.3.6–7). When democracy was restored, however, the measure was reproposed during the archontate of Euclid (403–402) in honor of the exiled Samian democrats (Tod *Greek Historical Inscriptions* 97). Seventy years later, Philip of Macedonia defeated the Athens-led coalition at Chaeronea (338 B.C.), and it appeared for a moment that the victor, famous for razing defeated cities to the ground, was about to march on a practically defenseless Athens. Hyperides, a democratic politician as "irregular" in his political alliances as in his extravagant lifestyle, suggested freeing 150,000 agricultural slaves and miners (frags. 27–29 Balss-Jensen) to cope with the situation. However, he was taken to court for such an "illegal" proposal by a fierce mob-leader, Aristogiton, who rose to defend democracy against such an undeserved increase in citizenship. The argument used by Aristogiton on that occasion was typical of Athenian democratic oratory: that "as long as there is peace the enemies of democracy respect the laws and are, so to speak, obliged not to break them; but in times of war they will find any pretext to terrorize the citizens by insisting that the city cannot be saved" unless "illegal proposals" are adopted (Jander *Oratorum Fragmenta* 32).

Toward the end of the fifth century, more precisely during the last thirty years, a phase of bloody conflict tore the Greek world apart. A general war involved almost all the cities, leaving little room for neutrality since it was fought between not only Athens and Sparta but all the cities that fell into their respective orbits. At the same time, as an immediate and inevitable consequence, there was civil war. These two wars, both inside and outside the state, fueled each other, with the ruling group in each city changing according to its position at home or beyond. With each new regime, massacres and mass exiles marked the rise and fall in power of the two factions. Civil war even penetrated the heart of one of the two leading cities, Athens, where, for a few months in 411 (seven years before the city's final defeat), the oligarchs seized power. But it soon slipped through their fingers because of the democratic and patriotic reaction of the sailors who had formed an anti-state in Samos in conflict with the mother city, fallen into the hands of the "enemies of the people." The long war, civil and otherwise, seemed to reach a decisive epilogue in 404: the military defeat of Athens, its renunciation of fleet and empire, and its humiliating entrance into the list of Spartan allies under an even more ferocious oligarchic government (the "Thirty"). However, the most significant moment of the entire period came after less than a year. The regime of the Thirty collapsed, and the Spartans found themselves encouraging the restoration of democracy in the defeated enemy city. Attica had refused to become a satellite of Spartan Laconia. The choice that had gradually consolidated itself since Cleisthenes thus became a structure that was deeply rooted in the political reality of Athens. The system based on guaranteeing the right of non–property owners to participate in citizenship had shown itself to be stronger and more long-lasting than the (original) nexus of democracy and sea power.

The "Cow"

One of the basic factors cementing the pact between non–property owners and the aristocracy was the "liturgy," the more or less spontaneous, and often large, contribution that the rich provided for the running of the community: from fitting the navy out to providing the considerable funds needed for festivals and the state theater. Classical "popular" regimes only adopted expropriation as a punishment for certain crimes. The rich were allowed to continue as such, on condition that they took the weight of an enormous social burden.

Arthur Rosenberg has commented, with an efficacious use of modern terminology, that "the capitalist was like a cow, which the community carefully milked to the last drop. At the same time, therefore, it was necessary to make sure that the cow received a substantial amount of fodder. The Athenian proletariat had nothing against a manufacturer, trader or shipowner earning as much money abroad as he wanted; the more he earned the more he would then pay to the state."

Rosenberg rightly concluded from this that the Athenian "proletariat" and "capitalist" agreed on the exploitation of the allies and, more generally, on an imperialistic foreign policy. "The voices that inveighed against a policy based on plunder faded out and the Athenian non–property owners, during the period in which they held power, supported without reserve the imperialistic plans of the city's entrepreneurs. It is significant that, immediately after the proletariat came to power, Athens launched itself into two wars of plunder: one against the Persians for the conquest of Egypt, from which one can see the ambitious plans that Athens was hatching at that time; and the other against Greece itself, in order to annihilate the two commercial rivals of Aegina and Corinth."

Rosenberg refers here to the thesis, which should not be undervalued, that the commercial clash between the two major maritime powers of Athens and Corinth was the basic reason behind the Peloponnesian War.

In order to acquire prestige and popularity, the Athenian gentlemen in charge of the system handed out their money, not only as liturgies, but also in generous donations from which the people could directly benefit. This was the case with Pericles' rival, Cimon, who wanted to make all his possessions available to the public. Plutarch wrote: "He removed all the fences from his fields so that those foreigners and citizens who wished to could freely gather the fruits that were in season. Each day he had prepared in his house a simple but adequate meal for large numbers of people, which was offered to all the poor who desired it; *thus, by satisfying their appetites without effort, they were able to devote their time to political activity"* (*Cimon* 10).

Aristotle (frag. 363 Rose) points out that such treatment was not provided indiscriminately by Cimon, but only for those in his deme. The problem of the daily meal was also solved to some extent by the festivals that the city organized. On these occasions, non–property owners had access to meat, an otherwise rare and expensive dish. The so-called Old Oligarch, the putative author of the *Constitution of the Athenians*, explicitly condemns the people's parasitism in his pamphlet: "The city sacrifices many victims at public expense, but it is the people who divide up and eat these victims" (2.9). Cimon also provided clothes. Plutarch wrote: "When he went out he was always accompanied by very well-dressed young friends. Whenever the group encountered a poorly dressed old man one of them would exchange his cloak; and this gesture was considered worthy of respect."

Pericles could not equal such generosity, although his family was certainly no less important than that of Cimon. Cimon was son of Miltiades, victor at Marathon, and the Thracian princess Egesipele. On his mother Agariste's side, Pericles was descended from Cleisthenes, the man who, with Sparta's help, had driven the Peisistratidai from Athens and instituted the geometrically structured Athenian democracy. Based on ten territorial tribes, this had undermined the earlier system of patrician tribes. It was also, however, the family that was said to have established links with the Persians at the time of the invasion of Darius, the very invasion that Miltiades, the father of Cimon, had repelled. The house of Pericles was illustrious but controversial, apart from anything else for the sacrilegious way in which it had dispatched the attempt made by Cylon, the famous athlete, to establish a tyranny during a period that Herodotus and Thucydides described in different ways. The family had been ruined during its long exile, humiliated by defeat, and reduced to bribing the Delphic oracle in order to obtain Spartan assistance. In its time, however, at the death of Peisistratus, it was ready to bargain with the tyrant's sons, to such an extent that Cleisthenes himself became archon in 525–524.

Naturally, Pericles was well aware of the tricks of the political trade. When Aeschylus staged the *Persians* (472 B.C.), the tragedy in which the still-to-be-exiled Themistocles was praised, it was Pericles who paid for the preparation of the chorus (*Inscriptiones Graecae*

$2/3^2.2318$, col. 4.4). Themistocles disappeared from the scene shortly after, and Pericles gradually aligned himself with Ephialtes, who proposed full rights of citizenship for non–property owners. From the outset, he tried to compete in generosity with Cimon. "But Cimon," as Plutarch observed, "exceeded him in the amount of his gifts, thanks to which he was able to win the sympathies of those without property" (*Pericles* 9). It was at this point, according to Plutarch, that Pericles chose the road that led to "demagogy," decreeing grants of money belonging to the state. The traditional image is that Pericles managed in this way to "corrupt" the masses, introducing state payments for participation in plays and on juries, as well as providing state funds for other public events and duties. The systematic adoption of this type of state salary molded Athenian democracy during its most flourishing period, consolidating the image of a *dēmos* devoted to politics, the law courts, the theater and festivals and freed to a large extent from physical labor. It is also the period when the greatest number of slaves entered the city. According to Lysias, even the poorest Athenian had at least one slave (5.5).

But the most powerful weapons of Pericles' "demagogy" were his openly personal use of state funds and his no less concealed policy of public works. His enemies' attacks focused on this point: "They protested that the transfer of public treasure from Delos to Athens was an abuse of power, inciting malicious gossip and prejudicing the good name of the Athenians." Pericles responded by "explaining to the citizens that they did not have to account to their allies for the use they made of state funds, since they had fought for them and kept the barbarians at bay." He also said that once money had been paid, it belonged to whoever received it and that its use in public works was therefore more than legitimate as soon as the city's defense had been provided for. Why should not such money be spent on works that "once built, will bring the city eternal glory and, *while they are being built, will provide real well-being for the citizens?*" He explained that public works could provide the driving force and epicenter of the entire system: "They encourage activities of all kinds and create many new demands, providing the arts with inspiration, hands with work, and almost the entire city with salaries. This means," he concluded, "that the city, while adorning itself, is also fed" (Plutarch *Pericles* 12). According to Plutarch, Pericles wanted everyone to participate in the well-being produced by the empire. While young soldiers acquired wealth on campaign, the mass of workers who were not part of the army should not be excluded from the profits, nor should they be allowed to participate unless they worked. He passed magnificent projects in the Assembly, whose execution required "many different skills and considerable time." As a result, "those who stayed at home would be as justified in taking a share of the wealth as those in the fleet, the army, or on garrison duty." At this point, Plutarch provides an impressive list of the many types of craftsmen involved in this "Rooseveltian" wave of public works: carpenters, sculptors, smiths, stonecutters, dyers, goldsmiths and workers of ivory, painters, tapestry makers and woodcarvers, not to mention those categories of workers involved in the importing and transporting of raw materials, from shipowners, sailors, and pilots to ropemakers, tanners, miners, and so on. "Each craft, like a general with an army under his command, had its own corps of unskilled workers." The original design for the Parthenon, conceived by Callicrates, the architect linked to Cimon (who had already used the booty from the battle of the Eurymedon to build the southern wall of the Acropolis), was abandoned, Callicrates dismissed, and the role of chief builder assigned to Ictinus, who, according to Vitruvius, even wrote a treatise on the building of the Parthenon (*De architectura* 7, par. 16).

Comedians' jokes (Cratinus frag. 300 Kock), the sarcasm of pamphleteers, and political attacks were all inevitable. The orators "near to Thucydides, son of Melesias," wrote Plutarch, "inveighed against Pericles in the Assembly, claiming that he squandered public money and frittered away the city's income." Pericles' reaction was typical. He asked the entire Assembly if he had really spent so much. "Far too much!" replied the Assembly as one. And Pericles said, "Very well, everything shall be put onto my account. But let the name on the votive inscriptions [which bore the name of the person who had made the offer] be mine" (Plutarch *Pericles* 14). His move had the desired effect. Pericles was given permission to draw on public funds as much as he chose, either because, as Plutarch commented, his generosity was admired or possibly because the people were not prepared to give up the glory of the city's works to him.

The Personal Conception of the State

The idea that the state was composed of *the people* who possessed citizenship, that the state's income was equivalent to their income, and that Pericles could do with the state's income what Cimon attempted to do with his massive personal wealth are all symptoms of a "personal" conception of the state, a conception in which the state has no autonomous legal character over and above the people, but coincides exactly with its citizens. This was the idea in force when Themistocles "transported" Athens to the island of Aegina at the threat of Persian invasion; it was the theory that Nicias, the besieger of Syracuse and himself besieged, used to encourage his sailors: "The city is not its walls nor its empty ships, but its men" (Thucydides 7.77.7).

This idea of the state has certain consequences, for example, when the community is divided by *stasis,* or civil strife, a frequent occurrence (with the exception of particularly stable communities such as Sparta, a virtue praised by Thucydides 1.18 and Lysias *Olimpiacus* 7). In these cases, communities sometimes broke up physically into two or more parts. This occurred a number of times in Athens during the repeated crises that punctuated the long war at the end of the fifth century. In such cases, part of the state became an "anti-state," declaring itself to be the only legitimate state on the grounds that it was more consistent with an undefined "ancestral constitution" (*patrios politeia*). This happened in 411, when, a hundred years after the expulsion of the Peisistratidai—it was Thucydides (8.68.4) who made a point of observing democracy's century-long grip—the city of Athens was still reeling from the shock of the Sicilian disaster. The oligarchs, always ready to overturn the despised democratic system, seized power. However, they were faced by the unexpected reaction of the standing fleet at Samos—the social base, in other words, of democracy, armed for war. The fleet formed an anti-state, electing generals and declaring that "the war goes on," while the oligarchs attempted to reach an agreement with Sparta. The fleet's act was based on the firm belief that the state was its people, and also on the deeply rooted conviction, intrinsic to democratic thinking, that "the *dēmos* is everything," as the Syracusan Athenagoras proclaimed in a speech rewritten by Thucydides (6.39). This might be regarded as mere sophism based on the ambiguity of the term *dēmos,* which meant at once the popular faction, its social base, and the community as a whole. It was nonetheless a sophism that demonstrated its efficiency, since it, too, referred to the personal notion of the state.

In 404–403, during the longest and most serious civil war in the history of Attica, a division into three parts occurred. First, there was the absolute supremacy of the Thirty, who wished to change

Attica into a pastoral Laconia remote from maritime concerns (in a well-known anecdote related by Plutarch [*Themistocles* 19.6] Critias wanted the *bēma* from which orators spoke "to be turned to face the earth"). They completely ignored the exodus of democrats and common people, which had been caused by their victory. But the democrats scattered over Boeotia and Megaris soon joined together and, after some military successes, barricaded themselves at Piraeus, where they formed a democratic anti-Athens. The oligarchs, shaken by their defeats, split into two, with distinct seats of power—one in Athens and the other at Eleusis—and governments. When the Spartans imposed a peace settlement in which the democrats returned to power on the basis of the old democratic constitution, on condition that there were no reprisals or acts of revenge, an oligarchic republic continued to operate in Eleusis for some years, providing a refuge for those who were unable to accept the compromise of the peace settlement.

The other side of this concept of the state can be seen when pacts are broken and an exile forms a coalition with the enemies of the city in order to return. The initial premise in such a case is that it is not the state as such (as an abstract, superhuman entity) that has expelled him, but other citizens. The victim feels that their decision is mistaken or evil and wages a personal war against his own city in order to correct the error and restore justice. This explains why Alcibiades went over to the Spartans in order to give vent to his anger with the Athenian political system (Thucydides 6.89.6) and why—on his return years later—his apology consisted in a painstaking presentation of why he had been right to act as he did, followed by an attack, not on the state, but on "those who had expelled him" (Xenophon *Hellenica* 1.4.14–16). This is why the "Old Oligarch" actually praised the fact that Athens was fortunate enough not to be an island; because if it were, he observed, the oligarchs "*would not be able to betray* the city by opening her gates to the enemy" (2.15).

The very notion of "betrayal" at this point becomes relative. Two centuries later, in fact, when Polybius considered the political experiences of the Greeks, in whose most extreme vagaries he, too, had played a part, he expressed irritation toward this idea of "betrayal": "I am often amazed by the mistakes men make in many fields, in particular when they become angry with 'traitors.' That is why I should like to take this opportunity to say two words on the issue, even though I am aware that it is a difficult thing to define and judge.

It is anything but easy, after all, to establish exactly who should be defined as a 'traitor.' "

After making these comments, Polybius dismisses the very concept of betrayal by observing that it is clearly not a question of "establishing new alliances": on the contrary, he observes, "those who, according to the circumstances, have created new alliances and friendships for their city" are often recognized as benefactors, in which case it is absurd to follow Demosthenes' habit of labeling any political enemy whatsoever a "traitor" (18.13–14). "Betrayal" is nothing more than a unilateral way of judging political behavior. This is clearly understood by those who, like Alcibiades, the Old Oligarch, or even Polybius, are hostile to the democratic belief that "the *dēmos* is everything."

Kinein tous nomous

However, if the "*dēmos* is everything" and the citizens, who constitute the state, are the one source of legality and thus themselves above the law, the only possible law, strictly speaking, is "that the people do what they wish." This was explicitly declared by the "mob" (*plēthos*) during the famous trial against the victorious generals at the battle of Argineusae (Xenophon *Hellenica* 1.7.12) and is the same formula used by Otanes in Herodotus (3.80) to define the power of the monarch. But if the people are above the law, then it cannot be regarded as unchangeable or independent of the popular will. On the contrary, it must adapt to them, even though "changing the law" (*kinein tous nomous*) is one of the most familiar of the accusations made by democrats against their traditional enemies.

Both groups claimed to represent "the traditional constitution" (*patrios politeia*). According to Diodorus Siculus (14.32.6), Thrasybulus, one of the leaders in the civil war against the Thirty, declared that the war against the tyrants would not cease "until the *dēmos* had recovered its *patrios politeia*." The Thirty, according to Aristotle, ostentatiously claimed to be following the *patrios politeia* themselves (*Constitution of Athens* 35.2). While one group attempted to restore a radical democracy, the other tried to put its policies into practice by destroying radical democracy: those laws, as Aristotle explains, that Ephialtes used to take away the power of the Areopagus and create radical democracy in the first place. Thrasymachus, the Sophist from Chalcedon to whom Plato attributed the brutal theory that "might is right" in the *Republic,* pointed out this contradiction in his ironic judgment of political oratory: "In the conviction that the one is maintaining a different position from the other, neither orator realizes that he is aiming at the same result, and that the argument of his adversary is contained in his own speech" (Dionysius *On Demosthenes* 3 = 1, pp. 132–34 Usener-Radermacher). The use of the same term in a programmatic sense reveals a more general phenomenon according to which democracy, whenever it "speaks," ends up by modeling itself on the dominant ideology. Recourse to the past as a positive fact in itself (it is no coincidence that the original "founder" of democracy was identified as Theseus) was linked to the negative connotations of changing the existing laws (*kinein*). But this desire for stability could and did clash with the need to place the *dēmos* above the law, as the final arbiter should changes have to be made.

Modifications in the law take place, in any case, with time, so that, as Aristotle observes, the end that must be pursued is not "tradition" (*to patrion*) but "the good" (*Politics* 1269a4). This is generally an alarming phenomenon for conservative thinkers, from the Pythagoreans (Aristoxenus frag. 19 Muller) to Plato's *Laws* (772D), even though Plato does not conceal the inevitability of change (769D). *Kinein* is an ambiguous term that describes both change and development (Isocrates *Evagoras* 7) and thus coincides with the notion of *epidosis* (= progress, in reference to *technai*). *Epidosis* is regarded as an inevitable phenomenon by Isocrates in the passage referred to above and by Demosthenes in a famous sketch describing the history of the art of war (*Third Philippic* 47) in which *kekinesthai* and *epidedokenai* are synonymous. It is also inevitable, on a much larger time scale, as far as the law is concerned, even though—as Aristotle points out—it might be very dangerous to create the precedent that laws can be changed, since people might become used to the idea (*Politics* 2.1268b30–1269a29).

In an aside whose obvious reference to the well-known "archaeology" of Thucydides is intended to show the breadth of time as a "theater" of change, Aristotle provides a sort of "archaeology" of rights, similar to the more general "archaeology" of Thucydides. The validity of the latter text can be seen from the references made to it, some decades later, in the Proem of Ephorus (frag. 9 Jacoby), as well as in Aristotle's comment. The conclusion to which Aristotle comes is the recognition that only a synthesis of innovation and conservatism can produce a structure capable of change. He even attempts to identify a measure, or criterion, that would make it possible to estab-lish when and how far to innovate and when, despite the presence of obvious flaws, we should refrain from innovation. His criterion is empirical and generic: "When the expected improvement is modest, considering the fact that it is an evil to accustom people to change the laws in a casual way, it is clear that it is in our interests to leave obvi-ously defective laws in force; since the advantage to be gained would not compensate for the disadvantage of creating a tendency to diso-bey the law."

Freedom/Democracy, Tyranny/Oligarchy

When Pericles began to describe the Athenian political system in a speech preserved by Thucydides, he differentiated between "democ-racy" and "freedom." He commented that, in the absence of other terms, the regime was generally defined as a democracy because many people were involved in the *politeia*. However, what was really being described was a free political system (*eleutheros dē politeuomen*). In a sense, the orator saw democracy and freedom as antithetical. The oration is clearly not the "monument to Athenian democracy" that some of its interpreters have maintained (including Plato, who paro-died it in the oration delivered by Aspasia in *Menexenus*). The praise of Athens contained in Pericles' oration has reached us by means of a double filter: the first is the literary genre of the funeral oration, with its inevitably laudatory tone; the second is how Pericles was seen by his historian, Thucydides. The historian believed that the politician had perverted the democratic system, preserving only its shell. Not even the word he uses (*dēmokratia*) is characteristic of democratic lan-guage, which, as we know, preferred *dēmos* with its various meanings (a typical democratic formula was *luein ton dēmon*: "to break down, or try to break down, democracy"). Originally, in fact, *dēmokratia* was a violent and controversial term ("the prevailing of the *dēmos*") coined by the enemies of democracy. It expresses the (violent) domi-nation of one group. This group can only be defined in terms of class, to such an extent that Aristotle, with extreme clarity, formulated the paradoxical *exemplum fictum* according to which the supremacy of 300 non–property owners (if that is their number) in a community of 1,300 citizens is nonetheless a "democracy." From this viewpoint, a democracy assumes the features of a tyranny, first among which is the demand on the part of the *dēmos* for a privilege that belongs to the tyrant: that of being above the law (*poiein ho ti bouletai*).

Athenian political language, however, contains another cluster of terms and concepts that identify, on the one hand, freedom and democracy and, on the other, oligarchy and tyranny. Once again Thucydides provides us with the evidence, in the chapter of his eighth book (8.68), where he weighs up the meaning and consequences of the oligarchic seizure of power in 411. He notes that it was short-lived and violent, bloody and, above all, unexpected—the first taste of oligarchy since the tyrants had been expelled a hundred years before. Having briefly described in an admiring tone the three people behind the coup, he comments, "Clearly only people at this level could accomplish such a grand undertaking: that of depriving the Athenian people of power a century after the banishment of the tyrants." It is clear that in this passage Thucydides identifies the democratic regime with the idea of freedom, just as, in the sixth book—where he evokes the widespread anxieties in Athens after the scandalous and mysterious mutilation of the herms—he defines the plot that Athenian democrats suspected was at the root of such a horrible and apparently inexplicable scandal as "oligarchical *and* tyrannical." Here the grouping of terms is absolutely symmetrical to that in the eighth book: on the one hand, liberty equals democracy (destroying democracy means depriving Athenians of the freedom they had won by banishing the tyrants); on the other hand, tyranny equals oligarchy (a plot aimed at government by the few, that is, the destruction of democracy, is both "oligarchical" and "tyrannical"). This language conflicts with the (historical) fact that the main force behind the banishment of the tyrants was the Spartan-backed aristocracy, while the form taken by archaic democracy was, in fact, tyranny.

This apparent uncertainty has a simple explanation, which takes us back once again to the compromise that originally gave birth to democracy in classical Greece: the compromise between the aristocracy and the people governed by the rationale, political culture, and language of the gentlemen who ruled the democratic city. For them, democracy was attractive insofar as it represented "freedom" (it is no accident that Pericles uses the word *dēmokratia* with detachment and, at the same time, claims that the regime in Athens is one based on "freedom"). It was a regime, in other words, without a trace of "tyranny."

This is the empirical origin of the now customary classification—made specifically by Greek thinkers—that divides all political forms into two subtypes, one good and the other bad. Greek thought responded to the uncertainty mentioned above very early on in its history. We can see such a division being proposed by Aristotle, who even adopts two different terms: he refers to the "good" democracy as *politeia,* while the democracy that does not respect freedom is called, as we might expect, *dēmokratia.*

But this distinction was already implicit in the constitutional discussion described by Herodotus. Throughout the three speeches quoted (particularly when regarded as a whole) runs the assumption that all political forms degenerate into their opposites and that this process of degeneration sets in motion a historical cycle in which a society passes from one constitution to another. The clearest and most important of the three speeches, in this sense, is that made by Darius, which explicitly raises the question of the division of each political form into its "idealized" form, on the one hand, and on the other, its concrete realization.

The "Cyclical" Theory

Darius points out that, in the context of their debate, each of the three political forms is described in two contrasting ways. Otanes outlines all the basic defects of monarchic power and exalts democracy with a few effective rhetorical strokes. He is immediately followed by Megabyzus, who shares Otanes' view of the monarchy but criticizes the positive image of democracy, exalting in its place the domination of the aristocracy. Finally, Darius sets out to emphasize the flaws of oligarchic government and returns to the starting point of the debate by delivering a radically subversive elegy to monarchic rule. Precisely because a complete picture of the six possible evaluations of the three systems is available to him, Darius begins his speech by saying that all three regimes are excellent "in theory" (3.80.1: this reading, which is the correct one, has reached us only through the indirect transmission of Stobaeus). In other words, he emphasizes that each model possesses a positive variant in which the "theoretical" assumptions on which it is based can operate without interference. This implies— as Darius immediately states—that, for democracy and oligarchy at least, their negative features emerge in the transition from theory to practice.

But Darius goes further than this. He offers two models for the passage from one constitution to another. In practice, he observes, actual democracies and "real" aristocracies both lead to a state of such civil disorder that the emergence of monarchy is the result. Monarchic power is thus unleashed by an often bloody *stasis* produced by the effective failure of the other two forms of government. On the other hand, Darius could hardly have been unaware of the fact that a bad monarchy also creates *stasis,* since he was speaking shortly after the catastrophe of Cambyses (the perfect incarnation of the tyrant) and the civil war caused by the usurper (the "Pseudo Smerdis"), during which Persian dignitaries discussed the political form that should be adopted in Persia after the collapse of the monarchy. Their discussion of other constitutional possibilities was the direct result of the monarchy's taking such a disastrous turn. It was thus clear, not only to Darius, but also from the context in which the debate took place, that each form of political constitution led to another, and that this involved the painful process of *stasis,* or civil war.

Darius emerges as the winner on a historical, though not dialectical, level. From an expositional viewpoint, his arguments are additional to those of the two preceding speakers, but do not exclude them. Dialectically, the debate was neither won nor lost. This was inevitable since an "open" verdict corresponded absolutely with the cyclical pattern of one "constitution" following on from another, building on its ruins as a result of its defects, in a process that could never reach a final conclusion. This is another reason for claiming that successive developments in Greek political thought stem from the debate described by Herodotus. When Thucydides, in his narrative account of actual events, was faced by the unique problem of accounting for the rapid decline of the oligarchic government of the Four Hundred—in spite of its being composed of "people of the first rank"—he had no other option than to return to the general explanation provided by Darius on the failure of all aristocracies, however "good": rivalry between leaders, all of the highest level but eager to acquire a position of preeminence (8.89.3). Thucydides also referred to the replacing of one constitution by another, itself destined to be replaced. Each constitution is therefore seen as a "segment" in a "cycle": "Thus," he observes, "an oligarchy that rose from the crisis of democracy itself falls into ruin."

This image of the constitutional process dominates later political thought, from the eighth book of Plato's *Republic* to the third book of Aristotle's *Politics*. In the latter, Aristotle supports his analysis with a multiplicity of examples drawn from his unparalleled knowledge of the constitutional and political affairs of hundreds of Greek states (the 158 *politeiai,* among which that of Athens has survived almost in its entirety). Trying to establish in what order constitutional succession occurred was the object of much speculation by later thinkers, from the late-Pythagorean Ocellus of Lucania to Polybius, in whose works empirical investigation was combined with the philosophical notion of a "return": a process that could be read equally well in reverse.

The eternal cycle could only be corrected by creating a "mixed" constitution; a system that, by combining the best features of all three models, was considered capable of canceling out the destructive or self-destructive effects of each single constitutional form. The idea that such a "mixed" form might be quite positive can be seen, briefly but clearly, in a comment made by Thucydides (8.97), when the historian surprisingly praises the short-lived political system that arose in Athens after the fall of the Four Hundred. In fact, this system— known as the rule of the Five Thousand—was hardly "mixed." It was an example of the kind of system that Aristotle would define as an oligarchy since it was founded on the limitation of citizenship to those who met a property qualification. In effect, the other hypothetical examples of "mixed" constitutions—over which Aristotle and, above all, his disciples (from Theophrastus and Dikaiarchos to Strato) racked their brains—were all marked by the absence of the main feature of democracies, that of full citizenship for non-landowners. They were thus, essentially, oligarchies. Nonetheless, the theme of the "mixed" constitution dominated Greek thinking, above all during the Hellenistic and Roman periods. Faced by the original and complex way that the *polis* of Rome dealt with the problem of citizenship and its relation to the need for a stable power, Polybius believed that Rome itself was the concrete and long-lasting answer. The sixth book of his *Histories,* placed specifically after the account of the disastrous Battle of Cannae in order to show how Rome was able to survive its defeat, is devoted entirely to the city's constitution as a perfect example of a "mixed" constitution.

But it is only fair that our attempts to describe the "Greek idea of politics" come to an end with Polybius. In contact first with the great Hellenistic monarchies and then with the Roman *polis,* Greek thought has now become Hellenistic-Roman thought and taken new paths. It is the beginning of another story.

Appendix of Texts

Herodotus "The Histories" 3.80–82

Five days later, when the excitement had died down, the conspirators met to discuss the situation in detail. At the meeting certain speeches were made—some of our own countrymen refuse to believe that they were actually made at all; nevertheless they were. The first speaker was Otanes, and his theme was to recommend the establishment in Persia of democratic government. "I think," he said, "that the time has passed for any man among us to have absolute power. Monarchy is neither pleasant nor good. You know to what lengths the pride of power carried Cambyses, and you have personal experience of the effect of the same thing in the conduct of the Magus. How can one fit monarchy into any sound system of ethics, when it allows a man to do whatever he likes without any responsibility or control? Even the best of men raised to such a position would be bound to change for the worse—he could not possibly see things as he used to do. The typical vices of a monarch are envy and pride; envy, because it is a natural human weakness, and pride, because excessive wealth and power lead to the delusion that he is something more than a man. These two vices are the root cause of all wickedness: both lead to acts of savage and unnatural violence. Absolute power ought, by rights, to preclude envy on the principle that the man who possesses it has also at command everything he could wish for; but in fact it is not so, as the behavior of kings to their subjects proves; they are jealous of the best of them merely for continuing to live, and take pleasure in the worst; and no one is readier than a king to listen to tale-bearers. A king, again, is the most inconsistent of men; show him reasonable respect, and he is angry because you do not abase yourself before his majesty; abase yourself, and he hates you for being a toady. But the worst of all remains to be said—he breaks up the structure of ancient tradition and law, forces women to serve his pleasure, and puts men to death without trial. Contrast with this the rule of the people: first, it has the finest of all names to describe it—equality under law—and, second, the people in power do none of the things that monarchs do. Under a government of the people a magistrate is appointed by lot and is held responsible for his conduct in office, and all questions are put up for open debate. For these questions I propose that we do away with the monarchy, and raise the people to power; for the state and the people are synonymous terms."

Otanes was followed by Megabyzus, who recommended the principle of oligarchy in the following words: "Insofar as Otanes spoke in favor of abolishing monarchy, I agree with him; but he is wrong in asking us to transfer political power to the people. The masses are a feckless lot—nowhere will you find more ignorance or irresponsibility or violence. It would be an intolerable thing to escape the murderous caprice of a king, only to be caught by the equally wanton brutality of the rabble. A king does at least act consciously and deliberately; but the mob does not. Indeed, how should it, when it has never been taught what is right and proper, and has no knowledge of its own about such things? The masses have not a thought in their heads; all they can do is rush blindly into politics like a river in flood. As for the people, then, let them govern Persia's enemies; but let us ourselves choose a certain number of the best men in the country and give *them* political power. We personally shall be among them, and it is only natural to suppose that the best men will produce the best policy."

Darius was the third to speak. "I support," he said, "all Megabyzus' remarks about the masses, but I do not agree with what he said of oligarchy. Take the three forms of government we are considering—democracy, oligarchy and monarchy—and suppose each of them to be the best of its kind in theory; I maintain that the third is greatly preferable to the other two. One ruler—it is impossible to improve upon that—provided he is the best. His judgment will be in keeping with his character; his control of the people will be beyond reproach; his measures against enemies and traitors will be kept secret more easily than under other forms of government. In an oligarchy, the fact that a number of men are competing for distinction in the public service cannot but lead to violent personal feuds; each of them wants to get to the top, and to see his own proposals carried; so they quarrel. Personal quarrels lead to open dissension, and then to bloodshed; and from that state of affairs the only way out is a return to monarchy—a clear proof that monarchy is best. Again, in a democracy, malpractices are bound to occur; in this case, however, corrupt dealings in government service lead, not to private feuds, but to close personal associations, the men responsible for them putting their heads together and mutually supporting one another. And so it goes on, until somebody or other comes forward as the people's champion and breaks up the cliques, which are out for their own interest. This wins him the admiration of the mob, and as a result he soon finds himself entrusted with absolute power—all of which is another proof that the best form of government is monarchy. To sum up: where did we get our freedom from, and who gave it to us? Is it the result of democracy, or of oligarchy, or of monarchy? We were set free by one man, and therefore I propose that we should preserve that form of government, and further, that we should refrain from changing ancient laws, which have served us well in the past. To do so would lead only to disaster."

[From the translation of Aubrey de Sélincourt]

The Granting of Athenian Citizenship to the Samians

Cephisophon of Paiania acted as secretary.
For the Samians who stood beside the people of Athens.
    The decision of the Council and Popular Assembly.
    The Cecropid tribe held the prytany, Polymnis was secretary and Nicophon of Athmonon was president.
    Proposed by Clisophus and the other prytanies:
    Praise to the Samian ambassadors, to those who came earlier and to those who have just arrived, to their generals and to all the Samians, for their courage and their willingness to defend the good. Praise to their acts, which benefit both Athens and Samos. In return for the service they have done Athens, the Athenians value the Samian people highly and make the following proposal: It has been decided by the Council and the Assembly that the Samians should be granted Athenian citizenship, that this decision should be carried out in the way deemed most suitable by both parties and that, when peace is achieved, the two cities will continue to act together. Samos will continue to enjoy autonomy and all existing treaties and conventions with Athens will be maintained.

[Tod Greek Historical Inscriptions 96]

Plutarch, "Life of Pericles"

But there was one measure above all that gave the greatest pleasure to the Athenians, adorned their city, and created amazement among foreigners, and that is today the sole testimony that the tales of the ancient power and glory of Greece are not falsehoods. By this I mean his construction of sacred buildings; and yet it was this, more than any other action of Pericles, that his enemies slandered and misrepresented. They cried out that Athens had lost her good name and disgraced herself by transferring from Delos into her own keeping the funds that had been contributed by the rest of Greece, and that now the most plausible excuse for this action, namely, that the money had been removed for fear of the barbarians and was being guarded in a safe place, had been demolished by Pericles himself. "The Greeks must be outraged," they said. "They must consider this an act of simple tyranny, when they see that with their own contributions, extorted from them by force for the war against the Persians, we are gilding and beautifying our city, as if it were some vain woman decking herself out with precious stones and statues and temples worth millions."

Pericles explained to the people of Athens that they were not obliged to give their allies an account of how their money was spent, as long as they carried on the war for them and kept the Persians away. "They do not provide us with horses, ships, or hoplites, but only money," he said. "And money does not belong to those who give it but to those who receive it, as long as they do what they are paid to do. It is only fair that after Athens has been equipped with all she needs to conduct the war, she should spend the surplus on works that, once completed, will bring her eternal glory and, while they are being built, will provide real well-being for the citizens. These works encourage activities of all kinds and create many new demands, providing the arts with inspiration, hands with work, and almost the entire city with salaries, so that the city, while adorning it, is also fed." What Pericles wanted was that, while those who were of military age could earn through war, thanks to the contributions made by their allies, the masses would also be able to benefit from the profits without sitting about and doing nothing.

So he presented the Assembly with proposals for immense public works, which would require many different skills and would take a considerable time to complete; in this way those who stayed at home would be as justified in taking a share of the wealth as those in the fleet, the army, or on garrison duty.

The materials used were stone, bronze, ivory, gold, ebony, and cypress wood, while the trades that fashioned them were those of the carpenter, sculptor, coppersmith, stonemason, dyer, worker in gold and ivory, painter, embroiderer, and engraver, not to speak of those involved in the carrying and supplying of these materials, such as merchants, sailors, and pilots for the seaborne traffic, wagon makers, animal trainers, and drivers for everything that came by land. There were also ropemakers, weavers, leatherworkers, roadbuilders, and miners. Each craft, like a general with an army under his command, had its own corps of unskilled workers, and these worked in a subordinate capacity to carry out the tasks that were required.

[From the translation of Ian Scott-Kilvert]

Pseudo-Xenophon "Constitution of Athens" 2.19–20

I for my part maintain that the people of Athens definitely know which citizens are good and which are rogues. With full knowledge of this they like those who are devoted and useful to them, even if these are bad, whereas they hate the good ones. For they do not think that the morals of these are innate in them to the benefit of the people, but on the contrary to its harm. On the other hand, there are a few who undoubtedly take the side of the people without being democratic by nature.

Personally I forgive the people for being democratic; for everyone must be forgiven for protecting his own interest. But anybody who, without belonging to the people, prefers living in a city under democratic rule to living in one ruled by an oligarchy has prepared himself for being immoral, knowing full well that it is easier for a rogue to remain unnoticed in a town under democratic rule than under an oligarchy.

[From the translation of Hartvig Frish]

Pseudo-Xenophon, "Constitution of Athens" 2.14–15

But the Athenians have one defect. If they ruled the sea as islanders, they could do as much harm to the others as they wanted without being injured themselves, without having their own territory devastated and without being assailed by their enemy. Now, however, the farmers and the rich Athenians are obliged to shrink before the enemy, while the people, who know full well that the enemy will neither burn nor destroy their property, live freely and without trying to ingratiate themselves with the enemy.

But they would be free of another fear as well if they lived on an island: that of the town being betrayed by a handful of people opening the gates, or by their enemies suddenly entering, or by a rebellion against democracy taking place (for how could these things happen if Athens were an island?). For if there should ever be a rebellion, it would occur by placing trust in the enemy, thinking that they could enter the city by land.

[From the translation of Hartvig Frish]

Aristotle, "Politics" 1268b–1269a

Now that we have touched on this matter it might be as well to say a little more about it, especially as there is, as I have said, debate on the point and a case could also be made out in favor of change. At any rate, if we look at the other sciences, it has definitely been beneficial—witness the changes in traditional methods of medicine and physical training, and generally in every skill and faculty. Now since we must regard statesmanship as one of these, clearly something similar ought to apply there as well. And so indeed we could claim to find some indication of that if we look at the facts and observe how uncivilized, how rough-and-ready, the old laws were. Greeks used to go about carrying arms; they used to buy their brides from each other; and traces survive of other practices once doubtless customary, which merely make us smile today, such as the law relating to homicide at Cyme, by which, if the prosecutor can produce a certain number of witnesses, members of his own kin, then the defendant is guilty of murder.

Generally, of course, it is the good, and not simply the traditional, that is aimed at. It would be foolish to adhere to the notions of primitive men, whether they were born from the earth or were survivors of some great catastrophe: we may reasonably suppose that they were on a level with ordinary, not very intelligent, people today, and lack of intelligence was said to be one of the marks of the earth-born. We might go further and say that even those laws that have been written down are best regarded as not unchangeable. On the analogy of other skills, to set down in writing the whole organization of the state, down to the last detail, would be quite impossible; the general principle must be stated in writing, the action taken depends upon the particular case.

From these considerations, it is clear that there are occasions that call for change and that there are some laws that need to be changed. But looking at it in another way, we must say that there will be need of the very greatest caution. In a particular case, we may have to weigh a very small improvement against the danger of getting accustomed to casual abrogation of the laws; in such a case, obviously, we must tolerate a few errors on the part of lawmakers and rulers. A man will receive less benefit from changing the law than damage from being accustomed to disobey authority. For the example of the crafts is false; there is a difference between altering a craft and altering a law. The law has no power to secure obedience save the power of habit, and that takes a long time to become effective. Hence, easy change from established laws to new laws means weakening the power of the law. Again, if changes in laws *are* to be permitted, it will have to be decided whether they may all be changed, and in every type of constitution, or not. And who is to make the changes? Anybody or only certain persons? We will now give up this discussion; it will be better resumed on other occasions.

[From the translation of T. A. Sinclair]

Thucydides 2.37

Our system of government does not copy the institutions of our neighbors. It is more the case of our being a model to others, than of our imitating anyone else. Our constitution is called a democracy because power is in the hands, not of a minority, but of the whole people. When it is a question of settling private disputes, everyone is equal before the law; when it is a question of putting one person before another in positions of public responsibility, what counts is not membership of a particular class, but the actual ability that the man possesses. No one, so long as he has it in him to be of service to the state, is kept in political obscurity because of poverty. And, just as our political life is free and open, so is our day-to-day life in our relations with each other. We do not get into a state with our next-door neighbor if he enjoys himself in his own way, nor do we give him the kind of black looks that, though they do no real harm, still hurt people's feelings. We are free and tolerant in our private lives; but in public affairs, we keep to the law. This is because it commands our deep respect. We give our obedience to those whom we put in positions of authority, and we obey the laws themselves, especially those that are for the protection of the oppressed, and those unwritten laws that it is an acknowledged shame to break.

[From the translation of Rex Warner]

Thucydides 6.38–39

But, as I tell you, the Athenians know all this, and I am quite sure that they are occupied in safeguarding their own possessions. What is happening is that there are certain people here in Syracuse who are making up stories that are neither true nor likely to become true. This is not the first time that I have noticed these people; in fact I am constantly aware of them; if foiled in action, they resort to stories of this kind or even more villainous fabrications, and their aim is to make you, the mass of the people, frightened, and so gain control of the government themselves. And I am really afraid that their continual efforts may one day be actually successful. We ourselves are too feeble: we do not forestall them before they act; we do not follow them up with vigor once we have detected them. It is because of this that our city rarely enjoys a period of tranquility, and is involved in continual party strife and struggles more within herself than against the enemy; and there have been cases, too, of dictatorships and of powerful groups seizing the government illegally. I shall make it my endeavor, if you will only support me, to see to it that nothing like this is ever allowed to happen in our days. And my methods will be to bring you, the masses, over to my way of thought, and then to come down heavily on those who are engaged in these plots, not merely when they are caught in the act (it is not so easy to catch them like that), but also for all those things that they would like to do, but cannot. When dealing with an enemy, it is not only his actions but his intentions that have to be watched, since if one does not act first, one will suffer first. And as for those who want an oligarchy, I shall show them up, when necessary, and I shall keep my eye on them, and I shall even be a teacher to them; for so, I think, I shall be most likely to turn them from their wicked path.

And now here is a question that I have often asked myself: What is it that you young men really want? Is it to hold office immediately? But that is against the law, and the law was not made to keep able people out; it was made simply because you are unfit for office. Is it that you do not want to live on the same terms as everyone else? But members of the same state ought, in justice, to enjoy the same rights. There are people who will say that democracy is neither an intelligent nor a fair system, and that those who have the money are the best rulers. But I say, first, that what is meant by the *dēmos*, or people, is the whole state, whereas an oligarchy is only a section of the state;

and I say next that though the rich are the best people for looking after money, the best counselors are the most intelligent, and that it is the many who are best at listening to the different arguments and judging between them. And all alike, whether taken all together or as separate classes, have equal rights in a democracy. An oligarchy, on the other hand, certainly gives the many their share of the dangers, but when it comes to the good things of life not only claims the largest share, but goes off with the whole lot. And this is what the rich men and the young men among you are aiming at; but in a great city these things are beyond your reach.

[From the translation of Rex Warner]

Notes

1. [The Penguin edition translations have been used, with some editing, for quotations from the works of Aristotle, Plutarch, Herodotus, and Thucydides. The texts from Tod, *Greek Historical Inscriptions,* are based on the Italian translation and have been checked against the notes of the original. The Pseudo-Xenophon texts are adapted and modernized from the translation of Hartvig Frish (Copenhagen, 1942)—trans.]

Bibliography

Baslez, M. D. *L étranger dans la Grèce antique.* Paris, 1984.
Canfora, L. "Studi sull'Athenaion Politeia pseudo-senofontea." *Memorie dell'Accademia delle Scienze di Torino* 5, no. 4 (1980).
Carpenter, R. *Gli architetti del Partenone.* Turin, 1979. Italian translation of *The Architects of the Parthenon* (London, 1970).
Corcella, A. *Storici greci.* Rome and Bari, 1988.
Farrar, C. *The Origins of Democratic Thinking.* Cambridge, 1988.
Gauthier, P. "Symbola: Les étrangers et la justice dans les cités grecques." *Annales de l'Est: Mémoires* 43, University of Nancy 2 (1972).
Gernet, L. "La notion de démocratie chez les Grecs." *Revue de la Méditerranée,* 1948, 385–93.
Gillis, D. *Collaboration with the Persians.* "Historia" Einzelschriften, no. 34. Wiesbaden, 1979.
Glotz, G. *Histoire greque.* Vol. 1, *Des origines aux guerres médiques.* Paris, 1925.
La Rocca, E., ed. *L'esperimento della perfezione: Arte e società nell'Atene di Pericle.* Milan, 1988.
Loraux, N. *L'invention d'Athènes.* Paris, 1981.
Meier, C. *La nascita della categoria del politico in Grecia.* Bologna, 1988. Italian translation of *Die Entstehung des Politischen bei den Griechen* (Frankfurt, 1980).

Mossé, C. "Le thème de la patrios politeia dans la pensée grecque du IVème siècle." *Eirenè* 16 (1978): 81–89.

Musti, D. "Polibio." In *Storia delle idee politiche economiche e sociali*, ed. L. Firpo. vol. 1. pp. 609–52. Turin, 1982.

Rodewald, C. *Democracy: Ideas and Realities*. London, 1974. An excellent anthology covering the period up to the late classical age.

Rosenberg, A. *Demokratie und Klassenkampf im Alterum*. 1921. Italian translation in L. Canfora, *Il comunista senza partito* (Palermo, 1984).

————. "Aristoteles über Diktatur und Demokratie. *Rheinisches Museum* 32 (1933): 339–61.

Rousseau, J.-J. Note 1 from the "Dédicace" of *Discours sur l'inégalité parmi les hommes* (1754). In *Oeuvres Complètes*, vol. 3, p. 195. Paris, 1964.

Vatin, C. *Citoyens et non-citoyens dans le mond grec*. Paris, 1984.

Weil, R. "Philosophie et histoire: La vision de l'histoire chez Aristote." In *La politique d'Aristote. Entretiens Hardt* (Geneva) 11 (1964): 159–89.

Von Wilamowitz-Moellendorff, U. *Staat und Gesellschaft der Griechen*. 2d ed. *Die Kulture der Gegenwart*, vol. 4, no. 1. Leipzig, 1923.

CHAPTER FIVE

Homo Domesticus

James Redfield

Sources: The Presence of an Absence

THE LATE ARNALDO MOMIGLIANO taught us that history is not about the sources. History is an interpretation of that reality of which the sources are "segni indicativi o frammenti." Obviously, we proceed by examining the sources, but we seek to look *through* them to the reality they represent—and also fail to represent, and misrepresent, and even conceal. This teaching of Momigliano's is especially of value when we come to the present topic, because the classical Greeks have left us almost no sources for their domestic life.

We have, in the first place, very little informal evidence from this period, by which I mean such items as personal letters, business documents, archival material, evidence produced in court proceedings. We have instead formal representations: shaped and painted images, literary narratives, historical accounts, philosophical analyses, and public speeches preserved as rhetorical models. We meet the Greeks, as it were, in their Sunday best; we do not catch them unawares but see them as they chose to represent themselves. These representations, further, are with few exceptions representations of public life. History, once it had reached its canonical mode with Thucydides, concerned itself almost exclusively with politics and war. The philosophical tradition from Pythagoras onward was generally (Aristotle is an important exception) hostile to domesticity; the household is seen as a sphere of wavering emotionality, antisocial tendencies, and low motives. Public action is more likely to be moral because, being visible, it is subject to evaluation by the public.

Public life goes on in public space. This rule has a curious reflex in the art that represented private experience and domestic relationships to the Athenian public, namely, the drama. In both tragedy and comedy, the scene is set in the open—in the street or its substitute. Characters emerge from the house—or from its equivalent (Ajax's tent, the Cyclops's cave)—and not infrequently provide some explanation as to why they have come outside to discuss their secret plans or mourn their private griefs. The drama, in other words, represents itself as the revealing of something normally concealed. This helps us understand why domestic relations in drama are universally represented as abnormal, as broken or in crisis. Insofar as it is a representation of domestic life, the drama is a kind of scandal.

Many of the characters in drama are women. In ordinary life, it was to the credit of an Athenian woman (as Thucydides' Pericles remarks) that we knew nothing about her; the women we can see on the stage are already somehow discredited or in danger by the time the audience sees them—because the audience can see them. What is normally concealed is when revealed evidently out of place.

The Greeks of the classical period did not produce the sort of naturalistic fiction that is such a rich source for domestic life in modern times. We can certainly deduce certain things from the representations we have; our view is rather like the plays, where sometimes a door opens and a messenger appears, or a character peers inside and tells us something of what goes on in that closed, invisible world. On the basis of such hints and fragments, it is possible to write accounts of the Domestic Life of Ancient Greece. In fact, it has been done. The present essay, however, adopts a different strategy. It will be an inquiry into the *idea* of domesticity among the Greeks (especially as we can trace it through myths and rituals), and more specifically, the place of that idea in the ideology of the city-state. From the point of view of this inquiry, the absence of evidence is itself an important piece of evidence. The selection exercised by a people in their self-representation tells us much—as much by what it conceals as by what it reveals.

The Supression of Domesticity

Let us begin with an obvious but puzzling absence: the classical Greeks did not leave us any love stories. Our most familiar scenario, the one that begins boy-meets-girl and ends they-lived-happily-ever-after, is unrepresented in Greek literature before Menander's *Dyscolus*, produced in 316 B.C., seven years after the death of Alexander the Great. Of course, it may be that some lost works—Euripides' *Andromeda,* for instance—followed this pattern, and there are some partial exceptions in surviving works, mostly involving gods: for example, Apollo's courtship of Cyrene in Pindar's ninth *Pythian,* and Homer's allusion to the premarital adventures of Zeus and Hera "when they went to bed together, escaping the supervision of their own parents" (2.15.296). But in general, the rule holds and is the more striking in that (unlike naturalistic fiction) love stories are told worldwide and have provided the basis for classics as diverse as the *Tale of Genjii* and *Sakuntala.* Love stories, further, form an important part of the common stock of Indo-European folktales, whether the story is of the youngest son who wins the beautiful princess or the hapless maiden rescued by her shining knight.

The Greeks, of course, told such stories, too—for instance, the story of how Jason won Medea, or Pelops won Hippodameia. But when they tell them in the classical period, it is not exactly as love stories. Pindar, for example, tells the stories of both Pelops and Jason. Pelops certainly is (in the first *Olympian*) a suitor, but we do not see him paying court to Hippodameia; rather, she is the prize in his struggle with Oenomaus, her father. Jason (in the fourth *Pythian*) does bewitch and seduce Medea, but she is not the prize he seeks; she is the instrument whereby he carries out a task that enables him to recover his patrimony.

Jason, in other words, is not in quest of a bride but in quest of his inheritance. Inheritance is the aspect of family life that preoccupies classic fiction. Haemon and Antigone in the *Antigone,* for instance, are an engaged couple—his love for her is critical to the plot of the tragedy—but the playwright does not bring them on the stage together; rather, Antigone becomes something for Haemon to quarrel with his father about. Clytemnestra murders one husband and marries another, but her tragedy is in her relation with Orestes, who has to kill his mother in order to recover his claims on his father's realm. Then there is Oedipus, whose troubles began when his father tried to kill him in infancy, and who therefore (accidentally) has recovered his patrimony by killing his father and becoming his mother's husband. Trouble arises when a parent tries to prevent the proper succession of the generations. Similarly, the strife between Pelops and Oenomaus became murderous because Oenomaus did not wish to allow the marriage of his daughter; therefore, he challenged each of her suitors to a chariot race. He gave the challenger a start and then overtook him with his wonderful horses and stabbed him in the back. So he killed twelve young men. Pelops, the thirteenth, managed (by different means in different versions) to kill Oenomaus, thus winning Hippodameia.

In one version, Oenomaus wished to marry Hippodameia himself, and this incestuous theme must be seen as latent in all the versions. To marry the daughter is like killing the son, a refusal to let go, to let the next generation take one's place.

The gods, being immortal, do not have this problem—or rather, being immortal they have this problem in reverse. Hesiod's *Theogony* tells at length how the two high gods, Uranus and Cronus, failed, each in his turn, to prevent the succession; finally Zeus, the third in line, stabilizes the cosmos. This he does by swallowing, rather than marrying, his first wife, Metis; Athena was therefore born from the head of Zeus (and was thus utterly loyal to him as both father and mother), while the birth of the son who should be better than his father was avoided. The eternal power of Zeus, in other words, is secured by an eternally virgin daughter and an unborn son.

Because we are not immortal, their myths tell the Greeks, we must allow our daughters to marry and our sons to live. Those who disregard this rule disturb the universe. A legendary example is Atyages the Mede, who learned from a dream that his daughter's son would replace him as king (Herodotus 1.108). Instead of rejoicing at this dream, which promised him an extra generation of rule (he would be replaced not by his son but by his grandson), he acted as if he expected to live forever and sought to kill the child. The result was Cyrus the Great and the Persian empire. Errors that on the domestic level produce tragedy, on the world-historical level produce prodigies.

The problem of inheritance is one way of thinking about the problem of culture and nature: by inheritance we perishable organisms— "creatures of a day," as the poets call us—act to transmit an enduring cultural order. We can do this only if we overcome self love; in this way, the cultural order becomes the gift of each generation to the next. The Greeks, to the degree that they interpreted the family in terms of this problem, saw it from the point of view of the city-state. The purpose of the family, from this political point of view, is to transmit property and social roles so that the political order survives the death of individuals. In terms of nature, the civic role of women was to produce citizens, that is to say, male heirs to the households that compose the cities; in terms of culture, women functioned as tokens in a transaction between father-in-law and son-in-law. This transaction was the *enguē* or *enguēsis*. This was an agreement between the woman's father or legal guardian and her suitor whereby control of her was transferred from one to the other. The same terms were used as for any giving of a pledge in security. The giving of the woman therefore was a token of a bond between the two men; the elder proffered her as a pledge in the active voice of the verb; the younger received her in the middle (*enguomai,* cf. Herodotus 6.130.2). The woman was not a party to the transaction.

The Attic formula was, "I give as a pledge my daughter for the begetting of legitimate children, and with her a dowry of [so-and-so-much]" (Menander frag. 435 Kock; *Dyscolus* 842 f.). The father gave away his daughter, and he also gave his bond to the son-in-law, and also gave a dowry with his daughter. (The dowry formally never belonged to the husband but was held by him in trust for his sons, and it had to be returned if the marriage failed. Nevertheless, it was undoubtedly often an attraction, since the husband had the management of it as long as the marriage lasted.) The new son-in-law did not have to give anything back; in the epic, we hear much of bride gifts, but classic marriage-exchange was reciprocal only within a texture of generalized reciprocity; the father had to give away his daughter because he had once received the daughter of another. The only stated condition of the transaction was "for the begetting of legitimate children." The father-in-law was compensated by the prospect of grandchildren. Here again, the focus was on inheritance. Marriage was conceived as the means whereby a man could have descendants through his daughter. The son-in-law, in return, acquired certain claims on his father-in-law.

Greek marriages were not "arranged" if we mean by this an arrangement between the parents of both bride and groom. The Greeks never recognized anything like the Roman *patrias potestas,* whereby adult sons were under the father's authority so long as he lived; therefore, the suitor, as a free adult male, negotiated for his bride on his own behalf. To marry was a form of acquisition, part of the "third function"; Hermes, patron of the transfer of the bride from her old to her new home, is also god of trade, theft, and found objects. Glaucon in Plato's *Republic* speaks of marriage as if it were a form of commerce; the perfect unjust man, he says, "will marry wherever he wishes, and give in marriage to whomsoever he wishes, and will make partnerships and contracts with anyone he wishes, and will come out ahead in all these transactions by taking his advantages" (362b).

All this placed marriage firmly in a man's world of public transactions, of the competition for honor and gain. To the extent that marriage was understood in this way, it was not understood as centering on the private relation between man and wife. A further consequence, I would suggest, was the absence of love stories.

Stories about courtship, it should be clear, are really stories about the ideal of the marital relationship, because the price one pays to be married provides an evaluation of the married state, and an account of the steps from the single to the married condition is a way of talking about the differences between the two. To put this more technically: a love story states the ideal structure of marriage in terms of a series of ideal events. Such stories need not mirror any actual courtship practices; this explains why they are so popular in cultures—those of South Asia, for instance—in which practically all marriages are arranged, and the bride and groom do not see each other before the day of the wedding. Nevertheless, the bride hopes she will be valued and therefore has a keen interest in stories of the wooing of women; the groom hopes he will be admired, and therefore likes stories in which the bridegroom fights his way to the bride. If the story is one in which the bride is a prize awarded to the most meritorious, it responds to the woman's desire to be treasured and the man's aspirations to merit. If in the story the bride is a rescued victim, this means that women are to be protected and men are strong enough to do so. They live in the stories happily ever after, as if, given the story, that went without saying; the stories are really descriptions of marital happiness.

The absence of love stories in Greek literature is therefore an aspect of the absence of any positive representation of marriage. The women of the tragedies, for instance, are either abused victims, like Iphigeneia or Io, or vengeful furies, like Clytemnestra and Medea; not infrequently they manage, like Deaneira and Antigone, to be both. The most contented married couple in all tragedy is probably (before the moment of truth) Oedipus and his mother! There is a bit more in Aristophanes to redress the balance—the hero of the *Acharnians* appears with his wife, and so, at greater length, does the hero of the *Plutus*—but the only really memorable scene between man and wife is that in the *Lysistrata* where Myrrhine refuses her favors. Of the surviving dramatists, Euripides seems to have been the most interested in marriage; the *Iphigeneia in Aulis* turns on a wedding (which is, of course, a human sacrifice in disguise); the *Andromache* and the *Orestes* end with betrothals, and the *Helen* and *Alcestis* with the reunion of husband and wife. But of these only the *Alcestis* can be taken as a play about marriage; marital happiness is there mourned in its absence.

When we turn from drama back to epic, however, we have quite a different impression. The *Odyssey*, after all, turns on the reconstruction of a marriage, and a marriage was also the *casus belli* of the Trojan War; the action of the *Iliad*, further, turns on the loss and recovery of a woman by Achilles, who himself points out the parallel:

> Do they alone love their wives, among mortal men,
> These sons of Atreus? Since any man who is decent and
> brave
> Loves his own and cares for her.
>
> (*Iliad* 9.340–42)

In Priam and Hecuba, Hector and Andromache, Alcinous and Arete, and Odysseus and Penelope—not to speak of Zeus and Hera—we have in Homer a whole gallery of married couples, and the representation of marriage is generally positive. It is only in later literature that this theme disappears.

When at last we come to the *Dyscolus*, further, we are not confronted by a tentative first attempt at a love story; this is already a developed example of the genre, with its sincere and passionate young hero, its virginal secluded maiden, its irascible father, its story of ordeals and misunderstandings surmounted. And after Menander, this kind of story becomes the staple of Hellenistic narrative. It is as if such stories had been latently present throughout—a surmise confirmed by the observation that there is a latent love story already in *Odyssey* 6 and 7. Odysseus' visit to the Phaeacians is carefully and quite explicitly made *not* to conform with an underlying scenario whereby the handsome stranger from the sea marries the king's daughter and inherits the kingdom. This alternative pattern for the story is in the minds of all the characters; it was clearly familiar to the poet and the audience.

This notion of marriage as a latent, which is to say repressed, theme in Greek culture is further confirmed by the fact that the authors who give the most naturalistic picture of marital life are Aristophanes (e.g., in Strepsiades' account of his wedding night, and the women's gossip in the *Lysistrata*) and Herodotus—(there often in the exotic East, beginning with Candaules of Lydia, but also in Greek settings). Aristophanes and Herodotus are the two authors in the canon who are evidently most free to discuss topics deleted from more respectable kinds of literature; both, for instance, liberally discuss things never mentioned in Homer, for example, urine and women's genitals.

This brings us to a point of chronology. The period during which marriage as a literary topic is suppressed is exactly the period during which the city-state functioned as a self-sufficient—or at least independent—frame for the life of the Greeks. Before Homer, it hardly existed; after Alexander, it survived only as a social and administrative unit under the rule of the Hellenistic kings and their successors. The city-state, further, is the frame of life most typical of the classical Greeks and that best characterizes them. To speak of Domestic Man among the Greeks, therefore, is to raise the question of the relation between domesticity and the city-state.

In tragedy, which was a civic art, domestic themes are set in a frame of heroic society, a society partly imagined, partly remembered from the time before the city-state, a time when, as we see in the epics, women were more visible and more independent. Heroic society is ruled by monarchies, and the families at issue in the plays are the families of kings and princes. (Some early tragedies were placed in the East; this was not such a different strategy, since the East was also monarchical.) The tragedies thus reflect the anxieties of the city-state through a transformation. The domestic problems of royal families have obvious political relevance. The telling of heroic stories therefore became (among other things) a way of reflecting on the political implications of the domestic order.

A recurrent theme in these plays is the threat of female power, the danger that the men might lose control of their women. This danger, further, has its comic counterpart in Aristophanes' fantasies of women's political action. Whether tragically or comically, female power is always treated as a reversal of the nature of things, a reversal, moreover, brought about by the folly and weakness of men. Whether the woman in question is the vicious Clytemnestra, the passionate Antigone, or the wise Lysistrata, the woman's claim to power is invariably taken—even by the women—as a sign that something has gone terribly wrong. Legitimate power in the city-state, the theater told the Greeks, was men's power; and this legitimate order was far from secure.

Greek legends also tell of women completely out of control; these are the maenads, literally, "madwomen." They leave the city and range around the mountains, ecstatic and violent; they live amid miracles, play with snakes, tear live animals with their bare hands, and can defeat men in battle. They are usually devotees of Dionysus, who sports with them as Artemis sports with her nymphs. Whereas the nymphs are immortals, however, maenads are mortals, the wives and daughters of ordinary people, and maenadism is not a normal form of religiosity. On the contrary, it is in the legends most often a punishment that comes on communities that resist the god. Typical is the story of the arrival of Dionysus in Argos, where he was not honored. He therefore sent the women mad. "They took their nurselings into the mountains and ate the flesh of their own children" (Apollodorus *Library* 3.5.2.3.). Maenadism is the negation of motherhood and inheritance; it is a plague, like famine, drought, or pestilence, and like these can only be healed by instituting some right relation with the god.

Argos is also the setting for the stories of the daughters of Proetus, told in many versions, in all of which, however, the girls run mad. Sometimes they also have resisted Dionysus; sometimes the god they offend is Hera. In Hesiod's version (Hesiod frags. 130–33 Merkelbrach and West), they become arrogant because they have so many suitors and in their arrogance offend Hera; she makes them uncontrollably lustful and then punishes them with leprosy and the loss of their hair. They then are healed by being driven from the Argolid. In a related version, they make all the Argive women mad along with them, so that the women kill their children. Melampus and Bias then drive the girls into a neighboring kingdom, killing one of the three daughters on the way; they heal the other two and marry them. Proetus then divides the Argolid with his two sons-in-law (Apollodorus *Library* 2.2.2.2–8).

In Hesiod's version of this story, the women's power that gets out of hand is explicitly sexual power; the arrogance of the girls comes from being much courted, from their marriageability. Hera punishes them first by pushing their sexuality beyond control and then by making them completely unattractive. In the Melampus story, the healing takes place through the expulsion of the girls; the result (with the sacrifice of one in three) is both marriage and a political settlement. Within the framework of the domestic and civic order thus established, the women will cease to kill their children and legitimate inheritance can again proceed. Everyone lives happily ever after. Taken together, the stories of the daughters of Proetus seem to tell the Greeks that marriage, by turning the sexual power of women to the end of inheritance, restrains that power and thus secures both the civic order and a right relation with the god.

The greatest literary representation of maenadism is the *Bacchae* of Euripides. In this play, maenadism is again a punishment for resistance to Dionysus, whose godhead King Pentheus of Thebes refuses to acknowledge. (Dionysus is actually Pentheus' first cousin, being born of Zeus and Pentheus' mother's sister, Semele.) The god therefore sends the women of Thebes out into the mountains, where they run wild, attack settlements, and carry off babies. They are replaced in Thebes by the Asiatic women Dionysus has brought with him; the god cares for these women, masquerading as his own priest. Pentheus attempts to arrest Dionysus, but the god escapes by magic, shaking the palace; he then clouds the mind of Pentheus and leads him to the mountain dressed in women's clothing. There Pentheus' mother tears him limb from limb.

The *Bacchae* is a black play; the characters do not seem to learn anything except that god (while not good) is great. There is praise in the play of intoxication and ecstasy, but this praise is undercut by the action of the piece, which displays to us the catastrophic results of improperly limited ecstasy and intoxication. The message of this play has seemed to many to be sheer terror.

We should, however, notice that Dionysus, who as a god characteristically transforms appearances and whose devotees experience altered states of consciousness, is also god of the theater. In the *Bacchae*, this connection is nearly explicit; the god himself plays a part within the play and painstakingly costumes his victim. The play, further, was like all tragedies produced at a festival of Dionysus. In production, moreover, the chorus of maenads were played by men, as were all the characters; the audience was also (probably) exclusively male. The play represented the dissolution of the city, but the representation was an orderly public, and religious, event. In the festival, I would suggest, the Athenians achieved a right relation with the god, and they achieved it by excluding women—who were present only in the form of representations. The festival was thus *within* the play as an alternative to the play, an antidote to the terror the play evokes. Anyone who looked about the theater would see that the men were in control after all.

More generally, we may observe that Athenian drama only permits the representation of domestic life as triply separated from immediate experience. Domesticity is represented in public (by man for men); it is represented as if it occurred in public (the scene is set in the street); it is transformed because it is represented as if it occurred in heroic time—or, in comedy, by fanciful suspension of time, space, cause, and effect. By these three separations, we can measure the Athenian need to protect the public from the intrusion of domestic reality, while the existence of the plays gives us a measure of the correlative need to interpret that reality in the light of the needs of the public. The suppression of domesticity from public consciousness, which entails the absence of naturalistic fiction, can be seen as cultural precondition of the city-state—even though (or all the more in that) this reality then reasserts itself in stylized form.

The Exclusion of Women

The Greek *polis* or city-state may be defined as a political body founded on the idea of citizenship, which is to say, it is a community that contains a plurality of persons with no juridical superior. Authority is vested in individuals, not as something proper to the person (as in monarchic and feudal regimes), but as proper to the office (even if the office is held for life). Citizens are able to leave office without loss of status and, in fact, typically do so: the citizens characteristically are capable of holding office and then yielding it to another, of "ruling and being ruled," in the Greek formulation. Sociologically, the city-state consists of a plurality of small households related through generalized reciprocity (mutual entertainment, generalized bilateral marriage-exchange, etc.). Economically, it is a private-property society in which wealth is held by numerous individuals, but subject to a tax on capital in times of public emergency. On all three levels, the Greeks themselves contrasted their society with the oriental model, where authority belonged to the king (often also priest or god), honor was bestowed by the throne, and the surplus was held in palace or temple for redistribution on a routine or emergency basis.

Greek citizens were never the population in general; in fact, there was probably no city-state in which they amounted to as much as one quarter of the residents. The full citizens were either all free adult males, in which case the regime was a democracy, or some of these (chosen either from members of certain families, or by a property qualification, or both), in which case the regime was an oligarchy. In any case, women, children, and slaves were excluded. Their place was in the home—indoors, unless they had work that brought them outside. They were members of the household, but not of the city, or only indirectly of the city; they were certainly at home there, but they were not members of the public.

The citizens formed a public, and civic life consisted quite concretely and literally of public meetings—in the Assembly, in the theater, for games, for rituals. The right of the citizen was precisely his right to take part in these public occasions, if not as an actor, then in the audience. (I leave out of account here statuses between free and slave, for instance, freedmen and resident aliens; however important they may have been in practice, they play almost no part in the theory of the city-state.) This right was the citizen's *timē*, his claim to be "valuable." A familiar sanction in Attic jurisprudence was *atimia*, which was the loss of this right to appear in public; it was a kind of internal exile, like being a banned person in South Africa, and reduced the citizen to the level of a woman or child.

It was not that all the full citizens were equal; they were only equally qualified for public appearance. That appearance always took the form of a competition, which tended to establish the *inequality* of the citizens. The competition might take the simple form of the display of wealth; in the case of a ritual, the superiority consisted in being chosen to bear a leading part, whereas in a game the status won or lost was determined by the outcome. In public debate and in the theater, the relation between visibility and status was more complex; actors, for example, ceased to be particularly reputable as soon as the poets stopped playing the leading roles themselves. Some highly visible political roles, for instance, that of demagogue, were disreputable. However, it remained the case that public space offered men opportunities to become reputable—*ariprepees* is the Homeric term; here the community came together and in the process differentiated its members. The Greeks generally took the view that only by participating in such a community of competing peers could one become a human being in the full sense. Therefore, only men could be (in the strict sense) human beings.

The privileged competition was war, in which men distinguish themselves selflessly, on behalf of the community. In the Homeric representation of war, it is conceived as a kind of game, consisting as it does of single combats from which emerge individual winners and losers. Classical Greek warfare could not be—probably no warfare ever was—individualistically competitive in this sense; the notion of competition was adapted to the collective tactics of the phalanx by making battle a competition in steadfastness, in which a man won by not being among the losers, by not giving ground. Those who broke ranks were marked for life and had harsh local names: the Athenian "shield-thrower," the Spartan "trembler." The formal punishment was *atimia*. Thus, steadfastness on the battlefield was a kind of minimal competitive qualification for public life, just as military training was the recognized initiation to manhood.

From Homer onward, the Greek political community is conceived as a self-governing band of warriors; warriors are men, and therefore the political community consists of men. War in the sense of active combat, further, is for young men; there was therefore a tendency to exclude the old, even though it was recognized that their experience could be valuable. Nestor has to remind his audience that he, too, was once a warrior. There are some indications that old men tended to be relegated to the house, like Laertes in the *Odyssey,* retiring to the home farm to work in the garden. It is in old age (as we learn from Plato's Cephalus) that we verify the proverb that "the rich have many consolations" (Plato *Republic* 329c). The old, in other words, retire to the enjoyment of their property; they can no longer take active part in the competition for honor that is the life of public space. Nestor in fact says (somewhat apologetically) that it is *themis,* accepted propriety, for an old man to stay in his house and receive news; he can no longer go about (*Odyssey* 3.186–88).

As war defines what it means to be a man, so manhood is the necessary qualification for war and public life in general. "War is for men" says the Greek proverb. But this means something more than that men do the actual combat. When Hector uses this phrase to Andromache (*Iliad* 6.492), he means that since she is not a warrior she is not qualified to have any opinion about the conduct of the war. The point is generalized when Telemachus adapts the phrase (*Odyssey* 1.358); he tells his mother to go back to the women's quarters, "speech is for men." The irrationality of this masculine claim to a monopoly of political intelligence was evident to Aristophanes, whose Lysistrata tells ruefully how the phrase comes pat to an Athenian male when his wife displays an interest in public matters:

We stood the previous war as long as we could;
We kept on our good behavior, whatever you men did.
You never let us grumble. But we didn't like it!
After all, we could see what was happening, and often-
times here at home
We heard about the dumb decisions you made—on the
biggest issues.
Although we were crying on the inside, we'd ask with a
laugh,
"What was decided about the ratification of the treaty
In your meeting today?" "What's that to you?" my man'd
say,
"Keep quiet." And I kept quiet . . . home and quiet.
Then we found out about some even worse decision,
And we'd ask you: "Honey, how'd you do something so
stupid?"
And he'd give me a straight look, and say if I didn't go
back to the loom
I'd soon have a faceful of tears, "War is for men."

(*Lysistrata* 506–20)

The exclusion of women from Athenian public life reflects the kind of circularity typical of cultural systems. Why do women not take part in public life? Because they don't do the kinds of things of which public life consists. Why do women not do those things? Because those are not things suitable for a woman to do. The premises are self-demonstrating.

Nevertheless, it seems unlikely that the *Lysistrata* (which like the *Bacchae* was produced by and for men) was so fanciful as to be merely puzzling; the play tells us that Athenian men knew that their wives had political opinions and suggests that the women sometimes even went so far as to express them. The Greek suppression of women—even at Athens, where in some respects it went farther than elsewhere—was far from absolute. The education of women was not encouraged, but it was not forbidden. While women were barred from those arts that required public performance (and their craftwork was limited to weaving), we do hear of quite a number of women who were lyric poets. Also women could in various ways make public appearances; we hear of women's athletic contests—not at Athens, it is true, but especially at Sparta, and not only there—and in the ritual sphere women had something like parity with men. The women of Athens were not so secluded that they could not be represented, for instance, on the Parthenon frieze; and in real life, rituals often gave the men a chance to get a look at women of other families. If a young man found a girl attractive, he could (after appropriate inquiries) propose himself to her father as a son-in-law. If the negotiations were successful, the girl would leave her natal family. At Athens, the Eleusinian myth of Demeter and Persephone spoke to the parting of mother and daughter—and to the need for a continuing relation between them—but the departure of the daughter was a loss to the father as well. The dowry, in fact, gave material form to his continuing interest in her, and his stake in her children.

The fact that Greek kinship, while formally patrilinear, was latently bilateral indicates that for the Greeks women were persons. The objectification of women among them was never anything like complete—as we hear of it, for instance, among the Zulu; there, we are told, in the houses of the kings women were kept merely as sexual objects and for the production and care of infants. The Greeks, on the contrary, excluded women from civil society only with a bad conscience.

Indeed, this bad conscience may have been precisely their contribution to the "woman question" as it unfolds in Western history. It seems that the city-state as it excluded women evoked from the start a fantasy of the alternative city of women, a fantasy given ritual form in the Thesmophoria, when the women for a time withdrew and formed a kind of ritual city of their own. In comedy this fantasy also has its place; the political action of women is a fantastic reversal, like the conquest of heaven or the return of the dead to life. But the fantasy is of course best known to us from the philosophical tradition, particularly from Socrates' utopia in the *Republic*.

Socrates, as he unfolds his utopia, remarks at a certain point that the guardians, being educated to moderation, will of themselves work out "the possession of women and of marriages and the making of children, that in all these matters, as the proverb has it, all the possessions of friends should as much as possible be made common" (423e–424a). That "all things of friends are common" was a Pythagorean proverb; the Pythagoreans sought to perfect their community by pooling their property. It is unclear whether they ever thought of extending this rule to women; it is in any case clear to Socrates that the elimination of private property will not be enough; the city can never be a perfect community so long as the rulers have their *own children*, and thus a private interest in the welfare of particular persons.

At the beginning of book 5, Socrates' audience demands that he say more; the community of women has, as we say, a "human interest"—like anything connected with sex. Socrates' response is in two parts. First he defends the notion of admitting women to the political life and the ranks of the rulers; then he goes on to deal with the question of the family.

The utopia is to be a community founded on nature; it might then seem that men and women must have different treatment in it, since they are clearly different by nature. But, Socrates responds to this objection that he himself has raised, this is to misunderstand the relevant meaning of "nature." The utopia is a state in which authority belongs to those capable of a specific education; the only relevant natural differences are those relevant to the educable aspect of us, for which the Socratic name is *psychē*, the soul. That women bear children while men do not is a fact about the body, and it is assumed that this difference is unconnected to any sexual difference in psychic capacity.

Not that Socrates considers men and women psychologically equal; on the contrary, his argument that there are no skills particular to women, and therefore no skills particular to men, is founded on the claim that men, overall, are better than women *at everything*—including weaving and cooking (455c–d). Nevertheless, this does not exclude the possibility that some women may be better endowed than some men with the capacities fit for the best education, and these women should be admitted to the ranks of the best. Obviously there will be fewer of them there than men.

Since these capacities are characteristically masculine, the women who qualify will be those who are most like men. Socrates has already asserted that the women admitted to the best education will do all the things that the men do, including the "bearing of arms and the bestriding of horses" (452c). In particular (and here Socrates begins to fear ridicule), they will like the men exercise naked—and not the young women only, but the old ones as well. After all, he says, these things are culturally relative; not so long ago the Greeks thought the public nakedness of males to be shameful, just as the barbarians do now. "Eventually the ridiculousness of the sight was displaced by the reason that testified to the best" (452d)—and so it shall be in this case also.

On this fantasy, the difference between women and men is dissolved all in one direction; certain women "with a capacity for gymnastics and war" (456a) become, as it were, honorary men. The women so educated, further, will be "the best of the women" (456e). In other words, Socrates asserts that the best thing a woman can be is a man.

Socrates then goes on to lay out his program for the elimination of the family. It has already been asserted that the guardians shall have no households or private property; now he goes on to tell how they shall be bred like cattle, their children reared in common. The greatest scandals of the *Republic* are in this section, particularly the permission of incest and the eugenic murder of infants. Socrates here takes the philosophic antipathy to domesticity to its greatest extreme.

Socrates is careful to deny any value to femininity per se. That women bear and suckle (cf. 460d) babies is to be treated as a kind of physical handicap, which must be recognized to some degree, but which will as far as possible be overcome and minimized. The equal display of the sexes in nude exercise is crucial because it will teach the guardians not to think sexual difference a thing of importance. Socrates' argument is not an argument against the exclusion of women from the political sphere, but rather an extension of it to (some of) the women; their femaleness is to be excluded from consideration, not allowed to count against them—and that is the manner of their inclusion.

However ironically these proposals are meant, by Socrates within the dialogue or Plato speaking through it, they do enable us by interpretation of their inversions, exaggerations, and denials, to draw a schematic of the city-state. We are shown a life divided between a public sphere, where men display themselves in the service of communal values, and private space about which, perhaps, the less said the better, a "space of disappearance," where babies are conceived and other things happen beneath the notice of the polity. The public sphere is masculine; it is a sphere of words and ideas, characterized by open competition for honors—that is to say, the recognition of one's peers. The body here is characteristically stripped; this "heroic nudity" (which in art was extended beyond athletic exercise to young males in general) presents the person as a minimal creature, a simple self-assertive social unit. In competition, these persons achieve differences; their community is therefore founded on their initial similarity. (At Sparta, the citizens were called *homoioi,* "similars.") Women were excluded by the same principle by which Socrates included them, namely, the principle that similarity (in the relevant respects, whatever those turn out to be) is the principle of the state. Concretely, this similarity was enacted in most Greek states by participation in a common military training and organization, the core of which was a body of hoplite soldiers, of identical training and equipment, effective not as an organized hierarchy but as a uniform mass.

In the private sphere, by contrast, difference was primary; femininity acquired a specific value there because men and women in marriage related to each other through their difference. The house was not a place of competition but of cooperation, not of ideas but of things, not of honors but of possessions, ornaments, furniture. The body here is characteristically adorned; this is the primary locus of both production and consumption, the place where the citizen made contact with his natural self and with the earth. The Socratic fantasy is precisely to sever this connection with the earth, to deny personality to the body and the natural self.

The Spartan Version

Our theme so far has been the disappearance of the domestic sphere— not its unimportance in practice, but its theoretical insignificance, as if the city-state wished away the private life of families so that it could get on with its self-representation as a self-sufficient society organized around the competition of identically qualified peers. This view suggests an ethnographic parallel with an Australian men's society, where the males gather in secrecy to rejoice in the special powers of their sex. Or, since the point of the city-state was not secrecy but appearance, we might suggest a parallel with the Bororo village described by Lévi-Strauss. Here we find a circle of huts in the forest. In the center of the circle is the men's house, where the adolescent males live; no woman comes here except the day she claims a husband. Should a girl casually wander by she is liable to be raped. Within this central circle, also, the men celebrate the rituals of the tribe, in particular its funerals, which involve dancing and games. These are watched from outside the circle by the women; the women keep to the huts, which demarcate the central area from the forest. The circle, in other words, is cultural space; it is inhabited only by men, who are privileged to be the cultural sex. Women inhabit the boundary between culture and nature. They give birth, which is the natural production of persons: the men are in charge of death, which is the transformation of a person into a memory, which is to say, into that most perfectly cultural thing, an idea.

The Greek city-state that best approximated this model was Sparta (notable for its royal funerals and its many cults of the dead), and it was perhaps precisely the Spartan creation of a closed men's world that made Sparta the prototypical—if at the same time the oddest—city-state, praised by everyone and imitated by no one, as Xenophon says. The Spartans, after an extended period of military training—extended, not because it lasted longer than elsewhere, but because it started much earlier—adopted on a permanent basis the life of an army in the field. They ate together in military companies, going home only to sleep, and their food and clothing were more or less standardized. Furthermore, their lives were passed in constant competition as each tried to show himself more Spartan than the others. This body of males, united by an education that was also an initiation, was both the army (or at the least, the elite units and the officer corps) and the government of Sparta. The Spartans, in other words, made of the political sphere a closed world of men, of the acculturated.

The Spartans, further, were separated from the economic sphere. They were not supposed to accumulate wealth. They did no work, passing their lives, when not at war, in hunting and dancing. They were forbidden to manage their property; their land was worked by helots who could be murdered without penalty—annually the Spartans declared war on their helots—but who could not be evicted; neither could their rent be raised. The Spartans and the helots were locked together in a frozen, almost ritualized combat (which not infrequently turned into general violence). This relation to the labor force forced the Spartans to maintain their military organization and at the same time secured the separation of the Spartans from nature; their fixed rents supported them as if by magic, without any attention on their part. Liberated from brute necessity, they were freed to govern their lives by patriotism and piety. As free male citizens, they were privileged to higher values.

The Spartans themselves maintained a myth of their society as somehow primitive; their perpetual war with the helots ritualized the myth of their original arrival as a conquering band, subduing together the land and its aboriginal labor force. Whatever the basis in reality for this myth (and it was slight), we should also notice that the Spartans had another contrasting myth of their society, one that made it a product of design by the lawgiver Lycurgus. In this story, Sparta had once been the worst of societies, and had made itself into the best only by overcoming its own negative tendencies; if among city-states Sparta was uniquely pious and patriotic, that was in reaction to its experience of impious individualism. This myth also was ritualized, in the Spartan education—by the rigor of which we can measure the forces it was intended to overcome. Those forces were at Sparta located in the private households in which every Spartan originated and that each Spartan reconstituted through marriage.

Tribal societies like the Bororo, which explicitly associate women with the natural sphere and enclose males within a protected cultural environment, are usually matrilocal. The adolescent males who inhabit the men's house are on their way from the huts of their mothers to the huts of their wives. And since the Bororo village is spatially divided between exogamous moieties, they are literally halfway in their crossing from one side of the village, where the mother's moiety lives, to the other side, where they will join the wife's moiety, to which their children will belong. In such societies, the women usually provide the basic subsistence, through collecting or gardening (while "special" foods, that is, more highly acculturated foods associated with ceremonials, are provided by males through hunting). Marriage ties are relatively weak, the man being free to go back to his mother if things don't work out, and children are reared by the mother's kin, particularly the mother's brother. It is true that at Sparta marriage ties were relatively weak; we have some anecdotal material about wives who were shared or borrowed, and couples do not seem to have set up house together before the children were born. All this was praised by the philosophers (cf. Xenophon *Constitution of the Lacedaemonions* 1.5–9); indeed, the popularity of Sparta in the philosophic tradition can be traced in large part to the illusion produced there of a life wholly devoted to the state, without domestic ties. Nevertheless, Sparta was not a utopia because, as the philosophers knew, this was only an illusion. It is precisely on this point that Socrates in the *Republic* (548a–b) distinguishes Sparta (which he calls the "timocracy") from his utopia. Spartan society was based on private property, and when a Spartan's property no longer sufficed to pay his dues to the men's society, his citizenship lapsed. (Non-Spartans could not buy their way in, and the number of citizens was continually decreasing.) Spartan civic emergencies were met by taxes on capital, just as in other Greek states; individuals did accumulate wealth there, and wealth brought status. Furthermore, this property was held by families of the normal Greek type; patrilinear and patrilocal. The Spartans, in other words, did not eliminate the usual kind of domestic life; they merely went further than the other Greeks in excluding it from view.

The detachment of Spartan males from their homes was proper to a life phase (albeit a prolonged one). Up to the age of seven, before the training of the boys began, they were reared at home—and given the need of the older men, including their older brothers, to be elsewhere, were raised predominantly by women. They were then evicted into the male world of asceticism and competition, and we may attribute to the abruptness of this change the rigid and yet uncertain self-control of the Spartans; for all their discipline, they were certainly (as we meet them in the histories) more than other Greeks subject to fits of rage and violence.

The household of origin of course continued to exist and to be some part—we cannot say how small—of their lives; if a Spartan's father died, he became responsible for his sisters. Then, at a certain age, he was expected to marry; because of the diminishing citizen population, marriage was compulsory. He thus acquired a wife and, later, daughters. He therefore had to negotiate marriages. In the absence of other commercial opportunities, Aristotle tells us, marriage-exchange became an important way of acquiring property (*Politics* 1270a). The Spartan's opportunities to marry and give in marriage, further, were evidently significantly shaped by his success in the sphere of masculine competition; Xenophon speaks of the disadvantages suffered by the coward: he is despised by all "and must keep the maidens who belong to him at home and endure their accusations of cowardice, must see his hearth barren of a wife and pay the penalty for this as well" (*Constitution of the Lacedaemonions* 9.5). We can well understand that the Spartan women took the lead in enforcing the warrior code on their menfolk: "With your shield or on it."

The effect of the Spartan regime on the women was ambiguous. They shared the insulation of the men from the economic sphere and did not work; they alone among high-status Greek women were not expected to spend their days in the production of textiles. The energies thus liberated seem to have been absorbed by the elaborate ritual order that sustained and shaped every aspect of Spartan life; women (there as elsewhere in Greece) achieved in ritual a parity denied them in other spheres. Spartan rituals, further, were characteristically athletic, and the Spartan women were legendary for their athleticism, from the archaic girls in Alcman's poems who "run like horses in dreams" to Aristophanes' Lampito, who could throttle a bull. "Thessaly for horses, Sparta for women," said the Greek proverb.

On the other hand, they were denied participation in the political sphere; legend said that Lycurgus had asked them to join in submission to the laws, but they had refused (Aristotle *Politics* 1270a). The women therefore were at fault; as they were held to continue that "worst of societies" that existed before the law, they became the vehicle for all the negative tendencies in Spartan culture. To the discipline and asceticism of the men was contrasted the disorder and luxury of the women. Women at Sparta could (as they could not at Athens) inherit and own property; paradoxically, this was another sign of their exclusion. The men had abandoned the households to them, securing their own superiority (it seems) by leaving to the women wavering emotionality, antisocial tendencies, and low motives.

The Contradictory Position of Women

Because Sparta was the extreme form of the city-state, the contradictions of the city-state appear there in extreme form. These contradictions center on the "woman question." The citizens were a body of men whose relations were defined by open competition; they were therefore a class in competition with itself that nevertheless had to maintain the conditions of its own competition. These conditions were maintained by kinship, which structured a (somewhat) stable society within which the competition could take place. Therefore, the utopian solution (however much it fascinated the Greeks in history) was not available; the elimination of families, as Aristotle saw (*Politics* 1262b), would exacerbate competition, not moderate it. The citizen had to take a longer view and be concerned for the common good because he was concerned for future generations. He reproduced himself through his sons, and through his grandsons, including his daughter's children. Each citizen originated in a family and at maturity constituted one. For the Greeks, inheritance implied marriage-exchange.

The utopian solution, as we saw it in Socrates' project, would eliminate women by turning them into men; the "Zulu solution," which would eliminate women by turning them into objects or domesticated animals, was also unavailable for much the same reasons. A free citizen had a legitimate origin, which meant that his mother was a free woman. The children of concubines were not citizens, or they had to be granted citizenship, like strangers. A free woman was one who had been transferred to her husband by a free man who was her father (or guardian). Therefore, the legitimacy of the son was in part the gift of the paternal grandfather. And the honor and dignity of the family was as much invested in the daughters as the sons.

The society that sustained the city-state was one of private property and generalized reciprocity; therefore, the "Bororo solution," whereby women, mediating between culture and nature, send away men and receive other males in return, was not available either. It would have implied the loss of male control over the households, or at least the loss of inheritance through males. The free Greek citizen was everywhere master of a household, even at Sparta. In Greek society, the primacy of males was pervasive; marriage was patrilocal as inheritance was patrilinear and authority patriarchal. Yet males were never more than "half the state" (Aristotle *Politics* 1269b). As often as the women were deprived of significance, they reasserted themselves. They were not (except at Sparta) heirs, but their free birth conferred legitimacy. They were not citizens, yet the city was a community of free men and women. They did not (at Athens) own property, but they (so to speak) animated it; a house without women was empty. At the symbolic center of the women's quarters was the marriage bed; this belonged to the man and was intended for his wife. In the marriage ceremony, the groom took the bride by the wrist and escorted her into his house and bed. In the *Odyssey,* patrilocality is symbolized by the bed Odysseus has made with his own hands, and with a secret sign: it is literally rooted in the earth. In the *Alcestis* (1049–60), Admetus ponders the problem of (he thinks) a female captive Heracles has left with him: if he puts her in the men's quarters, she will be molested, but if she is put in the women's quarters, she will have to sleep with him! The departure of Alcestis has left a space in the bed in which he continues to sleep.

The Greeks made no provision for the entertainment of female guests; women were not supposed to travel. Nevertheless, in the relation of marriage it is the woman, not the man, who is mobile. Once in her life she has to be disembedded from one household and placed at the center of another, where she, an outsider, becomes custodian of everything enclosed, protected, turned inward. In mythology she thus becomes identified with Hestia, the goddess of the hearth, who alone in Plato's myth (*Phaedrus* 247a) does not join Zeus when he traverses the heavens, but remains always within doors.

However, the wife's relation to the hearth is ambiguous; the ritual

that received her into the house (Iamblichus *Life of Pythagous* 84) did
not, it seems, associate her with the hearth but established her separation from it. The purity of the hearth is hostile to sexuality; Hesiod
warns the couple not to make love within sight of the fire (*Works and
Days* 7.33f.). Hestia in mythology is not a bride but rather an eternal
virgin; Zeus gave her the privilege of staying forever in his house
"instead of marriage" (*Hymn to Aphrodite* 28). She plays the role of
the daughter who is allowed to stay with her father, and in fact the
virgin daughter is the truest hypostasis of Hestia.

It is characteristic of the gods that they can play forever a role that
for mortals must be transient. The Greeks assume that all women will
marry; the virgin daughter becomes a bride and takes temporary cus-
tody of the hearth until she can produce a virgin daughter of her own.
In this alternation of roles, we find the essential instability of women.
The perfection of a woman, for the Greeks, is the moment of the
parthenos, the marriageable girl. But this moment is evanescent, not
merely because of the universality of age and death (which are for
males also) but because the role itself (unlike its male equivalent, that
of young warrior) is *for* another role. The father rejoices in his daughter only to lose her to another; the more valuable she is, the more
marriageable, and therefore the more certain to be lost, and soon. The
maximally ambiguous moment, for a woman, is also the moment of
her completion: when she becomes a bride.

The ambiguous status of the bride is signaled by the fact that the
Greeks had two types of wedding and normally employed them both.
One we have already discussed: the *enguē*. It is sometimes miscalled a
"betrothal"; this translation is doubly deceptive, since a betrothal is a
transaction between prospective bride and groom and is preliminary
to the wedding. The *enguē* was a transaction between father-in-law
and son-in-law and it *was* the wedding. No other ceremony was required to legitimate the children or make final the financial arrange-
ments. Nothing remained to make the marriage actual but its consummation, for which the Greek word is *gamos*.

The moment of consummation, the wedding night (which might
follow the *enguē* by a considerable time), was usually the occasion for
a celebration, also called the *gamos*. Although this celebration was not
compulsory, we may believe that few Greek brides of decent family
would have done without it. This occasion looked much like our idea
of a wedding. There was a large party; people got drunk, made toasts,
sang songs; the father of the bride spent a lot of money. But there
was no wedding, in the sense that no vows were exchanged and there

was no sacralization of the couple. The couple, or the bride alone, might visit a temple on the previous day to say farewell to maidenhood and seek the protection of the god for this new life, but at the actual *gamos* the gods were no more present than they were at any party. The *gamos* celebrated, and thus ritualized, the sexual initiation of the bride, which was also the most significant stage of her initiation into adulthood.

Most of the festivities took place at the bride's father's house; the groom might sleep there the night before. The bride was elaborately adorned for the occasion. The most significant moment of this phase was the *anakaluptēria,* the unveiling of the bride by the *numpheutria,* the matron who conducted the ceremony, and her presentation to the groom. The groom then took her, on foot or by mule car, to his home; this journey was accompanied by torches and the sound of flutes. The *numpheutria* went with them; the mother of the bride saw them off; the mother of the groom welcomed them. After a ritual of aggregation, the *numpheutria* saw the bride and groom to bed. On the following day, there might be a further procession, the *epaulia,* wherein the friends and relatives of the bride brought her trousseau to her in her new home.

The *enguē* was a transaction between men and centered on the groom, who was congratulated for his success in winning a bride; the bride did not even have to be present. The *gamos* was conducted primarily by women, and it focused on the bride, on her adornment. She was certainly the star of the occasion; specific ancillary rituals, for instance, the preliminary bath, might in different communities be for both bride and groom or for the bride alone, but never for the groom alone. The groom trailed in the bride's wake; the change of life was after all far greater for the bride. The *enguē* was the ceremony of her transfer, the *gamos* the ritual of her transformation. In the *enguē,* the marriage was seen from the point of view of the city as a link between patrilines; in the *gamos,* it was seen from the point of view of the household as the establishment in the center of the house, of a new beginning for a family. The woman acquired a new status with specific obligations and specific powers.

Men and Women

The original bride is Pandora; her story deserves to be told here at length, since it places marriage in the context of a general mythical account of our relation with the natural order. I follow Hesiod, combining his two versions (*Theogony* 507–612 and *Works and Days* 42–105).

In the beginning, we are told, life was easy; a man could live for a year on the work of a day, and men and gods feasted together. Then one day at such a feast, Prometheus arranged the shares of meat in a deceitful way; he took the meat and the hide and packed it into the stomach while he piled the bones up in a great heap covered with fat. Zeus complained that the division was unequal; Prometheus offered him his choice. Zeus (although he knew he was being cheated) took the larger pile, and that is why when the Greeks sacrificed they gave to the gods the bones and fat (which were burned) while they reserved the edible and useful parts of the beast for themselves. Sacrifice is therefore ambiguous; it reestablishes a connection between men and gods it continues our feast with them) and reenacts the moment of our separation from the gods (it continues sacrifice in the form that made Zeus angry).

Zeus then took away fire, making sacrifice impossible and the separation absolute. Prometheus retaliated by stealing fire, reestablishing the connection but through an act of defiance. Zeus thereupon had recourse to guile. He had made of earth a beautiful maiden; all the gods adorned her; because she received gifts from them all she was called *Pan-dora,* "universal gifts." He then sent her as a gift to Epimetheus, Prometheus' brother. Epimetheus had been warned not to accept any gifts from Zeus, but faced with Pandora's charms he forgot. He took her in, as well as a jar that she brought with her. When she opened the jar, there flew out all the evils: sickness, labor, strife.

Epimetheus does not merely entertain Pandora; he marries her. Everything that was hers—that she brings with her—becomes his. In Hesiod's telling of the story, marriage is parallel to sacrifice. Both enact our ambiguous relation to the gods. Marriage results from our connection with them (Pandora was the gift of Zeus) and is a token of our separation from them (the gift intended harm). Both involve a theme of deceit, but differently. In the sacrifice story, Prometheus, on our behalf, attempted to deceive Zeus; Zeus, although he was not deceived, punished us for his attempt. When Prometheus overcame this punishment, Zeus sent another, this time deceiving us. The sacrifice story involves a kind of trial of strength with the gods, an act on our side of what the Greeks call *pleonexia,* "seeking to have more than one's share." In the marriage story, the gods overpower us; we are the victims, and harm comes to us because of our weakness.

The Pandora story is a story of the fall, which, as in Genesis, is a fall into nature, and all the ills the flesh is heir to: sickness, labor, and death. Women in both stories bring the Fall; they are the emblems of our natural condition since they are the authors of the flesh. The father, after all, contributes nothing to the child except genetic information; the substance is all the mother's.

Pandora was the first woman; "from her is the race of female women" (*Theogony* 590). As she brought death into the world, so she brought birth. There is no explanation in Hesiod of how men came to exist before there were women; perhaps they came from the earth, more likely they simply lived forever. No explanation is needed because in this first time, the Golden Age, men had no relation to nature at all; they were purely cultural beings. The myth, in other words, is based on a conceptual inversion not so different from the state-of-nature stories of the Enlightenment. In both cases, what is developmentally prior is placed in a secondary position. In Rousseau, pre-existing autonomous individuals join to form a community (but in what language do they discuss the Social Contract?). So in Hesiod men first exist, then acquire a biology. In Rousseau the reversal is of the relation between the individual and the group; in Hesiod it is between men and women. Male culture is placed *before* the female mediation between culture and nature.

Hesiod places the story of Pandora within the frame of his general explicit misogyny. "He who trusts a woman trusts himself to deception" (*Works and Days* 375). Women, he says, are like the drones who sit in the hive all day and let the bees feed them (*Theogony* 594–600). This is bad economics; the housework and craftwork of Greek farm wives must have more than paid for their keep. And it is bad zoology, as Hesiod knows. The drones (his pronouns remind us) are male, while the worker bees are female; indeed, Simonides of Amorgos, the other great archaic misogynist, took the worker bee as his model for the (rare) good woman. But perhaps Hesiod means exactly this reversal: as between culture and nature the roles of the sexes are reversed. In nature males are nearly redundant; in culture females are, if not redundant, a token of culture's failure to achieve independence of nature. We thus see here interpreted on the level of economics the same earthbound condition that we saw before on the political level: the Greek citizen after all originated in a family and created one, and was politically dependent on the possession of a household.

If the Fall is into nature, the aspiration to redemption is to a purely cultural condition. In these terms, we can understand the Greek aspiration to treat public life as all of life. The Spartans, with their insulation from the economic sphere, can be seen as enacting a fantasy of the Golden Age: without labor, without women. By their inclusion in the polity of their divine kings, they actually achieved a kind of feasting with the gods.

At Sparta, also, we are told, the state would have been perfect if it had not been for the women. It is the women that made wealth important there (rather than honor) because, as Aristotle says, "they are actually controlled by their women, like most militaristic and warlike races. . . . Evidently the man who first told the story was not irrational to join as a couple Ares and Aphrodite" (*Politics* 1269b). Women are dangerous because they are attractive (and they were especially dangerous at Sparta because they were especially attractive to the Spartans). Pandora, similarly, is overpoweringly attractive; she is "sheer deception, against which human beings are defenseless" (*Theogony* 589).

Pandora's power is conferred by adornments. Athena gives her the art of weaving (an attraction in a woman; cf. *Illiad* 9.390). Hermes gives her "lies and wheedling words and a thieving nature" (*Works and Days* 78). Zeus instructs Aphrodite to spread grace upon her head, and "harsh longing and cares that devour the limbs" ibid., 66). In the event, the instruction is carried out by the Hours and Graces and by Peitho, who give her golden earrings and crown her with spring flowers.

The attractions of a woman are characteristically *poikilos,* variegated; they involve the shifting and complex surface that in Greek culture is characteristic of things deceptive and entangling. A woman's jewelry is the concrete representation of her wheedling ways. The whole woman's world, with its basketry, furniture, painted pottery, and fabrics, is entangling of a man; this symbolic point is enacted in the curious scene in Aeschylus in which Clytemnestra induces Agamemnon to walk on a piece of embroidered fabric before she murders him. The master symbol is Aphrodite's girdle, a piece of embroidered fabric that contains "love and desire and courtship, beguilement which steals the mind of even the steadiest person" (*Illiad* 14.216–17). The adornment of the bride included a girdle; indeed, one euphemism for the consummation of the marriage was the "unloosing of the girdle." The girdle, like the jewelry, is a symbol of sexual power. The bride, in other words, is adorned so that she can seduce the groom into marriage.

Hera in the *Iliad* borrows Aphrodite's girdle so that she can seduce her husband. The power of Aphrodite extends even over Zeus "who is greatest of all and has the greatest *timē*" (*Hymn to Aphrodite* 37). Zeus retaliates by making Aphrodite subject to her own power, so that she falls in love with Anchises. Women are also subject to sexual power; they are both seductive and seduciable. In the stories it is usually the man who takes the initiative; as Theseus seduced Ariadne and thus found his way through the labyrinth, so Jason seduced Medea, and Pelops, Hippodameia. The marriageable woman is characteristically the weak point in the system. In both directions, we should observe, the sexuality of the woman serves to undercut male power; her desirability conquers her suitor, while her desire overrides her sense of duty to her father. In the most current version of the Hippodameia/Pelops story, both are in play. Hippodameia loves Pelops and therefore cooperates with him against her father; her father's chariot is weakened because Myrtilus, his charioteer, replaces one thole pin with a dummy made of wax—and Myrtilus performs this act of treachery because he is promised the favors of Hippodameia's wedding night, either by Pelops or Hippodameia herself. In this last version, the bride uses the only power she has, her sexual attractions, to separate herself from her father and adhere to the husband she desires. In the myth, of course, everything is extreme: the father wants to marry his daughter and kill her suitors; he is betrayed by his own servant to whom his daughter secretly gives herself, and he dies. In actual life, the father and the bridegroom could usually work something out, the father felt only somewhat sad to lose his daughter, the members of the household who encouraged the girl to marry were motivated by quite proper affection for her, and the favors of her wedding night were promised and given—to her bridegroom.

The Hippodameia story represents the bride as an active participant in the marriage contract. Certainly in ordinary life Athenian girls were consulted and consented to the marriage. We know, for instance, of the existence of *promnestriai,* go-betweens or matchmakers, who went back and forth between the young people. Xenophon's Socrates says, "Once I heard Aspasia say that the good go-betweens bring back and forth good descriptions within the bounds of truth and in this way have the art of bringing about marriage alliances, but are unwilling to praise falsely. For those who are cheated will hate each other and the one who has gone between them as well" (*Memorabilia* 2.6.36). It is striking that the go-between is a woman, and that Socrates hears about her from Aspasia, who is his contact with the women's world. The marriage, the *enguē,* may be contracted between men, but it is the women's powers that make it work, particularly the powers of the most female of the gods, Aphrodite.

In marriage, the power of Aphrodite separates the girl from her father and binds her to her husband. This is as it should be. In all the stories we have been considering—Jason, Theseus, Pelops—the father is supposed to lose; the young man in seducing the daughter is pursuing a proper aim. Later on, of course, both Jason and Theseus abandon their brides, but this is not supposed to happen. Abandoned brides in Greek myth are powerful, dangerous figures; both Ariadne and Medea achieve something like apotheosis. Ariadne (in most versions) marries Dionysus; Medea (in Euripides) after murdering Jason's children goes off in a fiery chariot.

The prototypical abandoned bride is Hera, whose rage pervades the mythical universe—against Troy, Heracles, Io, Leto, against everyone Zeus has ever loved. In the *Hymn to Apollo* (300–355), her rage against Zeus for producing Athena causes her to produce—also asexually—Typhon. Typhon in Hesiod (*Theogony* 820–68) was the last monster Zeus had to overcome in establishing his power. The struggle continued into the next generation, however; the offspring of Typhon was the Hydra of Lerna, overcome by Heracles with the help of Athena (ibid., 313–18).

The loveless, sterile marriage of Zeus and Hera is the key to the stability of the cosmos; it is evidence that Zeus has broken the cycle of the generations in heaven and will rule forever. We, however, are not gods, and on earth it is just the opposite; we survive only by perishing and giving way to our successors, who are bred in fertile—and best bred in loving—marriages. In marriage, the father is replaced by the husband, and this is as it should be. The clearest statement of this point is probably the story of Hypermnestra. She was one of the daughters of Danaus, who were forbidden by their father to marry their Egyptian suitors; when the marriage was finally forced upon them, they were told to stab their husbands in the wedding bed. Hypermnestra alone disobeyed this instruction; "desire beguiled her" as Aeschylus says (*Prometheus* 853). She was then prosecuted by her father for this offense against patriarchy. On her acquittal on the charge of failing to murder her husband, she founded the sanctuary of Artemis Peitho (Pausanias 2.21.1).

Probably these events were represented in the last play of Aeschylus' trilogy *Danaids,* of which the *Suppliants* is the first. The only surviving fragment from that last play is a speech by Aphrodite, probably speaking in Hypermnestra's defense:

The holy heaven loves to pierce the ground;
There captures earth the love of consummation.
The rain, falling down from liquid heaven
Made earth conceive, and then she bears for mortals
The flocks of sheep and Demeter's gift of life.
The season of trees from this well-watered wedding
Perfects itself. And I'm part cause of this.
(apud Athenaeus 600b)

That a woman should love her husband, says Aphrodite, is very natural. If women are the tokens of our fall into the condition of nature, we should remember that this is the same nature that nurtures us. Women are the problem and also the solution; they are the sign of our mortality, and also make it possible for life to go on—literally, in their fertility, and also institutionally. Theirs is the power to feel and inspire love, which in the city-state becomes the power to move from hearth to hearth and originate new houses.

Aphrodite calls herself "part cause" (*paraitios*) of the wedding of heaven and earth. This word in the law means "accessory"; it might also be translated "catalyst" or "mediator." The difference between male and female is the most socially significant of differences; the mediation of that difference by love is the foundation of society.

So the repression of domesticity for the Greeks was also an acknowledgment of its secret power. If the males claimed for themselves public space and cultural values, it was with an understanding that this could only be half the story. Every dichotomy—between public and private, male and female, culture and nature—is accompanied by a mediation. In ritual we can see it in the doubleness of the wedding: *enguē* and *gamos*. In myth it is in the eternal playful contest between Zeus and Aphrodite. It is the play within the city-state between law and love.

CHAPTER SIX

Spectator and Listener

Charles Segal

Vision, Monument, Memory

THE GREEKS ARE a race of spectators. Naturally curious about one another and about the differences between themselves and the Other—the non-Greek or "barbarian"—they are good observers and good storytellers. Both virtues are everywhere in evidence in the two great narrators at the beginning and end of the archaic age: Homer, orally composing and reciting his great epics in the late eighth century B.C., and Herodotus, writing down his account of the Persian Wars of the 480s and with it his vast survey of the neighboring civilizations.

Both authors are fascinated by the visual details that play over the surface of the world, and both delight in capturing in words the endless variety of human behavior: dress, talk, rituals and worship of the gods, sex, marriage, the family, war, architecture, and so on. Both know, too, about the seductive power of curiosity, the desire to see and to know. The *Odyssey* opens with the hero who "saw the towns of many men and came to know their minds" (1.2). Early in his *Histories,* Herodotus tells the story of Candaules and Gyges, a tale that turns on the power of vision, the secret viewing of a woman's body, whereby the Lydian king, Candaules, would display to his lieutenant the extraordinary beauty that he possesses in this wife whom he loves (1.8.2). Herodotus, in fact, has Candaules preface his story with the generalization "Among mankind the ears are less trusting than the eyes" (1.8.3). But in the story that he thus sets into motion, it is vision that releases the chain of disasters, intertwining love, voyeurism, the betrayal of trust, shame, and deception. In Homer the visual impact of a woman's beauty is equally powerful and has equally disastrous consequences. When the elders of Troy "saw Helen coming to the tower," they liken her to an immortal goddess and for a moment waver in thinking that it is worth fighting the war over her (*Iliad* 3.154–60). The tragedians dwell on the visual impact of Helen's beauty. In Euripides' *Trojan Women,* for example, Hecuba urges Menelaus to kill her without looking at her "lest she seize you by desire, for she takes the eyes of men, destroys cities, burns houses: such charms does she have" (890–93). The tableau of Menelaus dropping his sword at the sight of Helen's beauty became proverbial.

In such scenes, we the audience become, in effect, spectators of the power of vision itself. Both Homer and Herodotus, to stay with our two examples, intensify and broaden their audience's vision of the world. The Homeric warrior stands before us, in the recurrent epic formula, as "a wonder to behold," *thauma idesthai*. His power is in fact conceived visually: he is surrounded by the radiance of bright metal, conspicuous by the terrible crest and plumes of his helmet, and often seen in rapid and powerful motion that invites comparison with striking visual phenomena of nature, like large animals, birds of prey, fire, lightning in the sky. Herodotus, analogously, selects and describes what is "worth seeing," *axiotheëton*. His work as a whole is a "display" or "demonstration," *apodeixis* (1.1). Like Homer, he is concerned to preserve the great deeds of men in a verbal equivalent to the monument.

Herodotus is still in the first wave of writers to compose extensively in prose and therefore to leave these memorialized traces of the past in the form of writing. But for the oral poet, too, the preservation of great deeds lies potentially in the realm of the eye as well as the ear. Hector, in challenging the Greek chiefs in *Iliad* 7, promises that his opponent's memory will live on in the form of a "far-seen marker," his burial monument (*sēma*) in the Hellespont. Here it will inspire other words as "some one of later-born men, sailing over the wine-dark sea in a many-oared ship, will say, 'This is the marker of a man long since dead, who once in his glory was slain by Hector.' So one will say, and never will my fame perish" (7.88–91).

The monument alone, "far-seen" though it is, cannot speak. It requires the accompanying voice of a man, which the poet supplies through the speech of Hector. The situation here is analogous to the early dedicatory statues whose accompanying inscription lends voice to the mute stone, saying, "I am the tomb, or monument, or cup of so-and-so." A marker that lacks such a voice is just forgotten; it has no story to tell, no *kleos* (fame, from *kluein*, to hear) to be "listened to" by men in aftertimes. It is just an inert object, like the marker that serves as a boundary in the horse race at Patroclus' funeral games, merely "the marker of a mortal long-since dead" (*Iliad* 23.331). The phrase used of the "marker" here is the same that Hector used in book 7; but it has no tale to tell, no memories to awaken, and so remains mute, merely an object that the chariots hurtle past.

What is "memorable" endures by being "heard," as *kleos*. The worst fate that can befall a man in Homer is to perish *aklees*, without leaving the story that could preserve his memory in a human community. It would have been better, Telemachus says in the first book of the *Odyssey*, if Odysseus had died at Troy, for then "all the Achaeans would have made a tomb for him, and he would have won fame (*kleos*) for his son after him; but now the Snatchers (Harpies) have carried him off without fame" (*akleiōs*). So, too, "what one will say" about a man in his city can become his main criterion for action, as in Hector's fatal decision to face Achilles in battle (*Iliad* 22.105–8). As the epic's fullest bearer of this new ethos of the *polis*, Hector is naturally the hero most concerned with his relation to this voice of the community.

This function of "hearing" as a mechanism of social control, however, is only a small area of the acoustic experience with which the epic is concerned. Homer and Hesiod dwell with obvious delight on the sweetness and clarity of the voice and of the lyre. Singing, telling, and listening to tales form an important part of the action of the *Odyssey*. In the *Iliad*, Achilles is "delighting his heart with the clear lyre, beautiful, crafted," at the moment of the embassy's visit (9.186 f.), a rare example of solitary song. There is pathos, too, in the two shepherds on the Shield, who are "taking delight in their pipes" in ignorance of the ambush that dooms them (18.525 ff.). Great crises are marked by powerful sounds: the thundering of Zeus at the end of *Iliad* 7, or Achilles' cry of grief at Patroclus' death that Thetis hears in the depths of the sea (*Iliad*, 17.35), or his shout at the trench that resounds like a trumpet around an embattled city (ibid., 18.207 ff.). In telling the story of his murder by Clytemnestra, Agamemnon adds the pathetic detail of "hearing" the voice of Cassandra being killed beside him as he dies (*Odyssey* 11.421 f.).

Survival in memory depends on the ear; but in the epic, as in tragedy, it is the eye that permits the strongest and most complex play of emotions. The long-postponed recognition between Odysseus and Penelope takes place through a delicate play of eyes, as he, sitting opposite her, looks down (23.91), while she sits in silence and looks now directly at him, now at his clothes (94 f.), and defends herself against Telemachus' impatience and anger by explaining that she can neither address him directly or "look straight at his face" (105–7).

Vision also dominates the climactic scene of the *Iliad*. Priam and Achilles exchange wondering and admiring glances (24.629–34). But vision in this passage also shows the precariousness of this suspended moment. Priam asks for his son's ransom "so that I may look upon him with my eyes" (24.555). Achilles, like Homer, knows how overwhelming can be the reactions to such a sight; and so he orders that Hector's body be washed in a place apart, "so that Priam might not *see* his son, lest he with grieving heart not keep down his anger on seeing his son, and the heart of Achilles be stirred up to kill Priam and thus commit wrong against the commands of Zeus" (24.583–86).

Spectacles of Glory: King, Warrior, Athlete

As Greek poetry is deeply rooted in the communal functions of song, story, and tale in an oral culture, the occasions of performance can themselves be transformed into spectacles of the social order, made visible before the assembled multitude. Hesiod's *Theogony*, for instance, describes the king giving judgments in the Assembly, where "all the people look upon him as he decides the ordinances of the law with straight judgments," and they "revere him as a god with honey-sweet reverence as he comes into the gathering" (84–86, 91 f.; cf. *Odyssey* 8.171–73). This spectacle of the king himself as the living, personal realization of the well-ordered city is characteristic of the social mentality of an oral culture, where norms and ideals are embodied in concrete, public situations of face-to-face contact.

To achieve public recognition is to become an object of special vision, to "stand out" among the multitude as *ekprepēs*. This is a goal to which all aspire and that the poets sustain. The statesman has before him the ideal of Hesiod's king in the Assembly; the girls in the choral dances have the model of the girls in Alcman's *Maiden Songs* (*Parthenia* 1.40–49); and of course the athletes in the games hope for the kind of celebrity that Pindar describes when he promises to make the victor "wondered at (*thaēton*) amid songs because of his (victory) crowns, among those of his own age and older men alike, and a concern (*melēma*) for young maidens" (*Pythian* 10.57–59). In tragedy, however, as we shall see, to be singled out as a spectacle is part of the hero's ambiguous relation to society; and the viewer's wondering gaze of admiration becomes one of pain, puzzlement, and pity.

The athletic events are among the most prominent spectacles of ancient Greece. These include not only the four great Panhellenic festivals—Olympian, Pythian, Nemean, and Isthmian—but numerous local games in individual cities, such as the Iolaea at Thebes or the Panathenaea at Athens. The odes of Pindar and Bacchylides that celebrate victories in these games hold up to the winner the image of the ideal hero as reflected in the paradigmatic myths that poet tells. The victory reflects the athlete's inherited excellence, discipline, forthright behavior, the willingness to take risks, and moderation in the exuberance of success. The celebrated bronze Charioteer at Delphi, a commemorative dedication for a victory in the early 470s, is a sculptural representation of many of these qualities. The victory odes seek to create a "monument" in words that has the solidity, beauty, and durability of such a dedication. Hence the frequent comparison of the ode to a temple or treasury (e.g., *Olympian* 6, *Pythian* 6 and 7; cf. *Nemean* 5.).

What the family does for private victors, city-states do for themselves in war, setting up dedications in Panhellenic sanctuaries like Delphi or Olympia. These shrines form a virtual theater of the rivalries and hostilities between the cities.

As this last point implies, the grandest and most involving spectacle for the city is war. Already in the *Iliad* war is such a spectacle; and Homer's audience shares the perspective of the gods as they look down on the events on the plain of Troy from Olympus.

In war the city presents its own power as a spectacle, both for itself and for other states. The setting out of a large army, with its glittering weapons, pack animals and wagons, campfollowers, supplies, and equipment was a stirring sight and afforded the citizens a unique view of their strength and resources. Thucydides gives us a vivid account of such a scene and the emotional excitement that it could arouse in his account of the embarkation of the Sicilian expedition in 416 B.C. (6.2.1–2). This most austere of all classical Greek writers allows us, for a moment, to view the war as a great, tragic parade of Athenian glory, brilliant but doomed.

Even here we are still not too far from the epic world. One may compare this description of a contemporary event, for example, with

Pindar's account of the departure of the mythical Argonauts from Iolcos (*Pythian* 4.191–98):

> When they hung the anchors over the prow, the leader, at the stern, taking in his hands a goblet of gold, called upon Zeus, thunder-speared father of the Heavenly Ones, and on the blasts of the waves and the winds and for kindly nights and sea-paths and days and for a friendly portion of return. And from the clouds a divine voice of thunder echoed back. And bright flashes of lightning breaking forth came to them.

Pindar's spectacle of martial power, naturally, pays more attention to gods and nature than to ships and equipment.

Herodotus' account of Xerxes' huge army setting out overland also has a spectaclelike quality (7.187), reinforced by Xerxes' role, quite literally, as a spectator of the fighting. At Abydos he erects a throne of white stone for viewing his land and sea forces at the same time (7.44). At Thermopylae and at Salamis, he makes himself a spectator of the battle (7.212, 8.86), accompanied by a secretary to note the name of whoever performs a remarkable deed (8.88.2). Like Thucydides, Herodotus composes in the age of tragedy. The king's role of spectator, like that of the Athenian people watching their army set out for Sicily some sixty years later, conceals his blindness about the real meaning of the events.

The end of a war is as spectacular as its beginning. The *tropaion* is set up on the field of battle. There are processions of victorious warriors, with their booty of armor, equipment, and prisoners; and of this a tithe is generally set aside as a dedication, to be made conspicuous to all in a temple at a Panhellenic sanctuary. In due course, monuments are erected to the fallen, prizes are awarded to the valorous, and an elaborate funeral speech is made over the dead. As we see from Thucydides' famous account of Pericles' funeral speech at the end of the first year of the Peloponnesian War, this event is one of the city's most impressive public spectacles. Two days before the speech, the bones of the dead warriors are laid out in a tent for public display. Then there is a grand procession in which the relatives of the dead, both men and women, march beside the wagons that carry the cypress-wood coffins. They go to the city's outskirts, where the bones are buried in a common grave (Thucydides 2.34). As part of the burial ceremony, a celebrated orator delivers the funeral oration.

The city in defeat is a spectacle of another kind, presented powerfully as theater in Aeschylus' *Persians* and in Euripides' *Trojan Women* and *Hecuba*. In Aeschyles' play, we see the defeated monarch return amid groaning and lamentation, his army lost, his splendid robes now torn. The brilliance of the setting forth now reveals its true meaning. Even Pindar depicts an analogous scene as a foil to the joy and celebrity of the victory. "For the defeated," he wrote in one ode, "no happy return was decided at the Pythian festival, nor did sweet laughter arise around them for their sake when they came home to their mothers, but they slink back, out of the way, in alleys, bitten by disaster" (*Pythian* 8.83–87). Instead of enjoying the fame (*kleos*) of the victor and his visibility as *thaëtos* or *ekprepēs*, "wondered at" and "outstanding," the loser suffers concealment and oblivion.

In the misguided embarkations of a great army, Aeschylus, Herodotus, and Thucydides also exhibit the pervasive Greek interest in the dangerous seductiveness of mass emotions. The Greeks were aware of the powerful effect that a spectacle could create in a mob, although the early period has nothing like the bloodshed of the circus riots of imperial Rome or Byzantium. When the tragedian Phrynichus presented his play, the *Capture of Miletus* in 493 B.C., the Athenians fined him a thousand drachmas because he reminded them of the sufferings of their fellow Ionians. "The theater broke into tears," Herodotus writes (6.21). The passage indicates the emotional involvement of the Athenian audience in the tragic performances, but it also shows the recognition of the special category of collective emotion.

The word that early Greek authors use for the public gatherings of such spectacles is *agōn*, which also has the secondary meaning of "contest." This in fact becomes the primary meaning later. The Greeks delight in competition, and so often structure their "gatherings" as "contests." Hesiod competed in one such contest at the funeral games of King Alcidamas with a poem, perhaps the *Theogony*, and won a tripod (*Works and Days* 650–59). Plato enumerates among the "contests" that "give pleasure to the spectators" comedy, tragedy, music, gymnastics, horse racing, and rhapsodic recitation (*Laws* 2.658a–b). The girls who sing Alcman's *Maiden Song* (*Parthenion*) set up a competition among one another (Alcman frag. 1 Page). The poetry of Sappho and Alcaeus at the end of the seventh century B.C. indicates that there were beauty contests for women on their island of Lesbos.

In a more solemn area, the mystery cults, particularly the Eleusinian mysteries, enacted religious dramas of death and renewal that reveal to the initiate a hidden knowledge of the hereafter and thus offer comfort about his fate after death. Because the rites were secret, the exact details are obscure, but the performances were almost certainly accompanied by music and hymnic poetry. A passage near the end of the *Homeric Hymn to Demeter* provides at least a hint of what the spectator of such rites might gain:

> Happy among men on earth is he who has had a vision of those things. But whoever is uninitiated and without a portion of these rites, never when he is dead does he have a share of like things beneath the moldy darkness. (480–82)

The importance of the visual experience in such rites appears from the fact that the initiate was called *epoptes,* "one who looks on."

Ear-Knowledge and Eye-Knowledge

By the end of the eighth century B.C., the Greeks had developed the North Semitic syllabary into an alphabetic writing far better suited to their own language than the Mycenaean syllabary had been. Nevertheless, because of the preceding centuries of oral culture and the limited technology of writing, the spoken (and sung) word continued to have a privileged place. The poets can even imagine the highest happiness in aural terms. In the *Odyssey,* the pinnacle of heroic glory is the song of the Muses, "with their lovely voice," at the funeral of Achilles, which moves the entire Greek army to tears (24.60–62). Peleus and Cadmus, as paradigms of "the highest bliss" because both marry goddesses, "hear the Muses singing on the mountain and in seven-gated Thebes" (Pindar *Pythian* 3.88–91).

Important as the aural experience is for memory and the transmission of culture, Greek thought tends to privilege vision as the primary area of knowledge and even of emotion, as we have seen in Homer. The eye is the locus of desire, which the poets regard as emanating from the gaze of the beloved or situated in the eye of the love object. "Whoever looks upon the beams flashing forth from the eyes of Theoxenos and is not drowned in waves of desire," Pindar writes in his exuberant encomium for this Corinthian youth, "has his black heart forged by cold fire from steel or bronze" (frag. 123 Snell-Maehler).

The knowing subject is constructed as one who sees; what is unknown is also unseen, be this the mist-covered gloom beyond the setting sun (*Odyssey* 10.190, 11.13 ff.) or the depths of Hades beneath the earth (Euripides *Hippolytus* 190 ff.). To be alive is "to look on the light of the sun." Forgetfulness or oblivion, *lēthē,* belongs to darkness, whereas glory or fame is surrounded by radiance (*aglaia*). Sophocles' two Oedipus plays are built around the equation of knowledge with vision, blindness with ignorance. For Plato knowing the suprasensual realm of the Forms is to have a vision of the luminous, eternal realm above the clouded, changeable earthly phenomena (cf. *Phaedo* 109b–110c; *Republic* 9.586a). "Every human soul," he writes in the *Phaedrus,* "has been a spectator of Being" (*tetheatai ta onta,* 249e). He goes on in the famous myth of the chariot of the soul to combine the two aspects of vision, vision as the source of desire and vision as the source of knowledge. The soul's sight of the Form fills it with desire, and at the same time gives it the knowledge of its true home (250a–252b).

From its early beginnings to Neoplatonism, philosophy "looks up" to the celestial mysteries and also perceives what lies hidden "in the depths," as Democritus says (frag. 68B117 Diels-Kranz). Aristophanes' parody in the *Clouds* brings together both forms of this visionary quest for the remote and the invisible. While the disciples stare down at the earth, Socrates is suspended in a basket, thereby improving the fineness of his thoughts about *ta meteora,* the things in the heavens (227–34). He has also lost "a great thought" when a lizard dunged into his mouth as he was "gaping upward investigating the courses and circuits of the moon" (171–73).

Aristophanes' parodistic imagination here catches an essential quality of the Presocratic philosophers who stand behind the Socrates of the *Clouds,* namely, a passion for the visual clarity of the phenomenal world. For the Ionian physicists of the sixth and fifth centuries B.C., from Anaximander through Anaxagoras and Democritus, the world itself becomes a spectacle, a vision of order understood through the systematic application of reason. For this process and its results, the Presocratics use the word *theōrein,* of which the root is *thea,* "vision." *Theōria* implies the same identification of knowledge with sight that is expressed in the common verb "to know," *oida* (of the root *vid-,* "see"). These thinkers use the word *theōria* for observing the heavens, "beholding the effects and essence of number" (Philolaus frag. 44B11 Diels-Kranz), "seeing" the quality of human lives (Democritus frag. 68B191 Diels-Kranz), and "seeing the arrangement (*taxis*) throughout the entire universe" (Anaxagoras frag. 59A30 Diels-Kranz, reported by Aristotle).

In conceiving of the universe as a visually intelligible whole (as this last passage implies), the Presocratics abandon or make metaphorical the mythic reality of gates, walls, roots, or springs in Hesiod's cosmology (*Theogony* 726–57, 775–79, 807–19) and instead rely on abstract spatial relations based on geometry (see Vernant, *Les origines de la pensée grecque,* pp. 100–118, 120–21 = *The Origins of Greek Thought,* pp. 102–18, 120–21). They thus fashion a "spectacle" (*theōria*) for the mind rather than for the sensual eye. To display the synoptic clarity in his view of the universe, for example, Anaximander describes his world picture on a table (*pinax*) or even makes a sphere, presumably a three-dimensional model, just as the Milesian geographer Hecataeus makes a map (frags. 12, A1, and A6 Diels-Kranz, from Eratosthenes, Strabo, and Diogenes Laertius). This process, which is decisive for the development of Western science, not only replaces *mythos* by *logos,* but also replaces anthropomorphic imagery by a more abstract "theory" (*theōria*).

Although tragedy operates with the material of myth, it is also indebted, indirectly, to the rationalistic "vision" of *theōria* that derives from Ionian philosophy, for it presupposes an underlying notion of discovering and visually displaying an emergent world order in a neutral geometric space where relations between conflicting forces and energies can be examined and understood. Ritual and choral performances, of course, also play an important role in the origins and nature of the dramatic spectacle (see below); yet the aims of tragedy, like the form of the city-state that houses it, owe a great deal to this confidence in the power of mind to shape *theōria* and to organize both the physical and the human world in terms of visual models of intelligibility.

Aristophanes' *Clouds* makes a joke of the distance between reality and the philosopher's gaze toward remote objects of knowledge. But this encounter between the tangible and the distant is also an aspect of what Eric Havelock calls the "literate revolution." The transition begins in the sixth century and intensifies in the fifth. Ear-knowledge depends on direct, personal contact, from speaker to listener, from tongue to ear. Eye-knowledge allows a more distanced, speculative, and impersonal relation to information, especially when this is transmitted through the written message of a speaker who is not physically present.

Oral productions (like the Homeric poems) emphasize the "pleasure" in specific details and in the ornamental elaboration of events. Writing encourages a mentality more attuned to the abstract, the conceptual, and the universal rather than the concrete and the particular. Whereas the spoken word is invisible and disappears with the breath that carries it, writing fixes details so that criticism and comparison can be made. The oral tradition easily tolerates multiple versions of tales; the definitiveness of writing develops a more exclusive notion of truth as unitary, difficult, and attainable only through a process of inquiry and examination. Thus in early Greek poetry "truth," *alētheia,* is associated with "non-forgetting" (*a- lēthē*) rather than with "accuracy" or verifiability.

For the historians Herodotus and Thucydides, hearsay, *akoē,* is potentially deceptive and requires further testing by vision, preferably autopsy. Thucydides opens his *History* by calling himself a "writer." In comparing his conception of history-writing with previous work, he contrasts his own striving after "accuracy" through "painful" scrutiny with the facile popularity of "the mythical," which is merely "heard" for "pleasure" in a "contest for the present moment" (1.22). Different as he is from Plato, Thucydides nevertheless shares the same privileging of the eye over the ear in a directed movement away from the oral tradition.

These conflicts take many forms in tragedy, as we shall see in more detail later. Not only does tragedy bring together both the aural and the visual experience in its complex and contradictory constitution of truth; it also calls attention to the meeting, exchange, and clash of sensory perceptions. Oedipus' insult to the blind Teiresias, "You are blind in your ears and your mind and your eyes" (*Oedipus Tyrannus* 371), reflects something of this crossing of voice and vision in the paradoxes of knowledge and error in this play. Euripides' Hecuba in the *Trojan Women* adds to the pathos of her sufferings by telling how she not only "heard" of Priam's death but "with these very eyes of mine saw him slaughtered at the palace altar and saw the city captured" (479–84). In Sophocles' *Electra,* the oral report of Orestes' death (though reinforced by the physical evidence of the burial urn) defeats the truth of what Chrysothemis has seen with her own eyes (883 ff.).

By exploring such contrasts, tragedy rings endless changes on the discrepancy between what one *is* and what one outwardly *seems* to be. In Euripides' *Hippolytus,* we see before our eyes the (legally) innocent young man convicted of a terrible crime by the written tablets that Phaedra has left behind at her suicide. This play is particularly interesting for the role of writing as a textual mirroring of this female reversal of truth and appearance. The play correlates the inversion of reality and appearance with the power of Phaedra's written, "silent" lie of her tablets to overthrow the voice of truth (cf. 879 f.). Concealment and revelation in Phaedra's first scene are displaced into writing in her last action, but the initial nobility of reluctance has now become murderous deception. Through this association (not unique to this play) between writing, the female body, (sexual) secrecy, plotting, and revealing what is concealed "inside," Euripidean tragedy asserts its capacity to display matters of the most intense privacy and the most hidden secrets of the soul in the public, theatrical space.

The deceptiveness of external appearances in tragedy builds upon a long tradition in Greek thought. "Hateful to me as the gates of Hades," says Achilles in the *Iliad*, "is that man who has one thing on his lips and another in his heart" (9.312 f.), and he addresses these words to Odysseus. The disguises of this hero in the *Odyssey* also raise the question of the relation between changing outer shape and the constant form, if any, of what "we" are. What sign can fix our identity, so much of which changes or remains concealed? Odysseus successfully disguises himself from his wife but cannot hide from his childhood nurse the old mark of his adolescence. Homer does not, of course, consciously articulate such issues, but they are implicit in his presentation of his many-faceted, much-disguised hero of *mētis* and in the matching guile of his ever-weaving and unweaving wife. Much later, Plato speculated on the ugly scars that evil leaves on the soul of a corrupt tyrant (*Gorgias* 524c ff.; cf. *Republic* 588d ff.). Invisible in this life, they are laid bare before the judges of the underworld. This same concern with discerning the hidden inner being through the external appearance marks Socrates' discussion (reported by Xenophon) with a famous artist about how to depict the character or *ēthos* of a man (*Memorabilia* 3.10).

The Magic of Pleasure: Performance and Emotion

In early Greek culture, the spectacles that matter most are neither objects of nature nor the individual soul, but the communal gatherings for festivals, music, athletic contests, and religious rituals. Even in the Bronze Age, the frescoes from the Minoan palaces on Crete and on Thera depict public gatherings in the great palace courtyards and the adjoining areas. Homer preserves the memory of such festivals in a simile comparing a choral dance on the shield of Achilles to dancing in Ariadne's palace at Cnossos (*Iliad* 18.590–92). In the *Odyssey*, there is a similar scene of young men dancing in Alcinous' palace (8.256–65).

The gathering of the Ionians at Delos described in the Homeric *Hymn to Apollo* is the perfect festival, and by extension the perfect performance. It creates a spectacle of delight, *terpsis,* for both the god and the mortal participants (146–55). The poet seems to identify the *terpsis* that his song bestows with the cumulative effect of the festival as a whole. In addition to the "boxing, dancing, and song" (149), there is the pleasure afforded to the eyes when "one sees the grace of everything" (153) and "takes pleasure in his heart looking at the men and the beautifully belted women and their swift ships and all their possessions" (153–55). The passage is a precious testimony from the early archaic period of the combined effect of visual and acoustic pleasure at the great festivals and also of the special admiration for the mimetic powers of the voice. The author of the *Hymn* singles out the oral skill of the Delian maidens as a spectacle in itself, "a great wonder, whose fame will never perish." This consists not only in the "spell" of their song but also in their ability to imitate "the voices of all men and the sound of the castanet" (156–64).

The oral performance engages its audience in a total response, physical and emotional as well as intellectual. Poetry recited or sung in such circumstances involves an intensely personal rapport between bard and audience. When Achilles tells Thetis of his quarrel with Agamemnon in the first book of the *Iliad,* he repeats what we have already heard; but telling his suffering to his mother as a first-person account gives him the satisfaction of communication with this engaged and sympathetic hearer. Odysseus' summary of his adventures to Penelope after their reunion in *Odyssey* 23 is a similar episode. Such scenes of involved narration and reception may perhaps be regarded as ideal analogies or models for the relation that the bard hopes to create between himself and his audience. As Ion puts it more crudely in Plato's little dialogue of that name, "If I make them weep, I shall laugh, making money; but if I make them laugh, then I shall wail myself, losing money" (*Ion* 535e).

Plato regards such a release of emotion as dangerous and would therefore exclude the poets from his ideal Republic, but the *Ion* gives us an idea of what such a performance would be like. We see the rhapsode exercising a quasi-hypnotic spell over his audience as he makes visible to them the epic scenes of his narrative (535c). Plato compares the effect to a magnet holding iron rings. The magnetic force flows from the poet himself to the rhapsode and on to the audience (533d, 535e). The reciter himself, when fully immersed in his art, is "outside himself" (535b). "When I recite something that stirs pity," the rhapsode says, "my eyes fill with tears; when it is fearful or terrible, my hair stands on end with fear and my heart pounds" (535c).

The Sophist Gorgias at the end of the fifth century regards these affective responses as the special result of the aural power of poetry. In his eulogy to the power of language in his *Helen,* he writes, "Into those who hear poetry there enter a shuddering surrounded by fear, and also pity with abundant weeping, and longing that loves mourning" (9). These physiological responses to language confirm what we can infer about the emotional responses to tragedy both from later reports and from the tragedies themselves. The crises within the plays evoke the vehement reactions of shuddering, trembling, hair standing on end, aphasia, dizziness, pounding or leaping heart, cold chills in the belly, and a tension in the whole body.

The very power of poetry to move the emotions makes it a danger as well as a blessing. As a "charm" or "spell," it exerts a kind of magic, and Gorgias so describes it in the *Helen* (10, 14). *Thelxis,* the term for this "spell," describes both the song of the Sirens and the seductive magic of Circe in the *Odyssey.* Pindar tells how the Siren-like magical figures on the pediments of Apollo's temple at Delphi sang so sweetly that men forgot their families and wasted away, enthralled by the song, so that the gods had to destroy the temple (*Paean* 8, frag. 52i Snell-Maehler).

As the Greeks tend to represent deception and seduction also in the form of visions, images, and phantoms, the magic of the spoken word can produce an entrancing surface beauty that in fact conceals lies. Like Hesiod's Pandora, tales may be "adorned in variegated falsehoods" that take us "beyond the true account" (Pindar *Olympian* 1.28 f.). Odysseus enjoys a better repute than Ajax because of Homer's skill, Pindar says in *Nemean* 7, because "upon lies and winged devices there sits something solemn; and clever skill (*sophia*) deceives, leading astray by tales. The largest mass of men have a *blind* heart. For if they could *see* truth, mighty Ajax would not have driven the smooth sword through his breast, deprived of [Achilles'] arms."

Homer's Sirens are early poetry's strongest image of the dangers of the aural magic of song. In enabling us to forget our sorrows, as Hesiod claims for his poetry (*Theogony* 54 f.), song also may erase the memory that links us to the past and gives us our human identity. The paradox of a power of remembering that brings forgetfulness is already a feature of poetry in Hesiod. But in the Sirens the paradox turns into a set of contradictory features that negates the purpose of song. The Sirens know everything that happened at Troy and indeed "everything that happens on the much-nurturing earth" (*Odyssey* 12.188–91); yet their island is surrounded by the putrefying skin and bones of men and is located far from the communities of men where memory has its meaning and function (12.45–47).

Like Pindar's golden "charmers," at whose song men "waste away far from wives and children," the Homeric Sirens are perverted Muses. They claim total recall, but their power of memory anomalously coexists with the foulest signs of mortal decay, the antithesis of the godlike immortality of fame that is "imperishable" (*kleos aphthiton*). In keeping with the grossly corporeal effects of their magic, their "spell," or *thelxis,* is only of the moment; it resonates in the ear, but does not live on the lips of men. It is purely acoustic, and so Odysseus can block it by the purely physical means of putting wax in his companions' ears and tying his body to the ship.

What was a magical spell to the early poets becomes a technical skill as the language arts become professionalized and rationalized in the late sixth and early fifth centuries. Teachers of rhetoric, such as Protagoras, Gorgias, and Prodicus, taught such skills for a fee; and Gorgias, in his *Helen,* self-consciously elaborated on the affinities between this art and magical spells and drugs. Those willing to pay the fees were thus able to acquire this art of persuading a mass audience by playing upon their feelings. Pericles, according to Thucydides, derived at least some of his political power from his ability to sway the mob (2.65.9). Both the historians and dramatists of this period show a new sensitivity to the crowd and its emotions—panic, hysteria, sudden impulses of generosity or compassion.

The theater even more than the Assembly or the law courts is the place where mass emotion finds its fullest release. Phrynichus, as we have seen, excited the wrong emotions and received a fine instead of the victory crown. In place of poetry's power of emotional excitation, Plato would, as he implies, set the philosophical dialogue; this would be the "poetry" appropriate to the ideal, philosophically designed state. In the *Laws* he establishes "as the noblest Muse she who gives pleasure to the best men and to those who are adequately educated." Choosing the judges of the plays by lot is the sign of "a base theatocracy instead of aristocracy" (3.701a). The philosopher-lawgivers are "the poets of the noblest and best tragedy," for their ideal state is the "imitation (*mimesis*) of the noblest and best life" and thus embodies "the truest tragedy" (7.817b).

Leaving aside their import for Plato's conception of his own educative role, these remarks can be read historically to indicate, in retrospect, the centrality of the theater in the Athenian community and the importance of audience response. The special pride of Athens in its spectacles is also confirmed by the remarks attributed to Pericles in the funeral speech of Thucydides. Pericles here praises Athens for its abundance of recreation from the daily toil, consisting in "contests (*agōnes*) and festivals throughout the year," the "delight" (*terpsis*) of which drives away pain (2.38.1). He goes on to contrast Athens with Sparta in its openness that does not exclude anyone from "any knowledge or sight" (spectacle, *theama*) as long as it does not directly aid the enemy (2.39.1). Thucydides' language is general and a little vague, but the civic spectacles of drama may well be included in the *theama* of which Pericles speaks; and those may be in his mind in the more famous remark shortly afterward, when he declares, "And so to sum up I say that our whole city is the education of Greece" (2.41.1).

Dramatic Spectacle: Origins and Character

However much Homer wants us to "see" the great deeds of the epic world with the eyes of "wonder" (*thauma, thambos*), he has no doubt that it is the spoken (and sung) word that is the true vehicle of communication and memory. As writing becomes increasingly important in Greece from the late eighth century B.C. onward, this relation between the eye and the ear changes. By the late sixth and early fifth centuries, poets like Simonides, Pindar, and Bacchylides, though they still profess (and sometimes have) personal connections with their patrons, move toward a more professional view of their art. Writing on paid commissions from many parts of the Greek world, they are far more detached from the face-to-face immediacy of the performance than the oral bard of the Homeric type. This freer relation to the oral performance also appears in the visual metaphors that Pindar and Bacchylides devise for their song. Unlike the vocal imagery of Homer and Hesiod, these figures often have little or nothing to do with the situation of performance or even with voice or music. The ode is a statue, a garland, an embroidered tapestry, a temple, a rich libation of wine, a fresh spring of water, flowers, fire, wings. The poet himself may be an eagle soaring in the open sky, an archer or javelin-thrower shooting a missile of song, a traveler on a broad highway, or a voyager on a ship cleaving the seas.

When Simonides said, "Painting is poetry that is silent, poetry is painting that speaks" (Plutarch *De gloria Atheniensium* 3.346F), he brings poetry into relation not with the oral performance but with visual experience in quite a different area. It is tempting to relate Simonides' analogical linking of visual and acoustic here with the interaction of sound and spectacle that tragedy was beginning to develop about the same time, particularly as Simonides is in many ways a precursor of the traveling Sophist and his freedom of rational speculation.

In tragedy, the organization of the narrative material of the myths by a written text makes possible a visual narrative of new power and expressiveness, in which voice and image are interwoven in complex relations. As a result of this new perspective, stage and theater become metaphors for human experience in general. In the *Philebus* Plato can write that life itself is comedy or tragedy (50b), perhaps the first formulation in Western literature of the analogy between the world and the stage made famous by the melancholy Jaques in Shakespeare (*As You Like It* 2.7). Epicurus remarked, "We are all a sufficiently great theater to one another" (quoted by Seneca *Epistulae* 7.11). In its widest formulation, "Longinus" in the treatise *On the Sublime,* perhaps at the end of the first century A.D., compares the entire universe to a great spectacle, into which man comes as a privileged beholder and in which he recognizes the greatness for which he is destined by the infinite reach of his thought (c. 35).

This passage, much influenced by Platonizing Stoicism, in effect appropriates for mankind what in archaic and classical Greek thought is the prerogative of the gods: to be the removed spectator of the sufferings and struggles of human life. Such, too, is the perspective of the philosopher's godlike wisdom in Epicureanism (cf. Lucretius *De rerum natura* 2.1–13). The audience of both epic and tragedy possesses something of this privileged perspective—figuratively in the epic insofar as the omniscient third-person narrator makes us privy to what the gods see and know; more literally in tragedy since we sit above the action and look down upon it from quasi-Olympian distance, if not Olympian detachment. In both epic and tragedy, this spectacle of human suffering only intensifies the awareness of the limits surrounding mortal life. The philosophical vision, however, aims at transcending just these limits.

Although the origins of tragedy remain obscure and controversial, Aristotle's connection of tragedy with the dithyramb is widely accepted (*Poetics* 4.1449a). Initially an excited choral performance in honor of Dionysus, the dithyramb, by the late sixth century, seems to have become a calmer, more lyrical form that narrated myths about the gods and later about the heroes. The connections between tragedy and Dionysus were a problem even for the ancients. Hence the proverb "Nothing to Dionysus" was interpreted as a criticism of tragedy's too great distance from direct worship of the god at his chief festival, the Greater Dionysia, the most important occasion for the dramatic performances. Though tragedy has its first beginnings under the tyrant Peisistratus (534 B.C. is the traditional date), it is taken over and perfected under the new democracy of the early fifth century. Dionysus' association with popular cult rather than aristocratic traditions may have encouraged its growth.

Dionysus is a god of vegetation, especially the vine and its fermented product; he is also associated with madness and religious ecstasy. He appears frequently on vases with an entourage of satyrs, goat-footed creatures, half men, half beasts, who give free rein to their animal nature in drunkenness, lewd gestures, and indiscriminate sexual appetite. The satyr dances, according to Aristotle, also contributed to the development of tragedy (*Poetics* 4.1449a); and at the Dionysia a lighter play with a satyr chorus was presented along with the three tragedies of each competing dramatist. Also accompanying Dionysus and in close (though not necessarily harmonious) association with the satyrs are the maenads—literally, "madwomen." They, too, embody an uninhibited release of emotional and physical energy in a total surrender to the god and his cult.

The associations of Dionysus with the irrational, with madness, with women, with excited dance and music, and with the fluidity of the division between beast, man, and god are all relevant to tragedy. Dionysus' association with the mask is a still more immediate link. Dionysus is in fact often worshiped in the form of a mask, sometimes hung on a tree or on a pillar, sometimes adorned with ivy, the plant sacred to the god. The mask makes possible the mimetic representation of the myths in dramatic form. The masked actor can also explore the fusion between different identities, states of being, or categories of experience: male and female, human and bestial, divine and human, stranger and friend, outsider and insider. The mask is thus central to the dramatic experience as a sign of the audience's willingness to submit to illusion, play, and make-believe, and to invest emotional energy in that which is marked as both fictional and Other. The frontal gaze of the mask, as Vernant has suggested, is also the mode for representing the presence of divinity among men.

For all of these reasons, Dionysus is the god under whom tragedy most naturally has its place and could take its characteristic form: the emotionally charged atmosphere of a mimetic spectacle; intense identification with the illusionistic world created and enacted by masked actors; the ability to confront the otherness of the bestial and the divine in human life and to acknowledge the irrationality and emotionality associated with the female in a male-dominated society; and the openness to the widest questions of meaning made possible by the presence of gods as visible agents in human affairs. The spell of the Dionysiac mask releases, in controlled doses, the fears, anxiety, irrationality that lie beneath the brilliant surface of Periclean Athens.

Tragedy redefines the role of the spectator. Instead of the delight, or *terpsis,* of epic recitation or choral performance, tragedy involves its audience in a tension between the pleasure expected of a highly wrought spectacle and the pain of its contents. Here and there the tragedians themselves call attention to this contradiction, the "tragic paradox," of the pleasure in suffering (cf. Euripides *Medea* 190–203 and *Bacchae* 815).

Tragedy not only gives a startling corporeal enactment to the old myths; it also refocuses them upon situations of crisis. In contrast to the relaxed, expansive narrative of oral epic, tragedy selects single points of crises and concentrates the fortunes of a house or city into a tightly unified action that unfolds within a limited time and space.

The components of tragedy all lay to hand in the poetry of the past: the poetic recitatives of the messenger speeches; the choral songs of joy, lament, or warning mythical exemplar; and to some extent even the dialogue. But these elements take on a new power when they interact in the new ensemble that is tragedy. Aeschylus uses the symmetry of choral refrain or responsion to suggest the terror of a frightened crowd, as in the *Seven against Thebes* (150–80). In the *Persians,* he combines the lyric responsion of the lament with the visual spectacle of the defeated king, displaying his torn robe, to portray the impact of defeat on the whole community (906–1077). The theatrical audience's identification with the threatened city through the mimetic enactment of the danger gives such scenes an intensity beyond anything in choral lyric. The ancient *Life of Aeschylus* stresses his power of *ekplexis*, "smiting" the audience with overpowering visual effects. At the appearance of the Furies in the *Eumenides*, the *Life* reports, children fainted and women miscarried. The accuracy of the anecdote is dubious, but it probably reflects the spirit of his art. His acoustic effects are equally powerful: the Danaids' shrieks of fear in the *Suppliants*, Cassandra's mysterious *otototototoi popoi da / ōpollon ōpollon* (*Agamemnon* 1072 f.), half terror, half prophecy; the Furies' groans and growls as Clytemnestra's ghost arouses them at the beginning of the *Eumenides* (119 ff.), to be followed soon after by the terrible chant of their binding song against their victim (307–96); or whatever sound Io's *ā ā e e* represents as she enters, driven by the gadfly's stings (*Prometheus Bound* 566).

Sophocles and Euripides are tamer, but they too have their whistling Sphinx (Euripides *Oedipus*, frag. 2 Austin), bellowing heroes (Sophocles *Trachiniae* 805, 983–1017; Euripides *Heracles* 869 ff.), lamenting or screaming sufferers (Sophocles *Electra* 826–30, 840–45; *Philoctetes* 730–57). At the opposite extreme, they could also use silence to equally powerful effect. Aristophanes makes fun of the long silences of Aeschylus' protagonists in their opening scenes (*Frogs* 911–20). Sophocles' silent exits of Jocasta, Deinaeira, and Eurydice (in *Oedipus Tyrannus*, *Trachiniae*, and *Antigone*, respectively) are the ominous calm before the storm of disaster breaks. In the *Oedipus Coloneus*, Sophocles suspensefully keeps the old Oedipus silent for a hundred lines, until his smoldering anger against his son Polyneices bursts out in terrible insults and curses (1254–1354). Utilizing the still recent innovation of the third actor, Aeschylus must have astonished his audience in *Agamemnon* when Cassandra, silent in the long scene between Agamemnon and Clytemnestra, suddenly utters her terrible shrieks of despair and prophecy. In the next play of the trilogy, Pylades is similarly kept silent until the climactic moment when he gives Orestes the crucial encouragement to kill his mother at the terrible crisis of decision—the only three verses he speaks in the play (*Choephoroe* 900–902).

Language and the Tragic Spectacle

The signifying power of language is a major concern of tragedy. Crucial ethical terms like justice, goodness, nobility, or purity are constantly being called into question and redefined. The paradox of an "impious piety" lies at the heart of the *Antigone*. The meaning of the "sound sense" (*sophorosyne*) and "wisdom" (*sophia*) is central to Euripides' *Hippolytus* and *Bacchae*, respectively. Works like Aeschylus' *Agamemnon* and Sophocles' *Oedipus Tyrannus*, *Trachiniae*, and *Philoctetes* owe much of their power to probing the failures of communication, both among men and between men and gods. The ambiguities of language in prophecies and oracles determine the events of these as of many other plays. In this respect, tragedy not only reacts to the intensive scrutiny of language in the Sophistic enlightenment but also anticipates Plato's concern with stabilizing ethical values in the unstable and untrustworthy medium of words.

How important the issues of language and signification are appears from the fact that they appear on the comic no less than on the tragic stage. Aristophanes' *Clouds* gets much of its humor from Strepsiades' initiation into the subtleties of Sophistic studies of grammar, gender, and morphology. The auditory delights of comedy are hardly limited to the human voice. The chorus of the *Birds* must have been a remarkable evocation of bird song (such as the archaic poet Alcman claimed to be able to imitate [frags. 39 and 40 Page]), although only the bare *torotorotorotorotix/ kikkabau kikkabau* in our manuscripts bears witness to the playful experiment (cf. 223 ff., 260 ff., 310 ff.). Puns, double entendres, endless plays on words fill Aristophanes' plays. Names offer numerous occasions for jokes, many of them obscene, like that which turns an Attic deme into a community of masturbators (Anaphlystioi and *anaphlan*, *Frogs* 427).

Word, music, and movement probably carried the main effect in tragedy, and this is in keeping with the subordinate role that Aristotle assigns to *opsis*, spectacle, in his *Poetics*. The dramatists had some stage machinery. The crane could represent flying chariots or flying heroes, like Perseus. The eccyclema could expose to view the results of the action—usually violent action—in the hidden interior of the house. Aeschylus, as we have noted, was the boldest of the surviving dramatists in devising dazzling effects of spectacle. On the whole, however, the staging of the plays was conventional rather than realistic, and it used relatively few props and simple backgrounds. The acting, by masked and elaborately robed figures, must have been rather stylized; and voice, delivery, and gesture was exploited for their full expressive value. Even in musicians, movement and gesture were appreciated. Of the celebrated flautist Pronomos, for example, Pausanias reports, "By the form of his facial expression and by the movement of his whole body he gave exceeding delight to audiences in the theater" (9.12.6).

The visual effects of Sophocles and Euripides seem somewhat more integrally related to the main themes of the play than those of Aeschylus and are also more expressive of the characters and situations of the protagonists: the blindness of Oedipus in the Oedipus plays, the dressing of Pentheus as a maenad in the *Bacchae,* the misery and sickness of Philoctetes. Euripides frequently pushes the action to the extreme of suffering and horror, and then ends abruptly with the appearance of a divinity (the *deus ex machina*). Sophocles uses this device only once, and in a very different way: in the *Philoctetes,* Heracles arrives from Olympus, the living voice and the personal embodiment of the heroism and generosity that had been dormant in the sick, embittered hero.

Aristophanes' frequent parodies of the visual effects of tragedy indicate how memorable they were to the Athenian audience. In a somewhat analogous way, Sophocles and Euripides echo scenes from Aeschylus, particularly of the *Oresteia,* in their versions of the myth. In the *Trachiniae,* the entrance of Heracles' cortège with the silent captive, Iole, is a visual echo of Agamemnon's entrance with Cassandra in the *Agamemnon*—a device that casts the shadow of the murderous Clytemnestra on the faithful, patient, Penelope-like Deianeira.

Euripides' *Electra* is perhaps the richest visual echoing of Aeschylean scenes. In this play, Electra lures Clytemnestra into her house for the matricide on the pretext that she, married to a poor farmer, has given birth and needs help with the rites of purification. Arriving with a chariot, finely dressed, and accompanied by the slavewomen of Troy as her maidservants, Clytemnestra here plays the role of the hubristic Agamemnon of the Aeschylean play, whereas Electra, luring the powerful figure into the house for a deed of horrible, polluted revenge, plays the role that her mother had in the *Agamemnon.* In both the Sophoclean and Euripidean *Electras*, the scenic echoes can suggest the fulfillment of retributive justice, but they also imply the continuation of the pollution and the perpetuation of criminal violence.

Spectacle and Narrative

Even in its fully developed form as spectacle, tragedy does not break completely with the oral tradition. The lengthy messenger speeches that frequently narrate the climactic events of tragedy would be familiar to an audience accustomed to the sustained verse narratives of epic poetry. The spirit of such narratives in tragedy, however, is quite different from that of epic. The battle between Eteocles and Polyneices in Euripides' *Phoenician Women*, for example (1359–1424), is closely modeled after the heroic encounters of the *Iliad*. But instead of the clear, sharp distinction of friend and foe, the tragic account tells of the curse, pollution, and fusion/confusion of the two brothers who can neither come together in peace nor separate cleanly in war. Hence the Homeric formula of "biting the earth with the teeth" in death is here combined with the tragic motif of kin murder and failed differentiation (1423 f.).

The most violent and painful events of Greek drama are narrated in such speeches rather than shown on the stage: Clytemnestra's murder of her husband and her death at the hands of her own children, the dismemberment of Pentheus, Thyestes' feasting on his children, Medea's poisoning of her victims and then her slaughter of her children with the sword, and so on. In tragedy, however, these events do not remain in the realm of speech only, for three reasons. First, the audience soon sees the results of the violent acts of which they have heard: the bodies of Agamemnon and Cassandra wheeled out of the palace on the eccyclema, or the entrance of the blinded Oedipus or Polymestor (in Euripides' *Hecuba*), or Agave's display of the severed head of Pentheus in the *Bacchae*. Second, the narratives often unfold in the presence of two or more figures who have exactly opposite reactions. In Sophocles' *Electra*, for instance, Electra and Clytemnestra have antithetical responses to the (false) news of Orestes' death. In both the *Trachiniae* and *Oedipus Tyrannus*, a messenger's speech has one meaning for a male protagonist (Hyllus and Oedipus, respectively), but quite another for a female figure, who then leaves the stage in silent grief to commit suicide (Deianeira, Jocasta).

Third, and most important, the narration of offstage violence calls attention to what is *not* seen. It thus gives a privileged status to this invisible spectacle by the very fact of withholding it from view. Such a negative spectacle, one could say, creates a counterpoint between the events seen in the clear daylight of the orchestra and the hidden events offstage. These latter thus acquire an added dimension of mystery, horror, and fascination by the very fact of taking place behind the scene. This offstage space, often representing the interior of the house or palace, functions as the space of the irrational or the demonic, the areas of experience or the aspects of personality that are hidden, dark, and fearful. Such, for instance, is the palace into which Clytemnestra lures Agamemnon for his murder, or the house in which Deianeira stores and uses the Centaur's venomous blood, or the tent where Hecuba and her women kill Polymestor's children and blind the father, or the underground prison where Dionysus' appearance as a bull begins to undermine Pentheus' rational authority.

The messenger's speech of the *Oedipus Tyrannus,* the most famous such account in Greek tragedy, richly exploits this contrast between what is "concealed" and what is "made visible." The reticence or inability to relate "the most painful things" (1228–31) envelops the scene in a suggestive semi-obscurity. The messenger's "memory" lets us follow Jocasta into her interior chamber, which she at once blocks to view by closing the doors (1246). The literal barrier of the closed doors and the figurative barrier of the messenger's hesitant remembering and recounting keep her last agony invisible; but we hear her "call" to the dead Laius and her evocation of her own "memory" of the acts of conception and birth whose horrors now surround her in that closed space.

The climax of the messenger's narrative is a mysterious, unexplained revealing as "some divinity shows [Oedipus] the way" (1258). With terrible shouts, he crashes through Jocasta's bolted doors, opening to us the fearful sight of Jocasta's body, swinging in its noose. The hidden "spectacle of woe" is at last revealed (1253 f., 1263 f.), but only to the eyes of those within the palace (and within the narrative), not to the audience in the theater. "Terrible were the things to see from there on," the messenger continues (1267), as he turns back to Oedipus who now "sees her," shouts, and strikes his eyes with the pins from her robes (1266 ff.).

The repeated motif of blocked or partial vision is appropriate to sight too terrible for speech or for public display. But the tension between a narrative of what is visible and what is hidden, what is heard and what is seen, is resolved in the full visual spectacle of Oedipus, who now has called for the opening of the gates "to show to all the Thebans" the pollution that he is (1287–89). The narrator supplies the stage directions: "These gates here of the palace are opening; soon you will see such a spectacle (*theama*) that even one who loathes it will feel pity" (1295 f.). Oedipus' self-consciously theatricalized appearance allows the pent-up emotions to find their public, communal expression in the cries of the chorus as they, like the audience, finally see for themselves what has been kept back as a purely oral/aural experience. "O suffering terrible for men to see," the chorus cries, "O most terrible of all that I have ever met."

This scene is characteristic of tragedy's self-conscious reference to the visual spectacle of its reversals from prosperity and power to misery and suffering. The noble but doomed King Oedipus, accepting his suffering, insists on being revealed to "all the Thebans" (1288) as a "spectacle" of the vision that was blind and of a happiness that was only a covering for the evils that lay hidden beneath (1396–97). Jocasta, by contrast, locked herself behind the doors of her chamber for her suicide, and Creon at the end would have Oedipus hidden away inside the palace from the light and from the public view (1424–31). The *Ajax* opens with a scene in which Athena "darkens" the eyes of the hero so that he cannot see his old enemy, Odysseus, who stands beside her onstage (69–86). Her divine "skill" or "art" (*technē*, 86) thereby imitates the art of the tragic spectacle that creates the fictional and mythical space that the audience can observe in godlike removal without being seen. After Ajax's suicide, the play emphasizes the ugly spectacle of his body, pierced by the sword. "A sight not to be looked upon" or "hard to look at," it is covered and then uncovered as an important part of the stage action (915–19, 1003–4). It is prominently described as still bleeding at the funeral rites that end the play and finally lay it to rest (1411 ff.).

Euripides develops this kind of self-reflexive visualization. The *Bacchae* in particular reveals what it is to be a spectator and enter the realm of Dionysus, a strange world in which one can experience the mysterious power of the gods and, as here, see "the mountain and wild beasts join in the bacchic revelry" with the maenads. Dionysus himself, god of the theater, the mask, wine, and illusion, operates directly on the action. He releases and uses Pentheus' desire to be "an eager spectator of the maenads" (829) in order to transport him from his role and behavior as king of Thebes and bring him under his spell. He brings him into the Dionysiac world of potential delusions and madness, but the god's realm also reveals the truths—sometimes terrible truths—hidden beneath surface appearances, in this case the potentially murderous violence within both the king and the followers of Dionysus.

Euripides often describes elaborately crafted artifacts, like the statue that Admetus would fashion of Alcestis (*Alcestis* 348–54) or the armor of Achilles in the *Electra* (432–86), that are emblematic of the mythical artifice of the play itself. The *Hecuba* seems to be alluding to the audience perspective when, in her plea for Agamemnon's aid, the protagonist asks him to "stand back like a painter" and look at her with the eyes of compassion (*Hecuba* 807–8). In the same play, her daughter, Polyxena, is likened to a beautiful statue when she bares herself to the sacrificial knife (559–65). In the erotic atmosphere of this scene, the violation of her body by the knife is parallel to a violation by the eyes as she exposes herself to the lustful male gaze of the unruly army (cf. 604–8). But Euripides also exploits the paradox that this figure, in its beauty and noble eloquence, strikes the spectators with pity, like the immobilized, silenced Iphigeneia, "standing out conspicuously as in a painting," about to be sacrificed in the parode of Aeschylus' *Agamemnon* (238–47).

In Euripides, the act of viewing often reflects back to the spectators their own role in the theater. Such scenes include the admiring public gaze on monuments of mythical narration in the parode of the *Ion* (184–221), the mysterious double vision of Dionysus' spell on Pentheus in the *Bacchae* (912 ff.), or the new bride's intimate viewing of herself in a mirror, "laughing at the lifeless image of her body" in the *Medea* (1161–62), just before the poison corrodes her lovely form into a shapeless, bloody mass, "a fearful spectacle" (1167, 1202). Through such scenes, Euripides contrasts public and private viewing and the domestic and the heroic worlds that his plays often juxtapose. In the beautiful third stasimon of the *Hecuba*, for example, the chorus-leader of the Trojan women describes her absorption in the "limitless rays of the golden mirror" as she prepares for bed, while her husband, lulled into false security by the stratagem of the Trojan Horse, does not see the Greek attackers (914–32). This intimate scene is more than decorative detail, for it depicts a fatal failure to see that dominates the last half of the play. The murderer Polymester is literally blinded by the vengeful Hecuba, and Agamemnon is figuratively blind to his own future murder in Argos that, mutatis mutandis, reenacts the vengeful guile of women here in the Troad.

In his *Electra,* Euripides systematically undercuts the visual proof that Aeschylus used in his *Libation Bearers* to bring Electra and Orestes together, only to fall back on a still more clichéd device, the scar that Orestes got chasing a deer in his father's house. This token, however, is deliberately emptied of all heroic meaning, for it refers to the scar that Odysseus got in his first dangerous exploit, hunting a wild boar on Mount Parnassus (*Odyssey* 19). The visual token, then, is not only a correction of Aeschylus but also engages with the whole heroic tradition (like the shield of Achilles, mentioned above) to point up this play's nonheroic tone.

Tragedy: Spectacle of the City

Although tragedy deals more or less directly with the marginal, the outsider, the irrational, every part of the theatrical performance reflects its firm place in the city and the city's democratic institutions. One of the chief magistrates selected the three tragedians whose plays were to be performed at the civic festivals of the Dionysia and the Lenaea. Unlike the Roman theater, the actors and chorus members were citizens; and in the early fifth century, the poets themselves acted in their plays. The judges were citizens selected by lot from each of the ten tribes. The theater itself was a public building. In it, on the day after the Dionysia, the Assembly met to determine that the festival had been conducted properly. Along with the dramatic performances at the Dionysia, moreover, the tribute from the allies was displayed; benefactors of the city were proclaimed; and the orphans of citizens killed in battle were paraded forth in their military equipment provided by the state. As suggested by both Thucydides in Pericles' funeral speech and Aristophanes in the *Acharnians* (496–507), the Dionysia was an occasion for the city to put itself on display to its allies and neighboring cities, to make a spectacle of itself.

Yet tragedy is no simple part of such a civic spectacle, for with extraordinary openness it enables the city to reflect on what is in conflict with its ideals, what it must exclude or repress, what it fears or labels as alien, unknown, Other. In this way, one may understand the tragedians' recurrent dramatization of the power and anger of women in the household (Aeschylus' *Oresteia*, Sophocles *Trachiniae*, Euripides' *Medea, Hippolytus,* and *Bacchae*), reversals of sexual roles, and the transformation of powerful rulers into defeated, suffering outcasts (Oedipus, Jason, Heracles, Creon, Pentheus, etc.). Euripides could idealize Athens as the just and pious defender of the weak (*Heracleidae, Suppliants*). Sophocles did so in his *Oedipus Coloneus.* But Euripides could also write works like the *Hecuba* and *Trojan Women,* implicitly criticizing the brutality of the city's war policies. Aeschylus' *Persians* could present the defeated invaders in a sympathetic light. Comedy could express the longing for peace directly in plays like the *Acharnians, Peace,* or *Lysistrata,* satirize institutions like the law courts or the Assembly (*Wasps, Ecclesiazusae*), or parody public figures like Cleon (*Knights*).

Charles Segal

Tragedy could stage, in symbolic form, contemporary debates on large moral and political issues, such as the restrictions on the Areopagus in Aeschylus' *Eumenides*. But its civic and political meaning could also be more diffused and indirect. The role of Odysseus in Sophocles' *Ajax*, for instance, validates democratic compromise over aristocratic authoritarianism and intransigence. Tragedy also raises questions about the dangers inherent in the exercise of power (*Persians, Oresteia, Antigone*) or shows the disastrous consequences of division or discord within the city (*Seven against Thebes, Phoenissae*) or demonstrates a basic moral structure underlying human events as we watch the slow, difficult, often painful working out of justice over many generations, as in the trilogies of Aeschylus.

Whereas the performance of choral lyric tends to reinforce the traditions and the values of the aristocratic families, the relatively new art of the dramatic spectacle is the distinctive form of the democratic *polis*. Indeed, with its civic setting, structure of dialectical debate, and constantly shifting relations between individual hero and the community represented by the chorus, tragedy is the logical art form for the democracy to have fostered after its Peisistratid beginnings. The aristocratic ethos of individualism, personal honor, and competitive excellence expressed in epic poetry is still very much alive in the fifth century. As is clear in works like Aeschylus' *Seven*, Sophocles' *Ajax* and *Philoctetes*, or Euripides' *Heracles*, one of tragedy's functions is to reexamine such attitudes in the light of a democratic society's need for compromise and cooperation.

The myths presented by tragedy no longer reflect the traditional values of a remote, idealized age. Instead they become the battleground of the contemporary conflicts within the city: older conceptions of blood-revenge against the new civic legalism (*Oresteia*); the obligations of family against those of the city (*Antigone*); the conflicts between the sexes and between generations (Euripides' *Alcestis, Medea,* and *Bacchae*); the differences between authoritarian and democratic rule (Euripides' *Suppliants*, Sophocles' *Ajax* and *Oedipus Coloneus*). For these reasons, too, the tragic performances are not conceived of as an entertainment that is available at any time (as is the modern theater), but are restricted to the two civic festivals of Dionysus and take place within the carnivalesque space associated with that god.

Above all, tragedy creates a feeling of community within the theater and within the city. Here the citizen-spectators, however diverse, become conscious of their solidarity within the civic framework and

211

within the civic building that have brought them together. Its spectators become spectators of one another as citizens as well as spectators of the performance itself. The community of the theater forges bonds of shared emotion and common compassion. At the end of Euripides' *Hippolytus*, for instance, the grief felt for the death of Theseus' son is "a common grief" that spreads over "all the citizens" (1462–66), despite the fact that Hippolytus had rejected political obligations for the private pursuits of hunting and athletics. This civic commemoration, moreover, is the consolation that a human community can offer, in contrast to the private, cultic ritual with which his goddess, Artemis, will honor his memory (1423–30).

Tragedy not only holds the distancing mirror of myth up to contemporary problems; it also mirrors some of the most important institutions of the city. Of these, the closest affinities are with the courts of law. Ten of the spectators, chosen by lot, are in fact judges of the plays. The rapid adversarial exchanges of tragedy resemble the argumentation and cross-examination of the courts. The tragedies in effect make their audiences in some sense judges of complex moral issues where both sides have claims to justice, and right and wrong are hard to sort out. The debate between Hecuba and Polymestor in the *Hecuba*, for instance, actually is a juridical situation (1129 ff.). We may think also of the trial scene of Aeschylus' *Eumenides* and the parody of a courtroom in Aristophanes' *Wasps*. Later writers even praise the tragedies for their lifelike approximation of legal debate (e.g., Quintilian 10.1.67 f.).

Even more broadly than the adjudication of guilt and punishment, tragedy is concerned with the problem of decision. Nearly every extant play shows its protagonist tormented by a difficult choice between conflicting alternatives or involved in deciding between safety and a dangerous or uncertain action. "What shall I do?"—*ti drasō*—is a recurrent cry at moments of crisis. Figures like Medea, Phaedra, or Orestes, hesitate, waver, change their minds. Intransigence may be as disastrous as vacillation or changeability, as Sophocles' *Philoctetes* shows. Situations like Creon's reversal of his position in the *Antigone* or the vehement anger of Oedipus toward Teiresias in the *Tyrannus* play out before the audience not only the destructiveness of quarrels within the family but also the consequences of hasty, irascible, or mistaken judgments. Such dramatizations of decision, reversal, rigidity, and the like would appeal to the audience's experience of the assemblies as well as of the courts. Thucydides' account of the Athenian change of mind after condemning the Mytilenaeans shows how much in real life could rest on such deliberations and reversals (Thucydides 3.36).

Tragedy and Writing

The tragedians may well have composed large portions of their plays in their heads, like the oral bards, and taught them orally to the actors and chorus. Yet the mentality of literacy and textual production seem almost indispensable to the structure of tragedy: the preplanned concentration of a complex action into a highly structured form, unfolding in a geometric, conventionalized, symbolic space.

Aristophanes' *Frogs,* produced in 405 B.C., dramatizes the clash between newer and older conceptions of poetry and performance. Aeschylus accuses his younger rival, Euripides, of disrupting the old morality by his intellectual subtleties, paradoxes, and displays of immoral women (cf. 1078–88). The older poet, closer to the oral culture of the past, is also closer to a more direct correspondence of word and thing and to the traditional role of the poet as the mouthpiece of communal values (1053–56). Euripides' art is associated with the Sophistic movement, with books, airy lightness, and the twisting glibness of the tongue. It is presented as disassociating language and reality ("Life is not life"). Aeschylus' speech, on the other hand, possesses the earthy physicality of the voice in the oral culture; and his utterances come from the "guts," "diaphragm," and "breath" (844, 1006, 1016). In the Battle of the Prologues, in which verses are weighed on the scales, Euripides' "winged" subtleties of Persuasion lose to the weightiness of Aeschylus's chariots, Death, and corpses (1381–1410). It is a culminating twist of the irony that Dionysus chooses Aeschylus with Euripides' own verse about the split between "tongue" and "mind" (*Frogs* 1471; cf. *Hippolytus* 612).

It may seem paradoxical to associate tragedy, which so powerfully combines visual spectacle, music, and poetry for an excited and often boisterous crowd of thousands, with the austere, monochromatic communication that we associate with silent letters. Yet the behind-the-scene power of writing makes it possible to organize sight, speech, and hearing into this multimedia performance. Tragedy's frequent use of synaesthetic imagery and its explicit orchestration of visual and acoustic experience into moments of high drama call attention to this interconnection of the different senses.

Both the graphic space of writing and the theatrical space of drama depend on creating a field of symbolic activity where the smallest signs can have great significance. Here attention is concentrated on a limited, deliberately miniaturized field. This microcosm is the model for a larger order, whether of the society or of the whole universe. Both writing and tragedy require a focused, interpretive activity in a restricted area. Both depend on the ability to operate within a system of conventions, to recognize and interpret signs, and to put them together in the correct sequence, "inferring the new by means of the old," as Jocasta says of Oedipus (with reference also to his riddle-solving skill) in the Oedipus Tyrannus (916). In Greek "to read" is to "recognize," anagignōskein, which is also Aristotle's word for the climactic moment of tragedy, the "recognition," or anagnōrisis.

Tragedy's unique power may well be due in part to its emergence at this transitional moment in Greek culture when the force of the myths is not yet eroded by the critical mentality that comes with writing, abstract thought, and systematic ethical philosophies. Comedy remained a vital and innovative form well into the fourth century, in part because Menander and his followers were able to refocus Old Comedy on more private and domestic concerns, draw on the emotionality of the late Euripidean recognition plots, and develop a style that was both colloquial and elegant. But no such transformation infused new life into tragedy. The tragedies composed after the fifth century were not judged worthy of preservation, and none have survived.

Fifth-century tragedy was able to combine the moral and religious seriousness and mythical imagination of the oral epic with the intellectual probing of an age of advanced literacy that was attempting bold conceptualizations of man and nature in science, medicine, philosophy, history, geography, and so on. In tragedy, as in philosophy, thought and vision reach into the unknown. Aeschylus compares "deep thought" to a diver's plunge "into the depths" or tries to grasp the mind of Zeus that is "a vision bottomless," something that eludes human understanding (Suppliants 407 f. and 1057; cf. Septem 593 f., Agamemnon 160 ff.).

Tragedy's stunning visual enactment of the ancient myths seems to privilege the surface appearances of sense perception, but it constantly explores the divisions between surface and depth, between word and deed, between seeming and being. Its very fullness of representational power, combining word, music, dance, and mimetic gesture, in fact sets off the elusiveness of ultimate truth and the difficulty, indeed, the painfulness, of grasping the complex nature of human behavior, the ways of the gods, the terms and limits of mortality.

However different their medium, the tragic poets are the spiritual brothers of the philosophers who, like Heraclitus, Democritus, and Plato, know that the surface of the world contains more deception than truth and search to understand why life is as it is, why suffering exists, how justice and moral action can be realized in society, and what larger order, if any, makes our existence intelligible. Tragedies continue to be written and performed after the fifth century, but the creative energy, ethical concern, and theological probing that produced the great works now move into philosophy and history. The spectators of Aeschylus and Sophocles are now also the readers of Plato and Aristotle.

Bibliography

Adrados, F. R. *Festival, Comedy, and Tragedy.* Translated by C. Holme. Leiden, 1975.

Connor, W. R. "Early Greek Land Warfare as Symbolic Expression." *Past and Present* 119 (1988): 3–29.

Detienne, Marcel. (1973). *Les maîtres de vérité dans la Grèce archaïque.* 2d ed. Paris, 1973.

———. *L'invention de la mythologie.* Paris 1981. English translation, *The Invention of Mythology* by M. Cook. (Chicago, 1986).

———, ed. *Les savoirs de l'écriture en Grèce ancienne.* Lille, 1986.

———, and Jean-Pierre Vernant. *Les ruses de l'intelligence: La métis des Grecs.* Paris, 1974. English translation, *Cunning Intelligence in Greek Culture and Society,* by Janet Lloyd. (Chicago, 1991).

Diels, Hermann, and Walther Kranz, eds. *Die Fragmente der Vorsokratiker.* 5th ed. 3 vols. Berlin, 1950–52.

Il Dramma antico come spettacolo: Atti del II congresso internazionale di studi sul dramma antico. Dioniso 38 (1967).

Eden, Kathy. *Poetic and Legal Fiction in the Aristotelian Tradition.* Princeton, 1986.

Else, G. F. *The Origin and Early Form of Greek Tragedy.* Cambridge, Mass., 1965.

Ford, Andrew. *Homer: The Poetry of the Past.* Ithaca, N.Y., 1992.

Gentili, Bruno. *Lo spettacolo nel mondo antico.* Bari, 1977.

———. *Poesia e pubblico nella Grecia antica.* Rome and Bari, 1984. English translation, *Poetry and Its Public in Ancient Greece and Rome,* by A. T. Cole (Baltimore, 1988).

Ghiron-Bistagne, P., and B. Schouler, eds. *Anthropologie et théâtre antique.* Cahiers du GITA 3. Montpellier, 1987.

Golder, Herbert. "Visual Meaning and Greek Drama: Sophocles' *Ajax* and the Art of Dying." In *Advances in Nonverbal Communication,* ed. Fernando Poyalos, pp. 323–60. Amsterdam and Philadelphia, 1992.

Goldhill, Simon. *Reading Greek Tragedy.* Cambridge, 1986.

———. "The Great Dionysia and Civic Ideology." *Journal of Hellenic Studies* 107 (1987): 58–76. Reprinted in *Nothing to Do with Dionysus,* ed. J. J. Winkler and F. I. Zeitlin (Princeton, 1987), pp. 97–129.

Havelock, E. A. *Preface to Plato.* Cambridge, Mass., 1963.

———. *The Literate Revolution in Greece and Its Consequences.* Princeton, 1982.

———. *The Muses Learn to Write.* New Haven, 1986.

Herington, C. J. *Poetry into Drama.* Sather Classical Lectures 49. Berkeley and Los Angeles, 1985.

Knox, B. M. W. "Silent Reading in Antiquity." *Greek, Roman, and Byzantine Studies* 9 (1968): 421–35.

———. *Word and Action: Essays on the Ancient Theatre.* Baltimore, 1979.

Longo, Oddone. *Tecniche della comunicazione nella Grecia antica.* Naples, 1980.

Loraux, Nicole. *Façons tragiques de tuer une femme.* Paris. English translation. *Tragic Ways of Killing a Woman,* by A. Forster (Cambridge, Mass., 1987).

Pickard-Cambridge, A. W. *Dithyramb, Tragedy, and Comedy.* 2d ed. Revised by T. B. L. Webster. Oxford, 1962.

———. *The Dramatic Festivals of Athens.* 2d ed. Revised by John Gould and D. M. Lewis. Oxford, 1968.

Pucci, Pietro. *Hesiod and the Language of Poetry.* Baltimore, 1977.

———. "Euripides: The Monument and the Sacrifice." *Arethusa* 10 (1977): 165–96.

Romilly, Jacqueline de. *La crainte et l'angoisse dans le théâtre d'Eschyle.* Paris, 1953.

Seale, David. *Vision and Stagecraft in Sophocles.* Chicago, 1982.

Segal, Charles. *Tragedy and Civilization: An Interpretation of Sophocles.* Martin Classical Lecture 26. Cambridge, Mass., 1981.

———. *Dionysiac Poetics and Euripides' Bacchae.* Princeton, 1982.

———. *Interpreting Greek Tragedy.* Ithaca, N.Y., 1986.

———. *Pindar's Mythmaking: The Fourth Pythian Ode.* Princeton, 1986.

———. "Tragic Beginnings: Narration, Voice, and Authority in the Prologues of Greek Drama." *Yale Classical Studies* 29 (1992): 85–112.

———. *Euripides and the Poetics of Sorrow: Art, Gender, and Commemoration in Alcestis, Hippolytus, and Hecuba.* Durham, N.C., 1993.

Stanford, W. B. *Greek Tragedy and the Emotions.* London, 1983.

Svenbro, Jesper. *La parole et le marbre.* Lund, 1976.

———. *Phrasikleia: Anthropologie de la lecture en Grèce ancienne.* Paris, 1988.

Taplin, Oliver. *The Stagecraft of Aeschylus.* Oxford, 1977.

———. *Greek Tragedy in Action.* Berkeley and Los Angeles, 1978.

Thalmann, W. G. "Speech and Silence in the *Oresteia.*" *Phoenix* 39 (1985): 99–118, 221–37.

Thomas, Rosalind. *Literacy and Orality in Ancient Greece.* Cambridge, 1992.

Vegetti, Mario, ed. *Introduzione alle culture antiche.* Vol. 1, *Oralità scrittura spettacolo.* Turin, 1983.

Vernant, Jean-Pierre. *Les origines de la pensée grecque.* 2d ed. Paris, 1969. English translation, *The Origins of Greek Thought* (Ithaca, 1982).

———. *Mythe et pensée chez les Grecs.* 3d ed. Paris, 1974. English translation, *Myth and Thought among the Greeks* (London, 1983).

———. *Mythe et société en Grèce ancienne.* Paris, 1974. English translation, *Myth and Society in Ancient Greece,* by Janet Lloyd (New York, 1990).

———. *La mort dans les yeux.* Paris, 1985. Translated in part in *Mortals and Immortals,* ed. F. I. Zeitlin (Princeton, 1991), pp. 111–38.

———, and Vidal-Naquet, Pierre. *Mythe et tragédie en Grèce ancienne.* Paris, 1972. English translation, *Myth and Tragedy in Ancient Greece,* by Janet Lloyd (New York, 1990).

———. *Mythe et tragédie deux.* Paris, 1986. English translation, *Myth and Tragedy in Ancient Greece,* by Janet Lloyd (New York, 1990).

———. "In the Mirror of Medusa." In *Mortals and Immortals,* ed. F. I. Zeitlin, pp. 141–150. Princeton, 1991.

Walsh, G. B. *The Varieties of Enchantment: Early Greek Views of the Nature and Function of Poetry.* Chapel Hill, N.C., 1984.

Wyatt, W. F. Jr. "Homer in Performance: *Iliad* 1.348–427." *Classical Journal* 83 (1987–88): 289–97.

Zeitlin, F. I. "Playing the Other: Theater, Theatricality, and the Feminine in Greek Drama." *Representations* 11 (1985): 63–94.

———. "The Power of Aphrodite: Eros and the Boundaries of the Self in the *Hippolytus.*" In *Directions in Euripidean Criticism: A Collection of Essays,* ed. Peter Burian, pp. 52–111. Durham, N.C., 1985.

CHAPTER SEVEN

Forms of Sociality

Oswyn Murray

MAN IS A social animal; Greek man is a creature of the *polis:* that is the meaning of Aristotle's famous definition of *his* man as "by nature a *polis*-animal" (*Politics* 1.1253a). But Aristotle's definition was embedded in a an ethical–biological theory, in which, in order to be fully human, one must exercise to the full all the potentialities inherent in human nature, and in which an ethical hierarchy privileged the mind over the emotions. His perception, therefore, of the *polis* as the form of social organization in which man's potentialities could be most fully realized, subordinated the claims of religion, family, and the emotional realm to their place within the higher order of the political.

The history of the study of Greek social organization has been of a more or less conscious struggle to escape from this Aristotelian vision of Greek society toward a picture that lays less emphasis on the unique phenomenon of the Greek *polis* and tries to "depoliticize" Greek man, to see Greek forms of social organization as related to forms found in other early societies. In a sentence, this is the history of the study of the Greek city from Fustel de Coulanges (1864) to the present day.[1]

The relationship between man and society is in all societies a dynamic one: any particular age of man has a past and a future; and there is not one Greek man, but a succession of Greek men, as Jacob Burckhardt portrayed them in the fourth volume of his *Griechische Kulturgeschichte*.[2] Following his example, I shall distinguish four ideal types, or four ages, of Greek man: heroic man, agonal man, political man, cosmopolitan man. Such rough chronological distinctions have of course no absolute validity, but they are necessary, because only by some form of diachronic analysis can we comprehend the synchronic relationships that create the forms of sociality. To trace developments across the centuries is to falsify cultural history by privileging causality over function, and to emphasize the continuities is to ignore the fundamental changes that take place behind the screen of language and institutions.

Sociality and Commensality

The phenomenon of sociality can be viewed from a variety of perspectives, but it is perhaps helpful to present it first in its relationship to the economy. Behind the facade of social forms lie economic relations expressed in the unequal distribution of goods. A Marxist analysis will see social structures (and hence social relations) as a consequence of the struggle for an unequal share of benefits in short supply. More recently, others have emphasized the abundance of natural resources in primitive societies, and the consequent importance of such social activities as the gift, the festival, conspicuous consumption, the display of wealth before others and before the gods.[3] Either way the surplus, small or large, is used to create a social structure, which supports communal activities, cultural, political, and religious: forms of the redistribution of a surplus through displays of altruism or power are what structure society.

Given the primacy of the land and its produce in early history, it is agricultural surplus that is most commonly used to build society and its attendant culture. Typically, the redistribution of this surplus through social feasting or religious festival creates in its ritualized use a framework of sociality that permeates the other relationships in society. In particular, certain products in relatively short supply become privileged symbols of social status; the feast is ritualized and serves to define the community as a whole, or a class within it. In Greece the most significant products are meat and wine, reserved for special occasions and consumed in special rituals.

Meat is a sacred food, reserved for the gods and for an earlier age of heroes; typically of a product in adequate but not abundant supply from the hills and mountains of Greece, it is primarily consumed on religious occasions, in connection with the sacrifice of the burnt offering: the gods receive the scent of the entrails, while the humans enjoy a communal feast of the edible parts of the animal, freshly killed and boiled to make it tender, these occasions are not rare events, but common occurrences, structured according to a complex festival calendar; and they serve to express the sense of community of the group of worshipers in a shared experience of pleasure and festivity, which includes both gods and men. The worship of the gods is a time of enjoyment and release from toil, which typically involves the whole community, or a natural subset of it (such as adolescents or women), and sometimes even opens its ranks to the outsider and the slave.[4]

Alcohol is preeminently a social drug, whose ritual use relates either to the bonding of a closed group or to the cathartic release of social tensions in a carnival of permissiveness. The power of wine and the need for social control over its use are explicit in Greek culture. Barbarians indulge in unstructured (and excessive) drinking; the Greek is defined by his ritualized consumption of wine, mixed with water, and drunk within a specific social context. For reasons discussed below, wine becomes a mechanism for the creation of small groups, specialized in function in relation to war, politics, or pleasure. The use of wine as a release mechanism is less obvious, but certainly occurs in various rituals connected with Dionysus. Women, excluded from the social use of wine, and therefore characterized as prone to secret and unstructured drinking, worship Dionysus in rituals in which all rules are set aside: the sacrificial victim is torn to pieces, not killed with the knife, consumed raw instead of being grilled or boiled, and wine is consumed in unmixed disorder. But this is no expression of sociality, rather a release of those tensions that the rituals of sociality have themselves created.

The importance of commensality and the rituals surrounding food and drink in Greek culture are reflected in the evidence available for its study. From Homer onward, Greek poetry belongs in the context of the feast, and especially in its archaic development, the *symposion:* in musical accompaniment, meter, and subject matter, early Greek poetry must be understood in relation to its place of performance, either (for choral lyric, danced and sung by groups of young men or girls) the religious festival or (for elegy and solo lyric) the aristocratic drinking-group. The art of Greek pottery and vase-painting primarily served the needs of such groups; shapes and decoration reflect the same social interests as those of archaic poetry. The ordering of public and private commensality in the archaic and classical periods with sets of rules and privileges written in the form of laws or decrees reveals how important commensality was in the activities of such associations. Later the development of a philosophical literature of commensality in the classical and postclassical world created an idealized vision of a social institution, no longer perhaps as central as it had once been, but that remained sufficiently distinctive of Greek culture to attract the attention of the antiquarian writers of the hellenistic and Roman periods. The *Deipnosophistae* of Athenaeus, an encyclopedia of Greek commensality of the late second century A.D., mirrors its subject matter in being structured as a conversation at a *deipnon,* in which the contents are ordered according to the activities of the imaginary participants.[5]

Heroic Man

The world depicted in the Homeric poems is structured around rites of commensality. The essential characteristics of the house of a heroic *basileus* are the *megaron,* or banqueting hall, and the storeroom, where the surplus produce of his society is kept, to be used either in feasting or in the presentation of gifts to guests of the same class as himself. Odysseus in disguise claims to recognize his own house by its use for the activity of commensality: "I see that many men are feasting within, for the smell of fat is there, and the lyre sounds, which the gods have made as companion to the feast" (*Odyssey* 17.269–71). The *basileus* entertains the members of his class in "feasts of merit"; by this means, in a world of competitive honor, he acquires authority and prestige. The group thus singled out is a warrior group, whose status is expressed and whose cohesion is maintained in the activity of feasting. In one sense, it remains a social rite, concerned with the processes of self-definition and group formation on the part of an aristocratic elite; but this elite is also the warrior class whose function is to protect the society.

Like the poetic similes of Homer, the lies of Odysseus are perhaps more truthful than the imagined narrative in which they are embedded, for (as a second order of fictionality) they are intended to recall to the audience their own experiences in life. The interplay between feasting and military activity, both public and private, is well illustrated by Odysseus' account of his life as the illegitimate son of a Cretan nobleman, who was cheated of his inheritance, but won through valor a place in the aristocracy as a professional warrior: he grew rich from the proceeds of expeditions overseas. These were private ventures, but when the Trojan War came, it was the people who demanded him as their leader, "nor was there any way of refusing, for the voice of the people was hard on me." After the war, he returned to his private exploits: "Nine ships I fitted out, and the people gathered swiftly; six days then my noble companions feasted with me, and I gave them many victims that they might prepare a feast for themselves" before they sailed to Egypt (*Odyssey* 14.199–258).

In such accounts, two types of venture are presented: the private raiding of a warrior elite, composed of aristocratic leaders and "companions" of the same class, whose ties of loyalty are formed in the activity of communal and competitive feasting; and the right of "the people" to call on this warrior class for leadership in more formal warfare. The expedition to Troy is a public one, with feasting at public expense for the participants, and public fines for those who refuse to go. Within the community, status is determined by food; in the famous speech of Sarpedon to Glaucus, he asserts that the two champions, honored "with seats of honor and full cups in Lycia" and a *temenos,* have a duty to fight for their community: then the people will say, "Our nobles that rule in Lycia are great men, they eat fat sheep and drink the best honey-sweet wine. But they are powerful men, for they fight with the first of the Lycians" (*Iliad* 12.310–28).[6]

The *Iliad* centers on the wrath of Achilles, which is expressed in his withdrawal and his refusal to partake in the rites of commensality; the *Odyssey* contrasts two models of commensality, that of the ideal world of the Phaeacians, and that of the suitors on Ithaca, where the breakdown of social values is expressed in the infringement of those norms of commensality that involve reciprocity and competition: "Leave my halls and prepare other feasts, eating your own belongings, going in turn from house to house," says Telemachus to the suitors (2.139 f.). The crime of the suitors in fact lies in their usurping the prerogatives of a warrior class in the absence of the warlord.

The complex relationship of this poetic portrayal to any historical reality need not concern us. The Homeric poems present an image of a past society that both establishes a "contemporary" mental image and influences the future development of Greek commensality. It is, however, true that this image is in all probability a partial one, ignoring the forms of sociality engaged in by the people, especially in relation to the religious festival.

Nevertheless, the characteristics of this mental image are important for the development of Greek sociality. The Homeric *deipnon* or *dais* is preceded by a sacrifice in which animal victims are killed as an offering to particular gods, often on some special occasion of festival, cult, or family significance. The meat is grilled on spits, and the meal takes place in a hall (*megaron*) in which male participants are ranged seated along the walls, with small tables before them, two to a table; occasionally portions and seats of honor are mentioned, but in general the emphasis is on equality in both respects. The uninvited guest, whether fellow aristocrat or beggar, also receives his due. Wine is mixed with water and served from the *kratēr*.

The poet presents an image of human happiness, expressed in a ritual of sociality; at the center of this ritual he places himself: "Indeed I declare that there is no more perfect pleasure than when *euphrosynē* holds all the people, and the feasters listen to the bard in the hall, sitting in order, while the tables are full of bread and meat, and the winebearer draws the wine from the mixing bowl, and carrying it round fills the cups. This is the fairest thing I know in my heart" (*Odyssey* 9.5–10). It is an image that claims to be both of the feast and expressed within the feast, for the Homeric bard is himself the singer with the lyre, who, from within the narrative, performs the narrative itself. We may find difficulty in the notion of the performance of epic within the feast, but it is clear that Homer intends us to believe in his poetry as the accompaniment of *euphrosynē*.

If the *Iliad* expresses the external social function of warrior feasting in the organization of military activity, the *Odyssey* is an internal epic, constructed as entertainment for the feast. Each episode in the travels of Telemachus is sealed by the experience of commensality: all action leads toward or away from the feast. The central narrative of the travels of Odysseus is presented as a performance at the feast, involving contrasted forms of commensality, among the Lotus-eaters, the Cyclops, Circe, and the underworld. On Ithaca, the simple feasting of the swineherd is contrasted with the evil feasting of the suitors, who despoil the house of the absent hero. The final action in this epic of commensality centers on the destruction of the suitors at the table, while they are themselves engaged in the activity of feasting. As the poet sings within the feast, he evokes the imagined horror of another feast, and the listeners become themselves involved: it is their hall that fills with night, their meat that drips red, as wailing and lamentation arise, and the walls and roof beams are spattered with blood (*Odyssey* 20.345 ff.).

The *Odyssey* creates from its own place of performance a narrative structure, involving its audience in the action of the epic itself: it is performance poetry intended for the feast and making its narrative from the feast. Thus the audience participates in the narrative itself: both poet and audience are part of a dual event, narrated and experienced. The role of this poetry within the realm of commensality is to express for the participants the meaning of the social ritual in which they are engaged.

This heroic feasting presents already most of the basic features that distinguish later Greek rites of commensality. On the one hand, it is connected externally with the social function of warfare, on the other, its internal focus is on pleasure (*euphrosynē*). In heroic poetry, it possesses a form of discourse adapted to performance within the context of commensality and capable of self-reflection on the activities of the feast. As yet, however, the image presented is only partially related to the needs of the community, and many of the specific characteristics of the later Greek rituals of socialization are absent.

Archaic Man

Two features are conventionally regarded as distinguishing marks of Greek commensality in the historical period; they are the practice of reclining, rather than sitting, and the separation between the activities of feasting and drinking. Both these features are part of wider developments in Greek commensality of the early archaic age.

Reclining as part of an established set of social customs is first attested by the prophet Amos in Samaria in the eighth century (Amos 6.3–7), and it may well have been a custom adopted by the Greeks from contact with Phoenician culture. The earliest explicit evidence for reclining in Greece does not occur until the late seventh century, in Corinthian art and the poetry of Alcman, but the practice can be shown to go back more than a century earlier.[7] It represents a fundamental change in Greek commensality, because it introduced constraints on the organization of the group. The reclining participants, lying one or two to each couch around the walls of a room, established an arrangement of "sympotic space," which determined the size of the group.[8] The *megaron* evolved into the *andrōn,* a room specifically designed to hold a fixed number of couches, often with its door offset to the left in order to accommodate the difference between the length and the foot of a couch. More important, the size of the group is limited by the ability to communicate across the room: the standard sizes allow for seven, eleven, or fifteen couches: The group is therefore normally a restricted one, of between fourteen and thirty male participants.

This physical arrangement can be traced most clearly in the development of public and religious architecture of the classical period, and through its use in Etruscan tomb architecture, where it is one of the most obvious archaeological indicators of Greek influence on customs of commensality in other ancient cultures. But its main importance is, of course, as part of a wider development toward the formation of small groups and the elaboration of specialized rituals.

One of these rituals concerns the separation of food and drink. Greek commensality of the historical period is divided between the *deipnon,* at which food and drink are consumed, and the subsequent *symposion,* at which the emphasis is placed on the drinking of wine with an accompaniment of light cakes. There is little discussion of the *deipnon* before the Hellenistic period; it seems to have been simple, and to have lacked ritualization outside the sphere of specific taboos on certain religious occasions. The elaboration of discourse and of social ritual belongs to the *symposion.*

Around the *symposion* there developed a complex furniture. The *andrōn* itself could be provided with fixtures, floor covering, and drainage; the *klinē* and side tables were often finely made and decorated with inlay; there were elaborate cushions and other coverings. A large proportion of the pottery shapes in archaic and early classical fine pottery are specifically sympotic shapes—the *kratēr* for mixing water and wine, the *psyktēr* for cooling the mixture, strainers and jugs for distributing it, and an immense variety of cup shapes for the actual drinking, each with separate names and specialized functions. The images on these vases present a visual commentary on the perceptions and activities of the social class that took part in the *symposion.* Heroic scenes, scenes of war, and scenes drawn from the poetic repertory are common, as are scenes from the aristocratic life of sport, hunting, riding, and homosexual courtship. In contrast, genre scenes of work or the activities of citizen women are rare, as are scenes of religious ritual. Particular emphasis is of course given to divine, heroic, and contemporary representations of sympotic activity: the imagery reflects almost the full range of activities associated with the *symposion,* from the most decorous to scenes of overt sexuality and drunken riot. This metasympotic commentary on the *symposion* reflects through imagery the self-absorption that is also found in sympotic poetry; the iconography that developed is complex and sophisticated.[9]

Poetry, performed to music, remained central to the *symposion.* Two main forms developed, corresponding roughly to two types of musical accompaniment. The double flute (*aulos*) was the instrument of the battlefield, and also of elegiac poetry in particular. Among stringed instruments, the Homeric *kithara* gave way to the deeper sounding *barbiton:* traditionally invented by Terpander, and favored instrument for the singing of lyric poetry, it is the badge of the professional sympotic poet like Anacreon. Poetic forms reflected the spontaneous competition and creation expected of amateur poets: the elegiac couplet is especially suited to the round, a theme taken up and developed by each participant in turn; the *skolion* is a more formal development. Short lyric poems with repeating metrical verses sung to simple tunes indicate a similar mode of performance. The earliest lyric poets, like Archilochus, Alcaeus, and Sappho, composed and sang their own poems in the first instance, and elegy seems generally to have remained in the amateur sphere. For such reasons, personal emotion, personal experience discussed *in propria persona,* and direct exhortation to the audience are common: the poet often uses the first or second person. In the sixth century there developed a class of professional poets, such as Mimnermus and Anacreon, who supplied a more sophisticated and subtle level of poetic diction, using the same techniques, but making the personal poem generic in reference.[10]

The themes of this poetry reflect the interests of the social group and its aristocratic lifestyle. Like the visual evidence of the pottery, they concern heroic exploits, warfare, and homosexual love. Hymns to particular gods appropriate to the *symposion,* both serious and in parody, are common, but again there is little reference to actual religious ritual. The family and the citizen woman are absent: the expression of sexual desire is open and related to female slaves and entertainers. Political polemic and incitements to political action extend from the defense of the ship of state to calls for civil war.

Such themes rest on the creation of a group ethic, a world in which participants are bound together by their loyalty (*pistis*) and common values. The activity is self-conscious, and a vocabulary of companionship in drinking emerges, symbolized by the word *sym-posion* itself. This language finds its fullest expression in the poetry of Alcaeus, composed for performance at the gatherings of groups of companions (*hetairoi*) among the aristocracy of Mytilene around 600 B.C. The surroundings are still "Homeric" in many respects—the great house shines with bronze armor—but a new style of *euphrosyné* is revealed in the emphasis on "wine, women, and song" (here conjoined for the first time). The function of the group is no longer that of external warfare in a stable environment, but of unity for action within the *polis* in defense of class privileges: the war in prospect is civil war; the call is for internal group unity in action against the tyrant. Alcaeus does not seek to persuade a wider public; his appeal is to those already within the group, who share his values and his aims. Such activity is characteristic of the early history of the *polis* and demonstrates within the aristocratic sphere the complete fusion of sociality with the forms of political action. The leadership of the community belongs by right to Alcaeus and his aristocratic companions but has been taken from them: it must be recovered by means of civil war and even with the help of barbarian gold. Such a close fusion of commensality and politics centered on the aristocratic conception of the *symposion* as an exclusive organization devoted to maintaining the dominance of a social class over the wider world of the *polis*.[11]

Throughout the seventh and sixth centuries, this aristocratic world was under threat, as it became marginalized by new political, economic, and military developments. Archaic commensality responded to the decline of the aristocracy and the increasing importance of the *polis* in two ways, which emphasize the two opposing aspects of Greek commensality.

Military commensality of the Homeric type could combine with communal male institutions such as those found in the traditional society of Crete, where continuity and adaptation are especially clear. Here the male community was organized into groups, with a "men's hut" (*andreion*) for communal dining: food was provided by the city from communal land as well as through individual contributions. The continuity of such customs is illustrated by the fact that the old habit of sitting rather than reclining was maintained; its significance for the definition of the community is shown by the careful separation of visitors at a special "strangers' table," dedicated to Zeus Xenios. After the meal, public affairs were discussed, and "deeds of war are described and brave men praised, to be an example of courage to the younger men." Pederasty was ritualized as an initiation rite, and the lover presented the beloved with the three gifts of manhood, a cloak, an ox, and a drinking cup, symbolizing his admittance into the adult community.[12]

Probably the earliest social function of elegiac poetry was the reinforcement of warrior values through exhortation, rather than through the indirect mode of description used in heroic poetry. Already this change demonstrates a tension and an attempt to reinforce traditional values and behavior, which is characteristic of a society in transition:

"How long will you lie idle? When will you put on your strong courage, young men? Are you not ashamed to abandon the boundary lands so easily?" says Callinus of Ephesus. War elegy recreates the heroic image for a wider military group, now at the service of the *polis*.

The most complete example of this "institutionalization of the feast" is that created in Sparta in the archaic period, at roughly the same time as her adoption of the new hoplite tactics of mass military formation. Spartan commensality may have derived from Dorian practices such as those in Crete, but it was radically transformed in the social and military institutions of "Lycurgus." After passing through the rigorous age-class system known as the *agōgē*, the young adult male citizen was elected into a *syssition*, a warrior group centered on the practice of daily communal feasting at the *phidition*. Each member was required to provide a fixed amount of food and wine from his land: inability to do so meant loss of membership, and therefore loss of full citizen rights. The relationship between commensality and military organization is described by Herodotus: Lycurgus created the laws of Sparta, "and after that their military institutions, the sworn bands (*enōmotiai*), groups of thirty (*triēkades*), and dining groups (*syssitia*)" (Herodotus 1.65). It was in these groupings, based on the numbers fifteen and thirty, that the Spartan army fought throughout the archaic and classical periods.

Such numbers reflect the archaic organization of sympotic space, based on seven or fifteen couches: the earliest explicit literary evidence of the *symposion* in Alcman relates to a Spartan context and attests the seven-couch arrangement. The Spartan meal follows the classical Greek division into two parts, called here *aiklon* and *epaiklon*. Both involve compulsory contributions and are therefore original elements in the ritual. In the Spartan system of values, however, the *aiklon* carried symbolic significations of continuity with earlier forms, and of claims to equality and unchanging austerity: the contents of the meal were fixed and consisted of barley cake, boiled pork, and the famous Spartan black broth. By contrast, the *epaiklon* registered differences in wealth, status, and prowess through a range of possible contributions; it therefore developed into a more elaborate form of *symposion* than the normal, which made use of a range of additional foods, especially nonsacrificial meat from the chase. Despite Athenian fourth-century attempts to suggest Spartan abstinence or at least moderation in drinking, wine played a prominent part in the ritual.[13]

This model of commensality is closely associated with the creation of the hoplite *polis* as a "guild of warriors" (Max Weber); it diverges from the Homeric model in universalizing an aristocratic prerogative and from the Dorian model in isolating and privileging the military function. It is not surprising, therefore, that the Spartan poet Tyrtaeus was both one of Homer's closest imitators and the perfecter of the new genre of military elegy.[14]

The opposite development of Greek commensality emphasizes its internal aspect as embodiment of the pleasure principle. It could therefore serve as a vehicle for withdrawal by a marginalized aristocracy into a specifically private world of *euphrosynē*. The symbols of a privileged and leisured class came to have increasing importance in the archaic period; as warfare and political control ceased to be their distinctive right, sport and *symposion* were elaborated to replace them. This is especially evident in the colonial world of the Greek west, where a new aristocracy of original settlers sought to define itself in the course of the seventh century: sympotic customs were particularly dominant there, and were in turn accepted by the emerging Italic and Etruscan nobilities as the necessary symbols of the aristocratic life.[15]

Pleasure came especially from the elaboration of rituals, the development of luxury and comfort, increased sophistication in poetic and other entertainments, and liberation of sexuality from social constraints. On the other hand, consumption of food and wine does not seem to have altered. In contrast to the world of the Persian empire, Greek forms of commensality remained simple, and *tryphē* was expressed through elegance and refinement, rather than through exotic or excessive food and wine. Sympotic ritual and poetry have in general already been discussed; there remains the question of nonpoetic entertainment.

The arts of entertainment that developed in the sympotic context were often trivial, involving professional entertainers such as flutegirls, dancers, acrobats, mime artists, and comedians; by the classical age, impresarios existed with teams of entertainers, and training in the sympotic arts was available for attractive young slaves of either sex. The figure of the buffoon or *aklētos,* the uninvited guest, who earns his keep by entertainment is standard in sympotic literature.[16] A number of sympotic games are known from the archaic period, the most famous of which is *kottabos,* the flicking of wine dregs from one's cup at a target, claimed as a Sicilian invention. The toasting of fellow participants was also a common feature, responsible for the common inscription on many cups of a man's name with the adjective *kalos*. The *proposis,* or competitive challenge, was a feature that later attracted unfavorable comment from moralists, who contrasted the Athenian indulgence in such incentives to heavy drinking with their absence at Sparta. The competitive element is characteristic of such activities in the age of agonal man.

It is in the area of sexuality that Greek commensality had its most striking impact. Homosexuality was of course natural in the male world of the warrior group and was often institutionalized as part of the initiation rites that the young adult might be expected to undergo. There is a strong element of idealization and sublimation in the bonding created in the rituals of courtship between young male *erastēs* and adolescent *erōmenos,* who might (as in the Cretan rites) receive his formal introduction to the adult world of commensality through such a love affair. Until they attained full adult military status, boys were not permitted to recline at the *symposion,* but must sit by the side of their father or lover. The expression of homosexual love within the sympotic context is thus often idealized and concerned more with pursuit or competition than with conquest; it remains embedded within the framework of an *éducation sentimentale* and is directly connected with other areas of young adult life, such as the world of sport. In the terminology of Michel Foucault, it is "problematized," made to serve the wider needs of the community.[17]

The element of free sexuality derives from the presence at the archaic *symposion* of slave attendants and entertainers. The myth of Zeus and Ganymede expresses the traditional relationship between male participant and the boy who stands by the *kratēr* and pours out the wine. Naturally, the presence of two distinct forms of homosexual love in relation to free man and slave complicates our perception of the phenomenon; the characteristics of sexuality directed at slaves can therefore best be understood in relation to women.

Citizen women were never present at Greek *symposia;* there is no evidence to suggest that they even attended wedding feasts and funeral feasts, two areas with which women are traditionally closely connected. Their own gatherings were concerned with ritual festivals from which men were normally excluded or with the training of religious choruses. The only occasion where we glimpse a sort of female community, in the poetry of Sappho, is deeply problematic and seems to suggest a dependence on male forms of commensality.[18] Yet Aphrodite and Dionysus are the joint deities normally invoked, in sympotic poetry, from the earliest evidence of "Nestor's cup" in the eighth century. The women present at such occasions were slave girls; they were often trained as entertainers, dancers, acrobats, and musicians. Like the boys who also fulfilled these roles, they were chosen for their youth and beauty and seem often to have performed almost naked, and (like the boys) they often ended up on the couches. In the case of women (but not apparently boys), they could acquire a special status by being the constant companion of one or more men, in which case they were called *hetairai,* in ironical reference to the male *hetairoi,* or full members of the group. *Hetairai* were often possessed of a variety of entertainment skills and seem often to have been jointly owned by two or more men.[19]

It is these social practices that give archaic Greek love poetry its particular characteristics. On the one hand, there is the romantic intensity of a homosexual love that is personalized and usually directed toward a younger member of the same social class: it is represented as unfulfilled, concerned more with the pursuit of a pure ideal of beauty than with sexual satisfaction, capable of arousing the deepest emotions of love and jealousy. On the other hand, there is the unsocialized and carefree poetry of love for young girls as sexual objects, involving no complications, transient and easily satisfied, raising only regret for the passing of youth and intimations of mortality.

In such ways, the world of the *symposion* created an order separate from and outside the rules of the wider community, with its own alternative values. The ritual release of inhibitions through consumption of alcohol required its own rules designed to maintain a balance between order and disorder. A *symposiarchos* or *basileus* is often elected to control the mixing of wine; behavior is strictly regulated, and participants sing or speak in turn; each *kratēr* mixed is marked by a different character. As the comic poet Eubulus put it,

> Three *kratērs* only do I mix for the temperate—one for health, which they empty first, the second to love and pleasure, the third to sleep. When this is drunk up wise guests go home. The fourth *kratēr* is ours no longer, but belongs to *hybris,* the fifth to uproar, the sixth to drunken revel, the seventh to black eyes. The eighth is the policeman's, the ninth belongs to biliousness, and the tenth to madness and hurling the furniture. (Eubulus in Athenaeus 2.36)

The archaic poet is the sympotic legislator: much poetry is therefore metasympotic, concerned with proper or improper behavior in the *symposion* and prescriptive of rights and duties. The mere description of a *symposion* in Alcman is also prescriptive of the ordering of the ritual; Xenophanes similarly describes and advocates a model of sympotic ritual from which heroic poetry and talk of civil war are excluded in favor of praise of courage. The Theognidean corpus contains many passages devoted to proper behavior at the *symposion* and the proper relationships between participants, in which the bonds of love and of trust are especially emphasized. Greek monodic poetry is indeed a product of the *symposion* and presents a complex series of reflections on the varied forms of archaic sociality.

Trust and oath-taking are an important part of the transition from the internal activities of the *symposion* to activities outside. The question of whom to trust and the truth that is revealed in drinking are important themes in Theognis; Alcaeus' bands of *hetairoi* are sworn to a particular enterprise. The unity of the group is regarded as an absolute moral imperative: even in the fifth century to break trust is the equivalent of parricide, according to Andocides (1.51, 2.7).[20] One way of enforcing such bonds is through antisocial or even criminal activity designed as a *pistis,* a pledge of solidarity. These attitudes reflect the tensions between group and wider community.

Disorderly behavior within the group is in fact a preparation for the display of drunken behavior directed at the wider community in the ritual of the *kōmos.* At the end of the *symposion,* the garlanded participants often parade drunkenly through the streets, dancing in wild disarray, and deliberately insulting passers-by, inflicting violence and damaging property in a demonstration of social power and defiance of the community.[21]

Such attitudes could lead to repressive legislation on the part of the archaic *polis.* At Mytilene, for instance, the lawgiver decreed double penalties for offences committed when drunk; at Athens, Solon attacked the behavior of the wealthy and created in the law of *hybris* a public crime for acts intended to dishonor the victim, which reflects the sympotic world in its attention to the rights of women and even slaves. Other cities regulated the age for drinking.[22]

In these aristocratic rites of sociality, the gods of course play a role. The occasion may be part of a specifically religious event, for the *deipnon* is often preceded by a sacrifice, and it ends with a libation of unmixed wine to Agathos Daimon. The *symposion* itself begins with the distribution of wreaths to the guests; libations to Zeus Olympios, the heroes, and Zeus Soter; and a paean sung to the gods. During the proceedings, Dionysus and Aphrodite are the gods most often invoked by the drinkers. At the end, there should be a libation to Zeus Teleios. Yet despite this ritual presence, the gods remain in the background; the occasion is largely secular in function and discourse. Specifically, religious feasting belongs elsewhere.[23]

Religious commensality is concerned with the community as a whole: the festivals relate to the gods as protectors and guarantors of the community, and to the regulation of the order of the seasons on which it depends. Commensality in the religious sphere is a public activity, and its ordering corresponds to the ordering of society, in which the priests receive special portions as due to their office, but the members of the community are regarded as equal. Its increasing focus is therefore the *polis*.

Each rite of religious commensality is carefully differentiated to correspond to the signification of the particular cult. Two Spartan examples will show this. At the main Dorian festival of the Carnea at Sparta, nine "shades" or shelters were erected in which nine men feasted, with three "brotherhoods" or phratries represented in each shade. This arrangement reflects the original social organization into three tribes and subordinate phratries; it is a symbolic renewal of a pre-*polis* form of Spartan commensality, recalling the foundation of the community. Again, certain festivals at the old pre-Spartan center of Amyclae and elsewhere included a special meal for foreigners called a *kopis*. Beside the temple of Apollo, they built shelters with brushwood couches, on which any stranger could recline; all comers, both Spartan and stranger, were served with goat meat, round cakes, and other simple food. The exclusiveness of the civic ritual of Sparta is relaxed in a special religious context. Such multiple variations of the phenomenon of religious commensality could be illustrated from every city; the recall of real or imagined primitive rites and the problem of the hospitality of strangers are recurrent themes; some rites relate to a time of withdrawal from the city to a nearby shrine; those that take place within the city may be divided into occasions where the sacrificial meat must be consumed within the temple precinct and those where it is consumed elsewhere.[24]

The separation between aristocratic *symposion* and public festival was not complete. In particular, the aristocratic tyrants of the archaic age sought to intensify the element of luxury and display in their own sympotic lifestyle, and to develop new forms of public festival modeled on their conception of a heroic world. Thus Cleisthenes of Sicyon created a unique blend of *symposion* and aristocratic *agōn* with games and public feasting, in a contest for the hand of his daughter, which ended after a year with a sacrifice of a hundred oxen and a feast for the suitors *and all the Sicyonians* (Herodotus 6.126 ff.): the feasting of the suitors at least was in the form of a lavish *symposion*. Such interplay seems to have been common in the age of Pindar, who composed his victory odes for aristocratic athletes in relation to occasions that seem to have combined both public festival and private victory feast.[25]

Even those who wished to proclaim their rejection of the normal world of the *polis* did so by forming groups defined through different rites of commensality. Thus the Pythagoreans in the early fifth century developed a way of life based on separation from the community through complex food prohibitions and a communal life that began with a five-year rule of silence: their perverse conception of ritual purity "can be interpreted as a protest movement against the established *polis*. Their dietary taboos impeach the most elementary form of community, the community of the table; they reject the central ritual of traditional religion, the sacrificial meal."[26] Yet their rites in special meetinghouses are essentially inversions of accepted forms of commensality. For some time they exercised control in Croton, but in the end their fellow citizens took revenge by setting their meetinghouses on fire and massacring the members of the sect.

The religious experience focused on the *polis* is also one shared by Greeks in general, and transferred to the great intercity festivals developed in the archaic age, which were often connected with games (Olympia, Isthmia, Nemea) or with oracles (Delphi); they might seek to relate alleged natural groups like the Ionians (the Panionion at Priene, or Delos). But they all had a tendency through festival and sacrifice to result in the creation of a sense of "Greekness" (*to hellēnikon*), as the possession of "common blood, a common language, common centers for the gods, and common sacrifices and customs" (Herodotus 8.144).

Political Man

The forms of sociality distinctive of the classical period are developments and adaptations of earlier forms; it is mainly the social context that changes, and the relation between sociality and the *polis*. To classical man, in the words of Aristotle, "all forms of association (*koinōnia*) seem to be parts of the political association" (*Nicomachean Ethics* 8.1160a9). Yet even this politicization of social forms is not entirely new; and the difference lies more in the complexity of inter-relations between different types of association than in the subordi-nation of one type to any other.

The changing emphasis brings into prominence aspects of com-munal activity that are less visible in the archaic period, but neverthe-less important. The origins of political sociality have often been traced to the conception of the "common hearth." The cult of Hestia and the existence of a "common hearth" for the *polis* are widespread (perhaps universal) phenomena in Greece.[27] The city hearth is related to the existence of an eternal fire, and both offer a symbolic image of the political community as family group; just as a bride takes fire from her father's home to the new household, so colonists took fire from the mother city to their new foundation. This symbolism may well be one of the earliest signs of an emerging *polis* consciousness: fire and hearth are preserved in a sanctuary or public building and are directly under the control of the magistrates of the early aristocratic city, in contrast to other forms of city cult, which are administered by priesthoods belonging to hereditary groups. In Athens and often elsewhere, the "common hearth" was located in the *prytaneion,* the official building of the chief magistrate, the "eponymous archon."

A related function of the *prytaneion* was as the chief place of public commensality; the other archons also had such dining places, but these were of lesser importance. Here the archons, acting as rulers of the city, entertained the city's guests; the practice claims continuity from the earliest heroic style of commensality, in that the synoecism of Theseus involved the abolition of local *prytaneia* and the establish-ment of a central *prytaneion* in Athens. The institution is aristocratic; the ritual does not involve communal or even representative dining, but the honorific dining of an elite. Dining at the *prytaneion* is indeed the highest honor that the democratic city can bestow, and it is an honor to which no ordinary member of the *demos* can aspire. That is the force behind Socrates' ironical and insulting request on his con-viction that, instead of punishment, he should be offered free meals for life in the *prytaneion* (*Apology* 36).[28]

The right to dine permanently belongs in fact to a small elite of aristocratic type, defined by law; a fragmentary Athenian law of the mid fifth century lists those entitled as the priests of the Eleusinian mysteries, the two closest descendants of the tyrannicides Harmodius and Aristogeiton, those "chosen by Apollo," those who have won a major contest at the four great international games and (probably) the generals (*Inscriptiones Graecae* I³. 131); the archons would also have been present. In addition, an invitation to dine at the *prytaneion* was a form of *xenia* offered to foreign ambassadors, to returning Athenian embassies, and to those whom the city wished especially to honor. These privileges were extended and used more frequently in the fourth century and became part of the regular honors voted by the Assembly to benefactors of the city; for instance, those given citizenship were invited to dine at the *prytaneion,* and by the late fourth century, a permanent and sometimes even hereditary right of *sitēsis* might be granted.

The religious laws of classical Athens also contain a number of references to others with a right to *sitēsis* at the *prytaneion* or elsewhere; these are called by the technical term *parasitoi,* and seems often to be official assistants of the archons or of the priest of a particular religious cult; the *parasitoi* of the *archōn basileus* were chosen from the official demes of Attica; they were responsible for administering the tithes of barley and possessed a building of their own. The derogatory use of "parasite" derives in fact from this official usage and is a popular response to the traditional aristocratic practice of those on public business dining at public cost.²⁹ The aristocratic character of such forms of commensality is well brought out in one poetic quotation:

> Whenever the state honors Heracles sumptuously, celebrating sacrifices in all the demes, it has never appointed the *parasitoi* of the god for these sacrifices by lot, or chosen at random, but has always selected twelve men carefully from those citizens born of two citizen parents, who owned property and lived well. (Diodorus of Sinope in Athenaeus 6.239d)

The practice of dining at the *prytaneion* is an early institution of the aristocratic state, retained and developed in the classical period as part of a system of honors. But it was never a form of commensality shared by the political community as a whole, either directly or symbolically through the selection of representatives of the people. The one counterexample that is known, the dining at the *prytaneion* of the people of Naucratis on certain festivals (Athenaeus 4.149 f.), refers to an exceptional *polis,* created from existing separate communities. This type of commensality therefore represents an adaptation of aristocratic customs to the world of the *polis.* It finds its architectural expression in the formal and public *hestiatoria,* rows of rooms for sympotic dining found in city centers and at major sanctuaries such as Brauron from the mid sixth century onward: these are surely reserved for the official dining of an elite of magistrates, important guests, and priests.[30]

The Athenian state possessed another focus of public dining, which was truly democratic. Since the institution of an annual Council chosen by lot to prepare business for the Assembly, fifty *prytaneis* at any one time were on duty, and were provided with a kitchen and a dining room in the Tholos. This circular building is an unsuitable shape for the reclining banquet, and cannot have held the number of couches that would have been required; its architecture recalls the temporary *skias* or shelter for popular use at extramural sanctuaries, and suggests a class distinction between seated and reclining commensality. The Council members were provided with sacrificial portions of meat, but also with a cash subsistence allowance. It is characteristic that we lack any detailed information about this practical and nonhonorific form of commensality.[31]

The Athenian democratic state never developed universal rites of commensality such as those of Sparta. Nevertheless "the lawgivers . . . made rules for the dinners of tribes and demes and *thiasoi* and phratries and *orgeōnes*" (Athenaeus 5.186a): the details for the regulation of state festivals show the extent to which the Athenian people legislated to create a complex network of customs of commensality that expressed the sense of a political community united in religious ritual. Five main stages can be discerned in this process, though it is seldom possible to determine when particular practices were introduced. The laws of Solon in the early sixth century established rules for *prytaneion* and perhaps the Council, and for aristocratic private and religious feasting; already a wide range of associations were recognized:

> If a deme or *phratores* or *orgeōnes* or *gennētai* or drinking groups or funerary clubs or religious guilds or pirates or traders make rules amongst themselves, these shall be binding unless they are in conflict with the public laws. (quoted in Digest 47.22.4)

The activities of the tyrants in reorganizing some of the great Athenian cults, the Eleusinian mysteries, the Panathenaea, and the Dionysia will have had some effect on communal sacrifice and feasting. More important was the organization by Cleisthenes (508/7 B.C.) of a network of official local institutions, demes, and phratries, which regulated entry to the citizen body under the general supervision of the city, and which all had (or soon acquired) rites of commensality. At the end of the fifth century, the religious laws of Athens were codified for the first time by Nicomachus, and it is to this period that most of our surviving quotations from the laws concerning religious associations must belong.[32] Finally, the restoration of traditional religious customs associated with the conservative democratic statesman Lycurgus (338–322 B.C.) involved a financial and religious reorganization and extension of the major rituals of feasting.[33] As a result of this long process, the fusion between civic institutions and sociality expressed in religious feasting is almost complete, and all public and private social groups such as those mentioned in Solon's law even conduct their affairs on the model of the Assembly of Athens, with officials, proposals, and decrees about internal organization or in honor of "benefactors," and formal accounting procedures, often inscribed on stone, as if these groups were miniature cities within the city.

The great communal festivals of Athens illustrate the complexity of these relationships. One of the main liturgies, or periodic duties, of the wealthy Athenian was that of *hestiasis,* the provision of a feast for members of his tribe during the festivals of the Dionysia and the Panathenaea. It seems that the city sacrifice provided the meat for a grand distribution: as many as 240 cows were sacrificed at the Dionysia of 334/3 B.C. The distribution was organized by demes in the Cerameicus, perhaps in the vicinity of the Pompeion, at the city gates where the great processions started: here both formal dining rooms and signs of popular feasting have been discovered.[34] The liturgy of providing dinners for a tribe was probably part of this occasion, the city providing the meat, the rich man arranging the rest of the event. Similarly, at the women's festival of the Thesmophoria, two wives of rich men were chosen to preside and had to provide the food for feasts organized in the demes. Thus the people required the wealthy to provide ritual meals for that section of the citizenship to which they belonged, as part of their civic duty.

Equally, it was the duty of a rich man to entertain members of his deme at wedding feasts. But it was chiefly the phratry around which the rites of passage of the Athenian citizen were centered, in a series of feasts connected with the old Ionian festival of the Apaturia. Officials oversaw the feasting, and had the duty of providing some of the food; but the meat would have come from the sacrifices offered by fathers on behalf of their children. Three sacrificial occasions at the Apaturia mark the stages of transition of the young Athenian toward full adult status: the *meion* on his original introduction to the group, the *koureion* at puberty, and the *gamēlia* on marriage; each of these occasions is marked by a feast for fellow members of the phratry, and it is this public event that serves as proof of the legitimacy of the act. Here can be seen how rites and acts belonging originally to the kinship group have been transformed by the city into a universal practice and now serve as criteria for legitimacy and citizenship.

All these manipulations of commensality within democratic Athens are evidence of a long process of the politicization of customs of sociality based on food within the developed *polis;* they may be seen in part as the continuation of earlier customs, and in part as the civic dissemination of customs previously confined to particular classes or particular occasions.

Private commensality of course persisted, centered on the institution and rituals of the *symposion.* This continued to be viewed as part of an aristocratic lifestyle: Aristophanes portrays his populist hero Philocleon in the *Wasps* as ignorant of the correct forms of behavior at a *symposion,* having to be taught how to recline and make polite conversation, and finally taking an overenthusiastic part in the event, stealing the flute-girl and returning home pursued by irate citizens whose property he has damaged on his drunken *kōmos* (*Wasps* 1131– 1264, 1292–1449).

These aristocratic groups combined sympotic habits with political activities in political clubs, or *hetaireiai,* organized to "influence law cases and elections" (Thucydides 8.54); a democratic politician such as Pericles or Cleon, whose power lay in the Assembly, is portrayed as having avoided *symposia* because of their aristocratic political connotations. Plato describes the true philosophers:

> who from youth do not know the way to the agora or where the law courts or the Council house or any other public building are; they neither see nor hear the laws and decrees spoken or written; the enthusiasms of *hetaireiai* for office, their meetings and their feasts and their *kōmoi* with flute-girls do not occur to them even in dreams. (Plato *Theaetetus* 173d)

In the late fifth century, such *hetaireiai* became the basis for an oligarchic revolution, organizing street murders of opponents and supplying the leadership for an armed coup in 411 B.C. The development from elitist political activity within the law to *stasis* was assisted by the role of the *pistis,* or pledge of solidarity (discussed above). In

411 B.C., the murders of political opponents were described as a form
of *pistis*, and already in 415 B.C. the systematic smashing of the ithy-
phallic herms outside the homes of Athenians was assumed to be the
work of *hetaireiai* plotting revolution; the subsequent investigations
revealed a number of aristocratic groups committing deliberate sacrilege by performing the Eleusinian mysteries at *symposia*. The restored democracy of the fourth century not unnaturally formally
prohibited *hetaireiai* formed for the overthrow of the democracy (Demosthenes 46.26); and the citizen oaths of other cities contain an explicit promise, "I will not join in a conspiracy [*synomosia*]." At Athens
this was, however, an exceptional period: normally drunken assault
and minor sacrilege, such as urinating on wayside shrines or stealing
and eating the gods' share of sacrificial meat were the limits of sacrilege; some groups also engaged in parody of religious *thiasoi*, calling
themselves by obscene names, and meeting on days of ill omen.[35]

This abnormal activity reflects the normal activity of religious *thiasoi* and *orgeōnes*, private or semi-public associations for the worship
of individual gods, which had of course always existed and were already recognized in the Solonian law; in the classical age, they proliferated, together with the worship of minor heroes and foreign deities.
The central act of all such groups was the communal meal conducted
after a sacrifice, according to practices determined by each cult, but
usually involving *deipnon* and *symposion*. Aristotle describes the purposes of such sacrifices and gatherings as "honoring the gods and
providing relaxation and pleasure to themselves," and classifies them
as undertaken for the sake of pleasure (*Nicomachean Ethics* 8.1160a).
Other groups may be classified by function: the *eranos* was originally
a feast organized on the principle of shared contributions; it developed into an important institution for mutual help, lending money
to members without interest, and was often centered on a cult and
involved communal feasting. Similarly, burial groups ensured the
proper burial of members after death, but performed a social function
during life.

Death was indeed a problematic area. In general, commensality
does not reach beyond the grave, but so important were such rites in
life that some cults attempted to create for their adherents a belief in
an eternal *symposion*. Plato describes the Orphic doctrines:

> Leading them into Hades in their account, and laying them
> down and providing a *symposion* of the holy, they make
> them pass the whole of eternity crowned with garlands and

drunk, in the belief that the highest reward for virtue is an everlasting intoxication. (*Republic* 2.363)

The chief motive for initiation into the Eleusinian mysteries was indeed that it provided a guarantee of sympotic life after death. But such beliefs merely serve to emphasize the general separation between the social pleasures of life and their absence in death. Only heroes could escape this mortal fate, and in the Hellenistic age this became an important factor in the spread of the cult of the heroized dead.[36]

The self-conscious literary portrayal of commensality in the classical period tends to ignore the religious dimension, and concerns itself primarily with the social significance of the rite. The earliest attempt at writing memoirs, by Ion of Chios, gives a prominent place to the various great men he has met at *symposia,* and he judges their characters accordingly to their behavior. A favorite topic was already foreign customs, as a means of showing the "otherness" of barbarians (Herodotus; Euripides *Cyclops*), who do not understand the rules of civilized commensality. The customs of different Greek communities are analyzed by Critias as evidence of their moral character. These, together with the portrayal of *symposia* in archaic poetry, are the forerunners of that philosophical genre of the *Symposium* established by Plato and Xenophon in their portraits of Socrates. In these works, the rituals of sympotic discourse and sympotic behavior determine both the structure and the themes of the discussion. For even among philosophers, love (especially homosexual love) is the only proper subject for discussion in a *symposion;* and Plato, at least, shows, by his ability to evoke a mystical vision of the power of love, his understanding of the atmosphere of the *symposion.* Later in the *Laws,* he offers an equally deep understanding of the power of wine and commensality to influence men's souls to social ends.[37]

So it is that the personal relations of love and friendship are for the Greeks social phenomena. Aristotle defines friendship in terms of the social group, for "every form of friendship involves association"; he lists the friendship of kin and of comrades, that between citizens, members of the tribe, companions of voyage, and that expressed in ties of hospitality. Each of these involves association (*koinōnia*), and the *polis* is defined in the same terms, as itself a *koinōnia* that is composed of a network of *koinōniai* (*Nicomachean Ethics* 8.1261b). The life of man is bounded at all times by the ties of companionship, expressed in social rituals, often embodied in commensality, but also involving religion, sport, education, and war. In practical terms, the meaning of such a life is best described by a famous appeal made in 404 B.C., in time of civil war:

> Fellow citizens, why are you driving us out of the city? Why do you want to kill us? We have never done you any harm. We have shared with you in the most holy rites, in sacrifices, and in splendid festivals; we have danced in choruses with you and fought in the army with you, braving together with you the dangers of land and sea in defense of common safety and freedom. In the name of the gods of our fathers and mothers, of the bonds of kinship and marriage and companionship, which are shared by so many of us on either side, I beg you to feel shame before gods and men and cease to harm our fatherland. (Xenophon *Hellenica* 2.4.20–22)

In such a society, the freedom of the individual in our sense does not exist, for the individual is always considered as a social animal; he is never alone with his own soul. Yet there is a difference between those societies created around a unified conception of commensality, such as Sparta, and the complex world of Athens. As Aristotle says, criticizing the simplicities of the Platonic ideal of the community as a universal family:

> Which is the better way to use the word "mine," that each of two thousand or ten thousand people should mean the same by it, or rather as we use it in cities now, when the same person is called "my son" by one, "my brother" by another, "my nephew" by another, and so with other relationships of blood or affinity or marriage, the speaker's own in the first place or those of his relations; and as well someone else may call him "my clansmen or my tribesman"? (Aristotle *Politics* 2.126a8–13)

It is the concept of the individual that is lacking in Athens, not that of his freedom. For there is a personal freedom, an ability to "live as one wishes," that is part of the Athenian ideal: it consists in the freedom to choose between a multiplicity of overlapping social ties, and so to find an individual place for oneself through a form of "interstitial freedom." Yet it remains a socialized freedom, a freedom that results from the security of belonging in many places.[38]

Hellenistic Man

Two contrasting forms of social organization dominated the Hellenistic world and had their effect on the rituals of sociality. These were the court life of the successor kingdoms and their subordinate officials, and the transformation of earlier civic rituals in the exclusive colonial *polis* organization that spread over the whole extent of the former Persian empire from Afghanistan and north India to Egypt and north Africa.

Macedonian royal commensality, on which that of the successor kingdoms was based, reflected far older Greek traditions. In many respects, it resembles the Homeric world, and though it adopted many later Greek customs such as reclining, it was always conceived on a larger scale. The king and his companions were an aristocratic elite who dined together, often with many guests; food was more lavishly provided, and the Macedonians wee notoriously hard drinkers. Certain traditional practices reveal the manner in which they had adapted Greek customs, such as the rule that a man must have killed his boar in hunting before he could recline rather than sit (which reflects the common Greek distinction between adults and young boys), or the use of the trumpet to signal the end of the *deipnon* and the start of the *symposion*.[39] The arrangement of the dining hall for such grand occasions is unclear; many of the large buildings found in the Hellenistic period have features that suggest a set of almost independent reclining groups within a single hall. The problems of reconciling the Greek tradition of equality between participants with the realities of a royal court are exemplified by two contrasting anecdotal patterns: one emphasizes the tradition of "free speech" (*parrhēsia*) on the part of courtiers in the *symposion,* and the acceptance of a convivial equality on the part of the good king; the other describes quarrels, drunken brawls, and even murders perpetrated by the king in his royal anger, the corruption of power, and the impossibility of true companionship between unequals.

It is this style of entertainment that is characteristic of the Hellenistic court, doubtless with an admixture of Persian customs. The king and his officially designated "Friends" constituted a group who often dined together, and also gave lavish public displays of royal luxury; such luxury (*tryphēi*) became in Persian style a royal virtue. The festival occasions were true pageants; a long description of one survives, provided by Ptolemy Philadelphus in Alexandria (Athenaeus

5.196 ff.).[40] It included an extraordinary procession and a royal *symposion* held in a pavilion erected for the occasion, which is described as capable of holding 130 couches arranged in a circle. The building was decorated with paintings, hangings, works of art, and ornamental weapons characteristic of sympotic rooms; two hundred guests were arranged on a hundred gold couches, with two hundred gold tripod tables. The jewel-encrusted gold cups to be used were displayed on a special couch, and the total value of these objects is given as 10,000 silver talents (about 300,000 kilos). Unfortunately, the actual banquet is not described, nor the precise mode of distribution of the large quantities of wine and sacrificial animals displayed in the procession; but for all the element of marvel, the event is structured around the traditional rituals of Greek commensality. Other kings could not perhaps rival the wealth of the Ptolemies, but their own court life was modeled on the same sympotic style, and they, too, provided such festival displays.

In the private sphere, Athenaeus also describes the wedding feast of a rich Macedonian noble (4.128 ff.), again Greek in style, but with entertainments and presents of gold and silver utensils so lavish "that the guests are now looking for houses or land or slaves to buy." It is often asserted that gold and silver tableware was rare in the classical period and became common only with the Hellenistic age, and certainly the greater Macedonian access to gold and silver must have created different customs, especially after the conquests of Alexander had opened up the gold and silver reserves of the Persian empire. It has even been suggested that the decline of artistic standards in Greek painted pottery should be connected with such a change. But while it is true that in the classical Greek period precious metal was largely confined to religious uses, and luxury was more widespread later, the extent of change in the Hellenistic age should not be exaggerated. In the first century B.C., Juba of Mauretania asserted that "down to [and including] the Macedonian period people at dinner were served from pottery" (Athenaeus 6.229c), and the use of silver and gold was a recent Roman innovation.[41]

The new Greek cities of the Hellenistic age were colonial settlements in an indifferent and sometimes hostile native landscape; their institutions reflected a desire to maintain and strengthen their corporate and cultural identity. Whereas in the classical period, Greek man had found his true expression in political action and therefore tended to subordinate other forms of sociality to this aspect of the *polis,* to be a citizen in the Hellenistic period was to belong to a Hellenic cultural elite. Appropriate forms of sociality developed around this new cultural conception of citizenship, and the civic feast was remodeled as cultural experience.[42]

In this process, education was of central importance. Already in late-fourth-century Athens, access to the citizen body had been organized through a formal period of initiation, the *ephēbeia,* in which all male citizens between eighteen and twenty engaged in educational and military training under state officials. These *ephēboi* constituted age-classes that tended to perpetuate themselves in rituals of commensality. In Hellenistic cities, a formal education was provided at the *gymnasion* under a state official, the *gymnasiarchos.* The right to participate in this training was closely related to citizenship, so that, for instance, many of the disputes concerning the claims of Jewish communities to full citizenship within a Greek city are couched in terms of the right of access to the *gymnasion,* and the consequent problems of having to study non-Jewish literary texts and exercise naked. The institution of the *gymnasion* was standard over wide areas and long periods of time: the same set of 140 commandments of Delphic origin have been found in the *gymnasion* of Ai Khanum in Afghanistan, on the Aegean island of Thera, in Asia Minor, and in Egypt. Groups of *ephēboi* and *neoi* therefore proliferated in a nascent age-class structure, with a strong emphasis on such activities of youth as sport and hunting.

The liturgic system of the classical period also developed, as wealthy notables were encouraged by public honors to compete in public and religious office with acts of "euergetism" for the people. The most common evidence in this period for forms of sociality consists of a decree establishing a religious festival to be undertaken by a rich *euergetēs,* or a vote of honors for past benefactions. These acts of public benefaction are often similar to the duty of *sitēsis* required of the rich at Athens, in being related to holding particular offices or particular festivals; but they also developed further, as rich men sought to commemorate themselves by funerary and other benefactions involving periodic distributions to the people of food or oil, or a feast in memory of themselves.[43] Much of this activity took place in relation to the *gymnasion,* as well as other public spaces and sanctuaries. This phenomenon of euergetism does not imply a descent into a form of clientship, in which the poor are dependent on the rich, but is rather an expression of community of values, which is both expected and (at least in ideological terms) freely offered as a mediation of the economic divide that increasingly separated the rich notable from the ordinary citizen; public spirit, denied its place in politics, was expressed in a ritualized conspicuous expenditure on behalf of the community. Those who benefited from the donations could be an exclusive group of fellow officials, councilors, or priests; they could also be members of a subset of the citizen body, such as the benefactor's tribe. But very often it was the whole community who was offered free gifts or invited to a *dēmothoinia*. The restrictions on such generosity vary: sometimes it is all those taking part in a religious festival; sometimes it is all male citizens of the *polis*. Slaves are never explicitly included, and women receive only gifts, never invitations to dine. Normally, however, the invitation is open to "all": male citizens, resident aliens and visitors, and sometimes as a special category "Romans," that is, Italians. Such invitations express perfectly the claims of the *polis* to belong to a wider cultural community of the Hellenes, for the invitation is not in fact open to any non-Greeks except for the privileged category of Romans: although of course citizens of other Greek cities are welcome, the native peasantry is excluded. In this way, the new cities of the Greek world sought to create through cultural forms a sense of community that in earlier ages had existed naturally; to view such practices merely in terms of continuity is to ignore the novelty expressed in their universalization and in their changed function.

Associations based on economic activity existed in the Greek *polis* in all periods; but in contrast to the Roman world and the late medieval city, they do not seem to have been a significant element in the social structure: this perhaps reflects the low status of banausic activities and the subordination of the economy to politics. Occasionally, the cult activities of groups such as bronzeworkers and potters are mentioned, but it is not until the Roman period that such associations emerge into the public sphere. Earlier the importance of associations of skill is largely confined to those professional activities outside the civic structure; precisely because they were itinerant, doctors had possessed a cult of Asclepius, centers of training (especially Cos), a concept of themselves as a profession, and a "hippocratic oath" at least as early as the fifth century. The Hellenistic period saw the emergence of "the *technitai* of Dionysus," guilds of professional actors whose activities are found scattered throughout the Greek cities. This phenomenon, like the existence of organized groups of resident aliens from particular areas in Athens and elsewhere, is an expression, not of the structure of the *polis,* but of the need for social forms that transcend it. Similarly, groups of military origin, often with a specific national character, were a natural consequence of the employment of mercenaries from Campania and elsewhere, who might often be granted citizenship or impose themselves on the *polis.*[44]

The organization of learning followed the traditional pattern of cult organization with common property and fellowship through commensality. The old picture of philosophy in the Socratic age drawn by Plato, with public lectures and private meetings in the houses of the aristocracy or in the streets of Athens, gave way to more permanent establishments associated with *gymnasia* (the Academy of Plato), public buildings (the Stoa) or shrines (the Lyceum of Aristotle). The nucleus of each school was a group of friends sharing the use of a building for meetings and teaching, with property such as books held for common use, although actual ownership was vested in the head of the school; they conducted common sacrifices and ate together regularly. Similarly, the organization of learning established by Ptolemy Philadelphus in Alexandria, the Mouseion, was a group of scholars defined by their membership of a cult organization and their common life together within the palace complex, and at the royal table; this was the age of the scholarly *symposion* discussing questions of literary or philosophical import, until 145 B.C., when in exasperation Ptolemy VIII expelled the intellectuals from his court. The Garden of Epicurus provides the most interesting example of such communal life: his disciples lived together in the master's house, "escaping notice in their lives," holding a monthly feast on their master's birthday. Married women and former *hetairai* were members of the group, as well as male and female slaves. They were organized hierarchically like a mystic sect into three grades—teachers, assistants, and pupils. Thus although withdrawing from the world of the *polis,* the disciples of Epicurus could not escape its social forms of the common feast and the cult of the master as hero.[45]

That was achieved only by the Cynics, whose withdrawal involved an absolute rejection of all social constraints; their conception of the simple life, however, failed to achieve a new framework for the freedom of the individual because it was a mere negative image of the forms of sociality from which they sought escape. The most interesting philosophical work of the early Hellenistic period, the *Republic,* written in his "Cynic" phase by the founder of the Stoic school Zeno of Citium, expounds an ideal state in opposition to that of Plato's *Republic,* in which the wise man rejects the ties of the *polis* because he belongs, not to any real community, but to an ideal *cosmopolis* of the wise. Such responses reflect the difficulties of escaping from the ties of sociality that in all periods defined Greek man.

Notes

These notes are deliberately brief and are intended merely to refer the reader to the most authoritative or the most recent discussion. Detailed bibliographies for their respective topics may be found in Detienne and Vernant, *La cuisine du sacrifice* (1979) (by J.Svenbro); in Schmitt Pantel, *La cité au banquet* (1992); and in Murray, *Sympotica* (rev. ed. 1994).

1. Fustel de Coulanges, *La cité antique* (1864).
2. Jacob Burckhardt, *Griechische Kulturgeschichte* (1898–1902); the relevant paragraphs in section 9 (volume 4) remain the best account of Greek sociality (festivals and forms of commensality) known to me. For the *symposion* see also Von der Mühll, "Das griechische Symposion" (1957).
3. See for example Engels, *Origin of the Family* (1891); Veblen, *Theory of the Leisure Class* (1899); Sahlins, *Stone Age Economics* (1972).
4. Detienne and Vernant, *La cuisine du sacrifice,* (1979); Jameson, "Sacrifice and Animal Husbandry" (1988).
5. For the history of the study of Greek commensality see my introduction to Murray, *Sympotica* (1990).
6. On Homeric feasting and its social function see Finsler, "Das homerische Königtum" (1906); Jeanmaire, *Couroi et courètes* (1939), chap. 1; Murray, "The Symposion as Social Organization" (1983).
7. See Dentzer, "Aux origines du banquet couché" (1971), on origins; he supports a seventh-century date for the introduction of the custom to Greece, but I shall argue for an eighth-century date in "Nestor's Cup" (forthcoming, 1994).
8. For the concept of sympotic space see Bergquist, "Sympotic Space" (1990).
9. Lissarrague, *Un flot d'images* (1987).
10. Reitzenstein, *Epigramm und Skolion* (1893); Gentili, *Poesia e publolico nella Grecia antica* (1984).
11. Rösler, *Dichter und Gruppe* (1980).
12. Athenaeus 4.143, 11.782; Jeanmaire, *Couroi et courètes* (1939), chap. 6.
13. Athenaeus 4.138–42; Bielschowsky, "De Spartanorum Syssitiis" (1869); Nilsson, "Die Grundlagen des spartanischen Lebens" (1912); Murray, "War and the Symposion" (1991).
14. Bowie, "*Miles ludens?*" (1990).
15. Ampolo, "Su alcuni mutamenti sociale nel Lazio" (1970–71); D'Agostino, "Grecs et 'indigènes' sur la côte tyrrhénienne" (1977); Dietler, "Driven by Drink" (1990).

16. Ribbeck, "KOLAX" (1883); Fehr, "Entertainers at the *Symposion*" (1990); Pellizer, "A Morphology of Sympotic Entertainment" (1990).

17. Foucault, *L'usage des plaisirs* (1984).

18. Calame, "La fonction du choeur lyrique" (1977).

19. The best account of the life of a *hetaira* is the Demosthenic speech *Against Neaera* (59); see also Athenaeus, book 13.

20. See also below, n. 35.

21. Lissarrague, "Around the *Krater*" (1990).

22. Murray, "The Solonian Law of *Hybris*" (1990).

23. See Nilsson, "*Die Götter des Symposions*" (1932), for the *symposion;* for the religious festival, Gernet, "Frairies antiques" (1928); Goldstein, "The Setting of the Ritual Meal in Greek Sanctuaries" (1978).

24. Athenaeus 4.138–39; Bruit, "The Meal of the *Hyakinthua*" (1990).

25. Van Groningen, *Pindare au banquet* (1960).

26. Burkert, *Greek Religion* (1985), p. 303.

27. Gernet, "Sur le symbolisme politique" (1952); Malkin, *Religion and Colonization in Ancient Greece* (1987), chap. 3.

28. Miller, *The Prytaneion* (1978); Henry, "Entertainment in the Prytaneion" (1983).

29. See the learned discussion of *parasitos* in Athenaeus 6.234 ff.

30. Börker, "Festbankett und griechische Architektur" (1983).

31. Schmitt Pantel, "Les repas" (1980); Cooper and Morris, "Dining in Round Buildings" (1990).

32. See the speech of Lysias *Against Nicomachos* (30).

33. On the reforms of Lycurgus, see Schwenk, *Athens in the Age of Alexander* (1985); Humphreys, "Lycurgus of Butadae" (1985).

34. On civic commensality, see Schmitt Pantel, *La cité au banquet* (1992); on the Pompeion as "Festplatz," see Hoepfner, *Das Pompeion* (1976), pp. 16–23.

35. On Athenian clubs and their political role see especially Calhoun, *Athenian Clubs* (1913); Murray, "The Affair of the Mysteries" (1990).

36. On the alleged artistic motif of the *Totenmahl,* the critique of Dentzer, *Le motif du banquet couché* (1982), is fundamental; see also Murray, "Death and the Symposion" (1988).

37. For the literary genre of the *symposion* in philosophy and literature, see Martin, *Symposion* (1931); for Plato, see Tecusan, *Logos Sympotikos* (1990).

38. Discussion of the freedom of the individual in ancient Greece begins from Constant, "De la liberté des anciens" (1819).

39. For Macedonian *symposia,* see Tomlinson, "Ancient Macedonian Symposia" (1970); Borza, "The Symposium at Alexander's Court" (1983).

40. Studniczcka, *Das Symposion Ptolemaios II* (1914).

41. These brief remarks do not do justice to the wide-ranging controversy concerning the relationship between silver and pottery begun by Vickers, "Artful Crafts" (1985).

42. For this section, see especially Schmitt-Pantel, *La cité au banquet* (1992), part 3.

43. The importance of euergetism is the subject of Veyne, *Le pain et le cirque* (1976): see especially part 2. On euergetism and funerary cult, see Schmitt Pantel, "Evergétisme et mémoire du mort" (1982). The most extreme manifestation of this form of commensality is the royal cult instituted by King Antiochus of Commagene in the late first century B.C., which established a series of banquets on the tops of uninhabited mountains in honor of himself and his ancestors, to which all his subjects were bidden.

44. For professional associations, see Ziebarth, *Das griechische Vereinswesen* (1896), Poland, *Geschichte des griechischen Vereinswesens* (1909).

45. Epicurean friendship in practice and theory is discussed by Rist, *Epicurus* (1972), chaps. 1 and 7.

Bibliography

Ampolo, C. "Su alcuni mutamenti sociali nel Lazio tra l'VIII e il V secolo." *Dialoghi di archeologia* 4–5 (1970–71): 37–68.

Bergquist, B. "Sympotic Space: A Functional Aspect of Greek Dining-Rooms." In Murray, *Sympotica*, pp. 37–65. Oxford, 1990.

Bielschowsky, A. "De Spartanorum Syssitiis." Ph.D. diss., University of Breslau, 1869.

Börker, C. "Festbankett und griechische Architektur." *Xenia* (Constance) 4 (1983).

Borza, E. N. "The Symposium at Alexander's Court." In *Ancient Macedonia III: Papers Read at the Third International Symposium,* pp. 45–55. Institute for Balkan Studies, Thessaloniki, 1983.

Bowie, E. L. "*Miles ludens?* The Problem of Martial Exhortation in Early Greek Elegy." In Murray, *Sympotica*, pp. 221–29. Oxford, 1990.

Bruit, L. "The Meal at the *Hyakinthia:* Ritual Consumption and Offering." In Murray, *Sympotica,* pp. 162–74. Oxford, 1990.

Burckhardt, J. *Griechische Kulturgeschichte.* Berlin, 1898–1902.

Burkert, W. *Greek Religion, Archaic and Classical.* Oxford, 1985.

Calame, C. "La fonction du choeur lyrique." In *Les choeurs de jeunes filles en Grèce archaïque,* vol. 1, part 4, pp. 359–449. Rome, 1977.

Calhoun, G. M. *Athenian Clubs in Politics and Litigation.* Austin, 1913.

Constant, B. "De la liberté des anciens comparée à celle des modernes" (1819). In *De la liberté chez les modernes: Écrits politiques,* ed. M. Gauchet, pp. 491–515. Paris, 1980.

Cooper, F., and S. Morris. "Dining in Round Buildings." In Murray, *Sympotica* pp. 66–85. Oxford, 1990.

D'Agostino, B. "Grecs et 'indigènes' sur la côte tyrrhénienne au VII siècle: La transmission des idéologies entre élites sociales." *Annales E.S.C.* 32 (1977): 3–20.

Dentzer, J.-M. "Aux origines du banquet couché." *Revue archéologique,* 1971, 215–58.

———. *Le motif du banquet couché dans le Proche Orient et le monde grec du VIIème au IVième siècle.* Paris, 1982.

Detienne, M., and J.-P. Vernant. *La cuisine du sacrifice en pays grec.* Paris,

1979. English translation, *The Cuisine of Sacrifice among the Greeks* (Chicago, 1989).

Dietler, M. "Driven by Drink: The Role of Drinking in the Political Economy and the Case of Early Iron Age France." *Journal of Anthropological Archaeology* 9 (1990): 352–406.

Engels, F. *The Origin of the Family, Private Property and the State* (1884). In K. Marx and F. Engels, *Selected Works*, vol. 3, pp. 191–334. Moscow, 1970.

Fehr, B. "Entertainers at the *Symposion:* The *Akletoi* in the Archaic Period." In Murray *Sympotica*, pp. 185–95. Oxford, 1990.

Finsler, G. "Das homerische Königtum." *Neue Jahrbücher* 17 (1906): 313–36, 393–412.

Foucault, M. *L'usage des plaisirs*. Vol. 2 of *Histoire de la sexualité*. Paris, 1984. English translation, *The Use of Pleasure*, vol. 2, *The History of Sexuality* (New York, 1985).

Fustel de Coulanges, N. D. *La cité antique*. Paris, 1864. English translation, *The Ancient City*, ed. S. C. Humphreys and A. Momigliano (Baltimore, 1980).

Gentili, B. *Poesia e pubblico nella Grecia antica*. Rome and Bari, 1984. English translation, *Poetry and Its Public in Ancient Greece* (Baltimore, 1988).

Gernet, L. "Frairies antiques" (1928). In *Anthropologie de la Grèce antique*, pp. 21–61. Paris, 1968.

———. "Sur le symbolisme politique: Le Foyer commun" (1952). In *Anthropologie de la Grèce antique*, pp. 382–402. Paris, 1968.

Goldstein, M. S. "The Setting of the Ritual Meal in Greek Sanctuaries, 600–300 B.C." Ph.D. diss., University of California, Berkeley, 1980.

Henry, A. S. "Entertainment in the Prytaneion." In *Honours and Privileges in Athenian Decrees*, pp. 262–90. Hildesheim, 1983.

Hoepfner, W. *Das Pompeion und seine Nachfolgerbauten*. Berlin, 1976.

Humphreys, S. C. "Lycurgus of Butadae: An Athenian Aristocrat." In *The Craft of the Ancient Historian: Essays in Honor of Chester G. Starr*, ed. J. W. Eadie and J. Ober, pp. 199–252. 1985.

Jameson, M. H. "Sacrifice and Animal Husbandry in Classical Greece." In *Pastoral Economies in Classical Antiquity*, ed. C. R. Whittaker, pp. 87–119. *PCPS* Supplement 14. Cambridge, 1988.

Jeanmaire, H. *Couroi et courètes*. Lille, 1939.

Lissarrague, F. *Un flot d'images: Une esthétique du banquet grec*. Paris, 1987. English translation, *The Aesthetics of the Greek Banquet* (Princeton, 1990).

———. "Around the *Krater:* An Aspect of Banquet Imagery." In Murray, *Sympotica*, pp. 196–209. Oxford, 1990.

Malkin, I. *Religion and Colonization in Ancient Greece*. Leiden, 1987.

Martin, J. *Symposion: Die Geschichte einer literarischen Form*. Paderborn, 1931.

Miller, S. G. *The Prytaneion, Its Function and Architectural Form*. Berkeley, 1978.

Murray, O. "The Symposion as Social Organisation." In *The Greek Renaissance of the Eighth Century B.C.: Tradition and Innovation*, ed. R. Hägg, pp. 195–99. Stockholm, 1983.

————. "Death and the Symposion." *AION Arch. St. Ant.* 10 (1988): 239–57.

————. "The Affair of the Mysteries: Democracy and the Drinking Group." In Murray, *Sympotica,* pp. 149–61. Oxford, 1990.

————. "The Solonian Law of *Hybris.*" In *Nomos: Essays in Athenian Law, Politics, and Society,* ed. P. Cartledge, P. Millett, and S. Todd, pp. 139–45. Cambridge, 1990.

————. "War and the Symposium." In *Dining in a Classical Context,* ed. W. J. Slater, pp. 83–103. Ann Arbor, 1991.

————. "Nestor's Cup and the Origins of the Symposium." *AION Arch. St. Ant.* 16 (1994): forthcoming.

————, ed. *Sympotica: A Symposium on the Symposion.* Oxford, 1990; rev. ed. 1994.

Nilsson, M. P. "Die Grundlagen des spartanischen Lebens. 1, Altersklassen und Sysskenien" (1912). In *Opuscula Selecta* vol. 2, pp. 826–49. Lund, 1952.

————. "Die Götter des Symposions" (1932). In *Opuscula Selecta,* vol. 1, pp. 428–42. Lund, 1951.

Pellizer, E. "Outlines of a Morphology of Sympotic Entertainment." In Murray, *Sympotica,* pp. 177–84. Oxford, 1990.

Poland, F. *Geschichte des griechischen Vereinswesens.* Leipzig, 1909.

Reitzenstein, R. *Epigramm und Skolion.* Giessen, 1893.

Ribbeck, O. "KOLAX: Eine ethologische Studie." *Abh. Sächs. Gesellschaft d. Wiss.* (Leipzig) 9, no. 1 (1883).

Rist, J. M. *Epicurus: An Introduction.* Cambridge, 1972.

Rösler, W. *Dichter und Gruppe: Eine Untersuchung zu den Bedingungen und zur historischen Funktion früher griechischer Lyrik am Beispiel Alkaios.* Munich, 1980.

Sahlins, M. *Stone Age Economics.* London, 1972.

Schmitt Pantel, P. "Les repas au Prytanée et à la Tholos dans l'Athènes classique. *Sitesis, trophè, misthos:* Réflexions sur le mode de nourriture démocratique." *AION Arch. St. Ant.* 11 (1980): 55–68.

————. "Evergétisme et mémoire du mort: A propos des fondations de banquets publics dans les cités grecques à l'époque hellénistique et romaine." In *La Mort, Les Morts dans les sociétés anciennes,* ed. G. Gnoli and J.-P. Vernant, pp. 177–88. Cambridge and Paris, 1982.

————. *La cité au banquet: Histoire des repas publics dans les cités greccques.* Paris and Rome, 1992.

Schwenk, C. J. *Athens in the Age of Alexander: The Dated Laws and Decrees of the "Lykourgan Era" 339–322 B.C.* Chicago, 1985.

Studniczka, F. "Das Symposion Ptolemaios II nach der Beschreibung des Kallixeinos wieder hergestellt. *Abh. Sächs. Ges. d. Wiss.; Phil.-hist. Kl.* 30, no. 2 (1914): 118–73.

Tecusan, M. "*Logos Sympotikos:* Patterns of the Irrational in Philosophical Drinking. Plato outside the *Symposium.*" In Murray, *Sympotica,* pp. 238–60. Oxford, 1990.

Tomlinson, R. A. "Ancient Macedonian Symposia." In *Ancient Macedonia:*

Oswyn Murray

Papers Read at the First International Symposium, ed. B. Laourdas and C. Makaronas, pp. 308–15. Institute for Balkan Studies, Thessaloniki, 1970.

Van Groningen, B. A. *Pindare au banquet: Les fragments des scholies édités avec un commentaire critique et explicatif.* Leiden, 1960.

Veblen, T. *The Theory of the Leisure Class.* New York, 1899.

Vetta, M., ed. *Poesia e simposio nella Grecia antica: Guida storica e critica.* Rome and Bari, 1983.

Veyne, P. *Le pain et le cirque: Sociologie historique d'un pluralisme politique.* Paris, 1976. Abridged English translation, *Bread and Circuses* (London, 1990).

Vickers, M. "Artful Crafts: The Influence of Metalwork on Athenian Painted Pottery." *Journal of Hellenic Studies* 105 (1985): 108–28.

Von der Mühll, P. "Das griechische Symposion." In *Xenophon: Das Gastmahl.* Berlin, 1957. Reprinted in *Ausgewählte kleine Schriften,* ed. B. Wyss, pp. 483–505. Basle, 1975.

Ziebarth, E. *Das griechische Vereinswesen.* Leipzig, 1896.

CHAPTER EIGHT

The Greeks and Their Gods

Mario Vegetti

ARISTOTLE DESCRIBES HOW the wise old Heraclitus, "addressing those guests who had wished to visit him but who, upon entering and seeing him warm himself at the kitchen stove, had halted, invited them in without hesitation. 'Here too,' he said, 'there are gods.'" (*De partibus animalium* 1.5).[1]

Aristotle's anecdote is significant for a number of reasons and helps us to understand religious attitudes among the Greeks. First of all, it reveals the widespread nature of the experience of the "sacred," its closeness to the routines and places of daily life. The domestic hearth, for example, around which the family gathered to cook and eat, was dedicated to the goddess Hestia, who protected the prosperity and continuity of family life. Each newborn child was carried around the hearth in order to mark its entry into the domestic space in a religious sense as well.

In Heraclitus' comment, this diffusion of the sacred is extended into a familiar relationship with the gods that characterizes much of Greek religious experience. The gods are not distant and inaccessible. On the contrary, their presence might be said to mark every significant moment of private and public life. They are encountered so often, in images, in the religious practices dedicated to their honor, and in domestic and public storytelling whose densely interwoven plots symbolize the meaning of life, that the question of whether or not the Greeks believed in their gods seems out of place. It would make more sense to ask how anyone could fail to believe in the gods, since such a failure would negate a large part of daily experience.

The widespread nature of the sacred and a general sense of familiarity with the gods are two elements present in Aristotle's anecdote. A third feature might be added, specifically regarding the intellectual approach of philosophers toward the sphere of the divine. This became increasingly identified as the principle and guarantor of order and regularity, as something that provided the natural world with its sense (Aristotle quotes Heraclitus' comment in order to give legitimacy to the theoretical study of nature, a clearly less noble sphere than that of the heavens, which was closer to the gods, yet nonetheless also governed by laws of order and value, and therefore equally "filled with the gods"). At least in its basic assumptions, this philosophical approach does not contradict the nature of everyday religious experience. It does, however, extend it by creating a new concept that transforms the familiarity of the divine into that of the inherent order of the world.

We shall be analyzing these features of Greek religious experience more closely below. However, in order to understand its fundamental and apparently contradictory character—that of being an all-pervasive and ever-present experience and yet, at the same time, something that had little psychological or social "weight"—we must begin by establishing more clearly exactly what Greek religion was not.

A Religion without Dogmas or Churches

In the first place, it was not founded upon a "positive" revelation conceded to the human race by the gods. Unlike the great monotheistic religions of the Mediterranean, it had no founding prophet or sacred book that expressed revealed truth and constituted the basis for a theological system. This absence of the Book led to the parallel absence of a group of specialized interpreters. Greece never had a permanent professional caste of priests (in principle, priestly functions were open to all citizens, usually for short periods of time). Nor did it ever possess a unified church, in the sense of a separate hierarchy with the right to interpret religious truths and to officiate at services. Finally, the Greeks had no compulsory dogmas to observe, whose transgression would lead to charges of heresy or impiety.

This system of absences extends into a particular, yet meaningful, silence. In the whole body of beliefs and narratives that deal with the gods, those referring to the creation of the world and of human beings play anything but a central role. In fact, with the exception of certain marginal and sectarian contexts, they do not even exist. In everyday experience, therefore, the gods and men had always lived together. Equally, there is no idea (apart from in the exceptional cases mentioned above) of an "original sin" from which people must somehow be saved. Unless they became blameworthy through a specific act, the Greeks were normally "pure" and, as such, were given free access to all sacred functions. The question of the soul's survival and of life after death was also regarded as marginal, at least at the level of civil religion, although it tended to emerge in the context of the mystery and initiatory cults, as we shall see.

These absences make it difficult to speak of Greek "religion," at least in the positive sense in which the term is used in the context of monotheistic tradition. The Greek language does not even possess a term whose semantic field coincides with that of the word "religion." [1] The nearest term, *eusebeia,* is defined by the priest Euthyphro in the Platonic dialogue named after him as "the care (*therapeia*) that men have of the gods" (Plato *Euthyphro* 12e). In this sense, the term covers the punctual observance of services in order to express respect toward the gods, during which proper signs of homage and deference are displayed. These services usually took the form of votive and sacrificial offerings. The Greek equivalent of the word "faith" is equally weak. In everyday language, the expression "to believe in the gods" (*nomizein tous theous*) does not indicate a rational conviction of their existence (as it will come to do in a more developed philosophical language), but "to respect" or honor the gods by performing certain acts. *Nomizein* thus comes to mean the same as *therapeuein:* to devote the appropriate ritual care to the gods.

The nucleus of the relationship between the human and divine spheres, between "religion" and "faith" in the Greek world, thus appears to consist in the observance of those services and rites prescribed by tradition. This does not mean, however, that daily life was pervaded by an obsessive concern with ritual. The sarcastic portrait of superstition (*deisidaimonia*) painted by the philosopher Theophrastus in his *Characters,* written at the end of the fourth century B.C., probably reflected a widespread attitude: superstitious people live with the constant fear of divine power and devote an absurdly large part of their existence to attempts to ingratiate themselves with the gods by performing rites, by manically trying to avoid impiety, and by purifying themselves of sin. This, of course, is the description of a theatrical "character." Theophrastus' satire leaves us in no doubt that an obsession with ritual was neither widespread nor regarded with favor in the context of Greek religious attitudes. This naturally does not mean that people were not profoundly afraid of the gods' ability to punish their sins throughout their own lives and that of their descendants. Such a fear is evident in all Greek cultural experience during the fifth century B.C. In the subsequent period, Epicurus, a philosopher who was more or less the contemporary of Theophrastus, thought that if philosophy was to restore serenity to the lives of men and women, one of its main duties was to free them from the fear of divine punishment.

Taken as a whole, the complexity of these attitudes can be seen in an ingenuous anecdote told by Herodotus. The anecdote was written in the fifth century B.C. but refers to the Athenian tyrant Peisistratus (middle of the sixth century). Herodotus describes a strategem invented by Peisistratus to reacquire the power he had lost in Athens: after disguising a girl in the clothes and armor of the goddess Athena, he sent her in a chariot toward the Acropolis, preceded by heralds who invited the people to take the tyrant back, conducted as he was by the very goddess who protected the *polis*. This cunning strategem was successful, and Herodotus expresses surprise at the Athenians' ingenuousness since, even more than other Greeks, "they were considered to be sharper and less gullible than the barbarians" (1.60).

This anecdote can be read in two ways. On the one hand, the Greeks' familiarity with their gods, as well as the daily contact they had with their images, explains how the Athenians could have "believed" in the appearance of Athena at the head of Peisistratus' retinue. There was no reason to doubt the evidence before their eyes or, at least, no reason to question the appearance of the goddess among themselves. But there is another aspect of the tale, which underlines the "lightness" of this belief and confirms the habitual gullibility that Herodotus attributes to the Greeks. The very familiarity that allowed people to "believe" also allowed Peisistratus and his followers to hatch their plot, imitating the goddess without fear of sacrilege or divine vengeance. The gods were too close to the people; the relationship that existed between them could inevitably be transformed into an instrument of play, deceit, and trickery. Credulity or incredulity, fear of the divine or a mood of relaxed indifference, are thus closely intertwined in Greek religious attitudes. Too much stress placed on one or other of these aspects would lead to serious misunderstanding.

The specific character of this approach can only be explained by returning to the birth of the sacred in Greek cultural tradition, a tradition that is, in certain respects, unparalleled.

The Sacred

Hieros, "the sacred," is a Greek word that might be related to an Indo-European root meaning "strong." The Greek experience of the sacred in general (similar, in this sense, to that of many other cultures) probably derived from a sense of the presence of supernatural forces in mysterious places (forests, springs, caves, mountains), in frightening or inexplicable natural phenomena (lightning, storms), and in crucial moments during life (birth, death). This primary experience later developed in two divergent, although not contrasting, directions. On the one hand, the "sacred" became attached to certain "powerful" places marked by precise boundaries, in which the supernatural could be felt. These places, which then became the focus of a cult that worshiped the forces found there, gradually turned into sanctuaries (*temenoi*), sometimes with temples dedicated to actual gods and, at other times, marking the boundaries of other places of worship (for example, the nymphs associated with springs, or the tombs of the "heroes": often Mycenaean burial sites that became talismans ensuring the prosperity of families or communities, such as the legendary "tomb of Oedipus" in the Athenian suburb of Colonus). The creation of boundaries around sacred places led to a series of restrictions and prohibitions that protected everything within them—most commonly whatever housed the sacred image, but also votive offerings to the gods and to their priests—from profanation or abuse. As an extension of this, "the sacred" therefore referred to everything that lay within the boundaries of the cult or that was dedicated to it, such as sacrificial victims, traditional rituals, and those who performed these rituals. This territorial marking out of the sacred, however, never assumed the form of taboo in Greece, as it did in other places. Prohibitions never excluded contact with people. On the contrary, they structured contact since the sacred depended on the existence of a collective cult. Because of this, the respect that underpinned the sacred in Greece was never transformed into the blind dumb terror that accompanied it in other cultures.

On the other hand, "the sacred" had a widespread and extended significance for the Greeks, describing everything that emanated from the supernatural powers and, more specifically, from the divine will. The natural order, the passing of the seasons, the harvest, day and night, were all seen as sacred, as were the immutable order of social custom, the following on of generation after generation ensured by marriage, birth, burial rites and veneration of the dead, the permanence of political communities and systems of power.

In both senses, therefore, the sacred was experienced essentially as power, or as a group of powers, intervening in the processes of nature and of life. Its intervention could be beneficent, a source of harmony and of natural or social order. Equally inscrutably, it might be disturbing, violent, or destructive, expressing itself through storm, death, or illness (the Greek language continues to refer to epilepsy, the most incomprehensible and upsetting of all illnesses, as "sacred"). It was natural, therefore, to attempt to propitiate the beneficent aspects of this supernatural power and to ward off its negative violence. This explains why the priest Euthyphro describes religious behavior as "servants caring for their masters" (Plato *Euthyphro* 13d). The propitiatory rite—an individual and collective act whose success depended on its being performed correctly, according to a traditional procedure presumed to please the god to whom it was addressed—consisted primarily in votive offerings accompanied by invocation and prayer. For the Greeks, these offerings included valuable objects, libations, and prestigious religious buildings. At the heart of the rite, however, was food, in the form of the sacrificial animal. As we shall see, the sacrifice assumed different forms, depending on the god and the social class of the sacrificer. In all cases, however, it expressed the renunciation by a group of people of one of its most highly valued foods. By offering it to the gods with "care," it was hoped that the sacrificers would then be treated with divine benevolence.

The success of the rite, it must be stressed, depended primarily on the fact that it was carried out according to tradition. The Greek calendar, therefore, above all at the beginning, was essentially a collection of rules concerning rites, and the names of the months would continue to refer to the religious ceremonies to be performed during that period of the year. The ritual event, in which the positive relationship between people and the gods was celebrated and ensured, was naturally a high point in the civil lives of human beings, a moment in which they celebrated the existence of their community. It was thus accompanied by the most significant events in Greek civilization, from banquets, dances, and the games to processions and theatrical events.

The rite, particularly when it involved sacrifice, thus guaranteed a harmonious relationship between the divine and the human sphere. This relationship, however, could also be disturbed and changed.

It was possible for people to invade sacred spaces, violate their privileges, and break the divine laws that regulated the social order. An example of this occurs in the *Iliad*, when the Greeks reduce to slavery the daughter of one of Apollo's priests, Chryseis, consecrated to the god at birth and thus part of his property. Another example is that of Oedipus' patricide, staining himself with the blood of his father, Laius. A historical example occurs when the family of the Alcmeonidai put to death Cylon and his followers, who had taken refuge in the temple of Athena (Herodotus 5.71). These are all cases of "pollution" (*miasma*). Pollution also occurs whenever a sacred vow is broken, human blood is spilled, and ritual laws are not respected. It is a sin that goes beyond the ordinary legal and moral limits and brings down divine vengeance on the head of the guilty person, spreading out to affect the whole community (the acts of Agamemnon and Oedipus bring plague to the Greek army and the city of Thebes in their entirety) and passing inexorably from one generation to the next, as can be seen in the ill-fated and tragic houses of Labdacus and Atreus. The idea of *miasma* probably has a concrete origin, representing the filthy, soiled state of someone who lives outside the standards of his or her community. In its most powerful sense, it refers to the bloodstained hands of the murderer or the sores of someone who might be seen as the victim of divine punishment. The original sense of actual dirt or stain was naturally transformed with time into a moral metaphor, representing "guilt" and the "curse" of the gods. Whoever was affected by such a curse was excluded not only from sacred ritual but also from the community, which risked contagion. An echo of this can be found in the ancient ritual of the *pharmakos,* which undoubtedly derives from oriental culture. Each year the community selected one of its marginalized members, afflicted by a mental or physical handicap, and banished him from the city. The victim was led in procession to the city gates, to be expelled with all the other instances of pollution that might be present within the community (a literary echo of this ritual can certainly be seen in the banishment of Oedipus, the incestuous and patricidal king, from the city of Thebes, the final scene in Sophocles' *Oedipus Rex*).

The origin of the concept of pollution is thus concrete. Equally concrete is the ritual form taken by the process of purification (*katharsis*). Essentially this involved washing with water (or, more rarely, fumigation). It was intended to restore the cleanliness and purity required by his or her society to someone who was soiled and impure. Purifying ablutions were performed whenever potentially polluting events such as birth, death, sex, and illness were encountered, even when no blame was involved. In the ninth book of the *Laws*, Plato prescribes the ritual also in cases of involuntary or legitimate homicide. People had to cleanse themselves between a sexual act and a religious one, and houses in which a birth or a death had taken place also had to be purified. In the case of the most serious *miasma,* the rite was carried out following the precepts of the priest of Apollo, the god associated above all others with purification (*kathartēs*).

In the religious and moral consciousness of the sects, which would later, as we shall see, influence philosophical thinking, the idea of purification developed alongside the idea of polluting guilt as a condition of human existence. The process of living itself was thus seen as a gradual purification from the body, so that the spiritual element, the soul, could finally be released from its earthly bonds. This extreme concept of *miasma* and *katharsis,* however, was the prerogative of religious minorities and peripheral, albeit influential, intellectual groups. It never became part of the mainstream of Greek religion.

The Gods, the Poets, and the City

The characteristics described above are not specific to Greek culture since they can be found in similar form in the religious experience of other traditional cultures. Nor can they be considered to constitute a genuine religious universe. Two cultural factors are responsible for unifying Greek religious experience and for making it specific. The first factor is epic poetry (in which Homer's *Iliad* and Hesiod's *Theogony* play a decisive role); the second is figurative representation, which, in this context, represents an iconographic supplement to the poetry.

The epic clearly grows out of the traditional mythical accounts of those gods and supernatural forces that inhabit and control the world.

These accounts, anonymous, widespread, and handed down from generation to generation, constitute a vast catalogue of religious imagery. Taken as a whole, they represent their society's knowledge of the gods. They are instantly believable, persuasive, and unquestionable precisely because of their anonymity, the fact that they can be found over wide stretches of space and time, and finally, their immense antiquity. But these characteristics also mean that the polytheism that emerges from the tangled web of myth is chaotic, confused, and without any evident form that can be comprehended or controlled. The most significant effect of epic poetry—primarily the *Iliad,* although Mycenaean precedents probably existed—was to select and organize this material. It gave the divine sphere the impression of an organic, visible form that would mark it indelibly from that point on. The way in which functional and power relations in the *Iliad* organize the anthropomorphic polytheism of myth is thus the sign of an extraordinary intellectual revolution, which welded Greek religion into its final historic form. Epic poetry, however, maintained and even, with its literary grandeur, reinforced the basic character of the mythical accounts. They remain, in other words, a narrative that describes the deeds and gestures of the gods, identifying the places in which they took place, defining the protagonists as individuals with names, personalities, and specific features. Rather than metaphysical abstractions, concepts, or even totemic figures, they thus become narrated characters. By the time Hesiod attempts to impose more order on Homer's religious universe by producing, in his *Theogony,* the first and only Greek religious "manual," he has no choice other than to build on this basic experience. Relationships between these god-characters are therefore based, not on theological concepts, but on the order of succeeding generations and shifts in power, an order that is created as living, acting individuals relate to one another.

The founding gesture of the epic, its shaping of the divine sphere in the form of an anthropomorphic narrative, must be seen in connection with aristocratic Greek culture and its determined attempts to colonize Asia Minor. This aristocracy made use of the epic to celebrate itself, its origins, and its heroes and to provide its gods with a form by projecting its own image. Snell has written that these gods do not derive from worship or priestly teaching but that "they are created through song, along with the heroes."

The projective element in epic poetry's creation of a divine universe, in the context of a heroic aristocracy, enduringly defines its imagined characters. The gods are represented as heroes at the absolute limits of excellence (*aretē*) for beauty, strength, intelligence, and in order that these gifts should continue to flourish, immortality. This naturally means that they must transcend the human condition, crossing a threshold that separates gods and heroes even more decisively than that which separates the latter from the rest of mankind.

This threshold is due to the fact that the poetic imagination producing the Homeric gods is itself the result of projection. It is constantly being crossed by the very intellectual gesture that created it. The act that produces the divine universe remains "artistic" and thus, to some degree, "artificial." Its reassuringly aesthetic origin establishes a mirrorlike relationship between the mortal nature of the aristocratic hero and the immortality of his gods. The threshold is crossed in the first place by genealogy, which ensures that the aristocratic families are the result of recurring unions between gods and goddesses and their mortal ancestors. This is followed by the constant presence of bonds linking the gods to human beings, with whom they are in constant contact. They are bound by family ties, affection, aversion, and if nothing else, the shared need to receive those honors to which they are entitled as all-powerful lords. As a result, the worlds of gods and men are constantly interweaving and overlapping; this is the salient feature of both the *Iliad* and the religious imagination of the Greek world that it produced. It is also the source of the Greeks' familiarity with their gods and of the way in which specifically human emotions are attributed to them. Gods can wound, and be wounded by, heroes on the battlefield. They experience love, jealousy, envy, and all those passions that rightly belong to human beings. This means that although the gods can be feared for their power, they can also be seen with the irony and sometimes even sarcasm that one might use in judging human weakness. It is for this reason that the *Iliad,* the founding poem of an entire religious universe, can also be defined, paradoxically but not mistakenly, as "the most irreligious of all poems" (Paul Mazon).

Plato was quite aware of this when, in the third book of the *Republic,* he deplored the fact that Homer portrayed the gods as victims of laughter, tears, and sexual desire: "We must stop telling such tales. We run the risk that they might encourage our young men to commit evil lightly" (391e ff.) Plato the educator thus proposed the amending of those pages of the epic that dealt with religion or, even better, the banning of Homer and his followers, with all their dangerous poetry, from the new *polis* (*Republic* 10). But Plato's program was never realized, and the religious experience of the Greeks continued to be modeled on those epic poems that lay at the roots of their culture.

Anthropomorphic polytheism, in which the deity is seen primarily as an actual character in a story, made visible by means of narrative, produces a series of significant consequences. On the one hand, it rules out the omnipotence and, in a sense, omniscience of both single gods and their king, Zeus. The existence of omnipotence clearly excludes the possibility of narrative, which requires a plurality of agents whose deeds and intentions act upon one another to produce the events of the story. Despite being the most powerful of the gods, Zeus was unable to decide immediately and independently the outcome of the Trojan War. He was forced to overcome opposition, make compromises, and work out complex plans.

On the other hand, it is clear that what distinguishes gods from men is essentially their power. They are by far "the stronger." This is the result of two factors: the primary experience of the existence of supernatural powers at work in the world, and the poetic act of representing the divine by projecting heroic qualities to their absolute limits. The gods are distinguished by the specific realm in which they exert their power, even though, as actual characters rather than abstract concepts, they are normally figures possessing a variety of functions, whose powers extend into many different areas, interweaving and overlapping. As a whole, as Dumézil has commented of the Greek religious imagination, "the relations that are formed between concepts, images, and actions create a kind of network into which, in theory, the entire stuff of human experience can be absorbed and distributed."

This plurality of functions is expressed in the many specific names that accompany the primary name of each of the gods, invoking their presence in relation to the different fields in which they exercise power and offer protection. Thus, we have a Zeus of vows, a Zeus of borders, a Zeus protector of suppliants and guests, a Zeus of rainstorms and thunder. Behind this plurality of functions, however, the figure of the god maintains his unity and individuality, which does not derive from his place in a theological system but from a narrative that identifies him as a character. (There are, however, exceptions to this whenever the name of an Olympian god is superimposed on a preexisting deity who resists identification. This can be seen in the case of Artemis, the virgin hunter of the poets who was also linked, at Ephesus, for example, to the eastern cult of the Mother Goddess.)

This unity can be briefly shown by considering the twelve most important Olympians. Zeus is the principle of legal sovereignty, uniting strength and justice in his own person and acting as the universal guarantor for natural and social order by virtue of his power. This, in fact, is the reason for Zeus' power, which does not derive from his birth but was acquired by a series of heroic acts. According to the genealogy of Hesiod (eighth–seventh century B.C.), Zeus brought an end to a dynasty of dark chaotic gods, whose last representative, Cronus, the father of Zeus, devoured his children. Rescued from his father's wrath by the cunning of his mother, Rhea, Zeus later deposed his father to become ruler of the gods himself. The new Olympian dynasty finally established its power when Zeus won the war against such primitive chthonic deities as the Titans, bound to the chaotic world of Cronus. With Zeus' ascension a clear distinction was finally made between earth and sky, light and shade, and the harmonious succession of generations was ensured. His wife, Hera, as the representative of legal marriage and of the family, a union that created legitimate descendants, is linked to the very existence of human society and civilization. Her presence ensures that it will never relapse into the disordered wildness of the natural state.

The brother of Zeus, Poseidon, is an ancient and powerful deity of evident Mycenaean origins. In the Homeric universe, his role is, to a certain extent, marginalized. Zeus is lord of the heavens and of the earth, while Poseidon is left with the depths of the sea and whatever lies beneath the earth. Poseidon was a greatly feared god and, as the protector of sailors, remained closely linked to this fundamental aspect of Greek life.

Zeus' favorite among his children was Athena. Born directly from his own body without female intervention, she represented the principle of patriarchy, insofar as such a male principle could be shared by a woman. In this sense, Athena is the repository of that practical intelligence that governs both the work of artisans and the typically female skill of weaving. Normally represented in hoplite armor, Athena is also *promachos,* a guide and armed protector. It is in this double role that she protects the fate of the Athenian *polis,* as a result of which she is particularly venerated (many cities, in fact, had patron goddesses, such as Hera at Samos and Artemis at Ephesus; this can also be explained by their maternal role as food-providers, guaranteeing fertility and prosperity to the city's people, alongside their other function as armed protectors).

Among Zeus' other children, Apollo had an extraordinary position. The great sun god and, originally, warrior, Apollo became increasingly the god of light, a healer and purifier. Endowed with the supreme gift of wisdom, Apollo could foresee the future and thus presided over the great oracular sanctuaries, such as that of Delphi. Linked to music and poetry, the essential cultural elements of Greek civilization, and guarantor of harmony, beauty, and the aesthetically defined order of the world, Apollo was considered, more than any other deity, the "philosophical" god. As a result, his prestige sometimes even eclipsed that of Zeus during the historical epoch.

At the opposite pole from Apollo was another important and ancient Greek deity (to whom the Greeks themselves attributed an eastern origin), Dionysus. The god of wine, Dionysus was linked to the experience of drunkenness, delirium, and madness. He controlled the dark region that preceded the ordered existence of civilization in which bonds are established between people, animals, and nature. His worship, which favored woods and mountains and attracted women and foreigners, was often regarded as subversive when compared to the order represented by the *polis*. Although he played a marginal role in epic poetry, where the heroic image of the gods prevails, Dionysus became the divine protector of tragic verse. He was often seen in contrast to the harmony and order associated with Apollo, as the figure of the Other—the other side of the sacred, disturbing and elusive rather than stable and regular. Nonetheless, Greek religious experience did all it could to integrate these two aspects without conflict. In the same sanctuary at Delphi, Dionysus was venerated alongside Apollo, as though they were brothers. In the religious life of the Greek city, Dionysus had his own specific role during festivals, in the carnival-like moments devoted to wine, and above all during theater festivals, whose function was to render the Dionysiac Other and the dimension of experience it represented comprehensible and acceptable to the social order.

Three goddesses and three gods complete the Greek pantheon. Artemis, Apollo's twin sister, is a virgin goddess, linked to spaces outside the city, such as the woods in which she loves to hunt with her bow and arrow, in contrast to Athena, armed as a hoplite at the city's heart. Artemis is connected to women's worship, presiding over the rites of girls during their passage from virginity to marriage, and protecting birth.

Aphrodite, the goddess of sex and generation, and probably related to eastern fertility goddesses, was very different. Connected to the experience of erotic desire (she was, in fact, the mother of Eros), Aphrodite remains outside the area of the family and marriage. Bound as she is to the uncontrollable and primordial dimension of sexuality, she represents in a sense the opposite pole to that of reproduction within marriage represented by Hera.

As the goddess of the earth's fertility and natural cycles, Demeter can be linked to Dionysus. Her realm, however, is not that of wine but of the cultivation of cereals. She is thus connected to the very origins of agricultural civilization. The story of Persephone—the daughter of Demeter who was kidnapped by Hades and taken to the underworld, the shadowy realm of death, later to be restored to the light of the sun each spring by her mother—celebrates the seasonal nature of sowing and harvesting, but also, more generally, the birth–death cycle. Because of this, Demeter is particularly closely linked to women's worship. The adventure of Demeter and Persephone also grants them, as we shall see, a central role in the Eleusinian mysteries.

One of the three male deities is the very unusual god Hermes, who plays the part of the messenger and traveler. The god of movement, connected to roads and open spaces, Hermes also represents the link between the worlds of the living and the dead since it is his task to conduct the souls of the dead to the beyond. His skills in the field of bargaining and making contact, combined with his ability to travel, make him one of the first gods of both commerce and culture, seen as the art of communication and understanding among men.

His opposite is Hephaestus, the god of crafts, connected to the enclosed spaces of the workshop and fire of the smithy. Hephaestus expresses the transforming and creative power of the maker. Although Hephaestus was often linked to Athena among artisans' cults, his real wife was Aphrodite, a union that brought together the sexual reproductivity of nature and the artificial productivity of the craftsman. Aphrodite, however, ignores her marital bond, neglecting the hardworking Hephaestus for the destructive primordial forces of Ares, the god of war. The much-feared deity of the battlefield, Ares was closely linked to the heroic values of Homer's warriors: rage and an uncontrollable homicidal urge.

The Greek pantheon naturally included many other deities apart from the twelve most important gods. Some of these minor gods are very ancient, such as Hades, the god of the underworld and the dead, Hestia, Eros, and Persephone. Others were added during the classical period as a result of a moralization process of the archaic religious universe, a process that had its roots in legal and political changes. As the iconic and narrative personalization of the latter came to seem increasingly inadequate when called on to express the growing complexity of social experience, new figures were integrated. These figures did not derive from the original poetic structure of narrated myth, but from a process of abstraction in which the values and problems of the new collective reality were sublimated. New divinities made an appearance, such as Dike, the goddess Justice, conceived as the daughter of Zeus in order to represent his direct involvement in ensuring the ethical and political values of social coexistence; or Eirene, Peace, a goddess expressing the need for harmony inside and beyond the borders of the *polis;* or later, Tyche, Fortune, whose cult would become increasingly important during the Hellenistic period because of a widespread feeling of personal and collective insecurity.

As a result of its contact with alien religious cultures, particularly that of Egypt, the Hellenistic world also witnessed the addition to the Greek pantheon of foreign deities, syncretically assimilated to more traditional gods. Thus Amon was united to Zeus, sometimes worshiped with the double name, Isis to Demeter, and Osiris to Dionysus.

Before this happened, however, the old Olympian gods had already undergone another, decisive, transformation. They had been integrated into the framework of the *polis* as representatives of a politicized civic religion. The appearance in classical Greece of the *polis,* an all-embracing social and political organism that was capable of restructuring collective experience and all aspects of public and private life, could hardly fail to affect relations between gods and men, and the role the former would play in human existence. The Olympians were integrated into the social spaces of public life. Like every active citizen, they were expected to render service in the human *polis.* This service—rewarded with acts of religious worship that were henceforth regulated, legalized, and financed by the political community—consisted first in ensuring protection and prosperity to the *polis,* a task that was assigned to all the gods, and second in advising, providing assistance, and safeguarding the city's activities. Wars and the founding of colonies, the passing of laws and establishing of treaties, marriages, and contracts: nothing could take place without the protection of a god, whose attention was attracted by the required acts of worship and sacrificial offerings. Above all, every social event, from festivals to the Assembly, was consecrated to a deity, in order to ensure divine benevolence.

The shared citizenship of human beings and gods is represented by the site where the city chooses to place the statues of its deities. At the center of the city, in the heart of its public space and clearly visible from all parts of the *polis,* the temple is open to the public and is the common property of all citizens. The worshiping community that attends the temple and its rituals is identified with the civic body at its most compact, since it is here that the unity of the city is cemented by the relationship of its members to the god. Thus Hestia, the goddess who presides over the sacred flame of the *polis,* is identified with the city's "very legality" (Xenophon *Hellenica* 2.3.52).

It was precisely because of this that the body of priests who administered the temples and carried out religious functions (*hiereis*) was never considered a separate structure, distinct from the civic body with permanent professional positions. The role of priest, like that of magistrate, was often assigned by election or by lot. In any case, the magistrates of the *polis*—the Athenian archons and the Spartan ephors—directly performed sacred functions. But even when hereditary priesthoods existed, such as those associated with the Athenian families of the Bouzygoi and the Praxiergidae, they were placed under the control of the *polis.* As temple treasurers, they were responsible for communally owned property and had to account to the city at the end of their term in office, which was, in any case, temporary and capable of being revoked. Nor were priests expected, given the basic nature of Greek religion, to have any particular competence as theologians beyond a knowledge of the heritage of myth and ritual that every citizen possessed. From the moral point of view, they simply had to be free of pollution and to carry out the necessary acts of purification before performing the rites and sacrifices.

Sacrifice to the Olympian gods was undoubtedly the focal point of what Plato defined as the "friendship between gods and men" (*Symposium* 188c) and thus, also, of that political friendship among men that the former friendship is called upon to guarantee. At the heart of the sacrificial act, as we have seen, lies the votive offering to divine power. But in the mythological elaboration and ritualization of sacrifice performed by the Greeks, there is something more specific. According to myth, the origin of sacrifice can be found in an act of trickery by Prometheus, who had given the edible meat of the animal to men and left the inedible part, which was destined to be burned, to the gods. This trick brought an end to the original practice in which men and gods ate together and assigned a different diet to each of the two groups: smoke and perfume for the immortal gods, and meat, with its associations of mortality, for men. The rupture caused by Prometheus was not removed by the sacrificial act—because it was impossible to return to the original practice of eating together—but harmoniously recomposed. The gods preside over the sacrifice and rejoice. Men, in their turn, are allowed to eat meat so long as they choose those animals whose flesh is purified by its consecration to the gods. The sacrifice is thus followed by the banquet, a communal meal in which the division of the meat sanctions and legitimizes the hierarchical ordering of society, with the best part going to the magistrates, priests, and most eminent citizens. The sacrifice and the banquet that follows it are carried out in a festive atmosphere, such as that of the Athenian Panathenaea. This event, represented in the friezes of the Parthenon, is one of the most extraordinary examples of self-celebration of the social body, in which the concord and harmony that reign not only among its members but also between the city and its gods is converted into spectacle. Plato wrote, "The gods, pitying the human race, which is born to suffer, conceded a truce and established it in the succession of festivals offered to them, and the companions of the festival offered the Muses and Apollo Musagetes and Dionysus" (*Laws* 2.653d). The truce was anything but short, if we consider that fifth-century Athens devoted about one hundred days each year to festivals accompanying sacrificial rites.

The public, festive, solar character of sacrifices offered to the Olympians is emphasized even more by their contrast with those dedicated to the gods of the underworld. These sacrifices still took place in the classical *polis,* however marginalized they might have become. They were carried out by night, without a raised and visible altar, on the bare earth. The entire body of the sacrificial victim was normally burned, leaving nothing for a communal banquet. The rite was therefore intended to ward off evil forces rather than to establish peaceful contact with a protecting god.

This dark side of the sacrificial rite casts a shadow over one aspect of Greek religious experience, those existential problems concerned with the fear of death, the invisible, and the unknown that the Olympian religion—in both its "heroic" form and later political metamorphosis—was unable to assuage, incorporate, or control. The difficult area of individual destiny and the anguish of uncertainty stands at the very edge of a religious system concerned with projecting a public, social image. It will find its place in a different kind of relationship to the sacred that constitutes a subterranean, but in some ways no less important, element in the religious experience of the Greeks.

Mysteries and Sects

For the Greeks, Hades, the god of the underworld and the dead, was a god without cult or temples. His exclusion from the sphere of Olympian visibility, along with the terror excited by whatever cannot be seen or spoken, and by all that is regarded as polluting, was precisely what encouraged the need for a different kind of religious experience, far removed from the places and practices of daily public worship. It was from this need that the mysteries were born (the term *mysteria* derives from *mystēs,* "initiated," and expresses the secrecy in which these cults were enveloped and the obligation their participants—or initiates—were under to maintain absolute silence about everything said and done during the rites). Before continuing, however, we must correct an assumption that easily arises, given the secretive nature of the mystery cults: any citizen could be, and generally was, initiated into these cults, including people who were normally excluded from the Olympian cults of the *polis,* such as foreigners, slaves, and naturally, women.

The mystery cults, therefore, were no more restricted than civic cults. On the contrary, in principle and in fact, they were far more open and their sphere of potential and effective initiates was considerably larger than that defined by the limits governing citizenship. This meant that they addressed people as individuals rather than as members of the *polis,* involving an area of experience that was more profound, deep-rooted, and extended than that concerning self-representation and the security of the civil body.

The need for a complex initiation procedure and the secrecy that enveloped the mysteries did not therefore involve selection among possible participants so much as a return to the profound, terrible, and inexpressible nature of the dimension of experience to which they were addressed. It is possible that the deepest roots of mystery religions lay in prehistoric festivals exorcising death, and in the ineffable experience of escape from the body and immortality that might have been achieved during these festivals by the use of hallucinogens. As far as the Greeks were concerned, we have some rare information (since the mystery surrounding initiation cults was generally maintained to a surprising degree) concerning the Eleusinian mysteries, celebrated in the context of the Athenian *polis* (although other important mystery cults, such as those of Samothrace, also existed). At the heart of the Eleusinian cult was the story of Demeter and Persephone: an obvious reference, therefore, to the natural cycle of death and rebirth, but also, and apart from this, to the dimension of sexual generation, to a hope in salvation, and to an escape from death, the limit of each individual experience.

"The things seen, said, and done" during the mysteries—according to the canonical expression defining the ritual—culminated in a vision, or series of visions, capable of evoking, either directly or symbolically, sex, death, and rebirth—capable, that is, of provoking an experience of primordial terror in those present (the heart of the ritual took place at night in a cavelike space lit by torches) and then, by means of the reassuring epiphany of salvation and rebirth, of healing and "purifying" the actor-spectators gathered at the rite.

However profound and radical the mystery cults were, since they were aimed at the individual rather than the citizen, they nonetheless formed a part of the Olympian religion, which was neither denied nor excluded by them. The Athenian *polis* safeguarded and administered the Eleusinian mysteries. They did not produce a type of man who was extraneous to the political community, since an initiate to the mysteries neither led, nor wanted to lead, a life that was different from that of other citizens (themselves normally initiates). The mysteries therefore touched a sphere of experience and psychological and religious problems that the public cults of the *polis* could neither express nor respond to. It was precisely for this reason that they represented a necessary and harmonious addition to those cults, without producing any private or public conflict between the citizen and the initiate.

This was not the case with those sects concerned with the possession of secret religious knowledge. These sects expressed the mystical or, perhaps more accurately, "puritanical" tendency of Greek spirituality.

The Orphic movement—named after Orpheus, a legendary bard, poet, and priest who was reputed to have descended into the underworld—was born in Greece during the sixth century B.C. in the same cultural and social circles in which the Dionysiac cults had developed. Echoes of the shamanistic tradition that had originated among the Scythians, alongside Indo-Persian beliefs in immortality, probably gathered here. From the social viewpoint, these religious protest movements seem to have been connected with areas of exclusion and unease produced by the formation of the politicized universe of the city: women, foreigners, peripheral communities, marginalized intellectuals. From the psychological viewpoint, these movements brought together the same needs that sought expression in the ritual of the mystery cults, needs that came from the most individual and deeply rooted levels of religious experience. However, the movements provided more explicit, articulated responses on both a religious and intellectual level. Finally, they offered themselves, not as something to be integrated into the Olympic religious practices of the city, but as a radical alternative to them.

This alternative was mainly expressed in its proposal of a way of life that contrasted with that of the citizen. It was composed of a complex set of duties and prohibitions, above all that of eating meat, the religious sense of which we shall be examining. Even more important, however, than the material content of these duties and prohibitions was their ability to establish a rigid set of detailed rules, creating a nervous zeal of observance and discipline among initiates. Rule and discipline alone ensured the purity of the sects' members, affirming their difference from other people, profane creatures in an impure and contaminated world. The meticulously organized and observed life led by these sects thus constituted the principle of exclusion that distinguished the few, who had chosen the path of purification and salvation, from the irreducible multitude of the impious, the world of the triumphant city that believed itself capable of segregating the weak and marginalized only to discover that it, too, as a result of the choice made by the sects, was being rejected and excluded.

But on what did these minorities, bound to social groups and cultural experiences that were extraneous to the *polis,* base their rejection of the city and its religion? The first thing to be rejected was its violent character, the cruel and murderous aspect that played a central part in the politicization of life. The city appeared to be structurally bound to the exclusion and oppression of entire social groups, to war between different communities, to *stasis* and *polemos* and to the killing (*phonos*) that inevitably accompanied them. In a word, the city was inseparable from the memory of the heroic violence of the *Iliad,* and this was visible even in its religious practices. At the center of the city's religion, in fact, was sacrifice, the slaughter of an animal and the spilling of its blood. It was a common belief among these puritanical forms of spirituality, and one that was destined, as we shall see, to assume theoretical form, that each sacrifice was potential murder and that, once violence had been unleashed, it became impossible to regulate and contain it in the symbolic act of sacrifice.

Social life was thus polluted by a bloody curse that perpetuated a more ancient double curse, branding all human existence on the one hand and, on the other, isolating one individual from another.

There was, in fact, an original act of murder. According to an Orphic myth, the Titans enticed the young god Dionysus to his death, then cooked and devoured his body. The Titans were struck by a bolt of lightning from Zeus to punish them for this act of primordial theophagy, and from their ashes, there rose the first men, stained from the very beginning by this dreadful pollution. The original sin was repeated, however, in each individual. According to Empedocles, an early fifth-century philosopher closely linked to both Orphic religion and Pythagorean thought, each life is bound in its mortal state to an immortal demon-soul, of divine origin but hurled from its celestial home because of a murder or act of perjury (frag. B115 Diels-Kranz) and obliged to expiate its sins on an inferior terrestrial plane. The life of man was therefore crushed beneath the weight of this triple curse, which branded the existence of humanity as a whole, of political society, and of the individual. Punishment for the crime consisted in the violence that polluted every human act, in the oppression and anguish that accompanied it, in pain, and in the dreadful waiting for death. But there was a path to salvation, an immortal joy capable of redeeming the very limits of the human condition. This salvation consisted in a double strategy. First of all, it contrasted the polluted mortal body with the soul, that divine and immortal element present in us all (the powerful concept of the soul in Greek culture derives precisely from this religious and philosophical context). We thus need to free the soul from the bonds of the body. At the same time, we must purify the soul of the sin that has cast it down from its state of divine demon into the human body. It can only achieve expiation for that sin by uniting with the very body that represents its punishment. For both purposes—purification from the body and purification of the soul—life must be led as a sacrificial exercise, based on renunciation and abstinence. The rules governing life within these sects were intended to ensure this. The first act of renunciation, from a symbolic viewpoint, was the rejection of meat-eating and, with it, of the sacrificial ritual that was inextricably bound to the religion of the city. This double renunciation symbolized the rejection of violence, of killing, and of the spilling of blood, all of which polluted human existence. It was accompanied by a series of rules imposing abstinence, beginning with a refusal to mingle body and soul in sexual activity. In the *Phaedo,* the Platonic dialogue that most obviously reveals the influence of Orphic and Pythagorean tradition, life is clearly described as a preparation for death:

> Purification (*katharsis*), as we saw some time ago in our discussion, consists in separating the soul as much as possible from the body, and accustoming it to withdraw from all contact with the body and concentrate itself by itself; and to have its dwelling, so far as it can, both now and in the future, alone by itself, freed from the shackles of the body. . . . Is not what we call death a freeing and separation of soul from body? (67c–d)

In Orphic thought, then, individual salvation was basically the salvation of the deserving soul by means of a purification that extended beyond ritual and determined an entire way of life: the god of Orphism is first and foremost Apollo Kathartes, the "purifier." Freed from the body, the purified soul can return to the blessedness of its original divine state. Adepts of the sect generally carried with them in the tomb small golden or horn tablets (such as those found in Locri in Magna Grecia or Olbia on the Black Sea). These affirmed that their souls had been purified and invoked the gods of the underworld to receive them.

The Orphics based their fundamental belief about the soul and its salvation on a theogony in direct contrast to that of Hesiod, just as their rejection of the cruelty of sacrifice was in opposition to the religious practices of the city. Orphic theogony is known to us in a fragmentary state (thanks, among other things, to the recent discovery of a papyrus at Derveni). While Hesiod presented the organization of the divine world as a passage from initial chaos to the orderly kingdom of Zeus (in which the world of the heroes and, subsequently, of the *polis,* could be recognized), the Orphics saw a process of decay from an initial order, symbolized by the unity of the primordial principle—the completeness of the cosmogonic egg and the indistinctness of night—to the disorder of multiplicity and differentiation, with all the conflict and violence that these introduced. A new order, however, was expressed with the arrival of Dionysus, his "passion" (in the theophagous act of the Titans), and his final recomposition; in man, Dionysus' passage was expressed in terms of original pollution, purification, and the salvation of the soul.

From the religious viewpoint of Orphism, therefore, Dionysus assumed a role that was at least as significant as that of Apollo. The relation existing between the ascetic, vegetarian puritanism of Orphism and the liberating frenzy of the Dionysiac rites constitutes a grave problem for interpreters. There was undoubtedly a shared reference to marginalized social strata and to forms of cultural and religious protest, alternative to the "official" religious culture of the *polis*. Apart from this, however, Orphism probably saw Dionysus as the god of lost innocence, and of reconciliation not only between men but also between man and nature—something that was jeopardized by the violence of war and political society. The innocence of Dionysian belief clearly involved a purification of the historical human condition in a downward sense, in a return, that is, to the natural innocence of animals, whereas Orphism aimed upward, toward the soul's recovery of its former divinity. Nonetheless, these opposing directions must have been experienced as the expression of a common rejection, a shared desire for order and peace that a religion based on politics could not ensure.

The philosophical tradition, however, that from the Pythagoreans to Plato takes up and elaborates in a theoretical sense the religious message of Orphism is absolutely dominated by references to Apollo, the god not only of purity but also of knowledge.

During the sixth and fifth centuries, the Pythagoreans developed the Orphic concept of salvation into an elaborate doctrine of the transmigration of the soul. The soul was seen as an immortal demon that passed through a series of incarnations in different mortal bodies, either superior or inferior according to the degree of purification achieved in the previous life. The soul was eventually able to detach itself entirely from this cycle in order to return to the divine world from which it came (according to one version of the doctrine). Alternatively, it could be reincarnated in the highest form of life conceded to man, that of the just king or sage, who by this point had been decisively transformed into the figure of the philosopher by a Platonic reelaboration of the tradition. In Pythagorean thinking, the ascetic purification demanded of the Orphic way of life had already taken on a new form. The highest form of "Apollonian" purification—a devotion to theoretical knowledge and to the study of its purest forms—had been added to abstinence and ritual renunciation. Mathematics, geometry, harmony, astronomy, cosmology, and philosophy—effectively the field of pure theory—integrated with and, in a sense, relegated to a secondary level the more specifically ritual and religious aspects of practices intended to purify the soul. Furthermore, they acquired a spiritual value in themselves, an Apollonian consecration that made the life of the thinker and of theory the highest forms of existence and those most pleasing to the gods. This tradition even affected a "lay" thinker like Aristotle, who, in the final pages of his *Nicomachean Ethics* (10.7–9), extols the perfection, blessedness, and near-divinity of the philosophical life.

In the course of this journey, however, the relationship between the attitudes of thinkers, philosophers, and intellectuals and religious beliefs was not always a question of integration and progressive shifts, such as those that occurred in the minority sectarian current that led from Orphism to Plato. This relationship was often destined to undergo moments of conflict and crisis.

The Criticism of Religion and the Division of Beliefs

For the Greeks, religious experience was always divided on two different but closely connected levels. On the one hand, there was daily ritual. On the other hand, there were the myths that provided the ritual with meaning. These myths were connected more or less directly to profound needs for order, sense, and value in both individual and social experience. Ritual observance thus required a certain amount of belief in the mythical universe. In an intellectual climate that was increasingly complex, filled with new problems, tools, and challenges, this belief was only made possible by shifting it to a place and time beyond the social space and historical time in which people lived. Its truth, in other words, had to be established autonomously. There could be no communication or bond with the historical, political, and intellectually governable truths of human life. In a sense, Aristotle was still able to consider mythical facts as events (*genomena*) that had actually occurred (*Poetics* 1451b15 ff.), but only insofar as they belonged to a space-time dimension quite distinct from the one in which historical experience unfolded and in which his intellect was able to operate.

The crisis of belief in myth and the tension that was created by the political and philosophical rationality that reigned over social life became apparent when reason tended to invade the space of faith in myth, or when belief itself encroached on the space-time dimension of history.

The first of these clashes took place when the increasingly abstract rationality of thinkers and philosophers began to invade the "other" space of myth. In this unequal conflict, myth's anthropomorphic religious imagery immediately revealed its intellectual limitations, as well as its poetic and ingenuously projective nature. Xenophanes had already impiously made this point in the sixth century: "Men think that the gods are born as they are, and dress as they do, and speak and look the same" (frag. B14 Diels-Kranz); "but if oxen, horses, and lions had hands or could draw with their hands or create works of art like men, the horses would make pictures and statues of gods like horses, and oxen like oxen" (frag. B15 Diels-Kranz); "Ethiopians assert that the gods have snub noses and black hair, Thracians that they have blue eyes and red hair" (frag. B16 Diels-Kranz).

This devastating attack on mythical anthropomorphism created an opening for philosophical abstraction. Immediately after Xenophanes, Parmenides established his single, motionless, and necessary being (the exact opposite of the mythical world's multiple narratives). After Parmenides, this "other" level above the world was gradually occupied by other theoretical structures. We finally come to Aristotle's cosmological theology, which, in his *Metaphysics,* casts a backward glance on its predecessors. "The first men understood these things in the form of myth and passed them down in this form to their descendants, saying that these heavenly bodies were gods, and that gods surround everything that is nature." Up to this point, Aristotle is understanding and indulgent. But he immediately adds, "The rest [that is, the names and stories of the gods] was added later, still in the form of myth, to persuade the mass of the people, to impose obedience to the laws, and for other practical reasons. They say, in fact, that these divine beings are similar to people or other animals, and they add other things, which derive from them or resemble them closely" (12.8). Aristotle thus makes a clear distinction between a core of truth, a "relic" of ancient wisdom—the faith in the divinity of the stars—and the structure of poetic myth, that anthropomorphic narrative around which the religion of the Greeks was organized. Once philosophical thought had invaded the space previously occupied by mythical tradition, it had no choice other than to provide rational explanations for its existence. The first was political: the gods of popular belief were invented—in their moralized version as guarantors of justice—in order to inculcate respect for the law and social values in the minds of the simple, who would have ignored these restrictions if they had not been afraid of divine wrath. Aristotle was not the first to say this. Toward the end of the fifth century, the oligarchical sophist Critias had written, "I believe that an astute, wise man invented the terror of the gods, so that the wicked would fear even those things they did, or said, or thought in secret. . . . Thus I believe that, to begin with, someone persuaded men of the existence of the gods" (frag. B25 Diels-Kranz). A long philosophical tradition, from Critias and Aristotle to Epicurus and Lucretius, made considerable effort to convince people of the absurdity of divine punishment.

The second rational explanation of myth was based on its allegorical nature. This also has a very long tradition, from the Presocratic philosophers to the Stoics and Neoplatonist thinkers. According to this tradition, myth expresses a core of philosophical truths in poetic form, to make them easier for simple minds to understand and also more beautiful. Thus the chariot of Apollo represents the motion of the sun, the justice of Zeus stands for the existence of a providential reason sustaining the laws of nature, the generations of gods represent the order of the cosmos, and so on.

The first clash between mythical beliefs and politico-philosophical rationality was produced, therefore, when the latter, as a result of its ability to create abstractions, invaded the remote space of the former. The second, however, occurred when those beliefs, as a result of their ability to influence the historical life of men by means of education, began to encroach on the space allotted to ethics and politics. As we have seen, Plato feared the harmful effects on education of the "theological" poetry of Homer and his followers, and proposed that the legislator of the new city should amend the texts in order to make them more edifying and then to banish poets from the *polis* forever. According to Plato, as long as it is believed that "Homer has educated Greece and that he deserves to be studied in the administration of human affairs and education," it will be impossible to live correctly or establish the good city. He adds, "if you admit the seductive lyric or epic Muse, pleasure and pain become your rulers, instead of law and the rational principles universally accepted as the best," in other words, philosophical reason (*Republic* 10.606a ff.).

Not only should the new city ban the wicked mythological religion of the poets because of its perverse effects on the education of citizens, it should also base its institutions and education on a new theology that responds to the dictates of philosophical reason. According to Plato's *Laws*, this new theology should be founded on a belief in the divinity of the stars and in the existence of a divine providence that guarantees celestial order and thus establishes the norms of human existence. Although this new philosophical theology would be considerably poorer in narrative content and imagery than its "poetic" predecessor, it would be far more demanding in a normative and educational sense and contain many more dogmatic assumptions. Behind this new theology was the recurring temptation to set up an apparatus of control and constraint, halfway between state and church, capable of imposing orthodoxy and punishing transgression. Thus, Plato thought of providing the religion formulated in the tenth book of the *Laws* with a governing body, the Night Council, able to punish impiety with death (*Laws* 10.12). In the third century B.C., the Stoic Cleanthes proposed the trial for impiety of the astronomer Aristarchus before a Panhellenic court, after he had expressed doubts about the centrality of the earth (and thus of men and their gods) in the system of stars and planets.

The *polis* attempted to defend religion and the pantheon on which it was based from these forces of disintegration—both sectarian and philosophical—in a number of different ways. As we have seen, it reacted to the worship of Dionysus by integrating it into civic religion, which made it possible to control its subversive potential and, at the same time, take advantage of its relation with "another" dimension of the sacred (unlike Rome, the Greek *polis* never forbade Bacchic rites; on the contrary, they were presented on the stage by Euripides in his *Bacchae*, in which King Pentheus received an atrocious punishment from the god for his impiety). The Orphics were forced into the marginal role of itinerant purifying magicians surrounded by an air of charlatanism, wandering from house to house in order to sell their books and bizarre rituals. At the most, they formed small communities on the borders of the universe represented by the Greek *polis*. The Pythagoreans were treated rather differently. When they made an attempt to convert their anomalous religion into a political regime with the aim of establishing sectarian puritanism—something that seems to have happened in Crotone, in Magna Grecia, toward the middle of the fifth century B.C.—they were bloodily repressed.

After this event, the Pythagoreans wandered throughout Greece, declining to the same level as the Orphics, although their intellectual influence was far greater.

The attitude of the *polis* and of its religion toward the challenge represented by philosophy is complex and difficult to interpret. Since the *polis* did not possess its own theological orthodoxy, it normally ignored philosophical transgressions and provocations. These, in any case, were restricted to a small minority of intellectuals with no real political weight. During the classical age, however, there were two dramatic exceptions to this general rule: the trials in Athens of Anaxagoras, in about 440 B.C., and of Socrates, in 399 B.C., on the grounds of impiety. The former was accused of having denied the divinity of the stars and, in particular, of the sun, which he interpreted as a red-hot stone. His punishment was exile. Socrates, as is well known, was accused of corrupting the Athenian young through his teaching, of denying, among other things, the divinity of the *polis* and of importing new gods that were possibly Orphic (the "demon") or cosmological (the "clouds" to which Aristophanes refers in his satire). For these crimes, Socrates was condemned to death. He refused to exercise his right to transmute the sentence into exile.

These two trials certainly encouraged a certain prudence among philosophers toward the *polis,* to the extent that Plato, Socrates' pupil, chose to leave Athens for a period, and Aristotle feared that he, too, might be tried. Contrary to what might be believed, however, the trials did not mean that the city was driven by religious intolerance to persecute heresy. The trials of both Anaxagoras and Socrates should be seen as episodes in the political struggle that gripped the city. The attack on Anaxagoras was intended to damage the political and philosophical circle surrounding Pericles, while Socrates' trial was aimed at the oligarchical group led by Critias, which had endangered Athenian democracy with its coup in 404. Nonetheless, in both cases, a popular jury representing the entire *polis* was persuaded to make a political condemnation for religious reasons. This means that the observance of the Olympian religion and its rituals was generally recognized as being in harmony with the very existence of the *polis* and its political structure. "Believing in the gods," in other words, was not so much a spiritual act of faith or theological respect as a concrete sense of belonging to the political community. Believing in the gods was ultimately the same thing as being a good Athenian citizen, just as it was in Sparta and every other Greek city.

It was precisely for this reason that the *polis* always reserved the right to make laws about the worship of the gods and the composition of its pantheon. The admission of new gods, such as Asclepius in 420 B.C. in Athens and, during the Hellenistic period, the recognition of numerous eastern deities and the cults of new monarchs, did not violate the city's order or stability as long as they were generally accepted by the community. Moments of religious integration between different cities and parts of Greece were equally regulated by the *polis*. These included the religious leagues (the amphictyonies), the Olympic games, and the acceptance of the Delphic oracle's authority in a whole series of public events. These moments of Panhellenic religious unity, although regulated by the *polis* in all cases, implied that accepting the Olympian religion, with its pantheon and rituals, also meant being not merely a citizen of one's own city, but of all Greece—it meant, in short, being a man. It is easy to understand, therefore, why a rejection by this religious community might produce a feeling of self-exclusion from the civic body, from Hellenic civilization, and from the very human community with which these were identified, a community that was quite distinct from the barbaric degenerations of other cultures. But since acceptance was confined to the public sphere, leading neither to private faith nor theological orthodoxy, it was possible to separate belief into a series of levels, and this happened more and more. "Believing" in the Olympian religion continued to mean the observance of common rituals and a participation in the body of narrated myth. These were the mark of belonging to a community, a culture, and a civilization in the same way as the use of the Greek language, a knowledge of Homer, and the shared customs of social life. At another level, this belief was quite capable of coexisting with monotheism or the immanence of a philosophical theology that gradually penetrated the upper classes from the fourth century B.C. on, in which the gods tended to be identified with the first god or, as with the Stoics, with the rational principle of order or an immanent nature. It could even coexist with the widespread religious skepticism among Greek intellectuals.

The tolerant polytheism of myths and rituals, if we disregard the political and social needs to which they were indissolubly linked, was therefore able to coexist quite happily in the Greek consciousness alongside the most far-reaching intellectual inquiries in theology, ethics, and science. This was certainly the case until new religious forms, endowed with a powerful theological orthodoxy and a coer-

Mario Vegetti

cive ecclesiastical structure, began to spring up. These new forms were as threatening to the world of myth as they were to that of intellectual inquiry. But at this point, we are moving away from the religious experience of the Greeks, even though the new monotheistic religions, Judaism, Christianity, and Islam, would draw to a greater or lesser extent upon its theological elaborations and its theories about the salvation of the soul.

Notes

1. [The Penguin edition translations have been used, with some editing, for quotations from the works of classical writers. The quotations from historical fragments are based on the Italian translation—trans.]

Bibliography

Bianchi, U. *La religione greca.* Turin, 1975.
Brelich, A. *Gli eroi greci.* Rome, 1958.
———. *Homo necans.* Berlin and New York, 1972.
Burkert, W. *Griechische Religion der archaischer und klassischen Epoche.* Stuttgart, 1977.
———. *Structure and History in Greek Mythology and Ritual.* Berkeley, 1979.
Derenne, E. *Les procès d'impiété intentés aux philosophes à Athènes au Ve et IVe siècles a. Chr.* Liège and Paris, 1930.
Detienne, M. *Les jardins d'Adonis.* Paris, 1972.
———. *Dionysos mis à mort.* Paris, 1977.
———. *L'invention de la mythologie.* Paris, 1981. English translation, *The Invention of Mythology* (Chicago, 1986).
———. *L'écriture d'Orphée.* Paris, 1989.
———, ed. *Il mito: Guida storica e critica.* Rome and Bari, 1976.
———, and J.-P. Vernant, eds. *La cuisine du sacrifice en pays grec.* Paris, 1979. English translation, *The Cuisine of Sacrifice among the Greeks* (Chicago, 1989).
Fahr, W. *Theos nomizein.* Darmstadt, 1969.
Gernet, L., and L. Boulanger. *Le génie grec dans la réligion.* 2d ed. Paris, 1970.
Girard, R. *La violence et le sacré.* Paris, 1972.
Guthrie, W. K. C. *The Greeks and Their Gods.* Boston, 1950.
Kerenyi, K. *Die Mythologie der Griechen.* Zürich, 1951.
Kirk, G. S. *The Nature of Greek Myths.* London, 1974.
Jeanmaire, H. *Dionysos.* 2d ed. Paris, 1970.
Momigliano, A., and S. C. Humphries. *Saggi antropologici sulla Grecia antica.* Bologna, 1970.
Nilsson, M. P. *Geschichte der griechischen Religion.* 3d ed. 2 vols. Munich, 1967–74.

Otto, W. *Die Gotter Griechenlands*. Bonn, 1929.

Des Places, E. *La réligion grecque*. Paris, 1969.

Rudhardt, J. *Le délit religieux dans la cité antique*. Rome, 1981.

Sabbatucci, D. *Saggio sul misticismo greco*. Rome, 1965.

Sissa, G., and M. Detienne. *La vie quotidienne des dieux grecs*. Paris, 1989.

Snell, B. *Die Entdeckung des Geistes*. 3d ed. Hamburg, 1963.

Untersteiner, M. *La fisiologia del mito*. 2d ed. Florence, 1972.

Vernant, J.-P. *Les origines de la pensée grecque*. Paris, 1962; 2d ed., Paris, 1969. English translation, *The Origins of Greek Thought* (Ithaca, N.Y., 1982).

————. *Mythe et pensée chez les grecs*. 2d ed. Paris, 1972.

————. *Mythe and société en Grèce ancienne*. Paris, 1974. English translation, *Myth et Society in Ancient Greece* (New York, 1990).

————. *Réligions histoires raisons*. Paris, 1979.

————, and P. Vidal-Naquet. *Mythe et tragédie en Grèce ancienne*. Paris, 1972. English translation, *Myth and Tragedy in Ancient Greece* (New York, 1990).

Vegetti, M. *L'etica degli antichi*. Rome and Bari, 1989.

Veyne, P. *Les Grecs ont-ils cru à leurs mythes?* Paris, 1983.

Will, E. *Le monde grec et L'Orient*. Vol. 1. Paris, 1972.

CHAPTER NINE

The Rustic

Philippe Borgeaud

THE RUSTIC, the primitive, the unsocialized, the bumpkin, the savage, the freak—all these figures haunted and fascinated the imagination of the ancient Greeks. They crowded the stage of that imagination in order to permit the inventors of *paideia* the pleasure of reflection on the conditions out of which a civilized balance might emerge. The rustic was of interest to the city in that he was central to the Greek meditation on the origins of culture.

This was already true in the earliest stories, the epics. Odysseus, set down on a beach of Ithaca by the Phaeacians, is wrapped in a mist that prevents him from recognizing his homeland. A young shepherd, who resembles the son of a prince, then appears, leading his flock. It is in fact Athena, who made the mist and who shows Odysseus the path to the real. This path goes through the realm of Eumaius, the "divine swineherd," who will carry out for his guest a first sacrifice, offered to Hermes and the nymphs by the well-known cave. The gradual recovery of the human world therefore begins with the pastoral. The rustic Eumaius, so pious and faithful (and how civilized!)—he is a slave, of course, but of noble birth—welcomes his master (whom he does not recognize), with the indispensable acts that have been lacking in the earlier personal encounters of that long voyage.[1]

The monster, the Cyclops, emerges in the *Odyssey* as the harbinger of what the city would soon do its utmost to deny so as to differentiate itself from it. Alongside the Greek schoolchild who learns the tale by heart, we must follow Odysseus' travels, his "exterior" journey. We must confront Polyphemus with him.[2] In the world of the

Cyclopes, the opposition is not set up (as it would later be) between the city and the countryside. It is seen first as an opposition between the little island and the land of the Cyclopes. The little island, upon which Odysseus and his companions land, the first humans to set foot on it, is an island of forests where "wild goats in hundreds breed,"³ the only inhabitants other than the nymphs, completely beyond the reach of hunters. Here there is neither cultivating or reaping. We are in the realm of the nonhuman. Opposite, within shouting distance, is the main island, the home of the Cyclopes. Although they are the sons of Poseidon, they know nothing of navigation. Close enough to the gods not to fear them, they live without planting or plowing, raising small livestock. Theirs is no longer the virgin nature of the little island, but neither is it truly compatible with the world of men. Their wine comes from the wild vines. "Giants, louts, without a law to bless them. / In ignorance leaving the fruitage of the earth in mystery / to immortal gods, they neither plow / nor sow by hand, nor till the ground, . . . [they] have no muster and no meeting, / no consultation or old tribal ways, / but each one dwells in his own mountain cave / dealing out rough justice to wife and child, / indifferent to what the others do." Here we have what would, after the fifth century B.C., be considered prepolitical society, characterized by the scattering of small dwellings.⁴ There are no social rules, no religion, either (and hence no sense of hospitality), in this little world close to the Golden Age and its ambiguities.

However, Odysseus disembarks in the land of a solitary creature. Far from his kin, Polyphemus is a savage among savages, a sort of Dyscolus before his time. He "slept in his cave alone, and took his flocks / to graze afield—remote from all companions."⁵ He is the opposite of a human being, of a good bread-eater. But in his cave, the drying racks are loaded with cheeses, the pens are crowded with lambs and kids, metal urns are filled with the milk from his animals. Like his kind he makes fire—a fire that is not used for sacrifices, and that seems to burn only to demonstrate that this strange world possesses the emblems of humanity. That this is a pretense is revealed by Polyphemus' behavior: he eats Odysseus' companions raw, and washes down his cannibal meal with milk. He is eventually defeated by three ruses that each in their own way relate to the imperatives of civilization: the pure wine, of divine provenance, which Odysseus offers him and from which he becomes drunk while devouring his gruesome meal (the union of the divine with the bestial); the olive tree stake (the tree of Athena), polished, worked over the fire, wielded under the command of a leader by the little group of sailors from Ithaca, by which he is blinded; finally, the verbal ruse (Odysseus' calling himself "Nobody") that denies him any social communication. Deprived of reason, sight, and language—"No one" has wronged him—at the end of his encounter with Odysseus, the rustic is nothing more than a violent brute, whose wailing is heard by one god alone, his father Poseidon, lord of great ocean storms, who takes over and carries off the cunning Odysseus.

Polyphemus does not leave the literary scene, and for a good reason. After Euripides,[6] he is found again in Alexandrian poetry as a shepherd in love with Galatea; he is clumsy, touching, his monstrousness having become pitiful. Through a play on words connecting Galatea to Galatians, Polyphemus discovers he is supposed to have fathered the Gauls, the barbarian invaders nervously ridiculed by the Greeks as those who flee panic-stricken from Delphi to Asia Minor. It is remarkable to see how the wild (and negative, though divine) strength of Polyphemus was destined to be transposed to the level of an ambiguous pastoral. This reinterpretation is not an abandonment of the monstrous, a loss of difference, but rather looks forward: the third-century Greeks were discovering certain values in the pastoral world, values that would continually recur in their tradition. From now on, the Homeric monster becomes a rustic.

When they are defeated by the power of a goatherd god (Pan, the instigator of panic), the Galatians, descendants of Polyphemus, are viewed in the context of the pastoral world, although their defeat in Asia Minor, when they are repelled by the lords of Pergamum, is on a cosmogonic scale, recalling the ancient battles against the giants. This coincidence of pastoral and cosmogonic themes, which is to say, a violence among rustics, begs an explanation. Idyll and epic remembrance alternate, two visions of the same thing. We have an ambivalent monster, both laughable and disturbing.

Looking briefly at another tradition—it, too, originally epic but starting from a cosmogonic point of view—leads us to a completely comparable observation. Everything begins, then, with Hesiod's *Theogony,* which allows us to examine another character, less expected in this context: Typhon. The process Hesiod describes begins on both a cosmic and a divine level, where one goes from formidable primal entities (Earth, Chaos, Eros, Tartar), filtered through genealogy and conflicts of succession, to the final establishment of a sovereignty won through a great struggle (that of Zeus). Defined as the guarantor of a balanced sharing among rival, but henceforth limited, powers, this sovereignty is also asserted in Hesiod's tale as a victory over the power of disorder, an enemy that appeared just when one believed the balance had been achieved: Zeus must still get rid of Typhon, the issue of primordial Earth, a menace that resurges after his victory over the Titans. This is a primordial moment: Earth gives birth to this monster and has thus not lost her cosmogonic fertility. Alternatives to an Olympian order can still emerge out of her, in the form of disturbing possibilities; from now on, however, what she produces will fall short. The conqueror of Typhon, Zeus swallows up Metis; he is henceforth convinced he will not be overthrown. His power rests on the assimilation of prudence, which remains, for all of Greek tradition, the best antidote for violent impulses.

From this point of view, the literary destiny of Typhon is of interest to us. This monster, whose defeat is portrayed in the *Theogony* in a battle that sets the universe on fire, while never losing his role as Zeus's adversary, in the Hellenistic period becomes a rather touching character, whose naivete leads him to ruin in an almost pastoral setting. After neutralizing Zeus in an initial battle, he is confronted with minor adversaries (Pan, Cadmus, or Hermes and Egipan), who trick him with the most elementary ruses. Having become a sort of rustic, the monster's attention can be diverted toward the pleasures of bucolic life, by an enticing smell of fish or the music of a pipe. The seriousness of the threat that weighs on the universal order is forgotten for a moment in a pastoral joust in which the monster, like a savage, allows himself to be entrapped by his desires. Zeus takes advantage of this, and regains the upper hand.[7] Is this sweetening of the myth simply an intellectual game? That would be too simple an answer. What is happening in fact is a carrying forward of the pastoral, of "rusticity," onto the concept of cosmic threat. The rustic is not identified with the cosmogonic monster but, at the end of a process that is not simply literary, he has become the logical heir to it. Beneath the neutral surface is the acknowledgment of a new function bestowed upon the pastoral image. Through his inevitable and indispensable presence, the rustic has among others the task of ensuring the dynamism of balance: a resistance, a threat, a process that continues to force the human, the political animal, to redefine himself in his distance from the gods and the beasts.

As we know, the situation is analogous on the heroic and human level: the space is not suddenly open to the undertakings of mortals; the *chōra* [countryside] must still be "tamed," "pacified." Hence the work, the suffering, of heroes such as Heracles and Theseus. Danger, in fact, will never be completely avoided: the foreigner, the barbarian, the absolute Other occupy not only the frontiers, but the still uncultivated regions of an otherwise civilized territory. In the heart of the political order, close to Zeus, Athena, or Apollo, the wild Mother of the gods sits on her throne, surrounded by lions, next to the Council of the Five Hundred;[8] while Dionysus, in his *boukoleion* ("sanctuary of the cowherd"), watches over the city of Athens.

In the second book of his *History,* Thucydides provides a brief historical account of the evolution of the city in Attica, explaining the upheaval that occurred in 431 after the influx of the rural population into the city of Athens, within the "Long Walls" that extended to Piraeus. It would obviously be wrong to believe that up to that time Athens was the only urban center in Attica. Many townships and even relatively large cities (for example, Thoricus or Marathon) had existed for a long time. The famous "synoecism," an urban joining together, which mythological tradition attributes to Theseus, suggests the existence of a plurality of urban establishments. The union was at first only administrative. Having become a political, commercial, and in some respects also a religious center, the city of Athens was not the home of the entire population. Naturally, most citizens continued to live within their own demes, following ancestral economic and religious customs. Thus the loss of political autonomy did not signify a loss of local ways. In the second century A.D., Pausanias points out that in the demes people still preserved traditions concerning the gods and heroes that were different from those reserved for visitors to the Acropolis.[9] This is why Thucydides, defining the situation as it was on the eve of the Peloponnesian War, specifies that "old habits still prevailed, and from the early times down to the present war most Athenians still lived in the country with their families and households (*en tois agrois*)."[10] The "country" here denotes the whole region that was not strictly speaking within the city of Athens, that is, the clusters of homes and towns, the demes, as well as the fields that were farmed.

The date 431 marks a fundamental rupture in the history of the ancient imagination. The Athenians very quickly felt it as such. With the abandoning of the countryside (temporarily, granted, but for long enough to give the impression that the situation was lasting forever), an entire vision of the world was transformed. Several of Aristophanes' comedies, and a few famous pages from Thucydides, show this clearly; the disruption, particularly during the plague of 430, was overwhelming: "Deep was their trouble and discontent at abandoning their houses and the hereditary temples of the ancient constitution, and at having to change their habits of life and to bid farewell to what each regarded as his native city."[11]

In his famous speech, Pericles describes the true nature of this change in mentality in a program of political and strategic action: "So that although you may think it a great privation to lose the use of your land and houses, still you must see that this power [Athen's maritime power] is something widely different; and instead of fretting on their account, you should really regard them in the light of the gardens and other accessories that embellish a great fortune, and as, in comparison, of little moment."[12] The ideal (always more theoretical than real) of an essentially agricultural Athens was soon challenged, and imperiously diverted, by the affirmation of the maritime and commercial destiny of the city-state. The (mythical) values of the land would certainly continue to assert their ideological role, but the center was henceforth to be elsewhere. The city, commercial and sophisticated urbanity, imposed new priorities on the citizen-peasant. Physically displaced by war into that new environment, he was justifiably at a loss, and his bewilderment often appeared as a generational conflict (for example, that between "right reasoning" and "false reasoning" in Aristophanes' *Clouds*). The old peasant, unable to adapt to his new surroundings, finds himself increasingly at odds with his son, a student of the Sophists (or of Socrates, who in the father's view is no different). The rhetoric of the *agroikia,* of the contrast between country and city life, thus originated in real historical situations.

Exasperated by his son's education, old Strepsiades indulges in an eloquent reminiscence:

> Oh! curses on the go-between who made me marry your mother! I lived so happily in the country, a commonplace, everyday life, but a good and easy one—had not a trouble, not a care, was rich in bees, in sheep and in olives. Then forsooth I must marry the niece of Megacles, the son of Megacles; I belonged to the country, she was from the town. She was a haughty, extravagant woman, a true Coe-

syra [the wife of Alcmaeon who came to settle in Athens in the twelfth century]. On the nuptial day, when I lay beside her, I was reeking of the dregs of the wine cup, of cheese and of wool; she was redolent with essences, saffron, tender kisses, the love of spending, of good cheer and wanton delights.[13]

Confronted with philosophical "clouds," Strepsiades is in fact called a rustic (agroikos), clumsy, and uneducated. He might be dismissed as a relic from another age, reeking of antiquity, if in other respects he didn't represent certain fundamental values: "If it be a question of hardiness for labour, of spending whole nights at work, of living sparingly, of fighting my stomach and only eating chick-pease, rest assured, I am as hard as an anvil."[14]

What one must remember regarding Greek tradition is that war gave a name to the opposition, which ultimately became conventional, between the rustic and the city dweller. We must look even deeper into history to see how the order described in the epics, where each lord ruled over a relatively autarkic, familial domain, became a city-based oligarchy whose property was worked by a servile labor force that ultimately rebelled (a situation seen in Megara in the sixth century and portrayed by Theognis, who was shocked at the idea that "serfs," poverty-stricken yokels, would be able to enter the city and take power).[15] What changed at the end of the fifth century, following a long Athenian experience (where the measures taken by Solon, then by Cleisthenes, were decisive), was the status of the opposition between the rustic and the city dweller: conceived against the background of a war that affected them jointly, that opposition became an instrument that enabled them to think about political space, social balance, and health. Peace, and the laughter it rediscovered, would for a long time preserve an honest and good odor of the farm within the heritage of that memory. "Georgia," "Farming," appears on Aristophanes' stage and is introduced in these terms: "I am the universal nurse of Peace. You can count on me in this role: nurse, stewardess, helper, guardian, daughter, sister of Peace" (frag. 294)."[16]

The opposition between the city and the country thus appears as an invention of the fifth century,[17] the issue of the unique situation created by the Peloponnesian War. Until that time, the Athenian citizen most often lived outside Athens itself in the demes, going into the city only to conduct business (economic, political, or religious). His life was tied to the working of his land. In the city, of course, he did encounter craftsmen and merchants, but their transactions played only a minor role in his life. The changes are evident on an archaeological level as well, and we begin to perceive an evolution of the individual dwelling. Until the end of the fifth century, luxurious houses were found in the countryside, that is, on estates where owners could flaunt their wealth and originality. As one approached the politico-religious center (the city), private homes became simpler compared to public, administrative, or religious structures. This simplicity reflected the ideal of political equality. After the end of the fifth century, the situation changed: landowners (even small ones) henceforth had their residences in the city and spent only certain periods of time in the country; rural residences became more modest, in a certain sense, secondary.[18] Permanent residents of the country (there remained some, of course) were identified as rustics, the *agroikoi,* at whom the New Comedy poked fun. Knemon, the gruff misanthrope in Menander's *Dyscolus,* is a good example.

The changes can readily be seen in the etymology of the relevant terms. The *agroikos,* as his name indicates, was the one who lived in the *agros,* that is, in Homeric Greek, the pasturelands, the uncultivated fields, which were distinguished from the *aroura,* cultivated land. The derivative *agroikos,* absent from epic poetry, did not appear until the fifth century, when it joined another, older derivative, *agrios,* applied in Homeric poetry to the world of the Cyclopes, among other places, and meaning "wild, ferocious." In a now-classic study, Chantraine has shown how *agrios* took on the meaning of "ferocious" by its homophonic association with the vocabulary of hunting, where one encounters *agreo,* "to catch," and *agra,* "the hunt" or "the game."[19] The opposition was thus established first between the regions where the shepherd encounters the hunter (on the borders, on the frontiers, and beyond the marked territory) and the areas reserved for farming. It was only in the fifth century that the opposition came to define the distance between rural space considered as a whole and urban space. This historical (and economic) evolution led from the epic poem to comedy.

Beyond the limits of culture, the *agrios,* the Homeric monster, was defined by the negation of elements that made up civilized life; going between these outer realms and the city, the rustic (*agroikos*) appears as a pivotal character, an intermediary, taking on all the ambiguity that role comprises. There is therefore nothing surprising in the fact that Pan, a god both rustic and bestial, was considered in Athens to be the son of Hermes, the Messenger.

We must show how different levels of this symbolization of space coexisted. The absence of the term *agroikos* from tragedy, for example, is significant. Tragedy remained faithful to the message of the old traditional tales, and of the still-active cults, that the cultivated land, as well as vine growing, guaranteed civilization. It was impossible in this system to place the primitive, the savage, next to the plow. He was more likely found alongside the hunters and the shepherds. Less dependent on myth, comedy invented the rustic, the peasant attached to his deme (which is anything but uncultivated). From then on, the rustic could not be viewed from one angle alone.

The figure of the *agroikos* appeared for the first time in literature in a play by the Syracusan Epicharmus, then in Antiphanes. These representations were only the most fragmentary indications of an interest that would eventually result in the full-blown rhetoric of the *agroikia,* centered on a complete "character." From Aristophanes to Quintilian, including Theophrastus, the portrait of the rustic was initially sketched very broadly and defined by a dual opposition: the *agroikos* preferred the thyme of his countryside to the myrrh of the elegant city ladies; he tended to speak loudly to his slaves rather than in the discreet tones appropriate to subtle political discourse. He was recognized immediately by the way he was dressed: in a goat or sheepskin (*diphthera*), he wore a leather Boeotian hat (*kunē*), and boots (*kabartinai*), when he wasn't wearing shoes held together with pins. His haircut was sloppy, his beard indifferently shaved with the knife he used to shear his animals. His filth and stench were always mentioned.[20]

The primary opposition, which was at the foundation of all others, was that of the country and the city. *Agroikos* was indeed contrasted to *asteios* ("urban"). Whereas the *asteios* appeared intelligent, quick, elegant, cultured, the *agroikos* was said to possess only negative traits: stupidity, slowness, boorishness, coarseness.[21] It is appropriate, however, to point out some subtleties. Just as urbanity, maintained within certain limits, was celebrated, the *agroikos,* when he did not sink into caricature, was revered as the holder of ancient values (as we have seen, by Aristophanes in particular). Courage and common sense appear on his side. So that even as he lost economic importance, he preserved a symbolic privilege, placed as he was at the crossroads of the wild and the civilized, and consequently knowing the paths that led from disorder to order, and back again.[22] Indeed, he occupied a liminal position between the "frontiers" (the *eschatiai*) and the urban center (the *astu*), between the heart and the limits of the marked territory (the *chōra*).

Aristotle contrasts the overrefinement of the city dweller, who sees humor in all things (the defect of the *bōmolochia*), with the uncouthness of the yokel, who takes everything seriously and who never laughs (the defect of the *agroikia*).[23] He is dealing with two poles, that is, two forms of excess. The two-dimensional rustic can neither joke nor be the object of a joke without getting angry. The city-dweller-turned-wit sinks into buffoonery and jokes about everything. Good quick-wittedness (*eutrapelia*) is an "educated violence" (*pepaideumenē hybris*).[24] The *agroikos* is indeed easy to confuse with the savage, the brutal, the *agrios*. He carries with him an element of violence, of hubris, which begs to be civilized, tamed. But too much education, too much urbanity, which causes one to forget one's roots, poses another threat: the pride of refinement, an exaggerated luxury, an overly sophisticated wit. A happy medium, "educated violence" avoids the two extremes. In this way for Aristotle it qualified a fundamental aspect of humor: neither vain laughter, at everything, nor the gross laughter of the peasant of the Old Comedy.[25]

While always defined, as it is here, by its dual relationship with the *agroikia* and with an education of violence, laughter was also understood as divinely inspired. The laughter of Pan, both goat and goatherd, resounds, signaling a return of the forces of life after the turbulence of war. Pan's is a disturbing laugh; this master of panic reveals the conjunction of sex and fear, where the human is confused with the animal. In the Greek imagination, the landscape in which Pan's laugh bursts forth is that of the remote countryside, near the frontiers or the mountains, where herds of small livestock sometimes take shelter in grottos, forcing the shepherd to reenter an Arcadia conceived as the threshold of the civilized.[26]

Take one example among the many we encounter, after the fifth century, in so many places: the grotto of Pharsalus. An hour-and-a-half's walk from the city, to the west, the cave opens a few meters from the base of a rocky wall, near the top of a hill. During the first decades of the fifth century, a certain Pantalkes had cleared out the grotto and the space around it, carving steps into the rock to reach the cave, planting and devoting a thicket to the nymphs, the goddesses. A century later, the place was still considered to be a sanctuary, where Pan, the son of Hermes, joined the nymphs and Apollo,[27] as well as other typically Thessalian "minor" divinities (Asclepius, Cheiron, Heracles). To the right of the entrance an inscription provides the words of the unspecified divinity (*ho theos*), an anonymous voice in a remote landscape, inviting the passer-by (the visiting city dweller) to pay ritual homage: the placing of an offering, the sacrifice of a small animal, a moment of peace and joy in the oppressive climate of domestic war that reigned at that time in Thessaly.

The god says:

> Greetings, passers-by, whoever you might be, female or male, men or women, young men or young girls. This place is a sanctuary of the Nymphs, of Pan and Hermes, of the lord Apollo, Heracles and the Companions, this grotto belongs to Cheiron, Asclepius and Hygeia.
>
> It is to them, through Pan our lord, that the very holy things belong, the trees here, the votive paintings, the statues and the many offerings. The Nymphs saw to it that Pantalkes, a good man, discovered this place and has watched over it. It was he who planted trees and who toiled with his hands. As recompense they have granted him a long life without hindrance. Heracles has given him energy and virtue, strength thanks to which he has cut stones, making the place accessible; Apollo, Heracles' son, and Hermes have given him health for the entire duration of a noble life; Pan has given laughter, good humor and just hubris; Cheiron gave him wisdom, and the ability to sing well.
>
> But now, accompanied by Good Luck, go into the sanctuary, sacrifice to Pan, make your wishes, rejoice: here you will find a suspension of all ills, the attainment of goods and a halt to war.[28]

Laughter (*gelos*), good humor (*euphrosynē*), and violence mastered by justice (*hybris dikaia*): such were the gifts granted to Pantalkes by the goatherd god; on the level of religious practice, within this rural cult for the use of city dwellers, they anticipated Aristotle's *eutrapelia* (*pepaideumene hybris*).

We know that Greek society, starting at the end of the fifth century, evolved toward a political negation of the rustic: Aristotle even wished to distance the peasant-citizen from the city in favor of slaves and immigrant workers.[29] This devalorization, this hiding of the *agroikos,* did not mean—far from it—the abandonment of a region that symbolically remained the producer of desires, of tensions, but also of civilization. Thus the cult, in the grottoes, of the god Pan, the symbol of primitive Arcadia, of eaters of acorns older than the moon, developed along with urbanization, just as the peasantry, in its most technical appearance, entered into literature.[30] As for the swampy territories, the slopes of mountains, wooded and wild zones, or the arid and dried out regions where one raised goats, hunted, fished, made charcoal, or where the ephebes watched the borders—they continued to be the object of a mythical discourse, even though their status had changed a long time before: they were no longer the *chōrai ēremoi,* the deserts, lands belonging to no one, but they were nevertheless always integrated into a group of ritual practices "which perpetuate the memory of the formation process of the territorial and political unity of the cities."[31]

Notes

1. With the exception of the Phaeacians, of course, who mediated between the other world, that of the journey into the inhuman, and the world of Ithaca: cf. Pierre Vidal-Naquet, "Valeurs religieuses et mythiques de la terre et du sacrifice dans l'Odyssée," *Annales E.S.C.* 5 (1970): 1278–97.

2. Homer, *The Odyssey,* trans. Robert Fitzgerald (New York, 1963), p. 148 f.

3. Ibid.

4. Cf. Plato *Laws* 3.680b, who cites the passage from the *Odyssey* relating to the customs of the Cyclopes. On the development of Greek ideas relative to the origins of civilization, let us note in particular Thomas Cole, "Democritus and the Sources of Greek Anthropology," published for the American Philological Association by the Press of Case Western Reserve University (Cleveland, 1967); and also Sue Blundell, *The Origins of Civilization in Greek and Roman Thought* (London, 1986), with bibliography.

5. Homer *Odyssey,* p. 150.

6. Whose satyr play entitled the *Cyclops* puts a chorus directed by Silenus on stage around the monster.

7. Cf. Marcel Detienne and Jean-Pierre Vernant, *Les ruses de l'intelligence: La métis des Grecs* (Paris, 1974), pp. 115–21; Philippe Borgeaud, *The Cult of Pan in Ancient Greece,* trans. by Kathleen Atlass and James Redfield (Chicago, 1988), pp. 113–15.

8. The author of these lines is completing a book on the Mother of the gods.

9. Pausanias 1.26.6.

Philippe Borgeaud

10. *The Complete Writings of Thucydides: The Peloponnesian War*, the unabridged Crawley translation with an Introduction by J. H. Finley, Jr. (New York, 1951), 2.16.1.

11. Ibid., 2.16.2.

12. Ibid., 2.62.3.

13. Aristophanes, *The Eleven Comedies* (London, 1912), vv. 41–52.

14. Ibid.

15. Theognis 1.53–57. In Pindar, too, "the agricultural land [is only envisioned] as the property of an aristocratic class and the source of wealth, not as the object of work" (Nathalie Vanbremeersch, "Terre et travail agricole chez Pindare," *Quaderni di Storia* 25 [1987]: 85).

16. [Cited in Victor Ehrenberg, *The People of Aristophanes: A Sociology of Old Attic Comedy* (Oxford, 1951), p. 69—trans.]

17. Cf. François Hartog, "De la bêtise et des bêtes," *Le Temps de la réflexion* 9 (1988): 60: "One can hypothesize about a correlation between the meaning and the values of the word *agroikos* and the ways the question of the relationship between the city and the countryside has been perceived and thought out from the middle of the fifth century to the third century B.C."

18. This evolution is demonstrated by Fabrizio Pesando, *Oikos e ktesis* (Perugia, 1987), pp. 20–25.

19. P. Chantraine, *Etudes sur le vocabulaire grec* (Paris, 1956), pp. 34–35.

20. The issue is presented and analyzed by O. Ribbeck, "Agroikos: Eine ethologische Studie," *Abhandlungen der königlichen sächsischen Gesellschaft* (*phil.-hist. Klasse*), t. 10, fasc. 8 (1885): 1–68.

21. The list of these traditional oppositions is drawn up by K. J. Dover, *Greek Popular Morality in the Time of Plato and Aristotle* (Oxford, 1974), pp. 112–14 ("Town and Country"); cf. Ehrenberg, *The People of Aristophanes*, pp. 82–94 (on the opposition between city/country).

22. This issue is admirably defined, starting with original legends of a bucolic genre, by Françoise Frontisi, "Artémis bucolique," *Revue de l'histoire des religions* 198 (1981): 29–56; cf., by the same author, "L'homme, le cerf et le berger: Chemins grecs de la civilité," *Le temps de la réflexion* 4 (1983): 53–76.

23. Aristotle *Magna moralia* 1193a.

24. The formula is found in Aristotle's *Rhetoric* 1389b11. *Eutrapelia* is not only a mastery of good humor. As its etymology indicates (*trepo*), it concerns a quality of intelligence that enables repartee and a reversal of the situation. It might be translated as "sense of humor," provided one recognizes its theatrical aspect, which is associated with the realm of the *mētis* analyzed by Detienne and Vernant, *Les ruses de l'intelligence* [note 7 above].

25. It is thus that Aristotle, in a development of the *Nichomachean Ethics* (1128a), becomes a source for a history of laughter, from the Old to the New Comedy. Concerning the relationships between urbanity, boorishness, balanced laughter, and the ridicule of ugliness, we refer to the study by Maurice Olender, "Incongru comme Priape: *Amorphia* et quelques autres mots de la laideur," to be published in N. Loraux and Y. Thomas, eds., *Le corps du citoyen* (Paris).

26. On Pan, the grotto, and Arcadia, cf. Borgeaud, *The Cult of Pan* [note 7 above].

27. According to the traditional grouping inherited from the Athenian model.

28. *Supplementum epigraficum graecum* 1, no. 248; cf. D. Comparetti, *Annuario della Scuola Archeologica di Atene* 4–5 (1922): 147–60.

29. Aristotle *Politics* 2.8.

30. On the genesis of this literature, see the very scholarly book by Stella Georgoudi, *Des chevaux et des boeufs dans le monde grec: Réalités et représentations animalières à partir des livres XVI et XVII des Géoponiques* (Paris and Athens, 1990).

31. Expression taken from the important work by Giovanna Daverio Rocchi, *Frontiera e Confini nella Grecia antica* (Rome, 1988), p. 31.

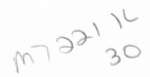